CRASH DIVE

TRUE STORIES OF
SUBMARINE COMBAT

EDITED BY LARRY BOND

A TOM DOHERTY ASSOCIATES BOOK
New York

CRASH DIVE

A Forge Book
Published by Tom Doherty Associates, LLC
175 Fifth Avenue
New York, NY 10010

www.tor-forge.com

Forge® is a registered trademark of Tom Doherty Associates, LLC.

ISBN 978-0-7653-4203-4

First Edition: April 2010
First Mass Market Edition: April 2011

Printed in the United States of America

0 9 8 7 6 5 4 3 2 1

CONTENTS

ACCIDENT ON *K-219*

THE DOMAIN OF THE GOLDEN DRAGON

IMPROVING THE BREED

FOR FURTHER READING

FOREWORD

by Rear Admiral Arlington F. Campbell,
U.S. Navy (Ret.)

Every boy and man needs heroes. Men he can look up to and strive to emulate. In my life I have had many . . . some of whom I have had the good fortune to meet and know personally, but I'm getting a little ahead of myself.

When I was growing up in the 1940s, most of my nonfamily heroes were characters from the radio or the movies. The Green Hornet, The Shadow, Hopalong Cassidy, Allan "Rocky" Lane with his faithful but equally renowned horse, Black Jack, and others provided that example of good triumphing over evil, however improbably.

As I moved on to the 1950s, my horizon expanded, mainly through television and sports. The 1954 Cleveland Indians and Otto Graham, the Hall of Fame Cleveland Browns quarterback, dominated in sports. TV introduced me to *Men of Annapolis*, Navy men in general via *Victory at Sea*, and submariners in particular through *The Silent Service*. Fresh in all of our minds was World War II, and then Korea was upon us. It was easy to find real heroes and I did, never thinking that one day I would be honored to meet and get to know some of them.

Holding this book in your hands indicates that you,

too, have some fascination with submariners and those who man them. Since I spent thirty-seven years in the U.S. Navy, all but ten of those years directly involved in submarines, I share your interest and even now, your fascination.

The chapters you are about to read come from a variety of sources, but most are directly from the submariners who lived these experiences themselves. If you have tried to write your own life experiences, you know that many stories are not easy to tell. Those who know veterans, especially those of World War II, know that getting them to talk of their experiences could be a daunting task. This gives you an idea of the enormity of the job of getting these events on the printed page. For many years after the war, their exploits remained highly classified, which precluded recording them for security reasons.

Reading has been my primary source of entertainment for years, particularly those years in the "boats." I have tried to read as many submarine-related books as I could, both factual and fiction. My hobby is to collect books of all types signed by the author. My most prized are those written by submariners. Many of those are represented in this compilation.

These you are about to read are just ordinary men doing their duty as they saw it. Events thrust them into roles they could never have imagined, but in which they performed well above the call of duty.

In time of war (hot, cold, or antiterrorism), the learning curve is steep. Those who can scale it successfully prosper and survive. These pages ahead are filled with such people, but allude to some who did not keep up or were overcome by events and did not survive.

Otto Giese survived; that alone was a major accomplishment. The German submarine force lost between seven hundred and eight hundred submarines during World War II. Toward the end, the survival rate of any particular submarine patrol was about 10 percent. Doing the math will quickly reveal the rate of surviving multiple war patrols. He did and lived to write about it.

Slade Cutter, whom you will meet aboard the USS *Seahorse*, seems to be an unflappable leader. What you see of his command tour does not in any way represent the first time in life he faced a significant challenge with steady nerves and a well-thought-out plan. While at the Naval Academy, he kicked a winning field goal in the Army-Navy game. Now, that shows a man with true nerves of steel.

In a portion of *Wake of the Wahoo*, you will be introduced to a Hall of Fame wardroom, an all-star team, if you will. The ship's yeoman (office administrator) with a gift for words gives marvelous insight into three of our top ten submarine skippers in World War II. The immortal "Mush" Morton, the commanding officer of one of the most successful boats, recipient of the Congressional Medal of Honor, but lost on *Wahoo*'s final patrol. Dickie O'Kane, his executive officer, who went on to command USS *Tang*, receive the Congressional Medal of Honor, and spend the last part of the war in a Japanese prisoner-of-war camp. George Grider, the engineer officer, who later led USS *Flasher* to near the top of the tonnage-sunk list by war's end. These three accounted for more tonnage by far than any other three skippers.

I trust that you will be thrilled and inspired by what you are about to experience. If so, I have taken the liberty to list a few of the best (in my opinion) books that I have read on submarining.

So . . . the heroes here are mine. I am proud of them and thankful for their service. Some of the most outstanding are Sam Dealey, Dick (Mush) Morton, Richard O'Kane, Gene Fluckey, Lawson P. (Red) Ramage, I. J. (Pete) Galatin, Edward (Ned) Beach, George Street, Hyman G. Rickover, and all submariners who lost their lives in the service of our nation, including my classmates and friends who were lost on *Thresher* and *Scorpion*, but most especially those on the fifty-two boats, which represent the highest percentage loss of any part of our armed forces, still on World War II patrol.

INTRODUCTION

by Larry Bond

Imagine working in a factory, surrounded by machinery. It's a high-tech installation, full of vital equipment. It's two stories high, and anywhere from 200 to 350 feet long. Space is at a premium, so the aisles are narrow, and equipment juts into the working spaces, with lots of corners and angles to bump into. It's dangerous, exacting work. A lot of the machinery can kill you if it isn't maintained properly.

The work is done in shifts, because the plant runs twenty-four hours a day. In addition to operating the equipment at regular intervals, which probably interferes with your sleep, you have to maintain and repair the gear, which takes up more of your time. And occasionally, at least once a day, all the workers have to get on the job at a moment's notice.

Now imagine that you not only work there, but also live there—but there's precious little space for people. Space is grudgingly granted for bunks (not enough for everyone, so you may have to "hot bunk" with another worker). You get a small locker for clothing and a few personal items. You share a few toilets with the rest of your coworkers, and there's barely enough water for infrequent showers.

You eat in a cafeteria, and luckily the food is pretty good, although you stock up every few months with so much food it covers the deck, and then don't get anything new for the rest of the time. Fresh food is rare.

It's crowded and smelly, and it can be noisy. There's no privacy, and here's the best part: You can't go outside for a stroll. In fact, the factory's surrounded by a hostile, demanding wilderness so dangerous that if you do leave, you'll be dead in hours.

The only outside air comes in the ceiling of the head office, and when it does, the whole factory moves— side to side, up and down, back and forth, and sometimes in a crazy combination of all three.

And by the way, you volunteered for this. You sweated months or years of school to get this job. In a time of slow business, the training required for this job could net you twice or three times your current salary if you changed to a more conventional employer. If business is brisk, it radically increases your chances of being killed, more than any other kind of employment.

I'm talking about submarine service, of course, putting it in familiar terms. Even as a former naval officer, it's hard to imagine life submerged for days or weeks or longer. I served on surface vessels, which can at times feel very much like an "outside" job. I spent one day on USS *Permit* (SSN-594). My ship (a destroyer) exchanged a few officers with her; then we chased each other around for a while. It was fun, we were treated well, and we learned a lot about how the other half lives, but there wasn't a moment that I wasn't in dire danger of bumping into something or somebody. It's *crowded*.

So what kind of person volunteers for the submarine service? And they take only volunteers. All navies, for as long as they've had subs, have taken only volunteers to serve in them. Even with the exigencies of military service, no navy will put a sailor in a boat unless he wants to be there.

I just used the word "boat." Now I have to explain. In naval parlance, commissioned vessels are always referred to as ships, regardless of their size. As I was informed roughly 3.2 milliseconds after being sworn in, "a boat is carried on a ship." The first subs, the Hollands and Lakes, were so small that they literally were boats, with only a handful of men in the crew. Even in World War II, they were smaller than most surface ships, with smaller crews, and they kept the term as a reminder of their uniqueness.

And that describes the men as well. The average sub sailor is more intelligent than his peers in the rest of the fleet. He still swabs the deck, but only when he's not operating a nuclear reactor or fixing a computerized fire control system.

He likes a challenge. Submarine service is dangerous, even in peacetime. Disasters like the loss of *Squalus*, *Scorpion*, and recently *Kursk* remind the public of the risk.

But there are benefits, too. Sub crews are small, and legendary for their closeness. The same thing happens to any group of men in a combat unit, but it's enhanced by the sub's isolation. Most misfits and shirkers are weeded out during submarine training. Those who are left work well together.

As special as the enlisted men were, they are still Navy sailors, and their duties and dangers are only somewhat different from those of their surface ship brethren. The officers on a submarine have to be a different breed entirely.

A surface ship, regardless of its size, is almost never alone. Small ships protect bigger ships, bigger ships protect the heavies, and the heavies get the job done. Nobody can do it by themselves, and they're not supposed to. A surface task force lives and breathes teamwork, spreading out the danger and backing each other up.

Officers on a surface ship know that if they're hit, other ships in the formation will come to their aid. Even a ship's captain, the most experienced officer aboard, knows that other men (the admiral and his staff) will guide his actions. They're the ones with the plan; he's just got to worry about his piece of it.

Submarine officers also follow the admiral's plan, but he's not on a flagship nearby. He's thousands of miles and weeks away. On a submarine, the skipper is truly on his own. Even if he's cooperating with a surface force, that cooperation will consist of staying in his patrol area and keeping as far away from the formation as possible. On a regular mission, he leaves port and won't expect to see another friendly face for weeks, probably months.

Combat on a surface ship needs teamwork. Information is gathered by the ship's sensors, collected and analyzed by the Combat Information Center, and distributed to the people who need it. The gunnery officer controls the guns, the torpedo officer fires the torpedoes, and so on. The captain sits above it all, acting only if things aren't happening the way he wants them to. It's called "command by negation."

On a sub, it's completely different. All information flows to the captain, who analyzes it himself. He maneuvers the boat, and controls its weapons. It's one-man control of a warship hundreds of feet long, weighing thousands of tons, and able to do terrible damage to the enemy.

A sub may patrol in enemy waters, attacking merchant ships, which are probably sailing in convoy. It may have to sail close to an enemy shore to gather intelligence. It may even have to land commandos or intelligence agents on that shore. None of these missions are easy, and most are outright dangerous.

A sub commander depends on skill and pure brass to outwit or evade enemy defenses and successfully attack the enemy, usually a target of his own choosing. A good submarine captain is a hunter, someone who aggressively and intelligently seeks out the enemy in order to do him the most damage possible. He also uses the boat's stealth to good advantage. Sub captains pride themselves on being sneaky, conniving types who will work every angle they can, and cheat on the rest.

Throughout this book, you will read of submarine skippers who are not satisfied with just patrolling a box and sinking whatever they encounter. They work hard to learn the enemy's methods and operating patterns, then go in at the cracks, or sometimes make the cracks themselves.

And they'll do it alone. If a plan fails because of poor judgment or bad luck, he and his crew will have to endure the consequences. At best, it's a missed shot, which is disheartening to everyone. It may mean pursuit lasting hours or days by an enemy that has many advantages over the now-exposed hunter.

A sub has no defenses except for the fact that it is very hard to see through water. After fifty years of technological progress, the primary ASW sensor is still sonar. Others sensors, ranging from sniffing diesel fumes to detecting neutrinos and Kelvin wakes, have not panned out. A sub simply depends on the opacity of water to conceal its movements, both on approach and as it makes its escape.

Surface ships expect to be shot at, and a large part of a surface ship's displacement is devoted to defense—armor, countermeasures, and defensive weapons. A sub's only armor is its stealth, which it can lose in a single unhappy moment. True, it can regain its stealth with proper tactics and a little luck, but in the meantime the enemy will do everything it can to sink it.

And they did sink subs. In spite of being hard to find and manned by each navy's best men, a lot of subs have been sunk. In World War II, 52 U.S. subs, 83 British subs, 128 Japanese subs, and somewhere between 700 and 800 German subs were sunk.

Of course, the submarine was the major arm of the German Kriegsmarine, which skews the numbers a little. The Germans built a little over a thousand boats of all types, but losses still amounted to about 70 percent of all the subs the Reich ever built! U.S. losses, by comparison, represented about 18 percent of its submarine force—still high.

And losses were almost always total. When a sub went down, it usually took its entire crew with it. Some tried escape gear or a free ascent to the surface, but however many tried, few succeeded.

And it's no better today then it was in World War I. *Komsomolsk*, a Russian nuclear submarine that was lost in 1989, was equipped with a sophisticated rescue sphere capable of holding her entire crew. In spite of this precaution, of the five men that used it, only one survived. Others, like *Thresher* and *Scorpion*, were total losses.

These men were some of the best we had, who chose an uncomfortable, dangerous service. Some of them did not come back. Those who did brought us these stories.

CRASH DIVE

BATFISH

FROM *Submarine!*

by Commander Edward L. Beach

We begin our tour with an excerpt from *Submarine!* by one of the most famous and decorated naval heroes of the twentieth century, Commander Edward L. Beach (1918–2002). Commissioned as an ensign in 1939, he attained the rank of commander before his retirement after twenty-seven years of naval service. He served throughout World War II in the Pacific theater, participating in the battle of Midway, and overseeing twelve combat patrols that sank forty-five enemy vessels. Afterward, he served on nuclear submarines, and commanded the USS *Triton* on its record-breaking submerged voyage around the world. He was awarded numerous honors and decorations for his valiant service, including the Navy Star, the Silver Star Medal, two Presidential Unit Citations, the Legion of Merit, and the National Defense Service Medal. After his retirement, he wrote both fiction and nonfiction, including the classic novel **Run Silent, Run Deep**, which was made into a film in 1958, and his autobiography, *Salt and Steel: Reflections of a Submariner*. He was also the coeditor of three editions of the *Naval Terms Dictionary* and wrote numerous articles for periodicals ranging from *American Heritage* to *National Geographic*. The Naval Historical Foundation History Prize has been renamed the Commander Edward L. Beach Prize in his honor.

It takes a certain kind of man to write about the everyday happenings aboard a submarine on war patrol, and make it as real as if you were standing right beside the men as it happened, and few do it better than Commander Beach. This excerpt is no exception, detailing the sixth war patrol of the USS *Batfish*, and bringing home the cramped, crowded, tense conditions under which its captain and crew played a deadly game of hide-and-seek with enemy submarines during the latter part of World War II.

USS *Batfish* got under way from Pearl Harbor on December 30, 1944, on what was to be her sixth war patrol. It was also to be one of the epoch-making patrols of the war, one whose influence may be discerned even at this late date. Her skipper was Commander J. K. Fyfe, a Naval Academy graduate of the class of 1936, who had already built up an outstanding record of successful submarine action. From the time when the PC boat escorting her out of Pearl Harbor was dismissed until she arrived at Guam, Jake Fyfe kept his ship at flank speed. He, in common with most submariners, saw no reason for delay in getting into the war zone, except the necessity of conserving fuel. The capture of Guam removed that necessity, insofar as the first leg of the trip was concerned. After leaving Guam or Saipan it usually paid to be a bit conservative, in case you ran into a long chase, or were given a prolonged special mission.

On January 9, 1945, *Batfish* arrived at Guam, and on the next day she departed en route to an area north of the Philippines. On January 12 she sighted what was probably her first enemy contact on this particular patrol, presaging the turn which the whole patrol would subsequently take. A periscope suddenly popped out of the water some distance ahead. Since you don't stick around to argue with an enemy submarine which has the drop on you, and since, besides, Jake was in a hurry to get to his area where he was scheduled for immediate lifeguard services, he simply bet on everything she would take and got out of there. Sightings of Japanese periscopes by our boats were fairly numerous during the war. The Japs never learned how *doubly* cautious you must be when stalking one of your own kind; we never learned a lesson better.

Between January 13 and February 9 *Batfish* had rather a dull time. She wasted two days looking for several aviators who were reported ditched near her track; investigated twenty-eight junks to see what kind of cargo they were carrying; dived at occasional aircraft alarms. Then, on February 9, while she was patrolling in Babuyan Channel, south of Gamiguin Island, the radar operator sounds a warning.

Something in his radar arouses his attention—he looks closely—there it is again—and again. It is not a pip which he sees; if it were, he would not wait to sing out "Radar contact" and thereby immediately mobilize the ship for action. This is something more difficult to evaluate. A faint shimmering of the scopes—a momentary unsteadiness in the green and amber cathode ray tubes—which comes and goes. Almost unconsciously he times them, and notices the bearing upon which the radar head is trained each time the faint wobble in the normal "grass" presentation is noticed. A few moments of this, and—*"Captain to the conn!"* No time to wait on ceremony. This particular lad wants his skipper, and he wants him badly.

A split second later the word reaches Jake Fyfe in his cabin, where he had lain down fully clothed for a few minutes of shut-eye. In a moment the skipper is in the conning tower.

The radar operator points to his scope. "There it is, sir! There it is again! I just noticed it a minute ago!" The operator is doing himself an injustice; from the time he first noticed there was something out of the ordinary to the moment Fyfe himself was beside him could not have been more than thirty seconds.

The captain stares at the instrument, weighing the significance of what he sees. This is something new, something portentous—there is a small stirring in the back of his mind—there seems to be a half-remembered idea there, if he can only dig it up—then, like a flash, he has it! If he is right, it means they are in grave danger, with a chance to come out of it and maybe add another scalp to their belts; if he is wrong, what he is about to do may make a bad situation infinitely worse. But Jake knows what he is doing. He is not playing some far-fetched hunch.

"Secure the radar!" he orders. The operator reaches to the cutoff switch and flips it, looking questioningly at his skipper.

"What do you think it is?" Fyfe asks the lad.

"It looked like another radar to me, Captain." The reply is given without hesitation.

"What else?"

The boy is at a loss for an answer, and Jake Fyfe answers his own question:

"Japanese submarine!"

Submarine *vs.* submarine! The hunter hunted! The biggest fear of our submarine sailors during World War II was that an enemy submarine might get the drop on them while they were making a passage on the surface. It would be quite simple, really. All you have to do is to detect the other fellow first, either by sight or by radar, submerge on his track, and let go the fish as he passes. *All you have to do is to detect him first!*

Our submarines ran around the coast of Japan as though they were in their own backyards. They usually condescended to patrol submerged only when within sight of the enemy shoreline in order not to be spotted by shore watchers or aircraft patrols, for you can't sink ships which stay in port because they know you are waiting outside. But when out of sight of land, and with no planes about, United States submarines usually remained on the surface. Thus they increased their search radius and the speed with which they could move to new positions. And it should not be forgotten that the fifty-odd boats doing lifeguard duty at the end of the war were required to stay on the surface whether in sight of land or not! Small wonder that our submarine lookouts were the best in the Navy.

United States submariners were, as a class, far too well acquainted with the devastating surprise which can be dealt with a pair of well-aimed torpedoes to take any preventable risk of being on the receiving end themselves. Submarines are rugged ships, but they have so little reserve buoyancy that a torpedo hit is certain to permit enough water to flood in to overbalance what remaining buoyancy there is. Even though the submarine might be otherwise intact, she would instantly sink to the bottom of the sea with most of her crew trapped inside. *Tang* was a prime example. Ordinarily there are no survivors from sunken submarines, with the exception of the Germans, who had a habit of surfacing and abandoning ship when under attack.

The submarine, which hunts by stealth, is therefore itself peculiarly susceptible to attack by stealth. But don't make the mistake of underestimating the enemy submarine crew. The fact that they are operating a submarine at all indicates that they are picked men, who know as much about the game, in all probability, as you do. The odds are definitely even, and it is a question of dog eat dog. The only advantage lies in superior ability and equipment.

Not counting midgets, the first Japanese submarine sunk by our forces was the *I-173*, which fell victim to the *Gudgeon* on January 27, 1942. The last such was sunk by the *Spikefish* on August 13, 1945. Between these dates twenty-three additional Japanese subs were destroyed by our own undersea warriors. And we regret to chronicle that some five of our own subs, it is thought, went down under the periscope sights of Japanese submarines. Unfortunately the Jap records are so poor that the precise manner in which all of our lost submarine vessels met their doom will never be discovered. The fact remains that our submarines were convinced that the Japs were sending the two-man midgets out at night, looking for them. And almost every patrol report turned in by our people toward the end of the war records that one or more torpedoes had been fired at them.

The most outstanding record of enemy subs sunk was the one hung up by *Batfish*, beginning that fateful February 9.

"Secure the radar!" Jake Fyfe turned to a shocked conning tower crew, and ordered crisply, "Battle stations torpedo!"

The helmsman instinctively had already extended his hand in the direction of the general alarm. Now he grasped it, pulled it out, and then down. The low-pitched chime of the alarm resounded through the ship, penetrating every corner, waking men who had turned in dead tired, vowing to sleep for a year— meaning only until their next watch—bringing them upright, fully alert, instinctively racing to their battle stations, all in the space of an instant.

What is it? What is it?

Don't know. Something on the radar.

Skipper says a Jap sub out there.

How does he know that?

The process of deduction by which Fyfe arrived at the conclusion that the source of the radar peculiarities was an enemy submarine was not at all illogical. The wavering of his radar scope was probably due to the presence of another radar. It was known that the Japs had radar, though of an inferior type to ours. If this radar came from a vessel as large as a destroyer, he should have been detected on *Batfish*'s radar before the emanations from his low-powered radar had been noticed. This, of course, was the usual case. Since the radar waves had been the first to be picked up, it followed that the ship producing them must be small and low on the water. Yet it must be a valuable ship, sufficiently important to rate one of the relatively few radar sets the Nips possessed. *Hence, a submarine.*

The reason why Fyfe ordered his own radar temporarily secured was simply to deny the Jap the same information which he himself had just received, while he and his executive officer, Lieutenant C. K. Sprinkle, USNR, broke out the charts and did some very rapid figuring.

The enemy radar emanations have been from 220, approximately southwest. Babuyan Channel runs more or less north and south. Therefore the target must be on a northerly course, approaching from the south.

To check this deduction, *Batfish*'s radar is cautiously turned on for only a moment. Sure enough, the bearing of the other radar has changed slightly. It is now 225.

"All ahead full! Right full rudder!" *Batfish* leaps ahead and steadies on a course calculated to get to the north of the approaching enemy vessel. She runs for a short time, every now and then checking the situation with her radar. All clear—no other ships around. Just the Jap, and his signals are becoming stronger, while his bearing is now drawing to the southward. This is as it should be.

But Fyfe does not, of course, propose to make his approach and attack on bearings alone. He wants to close the range, but on his own terms, with his bow on the enemy, his torpedoes ready—in short, with the drop on him.

Finally, Jake Fyfe and Sprinkle figure their position is about right. *Batfish* turns toward the enemy and ghosts in, keeping the darkest section of the midnight horizon behind her, and sweeping frequently, but at odd intervals, with her radar.

"Radar contact!" The word from Radar this time startles nobody—they have all been expecting it for several minutes. The tracking party now goes to work in earnest, with some concrete information instead of the rather sporadic and imprecise dope they have had up to now.

Target is on course 310, speed 12. The dials whirl on the TDC in the conning tower, where Sprinkle is in charge.

The range continues to decrease, the radar operator and the TDC operator tirelessly feeding in the essential information on the fire-control instruments. The plotting party also has its part in this, for all solutions must check before torpedoes may be fired.

On the bridge, the captain strains his eyes, and so do the lookouts up there with him. Suppose the Jap has somehow learned of the presence of the American submarine! It is possible. In this case, if he deduces what is going on, he might very logically turn the situation to his own advantage by firing his torpedoes first. After all, when you make an approach on another ship, there is a period during which you are in a much better position for him to shoot torpedoes at you than you at him—at a somewhat longer range, of course. Or, more probably, he might simply dive, thus spoiling the shot *Batfish* has worked for so long, not to mention making it immediately imperative for her to get the hell out of there!

Closer and closer comes the unsuspecting enemy sub. It is so dark that as yet he cannot be seen by the tense bridge party. As the situation develops, it is apparent that he will pass through the firing position at just under 2,000 yards' range. This is a little long for optimum torpedo fire, but Fyfe wants to take no chances of being detected. On he comes—only a little more now—then from the conning tower, "On the firing bearing, Captain!" This from the exec.

"Let them go when ready, Sprink. Shoot on radar bearings. I still can't see him from up here." From the skipper.

Silently, four torpedoes are loosed into the water. Four new wakeless electric fish start their run toward the target They have 1,800 yards to go; it will take a while. The watch hands crawl slowly and maddeningly around their faces. The wait grows longer, more anxious. *Something should have happened by now! Those fish should surely have arrived! We could not have been so far off that our spread missed also!*

But miss they do, all four torpedoes. Finally there is no escaping that conclusion. The whole careful and well-executed approach—wasted! All hands are bitterly disappointed. What can have gone wrong?

The question is answered by Plot, dramatically. "Target has speeded up! Speed now fourteen knots!" Too bad this was not detected a minute or two earlier. At least it explains the trouble, and allays the suspicious doubts which had already inevitably crept into the minds of both skipper and exec.

But the target continues serenely on his way, giving no sign of being aware of having been fired upon. Maybe *Batfish* will be able to try again.

No sooner thought than tried. The four murmuring diesels of the hunter lift their voices, and the submarine slips away through the water, seeking another position from which to launch her deadly missiles. But by this time, of course, the target has passed beyond *Batfish*, and in order to regain firing position it will be necessary to execute an end around.

Jake Fyfe has elected to remain on the surface for the whole attack, crediting to his superior radar the fact that he had been alerted before the Jap; and trusting to his belief that he could keep the enemy from detecting him. His plan is to get up ahead of the other submarine, and to head in toward him while the unsuspecting Nip is pounding along in nearly the opposite direction. Thus the range would close rapidly, and the amount of warning the other submarine could expect before torpedo junction would be very little. It was surprising that the Jap sub gave no indication of being aware he had been shot at. Whereas Fyfe had expected only one chance at him, he now finds another. "Obviously the fellow isn't as good as I gave him credit for!" And concurrent with this came the resolution to get in closer the next time, play his luck a little harder. If he could only sight the enemy, and fire on optical bearings instead of radar bearings, he would have a much neater solution to his fire-control problem—and thus greater certainty of hitting.

And besides, although Jake was morally certain the ship he was stalking was another submarine—and therefore Japanese, for he knew positively there were no friendly submarines in that area—he naturally wanted very badly to see him, just by way of confirming things. He had thought that visibility was good enough to see 2,000 yards—a mile—and therefore had settled on about 1,800 yards for firing range. Events had proved him too optimistic, and he had not been able to see him at that range. This time he *would* get a look!

All the while, *Batfish* is racing through the black night at full speed. She has pulled off abeam of her quarry, just within maximum radar range in order to be outside range of the less-efficient radar carried by the enemy, and she is rapidly overhauling him. Jake is still very careful with his own radar, searching all around and getting a radar range and bearing on the enemy as frequently as he dares, but he is not going to take a chance on being detected. All this time, of course, the radar emanations from the Jap have been coming in regularly, and their unchanged characteristics add proof that he is still sound asleep.

The skipper stands on the bridge of his ship during the whole of the new approach, for the situation could change so radically and so quickly that he must remain where he can take immediate action. So he must trust the coordination of everything belowdecks to Sprinkle.

Batfish has worked up somewhat ahead of the enemy's beam. Fyfe is trying to visualize the chart of the channel, for if he remembers rightly, some kind of a change is going to have to be made at the rate they are covering ground. The sea is fairly smooth, as it so often is in these southern waters, and hardly any solid water comes over *Batfish*'s main deck, although considerable spray is whipped across it by the wind of her passing. It is an absolutely pitch-black night. No distinction can be seen between sky and water—the horizon simply doesn't exist. All about is warm, dank, murky grayness, broken only by the white water boiling along your side. It is as though *Batfish* were standing still, dipping and rising slightly, and occasionally shaking herself free from the angry sea which froths and splashes beneath her.

In a moment Clark Sprinkle's voice is heard on the interior communication system: "Plot says target is changing course. They'll let us know for sure in a minute."

The skipper presses a large heavy button on the bulkhead beside him and leans forward to speak into the bridge speaker: "Fine! As soon as you're sure, we'll change too."

About a minute later a speaker mounted to the overhead of the conning tower squawks: "This is Plot. Target has changed course to the right. New course, zero one five."

"I've got the same, Sprink," says the TDC operator. "New course about zero two zero, though."

Sprinkle pulls a portable microphone toward him, presses the button. "Bridge, Plot and TDC have the target on new course between zero one five and zero two zero. Suggest we come to zero two zero."

"Right full rudder! Come right to new course zero two zero!" The order to the helm is sufficient acknowledgment.

"Rudder is right full, sir! Coming to zero two zero!" the helmsman shouts up the hatch.

Batfish heels to port as she whips around. Her white wake astern shows nearly a sharp right-angle turn as her stern slides across the seas.

Several more minutes pass. Fyfe is on the point of asking for more information, when again the bridge speaker blares its muffled version of Sprinkle's voice: "Captain, we've got him on zero two zero, making fourteen knots. Range is seven oh double oh, and distance to the track is two five double oh. This looks pretty good to me. Recommend we come left and let him have it!"

"Okay, Sprink. Give me a course to come to." The captain's voice has assumed a grim finality, a flat quality of emotionless decision. This is always a big hurdle; until now you really have the option of fighting or not fighting—of risking your neck or not—that is, if you can remain undetected. But when you start in, you are committed. You go in with the bow of your ship pointed directly at the enemy; you get well inside his visibility range, and radar range, too, for that matter; and you depend upon the quickness with which the attack develops to give you the opportunity to get it off. Keeping your bow on him gives him less to look at, a very important factor in the night surface attack; but if you change your mind and try to pull out of there you've got to change course, give him your broadside—and set yourself up for a beautiful counterattack on his part. Destroyers are supposed to be able to get a half-salvo in the air within seconds after having been alerted; submarines always carry one or two torpedoes at the ready, which can be fired instantly from the bridge. Small wonder that starting in is a crucial decision!

"Left full rudder!" Fyfe's command whips down the conning tower hatch to the helmsman.

"Rudder is left full, sir!"

"All ahead two-thirds!" Fyfe has waited a moment before slowing, in order to make the turn faster.

"Answered all ahead two-thirds!" Maneuvering room has matched annunciators with the conning tower, thus indicating that they have the word.

Sprinkle has been following things closely from the conning tower—checking bearings, ranges, courses, and speeds. He performs a rapid mathematical computation, drawing arrows this way and that, and measuring angles. Then he speaks into his little mike: "Captain, if we steady up on two four oh we'll have him ten degrees on our port bow, going across. His angle on the bow is now starboard forty."

"Steady on new course two four oh!" The ship has about thirty degrees more to swing, and the helmsman eases the rudder upon receipt of the command from the bridge.

"Steady on two four oh, sir!"

The exec speaks again. "Captain, he is on course zero two oh, making fourteen knots. Angle on the bow is starboard forty-five, and he now bears five degrees on our port bow. The distance to the track is two three double oh. Range, five oh double oh."

No answer from the bridge, but that doesn't bother Sprinkle. He knows he will hear quickly if the skipper isn't satisfied with the way things are going or the reports he is getting.

A few more tense moments pass. Again the speaker near the skipper's left elbow reproduces Sprinkle's familiar voice. "He's crossing our bow now. Range, four oh double oh."

"Come right to two five oh." Fyfe, who is working the same problem in his head that Sprinkle is solving mechanically in the conning tower, has the situation firmly fixed in his mind. He wants to keep coming around to head for the enemy, and has anticipated by seconds only the latter's recommendation.

"What is the distance to the track?"

"Two oh double oh, Captain."

"All ahead one-third." *Batfish* is closing the target's projected track too quickly, and the firing range will be too short, or the target might detect her before firing. Fyfe's brain is now in high gear, and he can feel every part of the problem falling into place. In fact, it is almost as if he could reach out and control the movements of the Japanese skipper also, and his mind wills the enemy to keep on coming, to keep on the course and speed as set up; to come unerringly and steadily on to his doom.

And on and on he comes, totally unaware of the trap set for him, totally unaware that he is springing the trap on himself, that any change whatsoever which he might make would be to his advantage, that the most serious mistake you can make, when it's submarine against submarine, is to relax—*ever*. Of course, to give him his due, the Jap doesn't know he is being shadowed. But he knows very well that he is proceeding through a submarine-infested area—and in this little game no excuses are accepted.

At 1,500 yards the keen eyes on *Batfish*'s bridge distinguish a blur in the gray murk, and at 1,000 yards the sinister outline of a Japanese I class submarine is made out—the first time during the whole evening that the enemy has actually been sighted. He wallows heavily in the slight chop of the sea—low, dark, and ungainly.

At 1,000 yards the Jap is broadside to *Batfish*: Fyfe's plan has borne fruit, for his own bow is exactly toward the enemy, and he has all the advantage of sighting. Furthermore, the darkest portion of the overcast is behind him.

Sprinkle is beside himself with eagerness. For about thirty seconds he has been imploring his skipper to shoot. He has a perfect solution and doesn't want to let it get away from him. "We've got them cold! Ready to shoot any time, Captain!" He repeats the same formula over and over, a veteran of too many patrols to say what he really means, which would be more on the order of, "*Let's go, Captain! What are we waiting for?*"

But Fyfe refuses to be hurried. He's worked too long for this moment, and he has already missed once, possibly because of a little haste in firing. Carefully he takes a bridge bearing and has it matched into the TDC, swings the TBT and takes another, to make sure there is no transmission lag which might cause an error. Then, for the first time using the word, he says, in a curious flat voice, "Fire torpedoes!"

"Fire one!" Sprinkle's voice is a split second behind that of his skipper.

Almost immediately the telephone talker standing under the conning tower hatch shouts loudly, so that his message is heard in the conning tower as well as on the bridge:

"Number one did not eject! Running hot in the tube!"

Something has gone wrong. The torpedo should have been pushed out of the torpedo tube by the high-pressure air ejection system. Instead, it has stuck in the tube, and the torpedomen forward can hear it running in the tube. This is critical, for it will be armed within a matter of seconds, and then almost anything could set it off. Besides, the motor is overspeeding in the tube, and it could conceivably break up under the strain and vibration—which might itself produce sufficient shock to cause an explosion.

But there isn't time to think much about possibilities. The skipper's reaction is instant. "Tubes forward, try again, by hand. Use full ejection pressure!" Full pressure is used only when firing at deep submergence, but this is an emergency.

The next command is for Clark Sprinkle in the conning tower. "Check fire!" Fyfe is not going to let the Jap get away while he waits for the casualty to be straightened out, but neither does he want the faulty torpedo to be ejected at the same time as a good one, and possibly interfere with it. If it does not eject on the second try, he will shoot the remaining tubes, and then return to the balky one.

"Number one tube fired by hand. Tube is clear!" The very welcome report is received after a few anxious seconds with a profound sense of relief. Only half a dozen seconds have been lost, altogether, and the situation is still good for the remaining fish.

"Resume fire, Clark!" But the exec has not needed that command. Number two torpedo is already on its way, followed a few seconds later by number three. Torpedoes number four, five, and six are held in reserve in case the first salvo misses.

Because these are wakeless electric torpedoes, Jake Fyfe, on the bridge, does not have the pencil-like wakes of steam and air to mark where they have gone. There is a slight disturbance of the surface of the water to show the direction they took, but that is all. Seven pairs of binoculars are glued to the Jap's low, lumbering silhouette and his odd-shaped bridge.

Down in the conning tower, the radar operator and the exec are staring at their screen, where the blip which is the target is showing up strongly and steadily, showing radar emanations still at the same uninterrupted interval. Suddenly, however, the radar waves become steady, as though the enemy operator had steadied his radar on a just-noticed blip, possibly to investigate it.

"I think he's detected us, sir!" whispers Radar. "See—it's steadied on us!"

Sprinkle has also seen. Eyes fixed on the cathode tube face he reaches for the portable mike to tell the skipper about this new development, when he drops it again. Before his eyes the blip has suddenly, astoundingly, grown much larger. It is now nearly twice the size it had been an instant before. Small flashes of light can be seen on the screen, going away from the outsized pip and disappearing. Then, swiftly, the pip reduces in size and disappears entirely. Nothing is left on the scope whatsoever.

At this moment a jubilant shout from the bridge

can be heard. "We got him! We got him! He blew up and sank!" Sprinkle mops his brow.

The watchers on *Batfish*'s bridge had hardly expected anything quite so dramatic as what they saw. One torpedo had evidently reached the target, and must have hit into a magazine or possibly into a tank carrying gasoline. The Nip sub had simply exploded, with a brilliant red-and-yellow flame which shot high into the night sky, furiously outlined against the somber, sober grayness. And as quickly as the flame reached its zenith, it disappeared, as 2,500 tons of broken twisted Japanese steel plunged like a rock to the bottom of the ocean.

There was nothing left for torpedo number three—following a few seconds behind number two—to hit, and it passed over the spot where the enemy ship had been.

Batfish immediately proceeded to the spot where the sub had sunk, hoping to pick up a survivor or two, but the effort was needless. Undoubtedly all hands had been either killed instantly by the terrific explosion or carried down in the ship. There had been absolutely no chance for anyone not already topside to get out. All Jake Fyfe could find was a large oil slick extending more than two miles in all directions from the spot where the enemy had last been seen.

Strangely—delighted and happy though he was over his success in destroying the enemy sub—the American skipper felt a few twinges of a peculiar emotion. This was very much like shooting your own kind, despite the proven viciousness and brutality exhibited by some of the enemy—and but for the superiority of his crew and equipment, the victim might have been *Batfish* instead of HIJMS-I-41.

The final attack on the Jap sub had been made at exactly two minutes after midnight on the morning of February 10. Then, an hour or so after sunset on the eleventh, at 1915—

"Captain to the conn!" The skipper is up there in an instant.

The radar operator points to his radar scope. "There's another Jap sub, Captain!"

Sure enough, there, if you watch closely, is the same tiny disturbance which alerted *Batfish* two nights ago. This time there is less doubt as to what action to take. The same tactics which were heralded with such signal success on the first occasion are immediately placed into effect. The crew is called to battle stations, the tracking parties manned, and all is made ready for a warm reception. The radar party is cautioned— unnecessary precaution—to keep that piece of gear tamed off except when a range and bearing are actually required.

If anything, it is even darker than it was the first night. Having found how ineffective the Jap radar really is—or was it simply that the Jap watch standers were asleep?—Fyfe determines to make the same kind of attack as before.

The situation develops exactly as it did before, except that this submarine is heading southeast instead of northeast. At 1,800 yards he is sighted from the bridge of the American submarine. He is making only 7 knots, somewhat slower than the other, and it takes him a little longer to reach the firing bearing. Finally everything is just about set. Sprinkle has made the "ready to shoot" report, and Fyfe will let them go in a moment, as soon as the track improves a bit and the range decreases to the optimum. About one minute to go—it won't be long now, chappy.

"Hello, he's dived! He dived right on the fire bearing!" Where there had been an enemy submarine, there was now only the rolling undulation of the sea. Nothing to do now but get out of there. *Batfish* must have waited too long and been detected. The Jap was keeping a slightly better watch than Fyfe had given him credit for, and now *Batfish* is being hunted. Just as quickly as that the whole situation has changed. With an enemy submarine known to be submerged within half a mile of you, there is only one of two things to do. Dive yourself, or beat it.

If you dive, you more or less give up the problem, and concentrate on hiding, which many skippers probably would have done. If you run away on the surface, however, there is a slight chance that he'll come back up, and you'll have another shot at him. Jake Fyfe is a stubborn man, and he doesn't give up easily: he discards the idea of diving. "Left full rudder!" he orders instead. His first object is to get away, and his second is to stay in action. Maybe the Jap will assume that he has continued running—which is precisely what Jake hopes he will do.

"All ahead flank!"

The Jap was on a southeasterly course before he dived. Knowing that his periscope must be up and watching his every move, Fyfe orders a northerly course, and *Batfish* roars away from the spot, steadying on a course slightly west of north. Three miles Fyfe lets her run, until he is reasonably sure to be beyond sonar as well as visual range. Then he alters course to the left, and within a short time arrives at a position *southwest* of the position at which the Jap sub dived.

In the conning tower, at the plotting station, and on the bridge there is some rapid and careful figuring going on. "Give the son of a bitch four knots," mutters Sprinkle to himself. "That puts him on this circle. Give him six knots, and he's here. Give him eight knots—oh, t' hell with eight knots!" Clark Sprinkle's exasperation is almost comical as he grips his pencil in sweaty stubby fingers and tries to decide what he'd do if he were a Jap.

The point is that *Batfish* wants to arrive at some point where she will be assured of getting a moderately long-range radar contact the instant the Nip surfaces, in a position to be able to do something about it. *But don't let her spot us through the periscope, or wind up near enough for her to torpedo us while still submerged.* This is where the stuff you learned in school really pays off, brother.

Naturally, *Batfish* cannot afford to remain overly long in the vicinity. Every extra minute she spends there increases by that much the diameter of the circle upon which the enemy may be; and even at that very moment he may be making a periscope approach— while she hangs around and makes it easy for him. But Fyfe has no intentions of making it any easier than he can help. Once he has put his ship in what he has calculated to be a logical spot to await developments, he slows down to one-third speed—about 4 knots. Then he orders the sound heads rigged out. With his stern toward the direction from which the enemy submarine would have to come, were he making an attack, and making 4 knots away from there, *Batfish* is forcing the Jap to make high submerged speed in order to catch her; she is banking on detecting him by sound before he can get close enough to shoot, or on detecting the torpedo itself if a long-range shot is fired.

Twenty minutes pass. Fyfe cannot guess how long the Nip sub will stay down, but his game is to outwit him. If his initial gambit of running away to the northward has fooled him, he'll probably show within an hour after diving. The soundmen listen with silent intensity, their headphones glued to their heads. The radar operator scrutinizes his scope with equal urgency. It would not do to miss any indication.

Suddenly, both sound operators look up at the same time. The senior one speaks for both. "Mr. Sprinkle! There's a noise, bearing zero one five!"

Clark is there in an instant. "What's it like?" He flips on the loudspeaker switch.

Clearly, a rushing sound can be heard, a sort of powerful swishing sound. It changes somewhat in intensity and tone, then suddenly stops. Like a flash the exec grabs the portable mike. "Captain," he bellows to the bridge. "He's blown his tanks, bearing zero one five. He'll be up directly!"

The blast from the bridge speaker nearly blows everyone off the bridge, for Sprinkle has a powerful voice. All binoculars are immediately turned to the bearing given. But the black night conceals its secrets well. Nothing can be seen.

The bridge speaker blares again. "Radar contact, zero one eight. That's him all right!"

Apparently convinced that all is clear, the Japanese submarine has surfaced, and is evidently going to continue on his way. *Batfish* is to get another chance. Whether the target saw them, or thought he saw them; heard them, or thought he did; detected them on radar, or simply made a routine night dive, will never be known. One thing Jake is definite on, however: He will get no chance to detect *Batfish* this time.

Once again *Batfish* goes through all the intricate details of the night surface approach—with one big difference. The skipper is not going to go in on the surface. The Jap detected him the last time. He's got more strings to his bow than that.

The Jap has speeded up and changed course slightly. *Batfish* again seeks a position in front of him, and when the range and distance to the track are to Fyfe's liking, *Batfish* dives—but not entirely. Since the radar antennae are normally on top of the highest fixed structure of the ship, it follows that they are the last things to go under when a submarine dives. All Fyfe had done was dive his ship so that these vital antennae were still out of water, although nearly all the rest of the submarine is beneath the surface. This is a good trick; that *Batfish* had been able to do it so neatly is a tribute to the state of training and competence of her crew. With her radar antennae dry and out of water, they still function as well as when she was fully surfaced, and the dope continues to feed into the fire-control gear, even though not a thing can be seen through the periscope.

And of course the Jap, probably alerted and nervous—maybe he has heard of the failure of one of his brother subs to get through this same area two nights ago—has no target to see or detect by radar, unless you consider a few little odd-shaped pieces of pipe a target.

So on he comes, making 12 knots now, fairly confident that he has managed to avoid the sub which had stalked him a couple of hours ago. He doesn't even notice or pay any attention to the curious structure in the water a few hundred yards off his starboard beam—for Jake Fyfe has resolved to get as close as possible—and four deadly fish streak his way out of the dark night.

Mercifully, most of the Nip crew probably never knew what hit them. The first torpedo detonated amidships with a thunderous explosion, virtually blowing the ill-fated ship apart. As the two halves each up-ended and commenced to sink swiftly amid horrible gurgles of water and foaming of released air and fuel oil, the second and third torpedoes also struck home. Their explosions were slightly muffled, however, as though they might have struck some stray piece of metal and gone off mostly in water; but they served to increase the probability that none of the enemy crew had survived the initial attack.

Three minutes later Fyfe logged two more blasts from deep beneath his ship, evidently some kind of internal explosions in the broken hulk of the sinking submarine. Eight minutes later one terrifically loud explosion rocked *Batfish*. First thought to be an aircraft bomb, the explosion was finally put down to part of the swan song of the Nipponese tub. All during this period, and for some time later, Sound heard the usual noises of a sinking submarine—mainly small internal explosions and escaping air.

This time Jake Fyfe was prevented from trying to rescue any of the possible survivors of the catastrophe by the presence of a plane, which was detected just as *Batfish* was getting ready to surface. It is highly doubtful, however, that there could have been any survivors, in view of the triple-barreled blow the submarine had received.

Shortly after midnight, some twenty-four hours later, one of the more irrepressible members of *Batfish*'s crew was heard to mutter, "What, again? Ho hum; here we lose another night's sleep playing tag with these slant-eyed submarines!"—as Captain Jake Fyfe rushed past en route to the conning tower.

For the third time in four days the radar operator has called his skipper—unfortunately the patrol reports of our submarines do not usually list the names of the crew, nor their stations—it would be interesting to know whether the same man spotted the enemy each time. From the times of the three contacts, however, 2210, 1915, and 0155, it would appear that one contact was made by each of the three watch sections, and that therefore the three men standing the radar watches each can lay claim to one Nip sub.

Naturally, the particular peculiarity in the appearance of the radar scope which had first served to alert *Batfish* had been carefully explained to all radar watchers, and they all knew what to look for. In this case, as in the last, the operator simply pointed to his scope and stated flatly, "There's another one of those Jap subs, Captain!"

One look at the screen, and Jake Fyfe raps out the command to sound the general alarm.

This time Fyfe himself gets on the ship's interior announcing system. "It looks like another Nip submarine, boys," be says. "We ought to be written right into their operation orders by this time. Let's see if we can't help him along the same road as the other two!"

Fyfe and his tracking party are pretty fine hands by this time, and it only takes a short while before the Jap is picked up for sure on the radar; and his course and speed are known. The United States submariners are fairly certain he will be on either the northerly course of the first sub or the southeasterly one of the second. It proves to be the latter—course one two zero, speed 7. *Batfish* heads to intercept, playing it cagily, as always, but a little more self-confident this time. Somehow these Japs don't seem to have as good equipment as our own—we can thank the home front for that—and they surely are not using what they have to the best advantage—for which we can thank *them*. And we will—in our own unique fashion.

But with the range still quite long, and before *Batfish* is able to get into attack position, the Japanese sub dives. Just why he does, no one knows. Possibly he detected an aircraft, or thought he did—although *Batfish* sees no planes on her radar—or perhaps he got a momentary contact on *Batfish* through some unexplained vagary of his radar equipment. The most probable explanation is that he has heard of the failure of two other boats to get through this particular stretch, and is attempting to make pursuit more difficult by diving occasionally.

But Jake Fyfe has the answer for this one cold. Last night qualified him in its implementation. He heads, despite this new development, to the spot originally selected for attack position. Then, instead of diving, he proceeds down the track at 4 knots, sound gear rigged out, radar sweeping steadily and deliberately, lookouts alerted and tensely watching.

Half an hour after the Jap dived, *Batfish*'s radar once again picks up the faint, shimmering emanations of the Nip radar. He's back up again, though this time no blowing of tanks has been heard. Fyfe, Sprinkle, and the tracking party start the same old approach game.

The first thing to do is to get actual radar contact; this wobble in the scope is no good for tracking, even though it does give a vague indication of the enemy's bearing. So *Batfish* heads for the source of what her radar operators now term the "wobbly," expecting to get contact momentarily. Several thousand yards are covered in this manner, with no result, except that the wobbly is getting stronger. Fyfe and his exec become worried over this development. They know the Jap is surfaced—or can he have thought of the same dodge they themselves used only last night? Suppose the Jap is even then in the process of making the same type of approach on *Batfish*! An unpleasant thought to entertain. The lookouts redouble their vigilance, especially directing their search at the water surface within half a mile around them. At the skipper's order everything else in the ship is subordinated to the sound watch. Fans and blowers are secured. Unnecessary gear throughout the ship is turned off. Most important, the diesel engines are secured and propulsion shifted to the battery. Silently, eerily, *Batfish* glides through the water, peering and listening for the telltale swoosh of a torpedo coming at her. If the Jap is very smart indeed, he will silence also, and will get so close before shooting that *Batfish* will not have a chance of avoiding the torpedoes, even though she might actually hear them on the way.

The lapping of the water alongside is excruciatingly loud in the unnatural stillness. The very air seems stifling and oppressive on the bridge, as it most certainly is down below, with all blowers turned off. Your breath seems to stop, and your heart beats with a muffled thump. The tiny blower motor in the radar gear whines insistently in the conning tower; impossible to shut it down because it keeps the radar tubes from overheating. Sprinkle makes a mental note to have it pulled out and overhauled at the first opportunity. Down below everyone talks in whispers, not that whispering could do any good, but in tacit recognition of the deadly desperateness of the situation. The Jap sub, submerged, possibly making an approach, and *themselves still on the surface!*

The basic problem, of course, is to compute how far the Jap sub can travel toward them, assuming his most probable course and speed for the time since he dived, and then to stay at least that distance, plus a little to be on the safe side, away from the spot where he submerged. Fyfe, straining for that elusive radar contact which his reasoned deductions say should come soon, allows *Batfish* to go as far as he dares before reversing course again. Just as he gives the order, someone in one of the engine rooms drops a wrench on the steel deck. The sharp noise is carried up the silent main induction pipe and hits the tensely waiting and watching bridge with a shock. All hands are visibly startled, and one lookout almost drops his binoculars. The skipper half opens his mouth, then shuts it again. It wouldn't do to show exasperation at this point.

And then, finally, with *Batfish* still swinging to her hard over rudder, it comes at last. "Radar contact, bearing three three six!" Fyfe's judgment and nerve have been vindicated again. The Jap was probably just being cagey himself, and had no knowledge of the presence of the United States submarine.

It happens that there are only two torpedoes left forward in *Batfish*, which really does not matter much since she is due shortly to depart station en route to Pearl Harbor. But it must be admitted that no one expected to run into three nearly identical situations like this—and until the third submarine was detected Fyfe had held no qualms whatever at being nearly dry forward. Now, however, a problem presents itself.

It is necessary to maneuver *Batfish* so that the Jap goes across her stern instead of her bow. Not too easy to do, since you have to be going away instead of toward the target. Fyfe plays his target slowly and carefully, somewhat like an expert fisherman campaigning against a crafty big one. The cast has been made, the fly has landed, the big fellow is nosing toward it, ready to head back for the deep water at the slightest suspicious sign.

This particular submarine has shown considerably more wariness than either of the other two. His peculiar actions on surfacing have proved him to be astute and careful, and Jake Fyfe is not the man to underrate his opponent. His recent scare is rather fresh in mind, and the ice is still mighty thin, measured as it is only in the superiority of United States equipment and alertness.

So *Batfish* tracks the target, gets his course and speed entirely by radar without ever having seen him, and finally submerges dead ahead of him, several miles away. Once again Fyfe uses the stunt of leaving his radar antennae out of water, so that the all-important information on the target's movements will continue to be available to his fire-control party and the intricate instruments they operate. Only this time he keeps his stern toward the target and moves slowly away from him, turning as he does so, with the result that the doomed Jap passes directly across his stern at the desired range, and three torpedoes are on their way to meet him. This is really a deliberate shot.

It also is slightly longer in range than the two previous attacks, and there is a longer wait in *Batfish*'s conning tower after the fish are finally sent on their way.

The skipper is watching through the periscope. He can now clearly see the long, low shape of the enemy, his odd-shaped bridge, and his peculiar undulating deckline. He is not a bad-looking ship, Fyfe must admit to himself, and most of these big Jap boats are pretty fast—at least as fast as our own. Not much is known about how they handle under water, however, and, like all United States submariners, Fyfe will reserve his judgment on that score. Our experience with big boats is that you pay for size with submerged maneuverability, and that the well-established theory about efficiency varying with the size of the vessel does not apply to submarines. The Nip is painted black, which makes him just a little easier to see against the gray night, and on the side of his bridge can quite plainly be seen a white rectangle with a dark disk in the center.

On he comes, ominous and a bit pathetic, entirely unaware of the three messengers of doom speeding his way. Fyfe, in the meantime, is a bit anxious. Without taking his eyes from the periscope, he calls out, "How long since the first one?"

Clark Sprinkle answers obliquely, "About fifteen seconds to go, Captain."

"Fifteen seconds! Damn!"

But the torpedoes run true and as intended, and Fyfe's impatience finally is brought to an end. "A hit!" he shouts. "A beautiful hit!" And so it is: a single hit which produces a brilliant orange explosion right in the center of the stricken ship.

Simultaneously, a wide diffusion of pips is noted on the radar screen, indicating that the target has blown apart. Then all the pips die away. The whole catastrophe has been silent; no sound whatsoever has reached the eager listeners in *Batfish*. A moment later, however, the noise of the explosion with its terrifying aftermath crackles over the sound gear into the headsets of the operators, and, indeed, comes right through the pressure hull, so that no man in the crew need have it described to him.

The loud WHAM of the warhead going off is followed instantly, and almost as though it were a single explosion, by a much louder and more prolonged WHRROOOM. This undoubtedly must be the enemy's magazines going up—and there exists a strong probability that he is carrying an extra-heavy load, possibly intended for the beleaguered Japs in the Philippines.

One of the three stopwatches is stopped with the first hit, and there is no doubt that this was the first torpedo, running the calculated range at exactly the calculated speed. But there are no further hits, despite the care with which the other fish had been launched on their way. This occasions no disappointment, however, since there is simply nothing left for the last two fish to hit.

As for *Batfish*, Jake Fyfe had her fully on the surface again within three minutes after the torpedo hit. Though he strongly doubted that there could possibly be any survivors of the terrific explosion he had witnessed, he was determined, as before, to give them a chance for their lives. It was nearly dawn, and no

good came from use of the searchlight, which Fyfe
had ordered turned on and played upon the water, so
the decision was made to wait until daylight, in hopes
that Jap planes patrolling the area would somehow
not be immediately in evidence.

Parenthetically, one cannot help comparing *Batfish*'s repeated magnanimous attempts to succor the
victims of her attacks with the treatment meted out in
similar circumstances by the Japanese. There is one
instance on record in which most of the crew of an
American submarine were picked up by a Japanese
destroyer; one man was injured, and was promptly
thrown overboard. Another had swallowed so much
salt water that he was retching heavily, and would
also have gone overboard had he not fought clear of
his saviors and joined the remainder of the group of
survivors. In the case of *Tang*, the pitifully small number of survivors were mercilessly beaten and clubbed
about the head and body. By contrast, *Batfish* deliberately exposed herself by turning on a searchlight to
assist in locating survivors of her night's handiwork,
and then voluntarily remained on the surface in these
enemy waters until long after daybreak, in hopes of
possibly finding one or two. Since her position was
well within enemy aircraft patrols, the unofficial rules
by which most United States submarines guided their
actions required that she be submerged during daylight.

Several of our submarines were enabled to rescue
enemy survivors in some manner or other, after either
they or someone else had torpedoed them. In more
than one instance American sailors or officers had to
go overboard after survivors and force them to accept their hospitality. In no case was such a prisoner

badly treated after rescue; most of them gained weight during their sojourn on board, and were so well treated that instructions had finally to be issued to treat them with greater severity in order not to "spoil" them.

With the dawn *Batfish* sighted much oil, bits of wood and paper, debris of various kinds, all newly in the water and quite evidently from the sunken submarine. No Japanese were seen, however—dead or alive. It appeared that once again there was to be nothing tangible to reward Jake Fyfe for his brilliant achievement, but finally a small wooden box recovered from the water was found to contain the Jap navigator's workbook and navigational instruments. Evidently he had just brought it topside, perhaps preparatory to taking a sight or two despite the not-too-favorable weather, but had not yet opened it.

Because the Japanese use Arabic numerals for navigational purposes, there was no difficulty in reading the workbook. Apparently the Jap departed Nagoya for Formosa, and had left there for Luzon—where he never arrived.

Batfish left her area for Guam three days later, and on February 21 she moored alongside the submarine tender *Apollo* in Apra Harbor, Guam.

To say that Jake Fyfe was received with open arms by the submarine brethren is putting it mildly. Though no public announcement of his magnificent feat could be made, owing to the well-laid policy of cloaking our submarine activities in anonymity, it instantly became known and broadcast throughout the submarine force. Here was another patrol nearly on a par with Sam Dealey's famous five-destroyers cruise. Here was additional proof that the spirit of the submarine force, so beautifully exemplified by Dealey and O'Kane and Morton, was still going strong, and that those who came after had not lost the touch of their predecessors.

There was, however, an even more important and far-reaching effect. To a nation like the United States, with its far-flung merchant marine, the submarine is perhaps the greatest menace to successful prosecution of war. That is to say, if and when we should get into another war our backs will immediately be up against the wall if the powers arrayed against us have a powerful submarine force. Witness what the Germans did to Great Britain in two world wars, and to us in World War II. In both instances the Allies won, but only by the narrowest of margins.

However, born of the imminence of defeat, a new type of submarine was developed in the closing days of World War II by the Germans. True, they did not invent anything extraordinary, but they put together several known but unused ideas to develop the high-speed snorkel submarine, and it may safely be said that this vessel has revolutionized previous concepts of anti-submarine warfare. It is virtually immune to the countermeasures we used so successfully against German and Japanese submersibles, and its efficiency in attack is trebled.

Fortunately, our military leaders have not neglected the challenge laid down by the fast submarine. A tremendous amount of thought has gone into the problem of how to get enemy subs before they can wreak their threatened damage upon our commerce—our lifeblood, so to speak. And every time the discussion in the halls of the Navy Department or the Pentagon—or even in the White House—has waxed long and earnestly, someone is sure to come up with a reference to Jake Fyfe and the fact that *Batfish* sank three enemy submarines within the space of four days with no damage and very little danger to herself. *Why not set a submarine to kill a submarine?*

The idea has grown until now, seven years after Fyfe's exploit, something is being done about it. It is obvious that the submarine will enjoy, in relation to another submersible, those same advantages which all subs always have had. That is, surprise, the ability of concealment, and so on. With one difference: Since the hunt is to take place in the natural environment of the submarine, *either one may become the hunter and either the hunted*. Prior detection will assume much greater importance than ever before—if that is possible. There is no question but that it will still be a nerve-racking occupation.

MERGUI ARCHIPELAGO

FROM *One of Our Submarines*

by Commander Edward Young

*O*ur next submarine captain-turned-author actually got his start in publishing before he even set foot on a submarine. Commander Edward Young (1913–2003) was selected by Allen Lane of Penguin Books to create their instantly recognizable avian symbol (he found his model at the London Zoo), as well as design the stylish covers for their paperback line in the late 1930s. When World War II broke out, he joined the Royal Navy Volunteer Reserve, where he was instantly commissioned as a sublieutenant owing to his previous sailing experience. During the rest of the war he saw service near Iceland, Malta, Sri Lanka, and off the Australian coast, earning the command of a submarine along the way—the first reservist to achieve this posting—and being awarded two Distinguished Service Crosses and the Distinguished Service Order. After his retirement, in 1945, he returned to publishing and wrote his gripping memoir, *One of Our Submarines*, which Penguin honored by making it their thousandth book in print, and it is still in print to this day.

Owing to their versatile nature, submarines were used in a variety of tasks during World War II, including attacking enemy cargo ships of all sizes. Instead of wasting torpedoes on the smaller vessels, the sub would find them, surface, and shell them to pieces with its deck guns. This sort of action is often overlooked in favor of the breathless underwater convoy hunts, but Commander Young details it with style to spare, and his pride in performing what some might think a less dangerous—but just as critical—mission during wartime is just as evident.

Our next billet was a submarine captain's dream—almost virgin territory (no submarine had visited it for nearly a year), and a roving commission to look for trouble along a 300-mile coastline studded with hundreds of islands. The area assigned to us was the Mergui Archipelago and the western seaboard of the narrow isthmus which joins the Malay Peninsular to Burma and Siam. It was suspected that, in pursuance of their policy of using small, shallow-draught coastal craft in place of larger deep-water ships, the Japs were working some of the many channels hidden behind the islands, and that the port of Mergui itself might be the departure point for seaborne traffic taking military supplies to Rangoon.

As we expected to use the gun far more than the torpedo tubes, it was decided to increase our outfit of ammunition. By converting a little-used trimming tank and various stowage spaces we finally managed to pack in twice as many rounds of three-inch shells as usual. We also organised a Boarding Party with a view to inspecting, and if necessary blowing up, junks and other small cargo-carrying craft. An edict had recently gone forth that all submarines in the Far East were to carry an additional officer for watch-keeping duties, and we were lucky in having appointed to us a young sub-lieutenant RN called Dicky Fisher, who was not only an extremely likeable fellow and a great asset to the wardroom, but also burning to distinguish himself in some personal fracas with the enemy. I imme-

diately appointed him Boarding Officer and told him
to decide for himself how many men and what equipment he needed. He entered into his commission with
enthusiasm and intelligence, selected five men, fitted
the party up with grappling-hooks, revolvers, demolition charges, and collected from God knows where a
most fearsome assortment of knives and daggers for
self-defence in case of treachery. When fully kitted up
for the first dress rehearsal they looked as bloodthirsty
a crowd of pirates as ever slit throats on the Spanish
Main.

We left Trincomalee on the evening of July 15th, and
after an uneventful passage entered the patrol area in
the early hours of the morning of the 20th. I had chosen to make a landfall in the vicinity of Tavoy, since
all the islands here are so steep-to that the navigational approach would be easy. We set course to arrive just to the north of Kabosa Island, and a good
radar fix was obtained off this and the neighbouring
islands before any land was sighted.

Patrol conditions during the first few days were
trying and depressing. A monotonous swell from the
southwest made depth-keeping difficult, and we had
heavy and almost continuous rain—as was to be expected in the wettest month of the monsoon period
on one of the wettest coasts of the Bay of Bengal. By
day the heavily wooded islands were half hidden by
the curtain of falling water, and at night on the bridge
we were miserable under the tropical downpour
which penetrated everywhere and rendered binoculars
useless. When it was not raining, the heat turned the
universal damp into a shrouding mist. Visibility was

always poor; there was no moon; and at night we had to rely entirely on radar for fixing our position.

The bad visibility foiled my first attempt to inspect the sheltered anchorage on the inside of Tavoy Island known as Port Owen, but on the 23rd I determined to try again. Diving before dawn a few miles out, we crept round the northern tip of the island and turned south towards our objective. The visibility was still down to about three miles, but I hoped it might clear later in the day.

At a quarter past nine the officer-of-the-watch suddenly saw a dim shape on the port bow emerging from the mist of rain. Examining it through the periscope, I could not at first make out what it was, but soon realised it was a small north-bound coaster of about 200 tons, heavily camouflaged with branches of trees and other foliage. I had never before met this form of disguise, an ingenious attempt to make the vessel hard to see when close in against the land.

I turned hard-a-port to bring the submarine on to a parallel course with the enemy, and gave the order,

"Stand by gun action."

This was the signal for a tremendous bustle and clatter as the gun's crew opened the lower hatches of the conning-tower and the gun-tower (situated over the wardroom) and clambered up the ladders to wait for the order to open up. Next to the wardroom, in the passage-way by the galley, the ammunition supply party were lifting the hatch-cover off the magazine under the deck and passing out the three-inch shells to be stacked on the wardroom table. Within a minute Blake was able to report, "Gun's crew ready."

I waited to let the coaster pass me, intending to surface on his port quarter.

"Target is a small coaster," I said. "Bearing Green 40. Range 800 yards. Open fire on surfacing. Point of aim the wheelhouse."

And then the coaster had drawn past our beam and the moment had come.

"Surface. *Gun action!*"

Number One at once gave the order to blow all main ballast. In accordance with the gun-action drill, the planesmen at first tried to hold the submarine down, but when the blowing tanks began forcing her up they reversed the planes and let her shoot to the surface like a cork. At fifteen feet, when the top of the gun-tower was still under water, Number One blew a whistle, the hatches slammed open, a little shower of water fell down the gun-tower, and then the men were climbing the ladders at the double. I had to wait until Blake and the gun's crew were clear of the conning-tower, so I kept my eyes at the periscope, watched the target still chugging along in the rain, quite unconcerned, and saw our bow rising out of the sea in a surge of whitened water. A moment later I was climbing the tower.

I got to the bridge just as the gun cracked away the first round. It was a direct hit, and made a shambles of the wheelhouse. There was no sign of opposition from the enemy, but although we pumped round after round into him, most of them along his water-line, he maintained his course and speed for some minutes with apparently no one at the helm. One shell produced a burst of flame from the deck-cargo of oil-drums. At last, after we had fired twenty-eight rounds, he came to a dead stop, so we ceased fire and closed slowly in towards him. There was still no sign of life, and I began to wonder if we had killed the entire crew, but as we approached figures began to emerge hesitantly from the after cabin and jump into the water. Some were Japanese, some Malays. Although the coaster had settled slightly by the stern he looked like taking some time to sink but as I was maneuvering *Storm* alongside to board him and blow him up with a demolition charge, the shattered vessel sank slowly aft and dived vertically stern first. As he did so, numerous oil-drums and odd bits of wood floated off the deck.

I decided to take only two prisoners. It was too early in the patrol to encumber ourselves with many passengers; the other survivors had plenty of debris to cling to, and land was less than half a mile away. We cruised slowly among the bobbing heads trying to select our prisoners. I was anxious to have one Jap if possible, but the first three we tried to pick up—all unusually large men for their race—swam away at our approach and could not be reached. However, one small Jap consented to be rescued, so he was hauled out of the water and taken below. We also picked up a Malay, whom we found to be wounded in the thigh; he was assisted down the conning-tower and handed over to the Coxswain.

I now decided on the spur of the moment to put into action a plan I had been toying with the previous day—to enter Port Owen brazenly on the surface. There was no large-scale Admiralty chart of the place, but at the last minute before I sailed George Perrin, the Staff Officer in *Maidstone*, had given me a plan prepared by the India Survey and Topography Division which charted the anchorage in great detail. Although this showed that the water inside was too shallow to allow us to dive in the event of serious opposition, I felt there was an excellent chance of getting away with it if we could achieve a tactical surprise.

It seemed to me that everything was now favourable for such an attempt. The rain, which was still falling heavily and which had thwarted my periscope inspection of the anchorage, would conceal our approach long enough to give us the advantage of surprise. Moreover, we had just tasted blood; the gun's crew were in buoyant spirits at their quick success; we were already on the surface and in a mood to stay there. It seemed unlikely that the noise of the action could have been heard as far away as the anchorage. I decided to go ahead.

It was ten o'clock when we left the scene of our sinking, proceeding southward, we found ourselves half an hour later at the northern entrance and able to see right across the harbour.

Three vessels were lying at anchor, close inshore. One of them was clearly the empty hulk of a large junk, but the other two were much more difficult to identify, being painted light grey and closer to the land. Blake and I began to have a nasty suspicion that they were submarine-chasers, and for a moment I lost my nerve, so much so that I ordered "Hard-a-starboard" to bring our nose pointing back towards the deeper water. However, on second thoughts we decided they were some kind of river gunboat or patrol vessel, and that having come so far and revealed our presence we must go ahead with the desperate enterprise. I therefore ordered gun action stations and kept the starboard helm on until we had come full circle back to our original course. The gun's crew had been fallen out after the previous action, but now came tumbling out of the hatches to take up their stations once more.

As we approached we observed great activity aboard the enemy ships and realised they were desperately trying to lift their anchors. One of them did in fact succeed in getting under way and turned towards us just before we opened fire at a range of 1,200 yards. This vessel was engaged first, hit and stopped with the third round, and after that every round was a hit. The enemy replied with machine-guns firing the alarming Japanese "clap-clap-clap" explosive bullets, which had at first so confused our troops in the retreat to Singapore, and with these bangs going off all round like Chinese crackers it was impossible to tell whether the firing was coming from the ships or the shore. Our shots were making a pretty good mess of the first patrol vessel, and presently the crew—all Japanese—began to leap overboard. As soon as we saw this we shifted aim to the second vessel, and after a bit of punishment her crew also took to the water. Further rounds were then fired at the first target and several water-line hits observed. Finally, as we swept past at a range of 400 yards, the second vessel was also punctured along the water-line.

At this point the breech-worker, Telegraphist Greenway, suddenly spun round as though kicked by a horse, and there was a cry of "Greenway's hit, sir!" from the gun's crew. I immediately sent him below, the second casualty for the Coxswain to look after within the hour. Fortunately, the action was in any case nearly over.

All this time I had been contending with the navigation of this constricted piece of water. I had no time to take bearings and put fixes on the chart, so there was nothing for it but to navigate by eye. As an extra precaution I ordered the echosounder to be started, with instructions that I was to be informed of the soundings every minute, or immediately they shortened to less than five fathoms. And what with the enemy machine-gun fire and watching the results of our own shots maneuvering the ship so as to bring the gun to bear with the best advantage, listening to the soundings coming up the voice-pipe, looking at the chart in the drenching rain to make sure we did not go aground, and passing my helm orders to the helmsman below, I was pretty busy.

Owing to the narrowness of the anchorage I considered it would be unwise to attempt to turn round and go back by the way we had come. When the gun could no longer be brought to bear, I broke off the action and set course to pass out through the southeastern exit. Before we could turn to port to make our getaway we had to go fairly close in to the shore on our starboard hand, and there under the trees by a large wooden hut we saw a group of Malays, women and children included, who waved gaily to us as we swept past them. Passing through the narrows towards more open water, we looked back at the anchorage in time to see the sinking of the second target; the other, which had received at least as much damage, was settling low in the water and would obviously be sinking very shortly.

These two successes had been achieved at a combined cost of only twenty-nine rounds of ammunition, not bad going in view of the opposition. It had all been very exhilarating, in spite of the torrential

rain and the navigational worries, but I was troubled
about Greenway; it turned out, however, that the bul-
let had passed straight through the fleshy part of his
right shoulder and left a clean wound with no complications; he was shortly able to resume his telegraphist duties, and when we reached harbour at the end
of the patrol, the wound, thanks to the Coxswain's
attention, was almost healed.

Not content with our two gun actions in the day,
we went off to look for more trouble, and found it:

1118 Set course southward on the surface to-
     wards King Island Sound. This involved
     crossing a six-mile patch of water too
     shallow for diving, but the risk was con-
     sidered worth while since it was intended
     to investigate the anchorage in King Is-
     land Sound, at the entrance to the Mergui
     River, before dark.

1334 Dived 9½ miles due north of King Island
     Sound and proceeded to close.

1615 Obtained a good view of the Sound and
     sighted it clear of shipping. A small fishing
     vessel was seen crossing the entrance.

1636 Sighted two landing craft proceeding
     down river from Mergui. One was ob-
     served to be armed with two light machine-
     guns, the other with one. Maneuvered for
     attack.

1700 Surfaced when both targets were in line
     and engaged the nearest one with gunfire
     at a range of approximately 1800 yards.
     This vessel turned stern on and showed
     no fight after we had obtained two near-

misses, but the other, the one armed with two machine-guns, turned towards and began firing. We had fired ten rounds at our first target, and were about to shift aim to meet this new menace, when the three-inch gun ceased fire, with the extractor apparently jammed open. The two Vickers guns opened fire successfully, but to my dismay the Oerlikon gunner could not get his weapon to fire. The three-inch failure was later discovered to be due to the new breech-worker (put in at the last moment to replace Greenway) holding down the breech-mechanism lever instead of releasing it, thus preventing the new shell from going home. The failure of the Oerlikon remains a mystery, as it was tried on the following day with the same magazine, and in subsequent gun actions never gave the slightest trouble.

1704 Not wishing to see my gun's crew mown down by the enemy fire, which was getting pretty hot by this time, I dived. Proceeded northwards at high speed for thirty seconds as deep as was safe (sixty feet). Half a minute after diving, much to my surprise, a depth-charge was dropped, followed by a second one five minutes later, the closest Storm has had yet. A few lights were put out, and one cockroach fell stunned on to the chart-table, but otherwise there was no damage. Our Japanese prisoner was very alarmed, and asked permission to visit the heads.

1711　In view of the navigational dangers, came to periscope depth shortly after the second depth-charge, to find one of the landing-craft ahead of me and the other astern. Decided, therefore, to escape through Iron Passage, the tide being on the ebb, and altered course westward accordingly. Neither of the enemy vessels seemed to be in asdic contact with me, and both eventually moved close in to the eastern shore of Iron Island, presumably hoping to be hidden against the land and tempt me into surfacing early.

1734　Iron Passage was successfully negotiated. The chart is correct in reporting "strong eddies"! The tide swept us through at a tremendous rate, and at one point the submarine was sucked down from periscope depth to sixty feet in a few seconds.

1830　Surfaced when clear of Ant Island and set course to pass round the north of Kabosa Island.

I now had a strong feeling that we had caused enough disturbance in the vicinity for the time being. In any case, the enemy would probably suspend the sailings of small craft for a few days and send out chasers to look for us. It would be advisable to spend a little time in the southern half of our huge area. That night, therefore, we shaped a course southward to pass outside the Mergui Archipelago until daylight, after which I intended to turn in among the islands and explore the inner channels as far as the Pakchan River, if possible on the surface.

There followed what were perhaps the most extraordinary two days of my submarine experience. From the time we turned in through Nearchus Passage to our emergence at the southern end of Forrest Strait, we moved everywhere on the surface, travelling freely among the innumerable islands, often in narrow waterways and always in full view of supposedly enemy-occupied territory. The absence of shipping in the inner channels of the archipelago, and the way we were able to proceed on the surface at will, even through Forrest Strait, were astonishing. We saw not a single aircraft. "It would even seem possible," I wrote in my patrol report, "for a large force of warships to approach the islands between Mergui and Pakchan unobserved, and to remain within their shelter unmolested perhaps for days on end. The islands appear to be largely uninhabited and contain numerous anchorages surrounded by steep-to hills."

Between some of the outer islands of the archipelago the seabed is in places only sparsely charted, so that on some courses we took a risk, like the old circumnavigators, of running onto uncharted rocks. In daylight, therefore, we always had a man posted on the periscope standards to keep a look-out for breakers, and by night we played for safety. Wherever possible, courses were set along lines of known soundings.

Moving still farther south, we spent two days patrolling dived off the Pakchan River in the hope of sighting small vessels carrying tin from the local mines, but without result. On July 28th we carried out a periscope reconnaissance of Hastings Harbour, an extensive anchorage formed by three islands which provided, by the looks of the chart, excellent shelter from both the southwest and the northeast monsoons, but although we had a good view into the anchorage through both eastern and northern entrances, no ships were seen, and we had to content ourselves with making panoramic sketches of both entrances through the periscope. That evening, having drawn blank for five days, I made up my mind to return to the Mergui area, and sent a signal to Trincomalee telling them of my intention to do so unless they had anything better to offer.

We had been steaming north for about four hours when we received their reply offering me the Puket area, farther south and outside my original patrol area, as an alternative if I wished. I immediately turned south, and informed them that I was doing so. Fourteen hours later yet another signal ordered us back to the northward again. It seemed they had new intelligence of some unspecified target arriving at the entrance to the Heinze Basin, to the north of Tavoy and again outside my area. All that night and the next day we travelled north, keeping just outside the islands, and at dawn on July 31st we were in position off the Heinze Basin. Here I soon came to the conclusion that it was not a good spot to wait for a target; in the prevailing bad visibility we could see the coastline only in patches, the shoaling water at the river-mouth making it impossible for us to patrol close in, and it would have been easy for a target to enter or leave the harbour unobserved by us. I accordingly began moving south, soon after midday, to patrol off the end of the Tavoy peninsula, where we could take up a better strategic position. The afternoon produced nothing, but we patrolled the same spot during the night, no more than two miles off shore, and on the following morning, August 1st, reaped our reward.

The alarm sounded at 0442. I shot out of my bunk and up to the bridge to find Number One and the for'ard look-out, Petty Officer Blight, peering to seaward through their binoculars. It was still dark, but the rain had stopped. Blight had seen a small light flicker for an instant in the darkness, and now Number One said he thought he could make out a black shape on the same bearing. A few moments later I could see it myself, a south-bound modern coaster with funnel aft.

I spoke into the voice-pipe. "Control-room ... *Gun action!* Tell the men to move as silently as possible. Anything from radar yet? Tell the operator we have a target bearing Green 40, range about 1,500 yards."

The gun-hatch opened quietly just below the front of the bridge, and the men climbed out on to the gun-platform in their sandalled feet, moving about the deck on tiptoe like a gang of conspirators; some came up the conning-tower and swung themselves quietly over the side of the bridge. Blake stood on the little raised step and in a low voice passed his orders down to the men round the gun.

There was still no report from radar. How I cursed the temperamental nature of this wonderful new invention! The set had so far given good results during the patrol and been a great assistance to the navigation, but now, on the first occasion when we badly needed an accurate range for a night gun action, it could not find the target which we knew was there.

I had in fact underestimated the size, and so the range, of the coaster, and consequently many rounds were wasted before we got our first hit.

The first crack of our gun seemed a desecration of the silence. In the darkness Blake could not see where the shot fell; it was not on the target, so he could only assume it had dropped short and raise the range by 200 yards. Another difficulty was that the gunlayer could not yet see the target and was obliged to lay his open sight on the muzzy line where he imagined the horizon to be. Our second round also whined away into the night and fell without visible trace, and it was not until the sixth or seventh round that we saw the little orange flash and heard the muffled *crumph* which indicated our first hit. After that we continued to hit the enemy with nearly every round. He came slowly to a dead stop, and then just sat there taking our pounding in silence. It was like murder, but our job was to sink enemy supply ships. By this time the dawn was coming up, and in the early light we saw that he was a steel ship, fairly new, and larger than I had originally thought. I put him at about 350 tons. We continued to pump shells into him until, after the expenditure of fifty rounds, he sank at last, going down slowly by the stern.

We had no time to stop to see if there were any survivors, for the vessel had hardly disappeared under the water when we sighted another ship on the horizon to the northward coming towards us in the gradually increasing light. We at once dived and ran towards him at full speed. I wanted to reach him before he was put on his guard by sighting the debris of the first sinking.

He turned out to be a small wooden two-masted

motor schooner of about 100 tons. When he was passing our position we surfaced and fired a round ahead of him, hoping he would stop and abandon ship. Instead, he increased speed and turned towards the shore with the obvious intention of trying to beach himself. I also speeded up, altered course to head him off, and resumed the attack. The crew soon jumped overboard, but the vessel kept on and did not slow down for some minutes. Closing to short range we poured into him a burst of Oerlikon fire which set the wooden hull ablaze from stem to stern, but although we riddled him with holes along the water-line with the three-inch gun we could not sink him. Finally I gave up the attempt and went alongside with the intention of placing a demolition charge for'ard. However, we could then see that he was thoroughly on fire below decks, and decided to leave him to burn himself out. He sank all right in the end, for when we came back to the same spot later in the day we could find no trace of him.

There were several heads dotting the water. I had previously decided that we would take one other prisoner, but no more; passenger space below was very limited. Again we found the Japanese were not anxious to be picked up, but we rescued an Indian who (unfortunately for the Coxswain) turned out to be suffering from two nasty wounds. As we began to withdraw from the scene our attention was attracted by a young Malay swimming a little apart from the others and waving and shouting in great excitement. I did not want to take on any more passengers, but I was impressed with the look of this lad and his obvious desire to be picked up, so in spite of Number One's ill-concealed disapproval I maneuvered close to him and took him on board. The Coxswain was even more disapproving when this man too was found to be wounded in the thigh: he now had four patients to look after.

However, I was very glad we had picked up this boy, whose name was Endi. He was extremely friendly and cooperative, and claimed to have been at the Malay RNVR Training School in Singapore before the Japanese arrived. In spite of his wound he was full of spirit, and delighted to be a prisoner of the British, even declaring that he would now be able to join the British Navy. He had been one of the quartermasters in the little ship we had just attacked, the *Kikaku Maru*, bound from Rangoon to Mergui with a cargo of rice. The crew consisted of the Captain, the First Mate, the Chief Engineer—all Japanese—and five Malays, two Chinese, and one or two Indians. When we surfaced and opened fire, he said, all the Malays in the crew went to the wheelhouse and tried to persuade the Japanese officer to stop and abandon ship. The officer shot four of the Malays out of hand, and compelled Endi to remain at the wheel and obey his orders. A moment later one of our shells hit the wheelhouse and blew him and the Jap overboard in opposite directions. Endi spoke excellent English, and later volunteered much useful information.

Meanwhile I decided to shift patrol northwards, a few miles along the coast. This last action had taken place within a short distance of the shore, and it was possible that the Japs had a look-out post at this focal point on the coastal traffic route. We ran for an hour or so on the surface and then dived fairly close inshore, just to the south of Oyster Island.

Nearly three hours later another coaster, of about

250 tons, was seen approaching from the north. I let him pass as usual, and surfaced for gun action astern of him. When I reached the bridge, machine-gun bullets were flying all round us and the enemy had turned in an attempt to ram. However, he soon changed his mind when our first shell demolished his bridge and a devastating fire from our Oerlikon and Vickers guns poured into him and set him ablaze. The crew, mostly Japanese, panicked and jumped overboard, and the vessel stopped, stricken and deserted. Soon the stern had slumped until the deck was awash, but then refused to sink any further despite all our efforts. Suddenly, while all this was going on, one of the look-outs called my attention to another vessel, coming towards us from the south. I immediately called off the action, dived, and proceeded towards this fresh target at high speed. This time I did not see how, if he was keeping a proper look-out, the new arrival could fail to sum up the situation ahead of him.

However, to my great relief, on looking astern five minutes later I found that our late target had finally sunk, leaving the usual mess of wreckage floating on the spot. The new target, a fine, new-looking coaster of about 300 tons, was still coming on, apparently unaware that anything was wrong. Once more I let him pass and then surfaced astern of him. Our first round went over him, the second splintered his bridge into a mass of wreckage. Figures were running for'ard to man the machine-gun mounted on the forecastle, but they never had a chance. Our third shell hit the deck in front of the bridge and set the ship on fire with an oily, billowing flame and high clouds of black smoke. This was the signal for the crew to abandon ship. We fired nine more rounds, until the whole ship was a writhing inferno. It was a most satisfactory result for the expenditure of only twelve shells, and as we were now running short of ammunition (only twelve more shells remaining in our magazine), I decided to cease fire and let the flames do their work.

At this point Number One asked to speak to me on the voice-pipe. It seemed that Endi believed our target to be an ammunition ship and urged me not to approach too close to it. I took his advice and retired to a safer distance. The information was correct. Shortly afterwards the vessel began to produce a succession of muffled explosions, bursts of enormous flame, shooting debris, and great columns of black smoke. This was such a wonderful firework display that I gave permission for the whole of *Storm*'s crew to come up on the bridge, two at a time, to enjoy the spectacle, which continued for the best part of an hour while we cruised backwards and forwards on the surface in full view of the shore. When the target sank at last we turned away southwards once more, and sat down to a long delayed lunch.

When I turned in that night and tried to sleep, visions of blazing ships came floating towards me in endless succession. But the patrol was nearly over. We had received our recall signal the evening before, and the following afternoon, August 2nd, we left the billet for the homeward voyage.

We now had altogether four prisoners on board, all of whom presented certain problems. Three of them were wounded and needed constant attention, a duty which fell to the Coxswain and proved to be such a full-time job that we had to relieve him of his watch-keeping. Besides these prisoners he had Greenway to look after. Poor Selby loathed this work, the tending of the torn flesh inducing in him a physical revulsion, yet so well did he perform it that two of his patients were soon able to get up and move about, and by the time we reached Trincomalee all the wounds were healing nicely. The MO in *Maidstone* said he had done a professional job. The fourth prisoner was the Jap. Altogether, we had him on card for a fortnight. He was not wounded, but we could not allow him to wander about the submarine of his own free will. He lived and ate in the fore-ends, with an armed sentry guarding him day and night, which meant that the watches were always short of one man. However, he gave no trouble. From a photograph of himself found in his wallet, we discovered that he was a soldier, not a sailor as we had imagined; presumably he had been taking passage to Rangoon when captured. Other articles found in his wallet were Japanese occupation currency notes, and two Chinese postage stamps. Besides the wallet, we removed from his person a Swiss-made watch, a key, a string containing wooden strips with inscriptions, and a folded paper chart bearing mysterious circles and probably representing a charm or prayer diagram. Every morning he was made to scrub the decks throughout the boat, and he did this job without complaining and more thoroughly than my own sailors. He was a little inclined to curiosity, and in the control-room would cast his eyes around at what was going on; once I caught him glancing at the chart-table as he passed it, and angrily sent him packing with an unwonted torrent of abusive language. At first I was taken aback by his hissing at me every time he came near me, but eventually tumbled to the fact that this was the Japanese indrawn-breath mark of respect. He spoke, apparently, almost no English, but the seamen for'ard discovered that his home town was Kobe and that he seemed to think we operated from Calcutta. In view of the language difficulty I decided not to interrogate this prisoner, as my questions might prejudice the official interrogation later.

The Malay whom we had picked up from the same ship became very friendly after recovering from his wound and his initial shock, and frequently volunteered for work in the engine-room. He lived aft in the stokers' mess and proved himself an expert draughts player. But he did not really like submarine life; it was a terrible shock to him when he discovered we were still off Mergui a whole week after his capture, for we had travelled so many miles in the meantime that he thought we must be nearing base.

The Indian survivor from the second coaster of August 1st spoke practically no English, had two nasty wounds, and seemed to be rather unhappy. He appeared to think he was going to be shot. It was obviously useless to attempt an interrogation.

On the other hand, the Malay lad Endi was only too eager to answer questions. He told us that the coasters travelling from Mergui to Rangoon usually carried ammunition and filled up with rice for the return trip; there was a large ammunition dump just north of Pakchan, the ammunition being transported thence to Mergui by rail; it seemed there was a good deal of traffic on this railway. He said that in place of balloon barrages the Japanese had stretched wires between the peaks of hills in the vicinity of Mergui and

Penang, that two American bombers had recently been brought down by this means and that the crews were now prisoners in the hands of the Japs. He also said the Japanese were laying traps in some of their junks in the Malacca Straits, the practice being to leave one man on board who would try to lob a hand-grenade down the conning tower as the submarine went along-side, while the remainder of the crew would pretend to abandon ship and leap overboard on the opposite side after fusing an explosive charge to scuttle the vessel and damage the submarine as well. When he was last in Singapore, about five months earlier, he had ob-served several Japanese warships: a battleship, three destroyers, three submarines, and some two-man sub-marines. He believed there were two torpedo-boats in Mergui. (We met one of these in our next patrol.) I was not sure how much of all this to believe. He was so anxious to please that he might have been inventing, or exaggerating, perhaps unconsciously, in order to produce information he thought we wanted to hear. I felt inclined to take some of it with a pinch of salt; on the other hand, none of it seemed to be the sort of thing anyone would make up.

We reached Trincomalee on August 7th. Going alongside *Maidstone*, with our black Jolly Roger flying from the periscope standards and spangled with seven new stars to represent our gun actions, we received a great welcome. We had the distinction of being the first submarine to bring back a Japanese prisoner, and tre-mendous curiosity was aroused by the sight of our pas-sengers being marched up the gangway ladder.

At the conclusion of my patrol report I was glad to be able to add the following general remarks:

1. The plentiful opportunities for gun action were seized on with avidity by the gun's crew and were popular with the entire ship's company. I wish to commend my Gunnery Control Officer, Lieutenant R. L. Blake, R.N., for his coolness and skill in conducting the shoots; also my Gun-layer, Acting Leading Seaman W. Taylor, for his accuracy, determination and spirit during the actions; and indeed the whole gun's crew for their coolness under enemy fire, even when one of their number was wounded.

2. I also wish to commend my Coxswain, Acting Chief Petty Officer F. Selby, for his skilful and patient attention to the wounded, one of whom was an unpleasant sight when brought on board.

3. During the patrol a total of over 4,000 miles was registered. The fact that during this long mileage the Main Engines were kept running without any serious defect arising reflects, in my opinion, great credit on the Engine Room staff as a whole, and in particular on my Engineer Officer, Mr W. H. Ray, Warrant Engineer, and the Chief E.R.A., R. Brown.

The only dissatisfied man was Dicky Fisher, who had had no opportunity of bringing his boarding party into action.

FIRST BLOOD

FROM *Pigboat 39: An American Sub Goes to War*

by Bobette Gugliotta

$\mathcal{T}$he world of submarines is dominated by men, but our next excerpt was written by a woman, and contains all of the excitement and danger of anything written by submarine captains and crewmen in the last seventy years. Bobette Gugliotta is the wife of former Navy crewman Guy Gugliotta, who sailed on the practically obsolete submarine *S-39* during its combat patrols in 1941, both before and after the Japanese attack on Pearl Harbor. Back home on Long Island, she also tells of life on the homefront, and of the particular burden of being a submariner's wife as she joins the women's volunteer services. She also wrote young adult fiction, a biography of Nolle Smith, and a history of the women of Mexico from the sixteenth through the nineteenth centuries.

Combat aboard a submarine is often difficult enough, but trying to fight the enemy aboard a leaking sixteen-year-old submarine with obsolete equipment brings new terrors to a crew every day. Despite the hazards of the job, the men aboard the "pigboat" *S-39* made do with what they had, and even found time to play practical jokes during their downtime, and explore the Philippines, where they were based. But when they are called to fight, the *S-39*'s crew is just as dedicated and driven to take the war to the enemy as any other submariners in the U.S. Navy.

Several attempts to better living conditions in port had been made by August of 1941, although there would not be much time left to enjoy the changes. At long last, enlisted men were given a club of their own, where they could have a drink without paying more than it was worth and without having a hostess sent over to double the costs. The club was in a new building on the Manila waterfront, constructed by the Philippine Commonwealth and rented by the U.S. If a man took on a load, or grew belligerent, he was less likely to end up in hot water than if he'd thrown a punch in a bar in town. No officer could use the facility unless invited by an enlisted man.

Submarine officers were allotted quarters in Manila free of charge. Each large, three-man room at the University Apartments came equipped with a bath, refrigerator, writing desk, couch, and Chinese maintenance help. The officers couldn't believe their luck—which lasted for a couple of months. Then, while the submarines were put to sea, the rooms were taken over by newly arrived reserve officers, and the disgruntled submariners traipsed back to the *Canopus*. Their quarters ashore were restored just in time for them to deposit their civilian clothes, golf clubs, and other gear and leave it all for the enemy.

Endless practice for warfare without actuality kept nerves on edge. The dives were long and tiring, watchstanding and workload had reached the reversed proportion of 16 hours on and 8 off. The submarines were now going to sea with torpedoes prepared as war shots, making realistic practice patrols with a full load in the torpedo tubes. There had been a few lemons in the crew, but Red Coe got rid of them; he might have far from perfect equipment, but knew he had excellent men. The captain was expecting orders in December but was aware that war might arrive before his orders did.

Larry Bernard, also counting the days, prayed that the conflagration would hold off until after January, which was his time to leave. His ulcers began acting up again. The skipper came down with a case of intestinal flu right after he wrote Rachel not to count on his being home for Christmas, and everybody noticed that his guts improved before his disposition did. Gugliotta had no hope at all of getting out before the explosion. He alternated between the comforting knowledge on the one hand that 39 was the best boat around and that his fitness report stated "would particularly desire to have him on board under wartime conditions," and the dreary realization on the other that his bride could be an old lady before he saw her again. To kick the blues, he went to a Chinese restaurant for fried *lapu lapu,* which he liked; saw the movie *Kitty Foyle* with Ginger Rogers, which he didn't like; then pigged it on candy bars, which he had never liked. Monk Hendrix, as a bachelor recently arrived, was less impatient, although his fitness routine accelerated.

Even the weather, seldom good, was extra capricious. Typhoons rolled in one after another with such fury that *S-39* was often forced to stand regular sea watches when in port. At times they had to leave *Canopus* and anchor separately because the boats banged against each other so hard in the wind that they couldn't stay moored. But the most obvious display of tension lay in the increase of nitpicking arguments. No statement, no matter how unimportant, went unchallenged. One afternoon in the crew's mess Bixler was describing the route from Olongapo to Manila. He declared, "The bus turns right as soon as you leave the gate and heads past the rifle range. Then in the valley you go straight until—"

"Oh no you don't," Nave, who had just come in, interrupted. "You forget that the goddamn bus makes a complete circle before reaching Subic and—"

"Fujigit, that's the Manila bus when it's going to Olongapo. What the hell do you know?" Bixler and Nave were now nose to nose, spit-spray from shouting mouths fogging the atmosphere. Half a dozen other guys joined in until the din reached epic proportions, and Schoenrock, very testy lately, pounded the counter with a soup ladle, yelling, "Shut up, you bastards. I don't need that flack in the galley." It worked, they all calmed down.

The cook had been sour on the whole bunch for some time. First, there was the monkey somebody picked up in Tawitawi and brought on board for a pet. His antics amused everybody except Schoenrock. With the seventh sense an animal has when somebody dislikes him, the monkey loved to wrap his tail around the overhead pipes in the galley and dip his bony fingers into Rocky's most beautiful creations, or carefully put a tooth through each cigarette in a pack the cook left on the counter before pushing them neatly back into the package. Then, when the cook wanted to enjoy a smoke, he couldn't get one lit no matter how many he tried. When Rocky discovered what was causing it, he went right to Coe with an ultimatum: "Either the monkey goes or I go." The captain responded by handing the monkey over to the Filipino crew of the laundry *banca*, but a few hours later the critter returned to his home away from home. He had leaped over the side of the *banca* and swum back to the 39. It took some doing to remove him permanently.

The antics of the little beast hadn't helped Schoenrock's sense of humor. One morning Allyn Christopher noticed Schab tucking one of the cook's huge, melt-in-your-mouth pancakes inside the front of his shirt. Christopher nudged his friend. "What goes, you saving pancakes for the long cold winter ahead?"

Schab chuckled. "When Rocky's napping after lunch, come to the galley."

Christopher wouldn't have missed it for the world. When Schab sneaked back to the cook's sacrosanct territory, along with Pennell, Matthews, and electrician's mate C.I. Peterson, Allyn followed them in.

"Hurry up," Schab whispered, "we gotta work fast. Sometimes he's only gone for ten minutes or so." Pennell hoisted a bucket full of lead weights onto the counter while Peterson climbed up on a chair and secured a strong wire to the overhead. Then Schab held up the stolen pancake, and Peterson carefully ran the wire through it, fastening the bucket of weights to the end. Everybody snickered. It looked as though a heavy-as-lead pancake were supporting the heavy-with-lead bucket.

Matthews, who wasn't big but had the appetite of a lion, thought of the future: "Rocky's not gonna like this." Zeke's motto was don't bite the hand that feeds you. The other clowns paid no attention. Tayco, bringing back a tray of dishes from the officer's mess, took one astounded look at the suspended flapjack and backed out of the galley, muttering, "I no want to be here when he see this."

Allyn went through the boat rousing up an audience; even the officers got wind of it, so that when Schoenrock walked into the silent galley, rubbing sleep out of his eyes and smoothing his tousled hair, there were many witnesses to his shame. His eyes circled the crowd, then caught the abomination hanging in his galley. Everybody guffawed. Rocky's mouth trembled, then spewed, "You're a bunch of goddamn ungrateful bastards. After all I've done for you." People would swear later that he had tears in his eyes as big as crabapples.

And, as if that wasn't enough, there was the boxing match. Mike Kutscherowski, the 39's peaceloving pugilist who became a killer only in the ring, had made it all the way to the finals for the middleweight championship, the culmination of the Army-Navy, all-Asiatic boxing meets. It was to be refereed by the former Naval Academy heavyweight champ, Moon Chappie. Betting was heavy, and the excitement had a tonic effect on tempers badly needing diversion. In the crew's mess, many men were promising Kutscherowski all kinds of treats if he won the title, to all of whom the good-natured fisticuffs expert made the same reply, "I'll do the best I can."

Schoenrock, a long-time devotee of the manly art, came up with what he considered the ultimate inducement. "Ski," he proclaimed, "I promise to cook you a deluxe dinner of your own selection if you win. You—can—have—any—thing—you—want." He paused between words to hammer into the boxer's scarred head the full implications of his offer. "Filet mignon, chicken

poached in wine, salmon with hollandaise." Kutscherowski's eyes bulged with the strain of trying to figure
out what the fancy names meant. "I'll do my best," he
said again earnestly.

The match took place on *Canopus* at an affair
called a smoker. It lived up to its name because everybody smoked like crazy: cigars, cigarettes, pipes, most
of which had been handed out free for advertising
purposes. A blue pall hung over the ring accentuating
the heat and humidity. Kutscherowski won. The 39
people went mad, shouting and screaming, pounding
each other on the back, collecting money, and making
plans to come through on all promises made to their
champion. Schoenrock waited for the tumult to subside; then, with his customary dignity, told the sweating boxer, "Ski, when you're ready for that victory
dinner, let me know what you want and when you
want it."

The champ's voice was still hoarse from his efforts.
"Gee whiz, Rocky, you know what I like best in the
world?"

"No matter, I'll make it for you," Rocky assured
him.

"I dunno why I like 'em. It just makes me feel good.
I never ate nothing like it back in the States. I think it
builds up my muscles." Ski's handler was untying the
gloves now. "I'd really appreciate a whole box fulla
papayas all to myself, but cold, see. I like 'em chilled."

The cook blanched. It was the final insult. How
could anyone prefer a plain product of Mother Nature to a consummately contrived dish conceived by a
master chef? Pennell tried to soften the blow. Knowing how much Rocky hated defrosting the ship's refrigerator, a job that came around all too often because

of the rapid build-up of ice from tropic heat and humidity, Pennell volunteered to do it for him. (The machinist's mate had devised a quick method; pumping hot gas through the evaporator coils caused the big accumulations of ice to fall off in minutes. It may have been the forerunner of automatic defrost.) But even Pennell's offer couldn't get a smile out of the disconsolate cook.

Rocky and Stowaway Johnson decided to go out anyways, and hang one on in celebration of the victory. During the course of the raucous evening, the cook offered to pay for any tattoo that Johnson wanted to add to his already picturesque collection—that is, if he could find space somewhere on his hide. Johnson located an empty upper arm and promptly had it embellished with three horse's heads whose nostrils flared realistically when he flexed his biceps. Not to be outdone and drunk enough not to care, the usually more conservative Rocky had a coolie and rickshaw tattooed on his thigh. Both men ordered tricolored jobs. Tops in flashy flesh.

A bright spot in the marking-time period was Fabricante's good luck. One morning he came aboard and said to Gugliotta, the duty officer, "Sair, I need to leave early. If you will say so today."

Gugliotta looked down at the tiny mess steward who seemed as pleasant, neatly dressed, and unruffled as usual. "I think that can be arranged. Any particular problem?"

"No, sair, no problem. I need only to put 5,000-peso check in bank." The ensign's mouth fell open. "Good grief, Fabricante, did you discover a gold mine?"

"No, sair," the little man was smiling now, "I won fourth place lottery."

Gugliotta did some rapid calculation. Five thousand pesos translated into $2,500 American, a sum worth having in anybody's language. "Congratulations, Fabricante, what are you going to do with all that money?"

"Well, sair, first I like for you to have this," Fabricante held out a 20-peso note, "half for you, other half for Mr. Hendrix."

Gugliotta stalled as he sought a way to refuse without hurting the generous mess steward's feelings. "Tell you what, Fabricante, you hang on to that money for now, and sometime soon Mr. Hendrix and I would be real glad to have you buy us a drink."

Fabricante agreed. When he deposited his check, the Philippine government only took 90 pesos in taxes. Presumably the Japanese government got the rest.

As tension mounted during the month of November 1941, the men of the 39 boat listened constantly to Manila radio station KZRF, which broadcast news in many languages. It did not have much to report that was encouraging, especially with the sinking by U-boat, in October, of the U.S. destroyer *Reuben James*, further straining relations with Germany. They also read the Manila *Daily Bulletin* with great care. One of the columnists got a lot of horse laughs when he said it would be ridiculous to expect a German invasion of Russia. But what really pissed them off was such statements from U.S. congressmen as, "Our navy will clean out the Japanese fleet in two weeks and burn up the island of Japan in one night," when they knew how their engineers sometimes had to work round the clock because the 39's engines had not been overhauled for a year and a half. There were leaks in the main ballast tanks and she often limped back to port on one engine. Her deepest dive, about 160 feet, always provoked leaks at various hull fittings. To keep everybody on his toes and the boat in readiness, Coe had called weekly inspections since the month of July. But if you can't make a silk purse out of a sow's ear, he certainly couldn't make a mechanically reliable vessel out of the patchwork pigboat.

At times the skipper became personally involved in the dirty work necessary to keep the prima donna functioning. One day during a torpedo firing run off Corregidor, Pennell, checking the motor room bilge, saw water coming in fast between the main motors, and 39 surfaced immediately for safety's sake. Before a hull inspection could be made to locate and assess the extent of the leak, equipment removal was necessary to dry out the narrow space. When everything was ready, Coe waved away other candidates and took on the job himself.

The captain kicked off his moulting straw sandals, hitched up his shorts, and motioned to Pennell to remove the metal floor plates. The welded grillwork beneath scarcely allowed a body the size of Coe's to insert itself into the motor-room bilge. In addition, the area was scummy-crummy with ancient grease and stagnant water that smelled like a dismal swamp. Down on hands and knees now, he asked Pennell to hang on to his ankles. The low pressure pump was at work cleaning the bilges, but noses wrinkled in sympathy as the redhead disappeared through the grillwork to probe for the leak below. Nobody could claim they had a skipper who balked at a dirty job.

On the brighter side, Pennell, who generally got

along with machinery better than with people, had so far been successfully nursing the important compressors. There were two in the motor room to jam air into the bank of flasks. This air was used to start the main engines and to blow out the main ballast tanks when surfacing. It was also necessary as a general source of power to operate certain equipment and to move water between the auxiliary ballast tanks. And in an emergency requiring prolonged submergence, such as wartime conditions or mechanical difficulties, it would be needed to replenish air for breathing.

The main engines were used to charge the batteries. During this operation the air compressors were run by clutching them onto the propeller shafts. When Pennell first arrived, he noticed that the process dragged on much too long; common sense and basic arithmetic told him the compressors were running at about 30 percent efficiency. He decided to do some overhauling on his own and found the Corliss intake valves way out of tune. His work brought the air compressors up to approximately 75 percent, a most important improvement considering the essential services performed by them. Blessings like these were carefully counted because the possibility of a complete overhaul for 39 matched the prognosis for peace in the Far East.

For many months Admiral Thomas Hart had been viewing with alarm the tendency of certain important U.S. politicians to make well-publicized, threatening speeches against the Japanese. He is on record as having written, "Nothing is ever gained by threatening the Japanese, their psychology being such that threats are likely to wholly prevent their exercise of correct judgment. Furthermore, such threats . . . tended to put the Japanese too much on guard against the preparations for war which were then being made in the Far East."

Hart did as much as possible with the limited material at hand to anticipate a surprise attack. Foreseeing the probable loss of Manila Bay, the admiral ordered the tenders to load all the spare ammunition, torpedoes, parts, and provisions they could carry. More torpedoes were stored in the tunnel allotted to the navy on Corregidor. Subic Bay and Manila Bay were mined, and by the end of November the tenders *Otus* and *Holland* had arrived, as well as a number of large fleet-type submarines from Pearl Harbor, bringing the total to 29 in the Asiatic Fleet; only the original six S-boats were vintage variety.

By 26 November the admiral had received a Navy Department dispatch indicating very serious developments in American-Japanese relationships. On the 27th an all-night practice blackout was ordered in the city of Manila. On the 29th there was a definite war warning from the Navy Department. This was the day of the Army-Navy game, traditionally a slack-off period for the services both at home and in far-flung places like the China Station. Celebrations had been known to go on and on, and there were some who thought the Japanese might choose this time to launch their offensive. They didn't.

By Monday, 1 December, *S-39* was underway for operations off the southern tip of Luzon near Masbate Island. Three or four men were arguing the merits of various night spots in Manila, Nave's foghorn voice claiming to have eaten frog legs bigger than chicken legs at the Arcade Cafe. In the officer's wardroom, Gugliotta and Bernard were involved in a hot game of cribbage. Between rounds, Gugliotta was describing a Saturday night dance in one of the more remote towns on Luzon. When he and some others got back to Aparri from a hike, they were lured by the squeaky sounds of a four-piece band coming out of a shed. Peering in, they were immediately welcomed and led onto the dance floor by local Filipinas.

"The band never stopped playing," Guy explained, "but the end of a dance was signaled by an old gent ringing a bell. He also chalked up the number of dances each of us had, then charged us ten centavos a dance. But the big event of the evening was eating *baluts*, unborn chicks in the shell. A soft boiled egg was cracked so that part of the shell could be removed, exposing the ugly and smelly chick. The woman I watched very delicately bit off a black glob, which turned out to be the head, then pulled off a tiny wing covered with feathers and ate it bones and all. She disposed of the remainder in one bite. Meanwhile, naked kids were standing around with big, hopeful eyes, and the woman finally gave one of them the empty half-shell. The kid slurped down the juice, then dug a gob of yellowy green stuff out of the bottom . . ."

"That's enough," Larry Bernard yelled. "You'll make my ulcers act up again."

Coe, who had come into the wardroom at the finale, said with a straight face, "Next time we go to Aparri, I'll challenge all of you to a *balut*-eating contest."

When the *39* anchored in Masbate Harbor, the quixotic Philippine weather had decided to be kind in the midst of the rainy season, but a shimmer of stars flung across the sky blinked and often went out as rain clouds scudded by. The topside of the old submarine was covered with canvas cots on which reclining bodies were flaked out. Most were clad only in skivvies to take advantage of cooling breezes on the prickly heat that never cleared completely.

In the wardroom, duty officer Hendrix dreamed of the day he would find the report of his selection for lieutenant junior grade in the official mail or maybe by dispatch. Gugliotta had received his commission just before leaving Manila, so Monk was now the only ensign. Drawing a pad of paper toward him, he decided to write a long overdue letter to his father. "I'm learning a lot of good submarine and am used to it now when the boat flops" (Monk's term for a dive). He had just finished explaining that the mail clippers had to navigate a latitude right through the center of the typhoon area, and wouldn't run unless sure of clear weather all the way, when he dozed off. He was awakened by a loud, "Sir, sir, Mr. Hendrix, sir."

It was 0330, 8 December. Pennell's urgent tone of voice snapped Monk's head up. As he read the words of the message, he jumped to his feet, as wide awake as though he were about to hit a home run. "Take this to the captain immediately," he said.

Pennell had been on watch in the machinery spaces and had just made one tour through the boat when Radioman Bill Harris handed him the message that now sent him scrambling up the hatch with all speed, Hendrix at his heels. Picking his way among the bodies on deck, he spied the red hair of his skipper as the clouds parted; it was the last time for a long time that any man on 39 would welcome a bright night. As soon as Coe read the historic words, "Japan has started hostilities, govern yourselves accordingly," he told Hendrix, "Make all preparations to get underway." Pennell was ordered to rouse the sleepers at once and to strip the lifelines, benches, stanchions—items that fell into the unnecessary or personal-convenience class. Their elimination would reduce noise while the boat was submerged, increase speed, and dispose of white elephants that could be blasted loose by depthcharging, float to the surface, and disclose the boat's position.

By the time the second message came from CINCAF (Commander-in-Chief Asiatic Fleet), about 15 minutes later, "Submarines and aircraft will wage unrestricted warfare," all personnel and cots were stowed away below. In 11 minutes more, *39* was underway for her patrol area; by 0445 they had rigged ship for dive, which took place at 0700 much to everybody's relief. Although nobody spelled it out, a submerged submarine in broad daylight was much more reassuring than one on the surface, especially when you were new at the war game and didn't know when the enemy might pop up. Larry Bernard kept telling himself, It can't be true, it can't be true, even though he and all the others had been expecting it for over a year. A feeling of unreality was strong among officers and men.

Their designated patrol area was San Bernardino Strait, about 40 miles from Masbate Harbor. As soon as the ship submerged, the radioman became the sound man. The equipment used was near-obsolete hydrophone (underwater sound) listening equipment. Harris was listening hard as they made their way when he caught the su-woosh, su-woosh of propellers and reported, "Ship noises, possible screws on the port quarter."

Gugliotta, OOW (officer of the watch), ordered, "Up periscope," and soon sighted the masts of a small ship about three miles away. He called the captain, and Coe, after taking a look, ordered, "40 feet"; at shallower depth he hoped to make out her type and size.

"It's a small cargo ship," he said, "but she's flying no flag. Take stations for Battle Surface but don't fire the deck gun right away. I want the signalman to bring up the searchlight and ask the vessel's identity."

Battle Surface was made, and as the dripping wet participants catapulted out, it was easy to see by their eager-cautious-fearful expressions that 39 did not have a blasé, hardened crew. The captain gave nothing away except by frequent tugs at his cap, even though the sun was not in his eyes. The signalman blinked "Who are you?" at the merchantman in international code but received no answer. The little vessel went right on going. Coe ordered, "Fire a shot across her bow."

This brought the desired result. The ship stopped immediately, hoisted her flag, and identified herself by searchlight as the SS *Montanez* of Philippine registry. Gun and gun crew were secured, and 39 submerged. Were they disappointed? Yes and no. At 1740 they surfaced and started battery charge. That was the first day.

The Japanese saw to it that the 39 quickly got used to being at war. On 11 December the boat picked up enemy masts 12 miles to eastward just prior to darkness. They had been hearing the distant boom of depth charges all day, but now an advance screen of enemy destroyers began heavy, random depth-charging while

Japanese cargo and troop ships made their way westward toward Albay Gulf. The explosions came closer and closer, and though 39 was pretty sure she was not being specifically tracked, she knew that a depth charge that found its target accidentally was just as lethal as one that found it on purpose. Pennell, whose Battle Station was in the motor room by himself, had noticed on the chart that the water depth in the area was 666 feet. Not given to flights of fancy, he had a sudden vision of one of the shattering crashes finding its mark and could feel the pigboat dropping, dropping, dropping to the depths, crushed like an eggshell with all hands aboard. When the session ended, those men who had been having trouble believing that a real war was in progress had become convinced.

With no fix since noon, meaning no chance to locate position by taking sights of celestial bodies or bearings of land or other charted objects, they did not know within a few miles where they were when they surfaced that night. The weather didn't help. Hendrix, OOD, was looking through his binoculars when he said to Quartermaster Rollins, "Take a look over there to the east."

"I see what you mean, sir, it looks like a submarine," the quartermaster said tersely, then turning to the lookouts asked, "What do you guys think?"

The two lookouts, training their binoculars on the same spot, said simultaneously, "I agree with that," becoming twins in the stress of the moment. "Okay," Hendrix said, "call the captain."

Coe was topside lickety-split, binoculars focused on the same location while rain beat down heavily. He didn't hesitate long. "Make ready number one and two torpedo tubes!" he said.

The two fish were fired, and everybody waited for the detonation. There was none. In the dark, and without navigational aids, they might have fired upon an object far beyond the limited range of the torpedoes, or a much larger mass whose distant outlines made it resemble a submarine close by. Charging batteries and running on the surface, Coe went close enough to discover, with the help of charts, that he had wasted two torpedoes by firing at Cajogan Island off the north coast of Samar. The novitiate had not yet ended.

By this time Japanese merchantmen as well as a considerable naval force were coming into Albay Gulf. Enemy transports and cargo vessels had no naval escorts until they were some ten miles northeast of Ungay Point, where destroyers out of Albay rendezvoused with them at dawn. The war was only five days old, but the men of the 39 felt as though they'd been seeing enemy masts for months without being able to do anything about them. At 0413, 13 December, S-39 was surfaced when she sighted an enemy submarine close aboard. This time it was real. The 39 dove immediately, but dark and rain resulted in zero visibility; she was unable to attack. Frustration was still the order of the day. And then came a little game of hide-and-seek as the Japanese sub began tracking by active sonar, which S-boats did not have. Sound waves sent by oscillator pinged against the old pigboat and echoed back; by calculating the amount of time it took to send and receive the signal, the enemy sonar could ascertain the range.

Then suddenly, at 0550, Hendrix, on the periscope in the control room, said excitedly to the messenger, "Call the captain. I've got a target out here on the port bow," and to Quartermaster Rollins, "Mark the bearing, range about 12,000 yards; down periscope."

Rollins responded, "Bearing 345 relative. I'm starting a plot."

Hendrix said, "Left full rudder, steady on course 005." At this point Coe walked in wearing only skivvy pants and the disintegrating sandals. He had been trying to grab a few minutes' rest. His blue eyes blinked away sleep rapidly as he said, "What's up?" Hendrix briefed him fast and told him he was heading for the target. Coe's face, bristling with blond stubble, lost its tired look. Larry Bernard had come in to take control of the dive.

"Pass the word Battle Stations Submerged," Coe said, then to Larry, "Come up a little bit more."

Quartermaster Rollins, scratching hard at the prickly heat on his rump that always flared up in moments of tension, passed the word on the public address system, while the telephone talker, Yeoman Smith, relayed orders to those concerned. Chief of the Boat Nave reported to the skipper, "All stations report manned at Battle Stations."

Coe, thoroughly awake now, asked Larry, "How's your trim?"

"Good, but I'd like to pump a couple of minutes." Coe nodded, and Larry said to Pennell on the trim manifold, "Pump 600 pounds from auxiliary to forward trim."

Pennell repeated the order, and when the action was complete Larry reported to the captain, "I have a good trim." Coe replied, "Stand by for a setup."

This would be Coe's first look at the ship he hoped to hit. As the only one seeing the target, he had to give as much information as he could to the approach party in the control room so they could determine the range, course, and speed. Accuracy was necessary to put the submarine in the best position for firing. The scene was reminiscent of the craze for seeing how many people could fit into a phone booth. The control room, 16½ feet fore and aft and 20 feet port to starboard, bristled with machinery, and a good chunk of it was taken up by the radio room. Battle Stations Submerged required that the approach officer, diving officer, assistant approach officer, plotting officer, chief of the boat, bow planesman, stern planesman, helmsman, quartermaster, trim manifold man, blow manifold man, telephone talker, messenger, and controllerman be present—14 in all, one-third of those aboard. Any quick movement dug elbows into nearby flesh. The claustrophobic could not survive long.

The skipper said, "Mark; angle on the bow 50 port; range three-quarter division high power; use 100-foot masthead height."

Rollins said, "Bearing 000 relative."

Assistant Approach Officer Gugliotta said, "Range 12,000. Can you make him out at all?"

Coe said, "Looks like a small freighter, 100 feet, and speed up, Larry. Give me the normal approach course."

During this period, until actual firing of torpedoes, observations were taken every few minutes with the speed kept as slow as possible to prevent a feather. This was the result of water running up the periscope, then down. Slow speed caused a dribble, fast speed caused a noticeable feather in the water, detectible by the enemy. But between looks, it was necessary to go fast to get close enough to fire. Less and less periscope was exposed above the surface as the range to the target decreased, and each observation was shorter, by now no more than five or six seconds. The mark 10 torpedoes used by S-boats had a maximum range of about 3,600 yards, but the ideal range for greatest accuracy was 1,000 yards. This was what Coe was hoping to achieve.

As Larry Bernard said to electrician Hiland, "Shift to series, 1,000 aside," and Gugliotta said to helmsman Norton, "Left full rudder, steady on course 275," both officers tied skivvy shirts around their necks to conserve their own sweat for cooling purposes, as well as to keep it from dripping onto the deck, where it turned slippery underfoot.

Hendrix, plotting officer, said, "I get him on course 240, we're about 8,500 yards off the track."

"Stand by for a look, 40 feet," Coe said.

Nave, for once as quiet as everyone else, started the scope moving upwards by means of a hand-held switch, stopping now and then at Coe's signal. As the scope rose, the skipper rose, coming off the deck until he reached standing position. The telephonic talker, with his trailing wires, kept them out of the way with the skill of royalty manipulating a train.

Bernard said to controller Hiland, "Shift to parallel, half-switch," and a minute later, "Forty feet."

"Stand by, mark, angle on the bow 55 port; down periscope, speed up, Larry," Coe said. "Range, a bit more than three-quarter division high power." Gugliotta put the information on the Iswas, a circular slide rule used to set the submarine course and also to set relative bearing and angle on the bow which gave target course. He converted the periscope range scale to yards with a slide calculator.

The quartermaster said, "Bearing 074 relative,"

and Gugliotta came back with, "Range 11,000." Bernard added, "Shift to series, 1,000 aside," while preparations began for another observation.

Coe, eye glued to the rubber eyepiece again, his usually rosy complexion fiery from rising temperatures and anticipation, said, "Mark, he zigged towards; angle on the bow 30 port; down periscope, 100 feet and speed up again, Larry. Range just short of one division high power."

"Bearing 093 relative," Rollins said. Gugliotta contributed, "Range 9,000," followed by Hendrix, "I get him on course 210 degrees (T) making eleven knots."

After consulting his Iswas, Gugliotta said, "Recommend course about 20 degrees to the right," to which Coe murmured, "Okay," and Gugliotta told the helmsman, "Right full rudder, steady on course 295 degrees."

The skipper asked, "Sound, do you hear anything? Target is near the starboard beam." But sound operator Schab, in the torpedo room, replied, "Nothing yet, Captain."

The approach party began discussing the probability that the target was heading for the entrance to Albay Gulf, which would put him on a base course of approximately 230 degrees (T) (true course by compass) to pass just north of Rapu-Rapu Island. The captain asked the quartermaster to break out the U.S. Navy publication on Japanese Merchant Silhouettes and, thumbing through, decided that #61, a cargo ship, most closely resembled the target. While this was going on, the tight-packed group took the opportunity to shift restlessly, dig a finger in an ear or up a nostril, pop a fresh stick of gum into a nervously working mouth, or hitch up the blue dungaree shorts that no matter how faded always looked black from grime.

But they all settled down quickly when the old man called for another observation and reported, "Mark, angle on the bow 30 port, range one."

Quartermaster Rollins said, "Bearing 092 relative," and Gugliotta, "Range 8,000." Hendrix reported, "No change, I get him on course 210 degrees speed 12, looking pretty good."

Larry Bernard knew what to expect, and he got it from Coe. "Speed up, Larry, we've got to get closer to his track, and I'm sure he's going to a more westerly course to head for the gulf entrance before long."

Sound operator Schab cut in: "I hear something, could be screw noises on the starboard beam but can't be sure."

"That's the target—stay on him and give us a screw count as soon as you can." Coe's voice stayed at the same pitch but his words came out faster than usual.

The next familiar "Stand by for a look" from the skipper was followed by, "Mark, he zigged towards; angle on bow zero; down periscope; stay at this slow speed, Larry. Let's head for him." The quartermaster replied, "Bearing 066 relative," and Gugliotta gave the range: "6,000 and right full rudder, steady on course 003." But it was slow work for impatient men. Three minutes later the bearing was 000 relative and the range 4,500.

At this point Schab reported, "I hear screws now, dead ahead, about 130 RPM."

"Good, stay on him and report any changes," Coe said. In a few minutes Schab came back with, "Target bearing is changing to the left. He may have zigged. I also hear more noise, screws at higher speed."

This brought "Up periscope" from Coe and, after

finding the target, "He sure did zig. Mark, angle on the bow 60 port, 100 feet, and pour on the speed, Larry. Torpedo room make ready number one and two torpedo tubes, and tell Sound that the high speed screws are a couple of destroyer-type escorts."

The range was 3,600 yards, bearing 350 degrees. Gugliotta said to Coe, "Recommend course 330 to give us a 105-degree track," got an "okay" from his captain, and said to helmsman, "Come left to 330 degrees." Hendrix, plotting, said, "Twelve knots is still good and checks with sound; target on course 250 degrees."

COB Nave relayed, "Torpedo room reports tubes one and two ready, zero gyro, ten feet depth set."

Coe said, "Okay, we won't get much closer, stand by for final setup and shoot. What's my firing bearing? Slow down, Larry."

Gugliotta fed him the information, 013: "I'll put you on it when you're ready."

"Up periscope. Mark, no change, angle on bow about 100 port. Down periscope," Coe said.

And for the last time this time, Gugliotta said, "Range 3,000" and the quartermaster replied, "Bearing 020."

The excitement in the control room was palpable. There wasn't a sound from those present as the skipper said, "Put me on the firing bearing"; Gugliotta turned the periscope to bearing; Monk said, "Setup checks, course 250, speed 12"; Coe said, "Up periscope, he's coming on, stand by."

A few seconds later the captain said, "Fire one." Nave, who as chief of the boat rated the honor, pressed the electric firing switch, and again when Coe said, "Fire two."

Torpedoman Bixler reported, "Both torpedoes fired electrically," and sound man Schab, "Both torpedoes running straight."

Now came the longest part of the 21 minutes since the approach had begun, the two- or three-minute interval between firing the torpedoes and knowing whether they'd found their mark. Coe kept wiping his palms on his skivvy pants but didn't bother to push back the strands of red hair that had come unstuck when he pulled away from the periscope. Nave kept opening his mouth as though he were about to say something, but nothing came. Larry Bernard folded his arms over his midsection and pressed down hard. He'd forgotten his belly, but now it was giving him trouble. Hendrix rubbed his eyes and blinked, rubbed his eyes and blinked. Some had clenched jaws; some were slack-mouthed. One man kept rolling his thumbs over and over each other. Each showed tension differently, but they were all listening, all breathing hard, all scared. Then two explosions were heard by all hands.

Coe, having a look through the periscope, said softly, "He's hit, going down by the stern and listing to port." Sickness stirred in the gut of every man present, but the memory of the baptismal depth-charging 39 had experienced put a brake on regret. The captain's next words stopped it completely. "Here come his escorts and one fired at our periscope; I just saw a splash nearby; 150 feet, Larry. Pass the word, rig for depth-charge attack." It was like a blast of cold air in the 100-degree control room. Schab's excited followup, "Two sets of high-speed screws approaching from vicinity of the target," caused further chilling.

They were in for it. There were four enemy destroyers, but instead of depth-charging they started echo-ranging and tracking. Coe and company figured that the Japanese submarine they'd encountered earlier might still be in the vicinity. The enemy couldn't be sure that the submersible they'd located wasn't their own. The Japanese sub couldn't be sure that the destroyers weren't U.S., so she was afraid to divulge her identity.

Coe ordered, "Rig for silent running." All electric motors not vitally needed were stopped. The gyro compass was kept running. The all-important but noisy battery ventilation motors were slowed as much as possible, as were the greatest noisemakers of all, the propellers. They had to be kept turning, though, in case it was necessary to make a knuckle. This consisted of a sharp turn and a burst of speed for just a few seconds, enough disturbance to create a mass of bubbles that would confuse the echo-ranging and enable the submarine to make a try at getting away. The sound waves that pinged against a target and echoed back were indiscriminate; a large fish, a mass of bubbles, or mud would sometimes do.

They were still at Battle Stations Submerged, which kept the best and most experienced people on watch. Silent running automatically meant that personnel movements were to be held to a minimum, especially in the engine room, where loose metal floor plates clanked when walked on. Sandals came off because callused soles were quieter than leather. A broken belt buckle on Tom Parks's sweat-soaked shorts was snipped because it scraped against equipment. The smoking lamp (a term stemming from early days when an actual little lamp was used to light pipes and cigars) had been out for some time.

The hourly cigarette break usually permitted when submerged was verboten. Air quality was a prime consideration in the relentless heat. Most of the men sat down on the deck right where they were to use as little energy and make as little noise as possible. The only people working hard were the helmsman and the planesmen, who had to operate the rudder and the bow and stern planes by hand now that power was secured.

In the torpedo room Ed Schab, still on watch, had shifted from the normal, powered JK listening gear to the SC, a long-range stethoscope mounted topside near the JK. As it was for everybody else, this was his first wartime experience with silent running. Wearing earphones, he was taking bearings when he began hearing something new, something other than the screws and the now familiar pings of the enemy's destroyers. He listened harder, moved around, took another bearing, turning the thick handle of the SC gear. Same thing. It didn't resemble the unmistakable explosion of depth charges; it was a very regular bang-bang, unchanging in tone and quality. Schab didn't like it. It was creepy the way it followed him, never varying no matter how he turned to lose it.

Coe was well aware that as long as they had four enemy destroyers pinging on them they were hardly out of danger, so he kept close check on the torpedo room. He had been sweating out the mystery sound with Schab for about ten minutes when his impatience became obvious. "Haven't you any idea yet what it might be?" he whispered.

Schab, who'd been having some unpleasant thoughts about the creepy noise, shook his head "no" just as Harris, radioman first class, came in. Ed handed over the equipment and Harris got down to the job. There was a touch of "We'll find out now that the expert is here" in Harris's manner as he set about covering the same territory Ed had. Schab sat back, praying that the leading radioman would come up fast with the solution. Waiting out the enemy still hovering above them was the worst part of the last five days. Everybody was exhausted, stubbly faces sagging from fatigue, the stinking air beginning to make eyes ache and temples throb from oxygen starvation. Expectations of living out the war were slim, but everyone had hoped to make it a little longer than this. To add the damned bang-bang and the fear of a secret weapon to the already existing misery seemed hitting below the belt.

"Well," the captain said impatiently to Harris, "do you still hear it?"

Harris gave the handle a big swing, a furrow of concentration between his heavy brows, beads of perspiration rolling down his jowls, listening, listening. "There it is again," he said. "I don't know what it is."

Schab, concentrating on every move the radioman made, suddenly caught sight of the metal tube leads that came through the hull; when Harris made a big, rapid swing, they twisted and banged together. Could it be? Ed wanted to shout as he watched it happen again when Harris trained around fast going from 15 to 90 degrees. Controlling himself, Ed tapped his skipper on the arm and pointed upward. Harris caught the action too. The mystery was solved.

For a few seconds it was almost reassuring to hear only pinging, but another hour went by and aching eyes had become red-rimmed and filmy. They were back to square one. Christopher, who kept having visions of a giant-sized, ice cold beer, thought to himself, How long, O Lord, how long? But nobody could answer that question. Increasing headaches were acting as a barometer of decreasing air quality inside the pigboat. Men who had been florid from heat were paling out from lack of oxygen. Nobody complained because there was no point in it. An S-boat was a great leveling agent; all suffered equally. Besides, why waste breath. It was too precious.

Depth-charging could blast you instantaneously out of existence, but pinging could wear you down until the lack of breathable air gave you the choice of surfacing or smothering to death. If you surfaced, you could shoot it out, hoping to do some damage and get away—not likely with four modern Jap destroyers on you. Or you could surrender and be taken prisoner, which was unthinkable. For 39 the point of surfacing and confrontation was getting near. Coe motioned Gugliotta to follow him into the wardroom. Guy silently picked his way across outstretched legs on the slimy deck; the only noisemakers were the enormous, dinosaur-vintage cockroaches plopping onto metal machinery.

"Guy, I want you to get all the confidential publications together," the captain whispered into his communicator's ear, "and if we have to surface, be ready to deep-six them."

Following instructions, Gugliotta went to the ship's safe, packed the confidential material into a canvas bag, and weighted it down with wrenches. Then he added his silent prayer to the rest of the silent prayers that he'd be taking them out and stuffing them back in the safe soon.

In the torpedo room Radioman Rice, who had relieved Schab, wanted to believe his ears but also wanted to be sure before he got everybody's hopes up that the pinging was getting farther away. Coming in quietly as a mouse, Coe took one look at the radioman's face and said, "There's a change. Have they given up on us?"

"It looks like it, Captain," Rice said cautiously. "The sound is getting further and further away. I haven't heard anything at all for the last couple of minutes."

The word got around fast. Faces brightened as 39 began surfacing, and by the time Quartermaster Rollins started cranking the dogs of the hatch cover, there were a few cautious smiles. If only they could get rid of the foul air, things might be okay. All eyes in the conning tower were on the hatch cover, still held shut by the latch and water pressure. Then the hatch was out of the water, and Diving Officer Bernard relayed the depth to Officer of the Deck Hendrix, who told the quartermaster, "Open the hatch."

Rollins pulled hard on the lanyard that tripped the latch. With an angry blast the foul air blew out and fresh replaced it as the main engines were started. Officers and men had never known anything so good. For the first time they realized that air tasted. They opened their mouths and gulped it. They rolled it around their tongues. They smacked their lips over it.

The relief didn't last long. They immediately made ready for a battery charge and found a considerable amount of water in the large main induction piping through which ventilating air was drawn into the boat when on the surface. The source of the leak was a distorted gasket on the main induction valve located in the bridge structure aft of the open bridge area; the shocks from depth charges on 11 December had un-seated the gasket. It had become badly crushed from opening and shutting since then, and no spare was carried on board. It was decided to force the dis-torted gasket into place, shut the valve, and keep it shut for the rest of the patrol. The hardest part would be to do the noisy job quietly and quickly in a patrol area crawling with enemy ships.

Bernard sent for Chief Machinist's Mate Paul Spencer and Jim Pennell to assess the task.

"Somebody will have to crank the valve shut from below because if it's operated by power it could cut off fingers," Spencer said. "It'll take three of us to force it into place and hold it there."

"I'll go get somebody," Pennell offered.

Coe had witnessed the rush of water when the valve was opened, and his concern brought him through the hatch to join the others on the bridge. It was a dark and hazy night, but the outlines of enemy vessels were discernible in the distance. In a few sec-onds Pennell was back with Earl Nave in tow. Though not a machinist's mate, Nave understood the problem from past experience on another submarine and had volunteered to help. He won a lot of respect for the action because a chief of the boat didn't have to do nasty little jobs like this. And most of them didn't. Some of the admiration given Nave was grudging, but all of it was genuine.

The three men got to work at once, unable to go as fast as they would have liked for fear of the noise. It was a hammer and screwdriver job. While the men worked, the skipper's eyes followed the pro-gress of a clipper-bow Japanese "tin can" (destroyer) that loomed closer and closer. The machinist's mates were finding Nave's experience invaluable as they tried to get the hard rubber disc back where it belonged and the word was quickly passed below that the honker was not only working quiet but keeping quiet. "A miracle, a miracle," somebody muttered. It was a night for miracles. Although the Japanese destroyer could be seen throughout the repair session, she never saw 39.

Frustration set in again next day. Albay Gulf was crawling with Japanese minelayers, transports, destroyers, and even a light cruiser. Visibility was poor because of rain and fog. The 39 sighted more cargo ships coming down from the north, but as they approached the entrance to the gulf, the enemy vessels were met by Japanese destroyer escorts to take them in. It was a very high-risk setup for a U.S. submersible, even if she could get close enough for a try. Excitement ran high when 39 sighted a transport on her stern, but it zigged away. The submarine could not close below 4,000 yards, which was beyond her torpedo range.

Then Coe got a wonderful idea. At least he thought it was and so did everyone else but Gugliotta. Except when his back was to the wall, Coe's philosophy was to be neither stupidly reckless nor overly conservative but to evaluate the situation and decide whether he had a chance of making a successful hit and staying alive to report it. Going in during daylight was out right now; surface approach at night was a problem for S-boats because their sonar couldn't be used unless submerged; going in submerged at night wouldn't do, either, because the periscope was inadequate after dark, especially in stormy weather. What to do?

"Guy, it'll be a natural for you," Coe said, "since

you're torpedo and gunnery officer. We'll go in submerged after dark but with the radio mast up; you can sit on it with binoculars and con the boat into firing position. You'll be much more accurate than the periscope, and you'll be in contact with me by telephone. This way we should get a good firing setup."

Gugliotta was a Naval Academy graduate who'd been trained to obey his commanding officer. The brown eyes met the blue ones, and Gugliotta said, "Yes, sir," but the plan didn't appeal to him. It wasn't so much the idea of being a human periscope, riding the radio mast all alone like the lookout on an old-time sailing ship while everybody else was safely below; it was the schools of viperish iridescent sea snakes he had so often seen in the warm waters of the Philippines. Did they sleep at night, or were they out to attack any legs that might be trailing through the water after dark? Gugliotta had a fix on snakes. He just didn't like them.

"Gee, that sounds great," Hendrix said, his big enthusiastic grin turned on his shipmate, who mumbled, "Yeah," and wished the skipper had asked for volunteers and Monk had been it.

But before the plan could be implemented, the order came to return to Manila. On the way back, Schab caught a Tokyo Rose broadcast. The velvet-voiced lady announced the sinking of the S-39 in her perfect, unaccented English, and there was pathos in her tone when she said, "The rest of you brave submariners want to be able to see your wives and sweethearts again, don't you? Why don't you surrender?" The quiver in the dulcet voice was heartbreaking as she added, "And now I'm going to spin a record for

you that will really make you think." The song was
"You'd Be So Nice to Come Home To," which provoked many a sigh from the crew. The women-hungry
men thoroughly enjoyed the sexy voice without taking her proposals seriously; they figured she didn't
either. What really upset them was to hear that the
Japanese had taken over Shanghai's International Set-
tlement on 8 December and that Blood Alley, a sail-
or's paradise, was no more.

That chaotic Sunday, to be known in history as Pearl
Harbor Day, would forever remain in the memory of
Bobette Gugliotta. At home with her mother and stepfather in Malba, Long Island, she had nothing special
planned. There would be the usual stroll down country roads lined with peach trees in this small community between College Point and the Whitestone Bridge.
There would be the *New York Times Book Review,*
roast beef, and snow flurries wafting across smudgy
storm windows. After dinner there would be radio
programs—such as Eddie Cantor's show with his famous sign-off, "I love to spend each Sunday with
you"—followed by writing to Guy, and winding up
with the usual long session of reading in bed. Bobette
was currently immersed in Upton Sinclair's Lanny
Budd novels and was about to finish *World's End.* It
was a curiously prophetic title. The world that the
22-year-old had known was ending, and a new era
was about to begin.

Word of the catastrophe came by telephone from a
friend. The next few days were hectic, with normal
people reacting abnormally. Charles Dixon, Bobette's
45-year-old stepfather and an ex–merchant mariner,

tried to enlist in the U.S. Navy on 8 December. His age, plus an X-ray that revealed an old tubercular scar, kept him out. Bobette's mother, Aline, opened a can of Japanese crabmeat and upon finding glasslike slivers in it called the FBI; the bureau made an analysis and found the slivers harmless preservative. Bobette, who had done nothing throughout the past year but write letters to Guy, send him books, visit his family in New Jersey, and lose weight from lovesickness, pulled herself together and joined the American Women's Voluntary Service. The most important job performed by the uniformed women was selling war savings bonds that helped finance badly needed equipment. Bobette worked out of a booth at the Jamaica, Long Island, racetrack and sold a good number of bonds to successful horse players who were put to shame by AWVS women beseeching them, in loud voices, to share their winnings with GI Joe so he could win, too. She was also good at collecting reading material, not so good at knitting socks, and no good at all at helping provide an honor guard for the dead. Unable to bear the sight of a flag-draped coffin with a naval officer's cap atop it belonging to a young aviator killed in training, son of an AWVS volunteer, Bobette left in the middle of the services. Sitting in the dressing room, she wept quietly, blaming herself for being a coward.

Caroline Bernard and her son were living with Larry's family in Deadwood, South Dakota. Although the town was well known for western characters such as Wild Bill Hickok, Calamity Jane, and Deadwood Dick, its current 3,288 citizens were true blue but not worldly wise. When the news of Pearl Harbor was broadcast, Caroline received many a commiserating call because Larry was in that awful place where all those battleships were sunk. The Philippines and Hawaii were lumped together in the minds of many townfolk, as they were in the minds of people in larger, more sophisticated centers. The U.S. was about to have a geography lesson. But Deadwood, highly patriotic, was eager to cooperate with the war effort, and when government rationing books were issued later, ranchers were doubly on the alert for cattle rustlers eager to make bucks in the black market.

Caroline didn't hear anything from Larry for some time, and knowing nothing of the routine employed to convey notice of death, she thought it would surely be by telephone, and quaked every time the instrument rang. Late one evening the harsh jangle of the wall phone struck terror into her heart, but it brought good news, a cable from Larry.

Corenne Ward was chatting and listening to the radio with friends in San Diego, including the English aircorpsman John Bellamy, still awaiting delivery of a plane. Suddenly the swing music of Artie Shaw stopped and a breathless voice kept repeating over and over, "Ladies and gentlemen, the Japanese have bombed Pearl Harbor."

"Let's drive down to the harbor and take a look around," someone suggested. Nobody knew what they expected to see, but the idea of movement was a relief in itself.

It was a mild, sunny day, the kind that made San Diego boast that it possessed the finest climate in the world. The group swung past the Civic Center and onto the Embarcadero, where tons of lumber were stacked up to build new housing for the swarm of defense workers who had recently invaded the area and were living in tent cities. Sighting the headquarters of the 11th Naval District, Corenne thought of Tom Parks—as she had the moment the awesome announcement of war came on the air. She had heard from Tom not long before and was pretty sure he was around Manila, but no announcements had been made concerning the Asiatic Fleet. She would call his mother later. If Mrs. Parks hadn't heard from Tom, she might have heard from his brother Jim on the carrier *Langley*. With a little shiver that had nothing to do with the weather, Corenne realized how hard it must be for Mr. and Mrs. Parks, whose only children were both in a theatre of war so far away. Corenne came back to the moment with a start as the car ground to a halt. "You've been dreaming," John Bellamy said, helping her out.

Corenne smiled. "I guess you're right. I didn't realize we'd driven all the way to La Jolla."

They stood on the wind-eroded cliffs, feeling mist upon their faces from waves that crashed against the strangely shaped rocks and sent watery fingers probing into caves underneath. As they looked out over the endless blue of a Pacific dancing with sun-sparkle, it was hard to believe that death and destruction lay beyond the horizon. It was their last opportunity to move about freely. Within a few hours the harbor was fenced off and the cliffs were declared out of bounds.

Corenne had no chance to become interested in a change of job, since she found out next day that the one she was in had been declared vital to the defense of the United States. By the time she arrived at the telephone building, there were guards at all doors. No calls to Mexico or anywhere out of the U.S. could

be connected without a monitor to warn customers
not to talk of weather conditions or troop movements. Callers were also warned not to speak Japanese, an order the employees considered little more
than a bluff, since 90 percent of the operators
wouldn't have known Japanese from Tagalog or
Hindi. Blackouts went into effect throughout the city,
and the major buildings were sandbagged. All military personnel were recalled to their bases, and people in the streets glanced over their shoulders first and
spoke in whispers if they had anything to say about
the war.

Corenne's friend Bellamy was a great help in those
first frightening weeks; he had gone through much
more in Britain, where London was taking the terrible
bombing that fortunate San Diego would never experience. Nevertheless, it took a while for the initial fear
to subside and for things to return to near-normal—
with the exception of rationing. The common folk
obeyed the law and took only their share of scarce
canned goods, red meat, tires, and gasoline. Of course,
the ever-present hoods and crooks immediately set up
a black market in ration stamps that spread from
coast to coast faster than maple syrup on hotcakes.

And then John Bellamy's plane was ready and it
was time for him to go. It was a difficult parting. Bellamy, to make sure Corenne's letters would reach him,
asked her to write in care of his home address in Sheffield, England, so that his mother could forward the
letters to his proper wartime address. He was to be
reassigned after he reached home and had no way of
knowing where he would end up. Corenne was very
fond of him, she wrote faithfully. But as the months
went by, she realized that John Bellamy's dowager

mother was not forwarding mail to her son from the American girl. Corenne's letters from John (and there were many before he became totally discouraged) asked again and again why she never wrote. Since John's letters bore no return address, after a while Corenne had to concede victory to Mrs. Bellamy.

Two stalwart crew members who had missed the S-39's first patrol were Schoenrock and Tom Parks. Parks had become the complete, dyed-in-the-wool, 100-percent devoted pigboat sailor by the time he got his dolphins. He had totally eliminated from his consciousness his old desire to be in aviation. After a night on the town, he met up with an aviation machinist's mate from a patrol bomber squadron. The encounter took place in the head at the barracks in Subic Bay. When the superiority of wings over dolphins came under discussion, Tom unfortunately did not have his pacifist friend Kutscherowski with him to keep him out of trouble. As the argument heated up, the aviation machinist's mate became abusive to the point of impugning the honor and respectability of Tom's mother, so the submarine sailor clopped his opponent in the jaw and was immediately decked by a punch to the solar plexus that left him gasping. By the time he caught his breath, the machinist's mate had shoved off. Tom realized that his hand hurt like hell, and it soon swelled up like one of Ski's boxing gloves.

Prewar tension had already resulted in a stab in the leg for Schoenrock during a fight on the beach. Coe had been able to finagle temporary duty aboard the *Pigeon* for the cook while his leg healed, but Tom's right hand was more serious. Parks went to the hospital, and the 39 went to sea. When he was released, 6 December, the hospital personnel office sent Parks to the USS *Holland*, one of the newly arrived submarine tenders, where he knew no one at all. Tom managed to persuade the personnel officer to endorse orders to Division 201 instead, familiar territory.

As he started across the bay, he caught sight of the old carrier *Langley* coming in and realized that he hadn't seen his brother Jim in over a month. And when he went aboard *Canopus* and found that the 39 was out to sea, he made a split-second decision that he never regretted: he went AWOL and spent the weekend aboard the *Langley* with his brother. Sunday night, as soon as he set foot on the *Canopus,* a heavy hand was placed on his shoulder by the master-at-arms. He was under arrest, spent the rest of the night in the brig, and after quarters in the morning was led out on deck for a captain's mast.

The informality and homey touches of an S-boat were lacking here—no sloppy shorts, bare chests, and sandals. The drizzly, gray light of the rainy season showed a grim-faced Commander Earl Sackett, his leading petty officer, a division officer, and the master-at-arms who had put Tom in the brig. With all speed Tom was set for a summary court-martial. He began to realize that his impulsive act could have serious results. He hoped and prayed that what he'd heard was true, that the Navy took into consideration your previous record. His was clean, and there were extenuating circumstances, in this case a desire to see his only brother. What he didn't realize yet was that a war had started. Within hours the Navy was too busy for minor things like courts-martial, and besides, it needed all the hands it could muster.

By the time the *Canopus* had sailed back across the bay and tied up at the President Lines pier, Tom had heard the news. Although not even Admiral Hart knew the extent of the damage at Pearl Harbor. Parks, like the higher-ups, thought the Philippines the main target. The area was alerted for air raids, and shortly after, sirens began their high-pitched, earsplitting whine. It was 10 December, the hour was 1210. Fifteen minutes later 54 Japanese bombers, accompanied by fighter planes, were sighted. Tom, mouth open and eyes wide as though in a trance, watched the faraway specks grow larger and break into two groups of 27 with the precision of an air show, before winging off into smaller units of nine with insolent ease. The flyers from Nippon knew they had nothing to fear by way of retaliation.

While Parks was wondering where the American fighter planes were, the first bombs began to fall, coming down at 1305 on Machina Wharf at Cavite, hitting minesweeper *Bittern* and submarine *Sealion*. That was only the beginning. The navy yard was bombed again and again, smashing ships and knocking out the power station so that no water pressure was available for firefighting. Parks was assigned to a boat gang ordered to take a fire-and-rescue party of 30 men to the navy yard. The trancelike feeling continued as they crossed the bay, and Tom stared in disbelief at red flames skyscrapering up through enormous black billows of smoke. But when he landed at Cavite, it was not the spectacle burning all around him that made war real but the sight of what shrapnel could do to a human body.

The Filipinos suffered most in the Cavite disaster; over 1,000 dockworkers and shopkeepers were killed outright, and 400 more would die later in the hospital. As Tom stared at the bloody remains of what had been live people a few minutes before, he grew sick to his stomach and felt the cold grip of fear for his own life. The barracks had taken a direct hit; the torpedo and machine shops were in ruins; the *Sealion* had gone down; and he could see the superstructure of the *Seadragon* pocked with holes. But none of that mattered like the helpless dead.

When the battered fire and rescue party went back across the bay to Manila the next day, Tom cried unabashedly from anger, frustration, and fright as he watched Japanese bombers overhead and saw the futile antiaircraft fire popping so far below the planes that it would have been funny if it had been happening to somebody else. He consoled himself by thinking, We'll even the score in a few days, we'll get back at them. He was still expecting a battle fleet from Pearl Harbor to steam in and save the Philippines. Nobody had yet told him how impossible that was.

Fleet submarines *Sealion* and *Seadragon*, when caught in the devastating attack, had both been undergoing overhaul. Lieutenant Commander Richard Voge, captain *of Sealion*, had issued orders the day the war started that all hands were to come aboard fast if an air raid alarm sounded, because there were no shelters in the navy yard and the submarine was the safest place to be. The Philippine workmen had been trying their best to complete the overhaul and by working like demons were ahead of schedule, but *Sealion*'s engines were still dismantled. Frank Gierhart, radioman second class from Cincinnati, Ohio, had been in the yard on business connected with *Sealion* when he heard the siren's wail. Running when he could and walking when he had to plow through the crowds of workmen and civilians frantically seeking shelter in a place which had none, Frank headed for home. He had put *Sealion* into commission and had been mighty glad to be on a new, up-to-date fleet boat after a two-year stint on the old *S-43* in Panama.

Frank scrambled across *Seadragon*, his heart beating louder than the wailing siren. He was scared. On the bridge Captain Voge urged Gierhart and others coming along behind him to get a move on. It was hardly necessary. By the time the bombers were sighted, the only men topside on *Sealion* were her skipper, the exec, and three gunners manning the machine gun. It was almost instantly clear that a single bantam-weight gun was impotent against 54 heavy-weight bombers.

As Frank dropped into the control room where most of the men were assembled, he heard the puerile ack-ack of Cavite's antiaircraft batteries, but not for long. The nine three-inch guns, with a range of 15,000 feet, might as well have been firing tennis balls into the air for all the impression they could make on high-altitude bombers. But it wasn't long before the holocaust taking place in Cavite stilled the sound of antiaircraft guns forever.

When the first bombs slanted down a few yards astern, Voge ordered all hands below, and minutes later two bombs hit *Sealion*, one completely destroying the machine gun mount just vacated. Fortunately, the first bomb exploded outside the hull, a few feet away from the crowded control room. If it had penetrated, most of the crew would have been killed. The impact shook the boat with the force of a giant hand, and three men in the control room were injured by bomb fragments piercing the pressure hull. But there was no time for tears because, almost simultaneously, a second bomb passed through the main ballast tank and exploded in the after engine room. The four electrician's mates working there were killed instantly. The room flooded immediately and the submarine settled in the mud, its sudden tilting slamming the men every which way as water started seeping through the bomb-fragment holes. All hatches were still above water, and the stunned and silent crew shot up them, escaping with all the speed of Battle Surface Drill, except the wounded assisted by their comrades.

It was worse outside than in. When Frank Gierhart emerged into the chaos of a thousand fires blazing like spin-offs from the fiery tropic sun and the explosions of zigzagging bombs wiping out people and landmarks before his eyes, he knew what terror was. The screams of the injured and dying were periodically obliterated by detonations, and the nauseating odor of cooked flesh was replaced by an oil stench when an errant breeze blew smoke from burning tanks through the hell that was Cavite. Gierhart was homeless now.

The day Cavite was bombed, another member of *Sealion*'s crew, Fireman First Class Leslie Dean, had been sent to Manila to buy or scrounge whatever supplies he could find. It was every ship for itself, and each one wanted to have as many spares and as much food as it could carry. Dean was a good man for the job. His farmer-minister-carpenter father had never made much money at any of his trades and during the Depression earned even less. This had made a realist out of his son, who joined the Navy in 1935 primarily to eat regularly and, by the way, to see the world. He'd never before been outside Mt. Vernon, Illinois. As soon as he could, he volunteered for submarines—extra pay the incentive. For the same reason he didn't mind being a messcook; the hat was always passed on pay day for services rendered and the extra bucks were worth a little sweat.

Like Gierhart, Les Dean had also put the *Sealion* into commission. Older than Frank, Les appreciated even more the pleasant life on a fleet boat; he had come up in the world and he wanted to stay there. Let newcomers to submarines live on the stinking pigboats; his four long years on *S-25* and *S-28* had made him a grateful graduate. Dean didn't get along with boatswain's mates but otherwise considered himself peaceable enough, not a personality to rub people the wrong way, somewhat forgettable in fact. He considered himself lucky as hell to have been in Manila when Cavite was bombed, but when he heard about *Sealion*, he took it hard. He was homeless, too.

Also in the Cavite Navy Yard when the war started was J.T. Lebow (no first name, just initials), another guy without a bunk to call his own. Lebow had six years of Navy experience; he had served on S-boats in Panama and then on the fleet boat *Cuttlefish* in Pearl Harbor. But when there was a shortage of radiomen in the Asiatic Fleet in early 1941, J.T. volunteered for the duty. He had bounced around on three different boats during the move to Manila, taking over temporarily for nonfunctioning radiomen. In the Philippines he had gone to the sub tender *Holland* as a spare. Filling in wherever needed, J.T. was as sought after as a substitute teacher and had served on *Scul-*

pin, *Sailfish*, *Spearfish*, and *Swordfish*. The conflict came as no surprise to him: back in Panama in 1940 he had predicted that war in Asia would involve the U.S. within a year. He was often right and not modest about it, which made him somewhat of a loner, except when it came to women.

In looks Lebow was not the traditional tall Texan but possessed the cockiness attributed to natives of the Lone Star State. In his spare time in prewar Manila, he had shot craps; guzzled scotch, beer, juleps; had some women and some fights. As the old saying goes, he was full of piss and vinegar, and behaved like many another sailor trying to do it all while he was still young and strong enough to enjoy it. He had a girl back home, Minnie Jeanne Nozero, but nothing definite had been settled between them. J.T. was too fond of the fair sex to ignore them in the warm and welcoming climate of the Philippines, or any other climate, for that matter. But like many another sailor who'd been blasted out of a nice setup by the war, Lebow would have to be on the move soon or take to the hills and learn to exist on bananas.

The crew of the *Sealion* and other displaced personnel found temporary refuge in the new Enlisted Men's Club on the dock in Manila. They were immediately set to work digging a trench around the club, wide enough and deep enough for a man to take shelter in. This was to be used only if they were unable to make the mile run to the wall surrounding the old city, which was considered a much safer place to be. After a few days a bombing pattern became obvious. With clocklike precision the Japanese came in twice daily, at 1300 and 0100; Gierhart, Dean, and others began grabbing a blanket to tote along for wee-hours session. The ground was hard, wet, and chilly at that time of the morning. They were supposed to go right back to the Enlisted Club as soon as the all-clear sounded, but many of them, worn out from recent events, fell asleep and stayed the night. Gierhart's and Dean's main preoccupation was thinking about what would become of them if the Philippines fell, which looked more and more likely. The rumor factory went 24 hours a day, ranging all the way from a Japanese bombing of D.C. that had killed President Roosevelt to the sinking of the fleet in Pearl Harbor. They believed the first more possible than the last, because all those big battleships and fancy cruisers and new destroyers in Pearl were supposed to come and rescue them.

And then came news that wasn't a rumor. Until two days before the event, General MacArthur "forgot" to inform Admiral Hart that Manila would be declared an open city on Christmas Day. In a hastily summoned conference with his flag officers, Hart told them of the imminent need to evacuate personnel, equipment, and the *Canopus*, the only submarine tender left in the Philippines. Though he tried to control it, his bitterness at the cavalier behavior of his peer showed; the lives of men were at stake, men of the fleet who deserved every chance to escape so that they might live to fight more effectively another day.

Tom Parks hadn't had much time to think about whether 39 would take him back when she came in but the thought loomed more and more important. There were a lot of homeless Navy men and Marines, an estimated 4,000 of them, and only small

vessels to put them on. Rear Admiral William A.
Glassford, Jr., had already departed for Balikpapan
with a cruiser, two oilers, and the *Langley*. When
push came to shove, which would be soon according
to scuttlebutt, space available for displaced men to
catch a ride would be the submarines and inshore
patrol vessels that were left. Whoever made it aboard
would be lucky; the rest, the bulk, could soon be in
the talons of an enemy swooping in like falcons sure
of their prey.

Ships from many countries had sought refuge in
Manila Bay, among them a modern French merchantman, *Marechal Joffre*, flying the Vichy French flag.
The top brass decided to take *Marechal Joffre* into
protective custody and put 100 U.S. Navy personnel
aboard to sail her to an eastern Australian port,
where she could be used by the Allies. But first a
boarding party had to be formed for the purpose, and
Parks was a member of the group chosen for the
takeover. He didn't know much about Frenchmen,
Vichy or otherwise, and was leery of the reception the
"pirates" would receive. As they climbed into motor
launches, he swallowed hard, recalling Errol Flynn
movies where the boarding party always encountered
gunfire and hand-to-hand fighting. The only thing
missing would be sabers—maybe the French still used
them.

When they neared the ship, the Americans could
see officers and sailors hanging over the rails watching their approach. They couldn't read the expressions on the faces. But as the first member of the
boarding party set foot on the *Joffre*, the skipper said,
"Allo," with a big smile. Then the French sailors waved

to the Americans, and Tom knew the takeover was going to be okay. He had one more hurdle to jump, and that was to find out if his billet was still available on the *39*.

ON PATROL IN
THE INDIAN OCEAN

FROM *Shooting the War:*
The Memoir and Photographs of a U-Boat Officer
in World War II

**by Otto Giese and
Captain James E. Wise, Jr.**

*O*tto Giese (1914–2001) lived a life intertwined
with the sea. At age nineteen, he began serving
aboard square-rigger sailing vessels and transoceanic
freighters, then went to the German Nautical Academy
for his mate's license. World War II was declared while
he was working aboard the ocean liner SS *Columbus*,
resulting in the ship being scuttled and his interment in
Angel Island prison near San Francisco. Promptly escaping, he returned to Germany, where he trained for
U-boat duty, serving in the major theaters of war in the
Far East, North Atlantic, and Indian Ocean. Captured
by the British during the war, he was interned in the
notorious Changi jail in Malaya, and not released until
1947. Afterward, he obtained his master's license and
began his own international shipping line, living first
in Cuba, then moving to the United States, where he
lived for the rest of his life. His papers chronicling his

life as a submariner are on file with the United States Naval Academy, and provide detailed insight into the history and everyday life of a German submariner.

The life of his writing partner on *Shooting the War*, Captain James E. Wise, Jr., is no less impressive. He served as a naval aviator, then an intelligence officer aboard the aircraft carrier USS *America*, and was the commanding officer of various naval intelligence units. He has also written and cowritten several books about the military, including an autobiography of James Arness, and *U-505: The Final Journey*, detailing the transportation of a German U-boat to the grounds of the Chicago Museum of Science and Industry, and then its transfer inside the museum itself. He has also written three books on the lives of actors who served in the armed forces, including *Stars in Blue: Movie Actors in America's Sea Services*, *Stars in the Corps: Movie Actors in the United States Marines*, and *Stars in Khaki: Movie Actors in the Army and Air Services*. His latest book is *Sole Survivors of the Sea*.

Although the Axis and Allied forces were bitter enemies during World War II, for the average soldiers and sailors, life was very similar on both sides of the conflict. German submarine crews functioned much the same as the U.S. and British crews—they sweated, suffered, lived, and fought much as their opponents did, and complained about the same problems, played practical jokes on one another, and served their country to the best of their ability, even after they knew that their homeland was going to lose the war.

On 16 March 1944 we said farewell to Bordeaux in company with the *U-196* (Captain Kentrat) and seven minesweepers. Captain Freiwald directed our departure smartly from the bridge. As we headed south we surfaced twice a day to charge our batteries, two hours shortly after sunset and two hours in the early morning. There was no sunlight for us anymore, only when we would glance through the periscope. At night the lights of the Spanish coast glittered. Numerous fishing boats caused us to proceed with great care. We ran a day routine at night and slept during the day. This was standard procedure for a long, submerged tour.

In the early morning of 23 March, while proceeding off Lisbon on a course for the Madeira Islands, we heard the high revolutions of a passing destroyer. We were at a depth of forty meters. Luckily, the destroyer didn't detect our passage.

After long hours under water the air would turn bad, 2.5 percent carbon dioxide. When the boat was surfacing, the pressure stabilized; before the conning tower hatch was even opened, one could see the bad air escaping. Boiling water in the messman's pots would suddenly surge up and vaporize. We would get up and salute when this stinking mess passed out of the boat.

Apropos saluting, there was no such thing as raising the arm in a "Heil Hitler." Space was too limited, and the saluter might have hit someone, perhaps the commandant, and nobody wanted to run that risk. If we saluted Nazi style among each other, we just plugged the thumb of the right hand into the pocket of our pants and raised the off hand. Otherwise we just stood at attention, leisurely, when we made a report to our chief. On the "bridge" we saluted in the old military manner, U-boat style, with slightly bent fingers to the cap, a grin on the bearded face, and some pointed joke on the lips. That's how it was with us, and that's how it must have been with all the salt-crusted U-boatmen on other boats.

One morning Captain Freiwald appeared in the central room with a bucket of hot salt water and his dirty clothes. We thought that he would call his orderly, but no—calmly and without a word he sat down and started washing. What a commandant! This gave me the idea to have a hot saltwater hose-down for the crew behind the diesels during our next two-hour surface run. What a delicious feeling it was! What a life!

We were now off Gibraltar. During our last nights in the Atlantic we often heard depth charges detonating, but they were far away. On 26 March we watched our first film, *Val Parez*, in the "bow theater." We closed the Madeira Islands on the twenty-eighth, marveling at their beauty through the action periscope.

It was now stifling in the boat. The air was dull and sultry. Our perspiration wouldn't dry anymore and our beards began to grow and get itchy. Only *Tosca* and our *Köllnisch Wasser* helped.

On 1 April we passed the Canary Islands. That same day we received a message from headquarters directing us to operate in an area southeast of Madagascar. During our short surface intervals I had my men overhaul the antiaircraft guns. They suffered from the constant underwater cruising. I had to do each hand grip myself to guarantee complete operational readiness in case of an emergency.

We celebrated the birthday of our navigation chief petty officer that first week in April. The "special occasion" record was played, and in the central room the commandant and the officer corps congratulated the young man. A bottle of liquor was passed through the boat to mark the event. Surfacing, submerging, up and down we went to receive orders from the BdU regarding our forthcoming rendezvous with a returning Monsoon boat, the *U-188*. Our poor engineer, Hille, was near exhaustion with no rest in sight. The daily paper *Typhoon* kept us informed about events on the battlefields. The Russians were at the German and Romanian borders. How will that end? we wondered. Something had to happen soon!

We were sure that our dear ones at home had been informed that we were still alive. Prior to our departure, we had organized a communications system whereby the commandant's wife, who received nonsensitive information about the boat, would pass on the news by telephone or letter to families of the officers, who would in turn contact relatives of the crewmen.

We passed the Cape Verde islands at Eastertime and our thoughts turned to home and loved ones. The canteen issued chocolate, candies, and fruit juice. We listened to concert music and had a film showing in our bow room.

The interior of the boat was by now so moist that the lockers streamed with water. Leather surfaces were soon covered with a thick layer of gray mold.

Nearly everyone had ailments—headaches, fevers, colds. We were now daring to surface for up to six hours at night. My dogwatch was exhausting because of little sleep, fresh air, and the strain of intense look-out duty. The night wasn't safe anymore in southern Atlantic waters. At any moment aircraft could appear from nowhere and toss a bomb down on our steel tube, which glowed in the otherwise pitch-dark tropical water.

On 22 April we rendezvoused with the *U-188*, a returning Monsoon boat. It was a memorable sight when two of the largest-type U-boats ran side by side, two ghostly shadows within calling distance.

After we received valuable information about our area of operations in the Indian Ocean, we parted and passed into the night with three short "Hip-hip-hurrah!"s.

By wireless we heard that the *U-488* (Captain Studt) was no longer responding to calls from the BdU. His young wife in Bordeaux was suddenly a widow. We were all anxious to take revenge.

Several days later, while submerged, we heard propeller noises on our hydrophones. It was 1400, my section was on watch. Going to periscope depth, we sighted a loaded freighter ahead of us. We surfaced and gave chase but had to dive when a plane was sighted. An hour later we surfaced again. We caught up with the freighter and positioned ourselves about 6,500 yards ahead of her. We attacked as clouds covered the moon. Our torpedoes found their mark and the ship went down fast. Only a few of the crew managed to get into the ship's lifeboats. When we approached them, I asked one of the men the name of the ship. He mumbled a name that sounded like *Be-*

navan. In fact, it turned out to be the British freighter *Janeta*.

On 9 May we celebrated the two-year anniversary of our boat with a half-bottle of beer for each of the crew. We were now entering the area of Cape Town, and the seas were getting rough. The boat plunged through deepening waves that sent sheets of swirling water over the conning tower. Oilcloth and leather clothing were changed in quick succession. The happiest hours on board were those of the afternoon coffeebreak in the officers' mess when we played games, or those hours after dinner when we would spin yarns and sip a small jigger of rice wine, a gift from the crew of the *U-188*.

We thought we sighted a smoke cloud but were disappointed. It was only the blowing of a whale. More excitement came soon. Our boat was rigged with a *Bachstelze*. This was a small, single, piloted helicopter attached to a long steel cable and lifted into the air by the speed of our boat while the cable was gradually reeled out. From his position aloft, the pilot had a 360-degree view and could report any vessels. One day, as I was busy on watch keeping the boat running against a strong wind while our aviator flew aloft, the man at the hawser reel yelled, "Sir, sir, look, the cable snapped!" I looked up. Our hapless pilot was spiraling down toward the water. Eventually he hit the surface with a huge splash. The pilot seemed okay. However, a new danger quickly appeared. Thinking he was a wounded fish, several large albatrosses and numerous seagulls descended on him, trying to peck his head. Before serious wounds could be inflicted, we picked up the stunned airman, who was received with roars of laughter by the crew. Nobody was sorry that the helicopter was gone. It had been more trouble than it was worth.

We rounded the cape on 17 May, Father's Day.

Our poor "Doc" Buchholz had little hair left on his scalp, and to keep what he had and perhaps grow more, he used a tonic known in the German navy as Trylisin. The bottle stood quite prominent in his open locker. In a moment of recklessness, one of the crew suggested that some ingredients be added to it while Doc was busy at the radar station. This we did, enriching the potion with liquor, sugar, and glue. At night, when all of us watch-free officers rested in our bunks, Doc would attend to the remarkable work of massaging his shiny scalp with his fingers. That night everyone watched from behind their curtains, hardly able to restrain their laughter when he poured the sticky liquid into his hands and started rubbing it over his scalp. The grimaces he gave the mirror when he combed his few remaining hairs and watched them depart with the comb! We asked him why Trylisin had so many sediments in it; he explained that the chemical formula was such and such, and that naturally here in the tropics the alcohol would evaporate . . . poor Doc.

But, in need of a scapegoat, we were not quite through with Doc. Another plan was shaped one night during an officers' meeting. We ground some carbon pills to a very fine powder and poured it into his heavy U-boat boots. Although he wore socks, his feet soon turned black. The carbon was not easily removed, not even with soap and a brush. What a painful situation for the ship's doctor, known as the neatest man on board, to have to wait each night until his fellow officers were asleep to start scrubbing his shamefully dirty feet. Only when we told him of our experience with Bordelaise powder, which stained our feet gray, did he catch on.

It wasn't long before he got even. Within days our toothpaste had acquired the bitter taste of quinine, and when we urinated the stream was either red or green. Not knowing the cause, we mentioned this discreetly to Doc, who told us the most horrible things about kidney and bladder trouble. We were in shock until he confessed to his revenge.

We finally reached our operational area, some two hundred miles southeast of Madagascar, in early June. We patrolled the shipping routes between Durban and Colombo, Aden, and Australia with no luck. The weather was almost too good, with beautiful sunsets and clear, moonlit nights. No smoke clouds appeared on the horizon.

Doc vaccinated the entire crew against cholera. My reaction was fever and the shivers.

On 6 June 1944 we received the depressing news that Allied forces had landed between Le Havre and Barfleur in France. They had launched an all-out invasion. But the reports added that the enemy had been thrown back, suffering heavy losses. The BdU ordered all U-boats to exert themselves to the utmost.

Finally on 19 June we sighted a distant freighter. The hunt was short. A single torpedo sent the Dutch ship *Garoet* to the bottom. Safety lights flared in the water. Rafts and boats bobbed up and down around us. The men in the boats answered my questions willingly, giving the name of the vessel, its cargo (sugar and coal), departure port (Bombay), and destination (Durban). In return, we told them the shortest route to the coast.

The southwest monsoon was blowing with force now. The constant rolling and eternal spray over the conning tower kept us more than busy wiping our glasses. No sightings . . . We were in low spirits. During these days it was over 50°C in the diesel room, damp and hellishly hot. One day, at the end of my watch, it started raining in torrents. I kept the boat under the dark cloud, and part of the crew, including Captain Freiwald, appeared on the bridge naked as God made them to rub off their coats of grime.

We passed the northern cape of the Laccadive islands, some two hundred miles from the mainland of India. The sky was covered with dark gray rainclouds. Enemy planes might have attacked us at any minute, but we remained on the surface. I couldn't get rid of a certain tension inside me. Perhaps it was the climate of the monsoon which strained my nerves.

On 15 July 1944 we arrived at a position about thirty miles off the coast of India. At 1815 a ship was sighted. The enemy was automatically zigzagging, and we had difficulty getting to a forward attack position. The night drifted in around us. Our *Naxos* (radar warning) detection system sounded at about 2200. We stayed surfaced, close to our prey, not wanting to lose her in the darkness. Then finally we attacked with two torpedoes, scoring two hits on the British ship *Tanda*. The detection signal got louder and louder, reaching a force 5. If it was a plane, it should have been on top of us. We dived, leaving the sinking ship behind. Two hours later we surfaced cautiously only to be driven down again by detection signals.

The next morning propeller noises sounded again. They were distinct, slow revolutions. Either a ship was running with caution or her crew was careless.

We waited and listened as the sound grew. Freiwald decided to take a look through the periscope. He saw nothing.

A hunting fever came over the officers. We talked of precedents in such situations and decided to surface and attack. Freiwald went directly to the bridge with the watch officer and five men. The atmosphere was tense. Below, we waited. The propeller noises continued. We began to wonder if they were real or some phenomenon of the sea around us. Then came the terrifying call from above: "ALAARRMM!" The men tumbled down from the bridge and we went into a steep dive. The watch officer looked at me with a sweaty face. "Twin motorplane out of the sun. Saw it too late." Everyone looked up, waiting for the explosions.

Four hammer blows rocked the boat when we reached forty meters. All electricity went off. A high-pressure pipeline burst and blew off into the central room with an incredible noise. Compressed air streamed fiercely into the compartment. The hydroplanes were jammed in a hard down position, giving the boat an increasing forward list; 20, 30, 35 degrees and still we continued down. The bottom was now some sixty meters below. The electrical motors suddenly stopped when a coupling failed to release. There was an immediate overload, and all the fuses blew.

Our disciplined crew acted and acted fast. Within seconds, the damages were pinpointed. The defective piping was turned off. Both hydroplanes were shifted to manual operation, new fuzes for the E-motors installed, emergency lights switched on. Minutes later the heavily battered boat was under control.

On orders from Freiwald, our chief engineer leveled

the boat at eighty meters. Then, gradually, we began to repair the worst damage as the boat crept along at three knots. The starboard fuel bunker was cracked and leaking. We had lost about thirty cubic meters of diesel fuel. We pressed the remaining fuel out and flushed the bunker with seawater. Our gyrocompass was badly damaged.

Six hours later, still submerged, the boat was rocked again by thunderous depth charges too numerous to count. Finally we escaped, but we remained submerged. Later we would discover that we had come under attack by Allied aircraft and the Indian sloop *Sutlej*.

After eighteen hours under water, we surfaced and headed for the safety of the Laccadives, where detection would be more difficult among the many islands. Freiwald masterfully guided the boat through the maze of atolls. Although badly wounded, we were in good trim again.

After a few days of surface running and continued repair work, the boat returned to routine patrol. One morning while we were on the surface and I was busy checking my sector ahead, Freiwald asked me softly, "Giese, please turn around!" It was 1044 on 20 July 1944 and our defective, temperamental hydrophone had not signaled any distant ships.

Pivoting, I watched as Freiwald and all the men smiled, then ducked below the bulwark of the conning tower. One of them pointed his thick thumb in the direction of starboard aft, and there, not four thousand yards away, was the broad silhouette of a vessel. I looked open-mouthed at Freiwald. "Alarm?" I asked. He shook his head laughingly and said, "Let's try showing them our back side."

Undetected, we quietly maneuvered the boat into a forward position and waited to attack shortly after darkness. We fired two torpedoes, both hit, and the British ship *King Frederick* went down.

We approached the men in the lifeboats and asked them the name of their vessel, their cargo, and destination. They were fearful and quiet. They appeared to have food and water and were capable of making their way ashore. We were mystified by their action. We learned later that they thought we were Japanese and feared for their lives because of harm done to other seamen by Japanese crewmen.

On 20 July 1944, the BdU declared a general alarm for the German navy following the attempt on Hitler's life. Hitler or no Hitler, we realized that the war was lost for us. Nevertheless, we were soldiers and bound to our oath. Our job was to sink tonnage and to fight to the bitter end. In fact, we hardly talked about the attack on Hitler's life. The radio messages were short. We felt that the sooner the situation calmed down, the better we would be able to prepare for the final fight and onslaught by enemy forces.

Freiwald sent a message to headquarters reporting our sinkings to date and our intention to proceed to Penang to repair our damage.

On our way eastward through the Straits of Malacca, we heard that Sabang had been attacked by British carrier planes and shelled from the sea. Furthermore, it was reported, a powerful British sea force of two battleships, two aircraft carriers, and several cruisers and destroyers was south of the Andamans, along our track. Hallelujah!

We heard by wireless that the *U-196*, which had left Bordeaux with us, was sending a series of short signals to the BdU. While the boat was in our vicinity, we worried that the signals would draw the attention of enemy forces, in which case we both might come under attack. Later, in Penang, when we met with Captain Kentrat (the *U-196*), we were told that he had tried at least five times to get a short signal through to the BdU before receiving a confirmation of his signal. However, he did exercise caution, diving after each signal and waiting for the following program time. He did not know that we were in the vicinity.

One night, in a dead calm, a long dark shadow loomed ahead. Our sharp night glasses revealed a conning tower. We watched each other for a few tense moments. Then the other boat dived and we departed at full speed.

At long last, we approached Penang and radioed our estimated time of arrival. Captain Junior *(Fregattenkapitän)* Wilhelm Dommes, chief officer in the Southeast, responded, warning us to stay alert and await a Japanese escort vessel where "the Slot" led into the straits off Langkavi Island.

On 8 August a German seaplane, an Arado, appeared out of the early morning haze and circled a few times over the boat. The pilot clearly saw the two broad stripes across our deck and the big swastika on the sides of the conning tower. The plane dipped its wings a few times in salute while the crew cheered.

Soon the Japanese escort was sighted. It was not what we expected. Looking for something like a powerful minesweeper or even a sloop we found ourselves welcoming a small motorboat that mounted a single small-caliber gun. Lieutenant Kölln, the German escort officer, stepped from the vessel onto our deck bringing baskets of fresh bananas and pineapples—precious cargo!

We asked Kölln to take off his lifejacket and invited him into the boat for a hearty brunch out of the last of our stores. He accepted reluctantly, declining to take off his lifejacket. We smiled, perhaps a bit too indulgently, as he strode around without much interest and appetite. It wasn't long before he told us in abrupt, rash words how it really stood with the "glorious and powerful Japanese navy" in the area. It had suffered devastating losses in recent dramatic sea and air battles in the Pacific, and as we went silently back on deck with him we mused that perhaps Goebbels' propaganda was nothing in comparison to the invention of victorious battles by our Axis partners down here.

"However, don't argue with the Japanese, gentlemen!" he warned as we stepped onto the deck. He left us then to take a long walk with Captain Freiwald on the sunlit deck. They were both deep in conversation while our boat zigzagged behind the small Japanese speedboat.

Luck was with us; nothing happened on the ten-hour trip. The crew enjoyed the fresh air and I had ample time to tell them about Japanese, Chinese, and Malayan manners and customs, which were so very different from ours. Most of all they wanted to know about love life in Asia.

The pier at Penang was filled with throngs of men, German and Japanese in white and khaki uniforms. The sun reflected from the glittering instruments of a large Malayan band. When a gust of wind blew music toward us, we were thrilled to hear German marches. In spite of a strong and unpredictable current, Freiwald brought the U-boat exactly where at the pier the Japanese admiral and his staff, the German officers and men, and the bandstand were positioned. As the German and Japanese national anthems sounded solemnly, all stood at attention. The German anthem was played a bit fast, like a foxtrot. "Banzai!" and "Hurrah!" rang out as the band played on. We had finally arrived at our distant post, anxious and excited about what lay ahead.

RETURN TO PALAU

FROM *Maru Killer: War Patrols of the USS Seahorse*

---

by Dave Bouslog

*F*or some people, the call of the sea is an insistent one, even if they have never served on a pigboat or any other submarine. Our next author is Dave Bouslog, who was born during World War II in 1942. During the summers between his college years he worked as a photographer and reporter for WHIO-TV in Dayton before joining the Montgomery County Sheriff's Department in 1965. After serving in Dayton for twenty-six years, he retired as a lieutenant in June 1991. He has been studying submarine history for over forty-five years, and it shows in his published first book, *Maru Killer*, which appeared in 1996 to rave reviews from men such as Captain Edward L. Beach, Jr., Captain Ralph Styles, and Nelson Cutter. Dave and his wife, Jolene, currently live in Sarasota, Florida.

Dave chose to chronicle the exploits of the crew of one of the most celebrated submarines in the Pacific—the USS *Seahorse*. Under the command of four different skippers during her combat patrols, including the

legendary Slade D. Cutter, she would sink dozens of
Japanese ships during the last two years of the war.
Although it doesn't appear that Dave ever served in
the Navy, his accuracy and attention to detail come
through on every page of the following excerpt from
Maru Killer, which tells of the masterful submariner
Slade Cutter's first patrol as captain of the *Seahorse*.

Hot skippers, those who were adept at sinking ships, could ask for and in most cases were given their choice of patrol areas. Slade Cutter was a hot skipper. Even though *Seahorse*'s second patrol was an unqualified success, Captain Cutter still had a bad taste in his mouth from the humiliating first patrol at Palau. He was a fierce competitor and did not take defeat well. Dick Voge, Admiral Lockwood's operations officer, called Cutter and asked him where he wanted to take *Seahorse* for her third patrol. Cutter didn't hesitate; he asked to be sent back to Palau. He explained:

> I chose Palau for a couple of reasons—one good and the other vindictive. The good reason was that I knew there was good hunting in the area; the bad reason was that I wanted to show up McGregor.

Because of its proximity to several Japanese convoy routes and its naval base, Palau was ripe with targets and, therefore, a coveted assignment. ComSubPac normally maintained a constant submarine patrol around Palau, but to honor Cutter's request, Voge allowed the area to remain vacant for six days until *Seahorse* could arrive.

A vastly different *Seahorse* departed Pearl Harbor on 6 January 1944. Unlike the timid *Seahorse* of the first patrol, she was now a proven fighter: aggressive and tenacious. She respected the potential of her Japanese enemy, but did not fear him.

Slade Cutter had passed the test with his superb handling of *Seahorse* on the second patrol. Spud Lindon summed up the feelings held by most of the officers and crew of *Seahorse*:

Slade possessed a rare combination of those qualities which made him an ideal wartime submarine commander. He was young and vigorous. He could operate continuously for several days with little or no sleep. At the same time he was mature and experienced. Aggressiveness was inbred in Slade, as exemplified by his tremendous athletic achievements at the Naval Academy.

Slade was also a prudent person. I don't recall a single instance where I considered that he acted rashly. His actions were well thought out and designed for maximum probability of success, making optimum use of the element of surprise.

Slade had an uncanny ability to relate individually to every member of the ship's company. His infectious enthusiasm and optimism were transmitted to all hands and reflected in their feelings of confidence and pride. Rarely was there a man more right for command in war.

Machinist's Mate Eugene Carl put it simply:

Slade Cutter was different than any officer I ever knew. To the young seamen, he was a father figure we all looked up to and admired.

Seahorse was a happy ship and, although it was not exactly Navy issue, installation of a new piece of equipment during the refit made the crew even happier. Spud Lindon explains:

> When the boats built in Manitowoc, Wisconsin, started to come through Pearl Harbor, some of them had brand new slot machines. Someone had talked a police department in the Manitowoc area into giving to the submarine service some confiscated slot machines for the purpose of contributing to morale and the furtherance of the war effort. It was done with the understanding that the slot machines would be used only when the sub was in international waters. *Seahorse* didn't have any state-side connections, but somehow, using the submariner's gift for ingenuity, with possibly some help from the Honolulu Police Department, the crew came up with a slot machine for *Seahorse*. It was, however, not a new one, it had a lot of miles on it. The fire-control technicians were given the added duty of keeping the slot machine running. As I recall, the fire-control technicians spent more time maintaining that slot machine than they did handling their normal duties.
>
> We had an arrangement that every bit of money the slot machine made, which was considerable, was put into the ship's recreation fund. This was for ship's parties and the general welfare of the crew. The machine was placed in the after battery near the galley. The Chief of the Watch was given instructions that when anyone hit the jackpot, he was to give them an added amount of money from the rec fund to sweeten the pot a bit. The machine was a big hit with the crew.

I remember one of the other submarines which
had a slot machine had a sign over it which read,
"During depth-charge attacks, stand under this
machine. It has never been known to be hit yet!"

On 6 January 1944 *Seahorse* stood out from Pearl
Harbor for her third war patrol outfitted with a valuable new piece of equipment. Captain Cutter now
had the PPI scope for which he had wished. The
scope would enable him to see the complete tactical
picture surrounding his submarine during approaches
and attacks, giving him a distinct advantage over the
enemy.

Seahorse and her crew were in peak condition
when they arrived at Johnston Island. The submarine
topped off her fuel tanks, then immediately sailed for
her patrol area.

During the passage, *Seahorse* crossed the International Date Line, which according to Spud Lindon
always prompted this message to be passed over the
IMC: "Now hear this. Today is tomorrow!" or "Today is yesterday!" depending upon whether the sub
was going east or west at the time.

Seahorse entered her patrol area on the thirteenth
but encountered no enemy activity for the first three
days. The drought ended on the morning of the sixteenth when a smokey maru was sighted. Captain
Cutter sent the crew scurrying to battle stations and
commenced an end around to get ahead of the target.
After a short run, *Seahorse* slipped below the surface
to lie in ambush. Cutter raised the periscope and
watched the target draw nearer, noting that it was a
freighter of less than a thousand tons. Under normal
circumstances Cutter might have let this small fry

pass unmolested, but the fact that the vessel was accompanied by four escorts suggested the possibility that it was a valuable target. Cutter described the scene to his officers in the conning tower. Their discussions soon centered on the possibility that this ship was a trap.

Q-ships were vessels of very shallow draft designed to lure a lurking submarine into firing torpedoes, which would usually be set too deep to hit. The escorts would then locate the submarine by following down the wakes left by the torpedoes and conduct a coordinated attack. Q-ship tactics were highly successful during World War I, but in this war had achieved few positive results.

Cutter decided that it was a Q-ship, but opted to attack anyway. *Seahorse* had a new weapon in her arsenal for this patrol. The new Mark 18 electric torpedo was a wakeless torpedo whose advantage lay in the inability of the enemy to track it back to the firing submarine. The downside to the electric torpedo was its slower speed. Having the electric torpedoes erased from Cutter's mind the intimidation factor posed by the presence of four escorts.

The Mark 18s were housed in the after torpedo room, and it didn't take *Seahorse* long to maneuver into excellent firing position for a short-range stern tube shot.

All four of the freighter's escorts were now on the same side as *Seahorse*, making the shot more difficult. Just as Cutter was ready to fire, the small freighter zigged away, ruining an ideal setup. Because of the Mark 18's slower speed, the torpedo run was longer than Cutter desired. Not wanting to waste torpedoes, he held fire.

All four escorts were actively pinging within a mere 600 yards of *Seahorse*. Two of them passed ahead, and two passed astern of the submarine as she went deep to let them go by. Cutter planned to come up for another end around when the escorts departed. One wily escort captain, however, put a crimp in Cutter's plan when, for an unknown reason, he stayed behind, circling the area. The Japanese skipper must have suspected the submarine's presence, and soon had *Seahorse* solidly pinpointed in his probing beam of sound. WHAM!—a single depth charge exploded very close to the submarine's hull. A minute later, WHAM!—another near miss rocked the sub. Four minutes later, a third and forth underwater bomb shook *Seahorse*. All of these depth charges were extremely close. Five minutes elapsed before the next depth charge fell, and this one was, as Captain Cutter termed it, "a blockbuster!" Glass from broken light bulbs, cork dust, and paint chips flew from bulkheads, and personnel not hanging on tightly to something were knocked from their feet. This patrol boat skipper was very good, and he had definitely found the range.

It appeared that *Seahorse* was in for a rough time, but, just as suddenly as it had begun, the escort discontinued the attack, and the search, and sailed for the horizon. The crew of *Seahorse* was left badly shaken but alive. A little more persistence on the part of the escort commander might have proven deadly for *Seahorse*. A great many American submarines were undoubtedly saved from destruction by the tendency of many Japanese anti-submarine vessels to break off attacks prematurely.

Cutter gave the escort time to clear the area, then

brought *Seahorse* to periscope depth for a look around. He found the seas empty, so he surfaced and renewed pursuit of the fleeing target.

Half an hour passed before the enemy's smoke was again in sight. Cutter ordered another end around, and by 1944 *Seahorse* was in position 12,000 yards ahead of the target. The wary maru was making small zigs off her base course of 180 degrees, while the escorts patrolled on station. Just as the submarine settled into another favorable attack position, the maru changed the setup again, this time with a major zig toward *Seahorse*. The night was pitch black, and the officer of the deck didn't notice the target's change of course.

In his patrol report, Cutter praised Lieutenant Bill Budding, his TDC operator:

> With target bearing information from the SJ radar the TDC operator detected it [the change of course] at once and in a few seconds had the correct solution. It was Lieutenant Budding's first attack as TDC operator, and he did an excellent job. The many hours that he spent at the attack teacher between patrols paid big dividends.

Budding had learned the TDC operation from Lieutenant Ralph Pleatman during the second patrol. Because of Budding's alertness, Cutter quickly countered the target's move and settled *Seahorse* into an even better firing position.

At 2010, as the unsuspecting freighter crept closer to destruction, four torpedoes flashed from the bow tubes (the change in firing setup made use of the electric torpedoes in the stern tubes impossible). Running hot, straight, and normal, the fish took two minutes to reach their points of aim. At the correct time, and because they had been fired simultaneously by accident, torpedoes numbers one and two ripped into the freighter's engine room just a fraction of a second apart, disemboweling her. Torpedo number three struck with deadly force under the bridge, blowing it completely off the ship. Three minutes after the torpedoes broke the target's back, *Seahorse*'s aft battle lookout reported that both halves of the victim had sunk. The 784-ton *Nikko Maru* was the first success of the third patrol and the seventh so far to succumb to *Seahorse*'s death-dealing torpedoes. The true nature of the *Nikko Maru*'s cargo and purpose was never learned. Her secrets and eight of her crew lie at the bottom of the Pacific.

The escorts immediately began their usual tactic of milling around in circles, dropping depth charges. With the aid of the PPI scope, Captain Cutter was able to plot the position of each escort and extract *Seahorse* from their midst without being noticed. Depth charges rumbled in the distance as Cutter set course for Fais Island.

During an attack, men not assigned to the conning tower or control room rarely knew what was happening. Sheldon Stubbs, an electrician's mate from Portland, Oregon, was making his first war patrol in *Seahorse*. He remembers Captain Cutter going through all of the boat's compartments after each attack telling the crew about the action. This gesture was greatly appreciated by the crew.

Cutter attributed the simultaneous firing of the two torpedo tubes to "buck fever." *Seahorse*'s firing doctrine called for a torpedoman to stand between the torpedo tubes and fire the torpedoes by hand at the same time they were fired electrically from the conning tower. This practice prevented a misfire in case of electrical failure. Joe McGrievy recalls:

It was young Torpedoman-Striker John Rhode's first time at this position. He was a real gung-ho kid. He did everything a striker was supposed to with genuine enthusiasm, diving bilges, cleaning tanks and tubes, painting the bilges, and other important, but menial tasks.

As phone talker at battle stations, John was stationed between the torpedo tubes at the breach. His job was to hit the firing key on the tube when the firing circuit was closed in the conning tower.

During the entire time on watch, eight hours each day while en route to the patrol area, John would stand between the tubes, facing forward and practice: "Fire one. Fire two. Fire three." He repeated this over and over again.

At the first sounding of the battle stations klaxon, John jumped between the torpedo tubes and manned his phone. As the approach on the target continued, no one, especially John, noticed that he was facing aft, and not forward as he had rehearsed. When the firing point was reached, Captain Cutter ordered "Fire one." In the conning tower I hit the firing button for number one. Doing his job in backing up the firing of the fish, John hit the key for number two, because in his excitement, he was facing the wrong direction. John took a fair amount of good-natured ribbing about this from his shipmates for a time.

When *Seahorse* surfaced the next afternoon, the after lookout discovered that the submarine was leaving a considerable oil slick in her wake. The damage had probably been done by the previous day's depth-charge attack. This was a dangerous situation since the trail of oil could lead the enemy right to *Seahorse*. A wild storm was in progress, and the sea was too rough for anyone to go on deck to inspect for and repair the leak. The slick would have to remain until the weather abated.

The next day, not only was the oil leak still with her, but another major problem developed. The main induction commenced flooding as *Seahorse* dived. Quickly, the ballast tanks were blown, raising the sub back to the surface. The sea had calmed, so crewmen combed the boat's superstructure, and soon found the sources of both problems. The main induction gasket was pulled out of the groove in the valve disc in two places, each about eighteen inches long. Temporary repairs to it stopped the flooding. The oil leak was simpler. The cap on the forward fuel filling connection had worked loose. It was simply tightened and that problem was solved.

Per her patrol orders, *Seahorse* was to reconnoiter Fais Island, which she reached on the nineteenth. Cutter stayed 3,000 to 4,000 yards off the beach while he inspected the island's rugged coastline through the periscope. Along the north coast of the island he observed what appeared to be the muzzle of a four- to six-inch gun silhouetted against the sky. Cutter moved the submarine to within 1,800 yards of the beach to verify the gun's emplacement. Through the periscope the gun looked like the real McCoy, so Cutter called for the camera. It was fitted to the periscope and a series of photographs was taken of the gun emplacement and complete panoramic views of the coastline. In his patrol report Cutter noted, "The one gun sighted was remarkably well camouflaged, and because of the terrain, offered excellent cover for other gun emplacements which likely exist."

A standing order for every submarine assigned to this area was the task of bombarding the phosphate plant at Refinery Point on Fais Island. Cutter took a good look at the phosphate plant through the periscope. Seeing no indications that the plant was in operation, he decided not to attack. He was not keen on the idea of sitting on the surface off the coast of an enemy-held island in daylight exposing his guns' crews and his submarine to sudden air or artillery attack just to lob a few shells onto a target for harassment purposes. There appeared to be no shipping in the area, so Cutter set course back to Palau.

Designated No. 8 Wewak, a convoy consisting of two transports, *Ikoma Maru* and *Yasukuni Maru*, and two subchaser escorts, No. 32 and No. 47, left Palau en route to Hollandia, New Guinea, on June 20, 1944. Both transports carried vital war materials including gasoline, ammunition, provisions, and mail. *Ikoma Maru* also had human cargo aboard. Carried on the manifest as an "Independent Brigade" were 611 men of the Indian Army. Faced with a choice of being prisoners of war or joining the Japanese against the "Imperialist British," they chose the latter. The treatment they received from their captors, however, was little better than that received by POWs. Worse was ahead for them.

United States Naval Intelligence's ability to decrypt the Japanese naval codes enabled it to garner strategic information from Japanese radio traffic. Decoded information having to do with the movements of Japanese naval and merchant ships was sent to American naval vessels in a position to intercept them. This highly secret information was sent to the receiving submarine or surface ship in the form of an "ULTRA" message. ULTRAs were for the commanding officer's eyes only. In most cases, only the ship's captain had knowledge of the source of this intelligence info, and ULTRAs were never mentioned in a submarine's patrol report.

Responding to an ULTRA on 21 January, *Seahorse* patrolled the Palau-Wewak convoy route on the surface. The periscope watch sighted one puff of smoke at 1231, and Cutter turned his submarine in the direction of the contact, No. 8 Wewak convoy. A ship was soon sighted, and *Seahorse* began the familiar end around procedure. In less than an hour, the masts of two ships were visible through the periscope lens. Tracking the targets, however, was a difficult task. The ships were not making much smoke and were frequently masked by the numerous rain squalls in the area.

The convoy's escort was sighted at 1411. The patrol boat was 15,000 yards off the convoy's track and on the same side as *Seahorse*. This forced Cutter to conduct an end around on the escort also. The great distance she had to stay from the escort to remain unseen caused *Seahorse* to lose sight of the convoy for the next several hours, during which time she raced ahead on the convoy's assumed course. Two hours later the enemy ships were back in sight, and the submarine dived to conduct a submerged approach.

As the range decreased, Cutter saw that both targets were heavily laden with crates of cargo piled high on their decks. He preferred to make a simultaneous attack on both ships, but found that their relative positions made that tactic impossible. Attacking on the surface at night was his best chance of getting both mams.

With darkness above, *Seahorse* slipped silently to the surface and made a radar approach on the convoy. Four pips, two large and two small, dotted the green radar screen. Two escorts had joined the merchantmen. As the range dwindled, the bridge personnel could see the large freighters through their binoculars. About this same time, the SJ radar detected a third escort trailing 1,500 yards astern of the convoy. The other two escorts were stationed 2,500 and 4,000 yards ahead of the two AKs which continually zigzagged independently of each other. This setup complicated Captain Cutter's attack plan.

The largest ship appeared to be about 5,000 tons. *Seahorse* positioned herself abeam of the target and started her firing run. When the range closed to 2,900 yards, the big target zigged forty-five degrees toward the submarine. This put *Seahorse* uncomfortably close to the ship under good visibility conditions. Cutter quickly reversed course and opened the range before renewing his attack. He wanted to shoot both ships at the same time but they were still not properly aligned. Resigned to picking them off one at a time, he centered the target bearing transmitter (TBT) on the largest maru. At 2137, Cutter commanded, "Fire four! Fire five! Fire six!" The three missiles lunged from the bow tubes, and Cutter turned his attention to the second target.

The torpedo run to the first freighter was 2,800 yards. The second ship was in line of bearing just to the left of the first at a range of 3,600 yards. Two minutes after firing, two great explosions thundered as the first two torpedoes ripped open the steel port side of the large Japanese cargo ship. *Seahorse* was just reaching firing position on the second target when the third torpedo, to everyone's surprise, slammed into her stern. Cutter noted in his patrol log, "The Japs were no more surprised than we, as we entertained no hopes whatever of hitting the second ship with our first salvo."

Both enemy ships immediately went dead in the water. Observers on the submarine's bridge watched as figures on both of the stricken ships ran to man their guns. The Japanese fired wildly in all directions with no clue as to their attacker's location. The bewildered escorts dropped random depth charges, which killed a lot of fish, but didn't come close to *Seahorse*. She sat on the surface a short distance away watching the pyrotechnic display, waiting to see what developed.

It appeared to those on the submarine's bridge that the second target was sinking. The larger freighter, however, though low in the water, was still on an even keel. Cutter decided to hasten her demise by putting two more fish into her rusty carcass. Sitting dead in the water, the freighter made for an easy, can't miss shot, but miss they did! The torpedoes from tubes five and six sailed harmlessly past the AK. One of the escorts saw the torpedo wakes but chased them down away from *Seahorse*. The submarine's fire-control team huddled in the control room to find the reason for the misses.

The small maru was well down by the stern with only her forward half showing. Her sinking was assured. The large, stubborn maru was another matter. Cutter lined up the TBT on the wounded ship and fired two more torpedoes from a range of 2,600 yards. Once again the sitting duck thumbed her nose at *Seahorse* as the torpedoes failed to strike home.

Another summit was held by the fire-control brain trust, and this time the problem was identified. The TBT, through which the torpedoes were being aimed, had been knocked out of alignment, probably during the earlier depth charging of *Seahorse*. The gremlin having been found and adjusted, the business of sinking ships resumed.

The unlucky freighter was now lower in the water, but still on an even keel. Cutter felt it was worth spending two Mark 18 electric torpedoes to ensure that this valuable ship couldn't be salvaged by the Japanese. The escort was not a problem. It had chased down the last pair of torpedo wakes in the wrong direction and was wasting depth charges blasting holes in the water some 6,300 yards away from *Seahorse*. The other two escorts were nowhere in sight. They had been patrolling so far in front of their charges, it was possible they were not even aware of the attack. Cutter maneuvered *Seahorse* to get a better angle on the bow, then backed down on the target to reach the desired 2,200 yards firing position. During this positioning, the smaller freighter took her final plunge to the bottom, stern first. Cutter fired stern tubes eight and ten at 2324. As the torpedoes raced to put the finishing touches to the maru, *Seahorse* went ahead full to exit the scene of her double triumph. At exactly the correct time, the first torpedo struck the target abaft her stack, erupting in brilliant flames. The brightly illuminated vessel then suffered the killing blow of the second torpedo just forward of her bridge. This was too much for the mortally wounded ship. Her burst seams drank in the killing sea water, which filled her compartments and dragged her to the seabed.

Seahorse witnessed a spectacular follow-up show. Oil from the sunken ship's bunkers blazed on the ocean's surface. Her deck cargo of gasoline drums, now floating in the fires, exploded one by one, thundering and marking the dead ship's grave with a mass of burning fuel. As *Seahorse* retired from the area, Cutter permitted all hands "an opportunity to witness the spectacular show, and enjoy the unique experience of 'below-decks-men' actually seeing the results of their hard work." That work was the destruction of *Seahorse*'s eighth and ninth victims, the 3,021-ton Army freighter *Yasukuni Maru* and the 3,156-ton Army transport *Ikoma Maru*. Forty-nine crew members and 480 passengers also went down with the two enemy vessels. Among them were 418 of the Indian soldiers.

The TBT was inspected the next day and found to be several degrees out of calibration. This accounted for the torpedo hitting the second ship, which hadn't been fired at, and for missing the sitting duck maru, which had.

A typhoon raged around Palau on 22 January, so Cutter took his boat to the Wewak-Palau and Rabaul-Palau convoy routes, spending an unproductive day in the area. The weather improved late on the twenty-third, so *Seahorse* returned to patrol off Palau's Malakal Passage.

The twenty-fifth was a frustrating day. The SJ radar broke down. Technicians littered the deck of the conning tower with disassembled parts and worked feverishly to repair this vital piece of equipment.

In the early morning hours, sound reported pinging in the distance, and Captain Cutter changed course toward the bearing. At 0607, two PC-type escorts were sighted. *Seahorse* remained at periscope depth and followed the pair. Cutter hoped they were going to rendezvous with an incoming convoy.

Two pesky sampans dogged the submarine all morning, making observation with more than a couple of feet of periscope impossible. At 1019, the smoke of a convoy drifted above the horizon, but *Seahorse* was too far off the track to reach its position. The convoy had air cover which precluded the submarine from surfacing to pursue.

The next day, *Seahorse* maintained a surface, high periscope patrol along the shipping lanes southeast of Palau, while the electricans continued their work on the radar. That evening, they had the SJ back on line, and Cutter took his boat back to Malakal Passage.

On the twenty-seventh, Palau was picked up on radar at the extreme range of 60,000 yards. Cutter praised his technicians, noting, "This is by far the best result yet obtained by our equipment." The radar was fixed just in time; at 1301, the screen showed a ship coining out of the Passage.

Battle stations chimed, and the crew raced to their assignments. Captain Cutter started an approach on the target, but he experienced déjà vu upon identifying the intended target as a properly marked hospital ship. This was *Seahorse*'s third encounter with one of these untouchables around Palau.

Action loomed again the next afternoon. Three trawler-type patrol boats enthusiastically made a thorough anti-submarine sweep off the entrance to Malakal. Loudly echo-ranging, they came within 1,500 yards of the lurking submersible, but did not make contact. The patrol boats seemed to be clearing a path for an outbound convoy, so *Seahorse* lay in wait.

The evidence proved solid; at 1719, three sources of smoke appeared on the horizon. As the convoy approached *Seahorse*, a patrol plane darted and weaved over the ships looking for enemy submarines. Forty-five minutes later, *Seahorse* lookouts counted three freighters and five escorts coming out of Malakal Passage. Soundman Roy Hoffmann reported that three of the escorts were echo-ranging. Cutter initiated an end around to gain position ahead of the convoy by 2110.

Moving at eight knots and zigzagging, the convoy lumbered toward its unseen stalker. The escorts kept close watch on their flock: two patrolling on the port flank, two on the starboard flank, with one astern. Between 2110 that night and 0416 the next morning, *Seahorse* made six attempts to attack the convoy: one from ahead, one on each bow, one on each quarter, and one from astern. Every attempt Cutter made was foiled by the presence of an escort, which put itself between *Seahorse* and her target. Cutter found it impossible to get into position for an effective shot.

Cutter was puzzled by the escort's tactics. He was sure they knew of *Seahorse*'s location at all times, but, contrary to their normal tactics, did not come after her. The patrol boats seemed perfectly satisfied with passively defending the convoy, interjecting themselves to block the submarine from attacking. Cutter speculated that the convoy commander was afraid that his charges were surrounded by a "wolfpack" of submarines, and having a speed disadvantage, he didn't want any of his escorts to be drawn out of position. If this was his strategy, it was entirely effective.

Not one to give up easily, Cutter changed his tactics. He worked ahead of the convoy, remained on the surface, and waited for the normal daylight change of base course.

At 0600, the masts of the ships again hove into sight. Little more than an hour later, a Japanese twin-engine bomber escorting the convoy flew at *Seahorse* and forced her to dive. The submarine remained under until 0915, then returned to the surface. Forty-five minutes later, she was again forced to dive by another bomber.

Slade Cutter was a patient man, but he was beginning to get annoyed. He had never encountered such an efficient air-sea convoy escort team. Using periscope observations and sound bearings on the pinging escorts, *Seahorse* trailed on the convoy's beam at six knots. Cutter was tired of this cat-and-mouse game. He decided to follow the convoy until sunset, then surface and drive his submarine in and make a determined effort to erase the enemy ships from the ocean's surface.

With the sun well below the horizon, the dark-hulled submarine emerged from the depths and advanced toward the convoy. Cloaked in darkness, *Seahorse* moved into position ahead of the oncoming merchantmen. Conditions were perfect for a night surface attack, and a determined Slade Cutter bored in to strike.

Three times he skillfully placed *Seahorse* in excellent firing position, and just as skillfully, an escort placed itself between the target and the aggressor, ruining the setup. Perplexed but undaunted, Cutter decided to trail the convoy and wait patiently for a window of opportunity to open.

The exasperated sub skipper got the break he was looking for at 0132 on the thirtieth. The convoy made a sudden zig to the right. Cutter was in the conning tower watching the TDC when he saw in its information the radical zig. He immediately realized that the escorts were thrown out of position by the zig, and that the convoy's flank was wide open. He jumped up and yelled, "Battle stations, torpedo," and turned *Seahorse* to attack. Cutter had his opening. Now it became a race to see if he could reach firing position before the escorts could recover and intervene.

On the surface, *Seahorse* had a decided speed advantage over the older and slower patrol boats which enabled her to win the race. She reached firing position with little time to spare.

The lead ship passed 2,600 yards in front of the submarine's bow tubes at 0149, and was greeted with three torpedoes. Two of them arrived at their points of aim. The first fish blasted a hole in the side of the maru and set her on fire. The third torpedo blew the stern from the rest of the hull. Silhouetted by a huge gasoline fire, the mortally wounded freighter took on a large angle down by the stern. Her bow stuck high in the air, paused momentarily, as if to get a last look at the sky, then slid gracefully to oblivion. Victim number ten was the 2,747-ton Army freighter *Toko Maru*. Her passengers were soldiers of the 31st Infantry Regiment and the 4th Field Hospital being taken to Manus Island. Four hundred and fifty-seven of them were killed in the explosion and fire, or were drowned. Tenacity, patience, and persistence, three trademarks of Slade Cutter and *Seahorse*, had paid dividends.

In an ironic twist, the escorts, who earlier had been so efficient in knowing the submarine's location and keeping her from the convoy, now had no clue as to her whereabouts and could not retaliate.

With the coming of the morning light, *Seahorse* was forced to open the range to avoid being detected. She continued to maintain radar contact with the convoy. Near sunrise, radar contact was lost. Sound tried to locate the enemy ships by listening for the ping, ping, ping of the escorts' sonar, but nothing was heard beyond the normal sound of the ocean and its biological inhabitants. It seemed that the convoy was lost. In a short time, however, *Seahorse* got a break. An escort vessel was sighted running at high speed in *Seahorse*'s direction. Thinking the escort was headed for the convoy, Cutter turned his boat to follow in its wake. At 0934, Cutter was shocked to find the convoy back in the location of his previous attack on the same group of ships.

Shortly after sighting the convoy, *Seahorse* was forced to dive by the approach of a Japanese bomber. With aircraft overhead Captain Cutter had to limit his periscope exposures. The escorts' pinging, however, enabled *Seahorse* to keep track of the group by sound while she continued her methodical approach to the remaining freighters. The submarine's slow underwater speed prevented her from closing the track sufficiently to fire, so Cutter settled for trailing the convoy to wait for another window of opportunity to open.

At dusk, the air cover which had persisted all day was gone. Half an hour later, the convoy split up. *Seahorse* trailed the nearest ship and escort, tracking them with radar. That evening, the radar's performance became erratic, and at 2100 contact with the ships was lost. The submarine began an immediate search to relocate the enemy, an effort which took fifteen hours. Just after noon on 31 January, contact with the convoy was reestablished, and the game started all over again.

A patrol bomber flew protectively above the enemy freighter, while somewhere in the vicinity of the convoy a series of sixteen depth charges exploded. These charges were probably meant to keep submarines at a distance, but *Seahorse* wasn't intimidated, and began another end around.

That evening, the radar began functioning again and quickly had the convoy plotted. It took another four hours, however, before the submarine was in position 16,000 yards ahead of the ships. A bright moon provided more than enough light for the bridge personnel to see the targets, and Cutter decided to hold his position until the moon set. He didn't want to risk exposure in the brilliant moonlight.

The moon dipped below the horizon at 2300, and *Seahorse* resumed her approach in total darkness. The SJ radar chose this moment to act up again, showing neither the target nor the escort on its screen. Cutter ordered, "All stop," and had the sound head lowered to get bearings on the escort's pinging. Just as the sound operator found the convoy, the SJ blinked back into operation, so Cutter continued his approach. The troublesome radar quit again just as the submarine settled into a suitable firing position, leaving Cutter blind. Exasperated, Cutter had no choice but to wait while the technicians did their best to fix the equipment. The electrician's mates did a good job in getting the radar working in just eleven minutes. The screen came alive again with blips, and *Seahorse* charged at the enemy.

Since six torpedoes remained in the after torpedo room, while the forward room had only two, *Seahorse* maneuvered for a stern tube shot. Nineteen minutes after midnight on the first of February, Cutter launched a four-torpedo assault on the surviving Japanese freighter. The entire crew was exhausted from this long ordeal, and Cutter wanted to end the contest, but it was not to be. After the fish were in the water, the target suddenly zigged away, and the torpedoes missed by a wide margin. All four then exploded at the end of their runs, which alerted the convoy to the submarine's presence. The only good news was that the enemy couldn't find *Seahorse*.

Using the radar and the extreme darkness, Cutter skillfully placed his submarine in a new firing location. By 0200 he was ready to shoot again, this time using the two remaining bow torpedoes. "Fire one! Fire two!" Cutter ordered. All hands prayed that these would be their parting shots, but again the freighter zigged, leaving the torpedoes out in left field, their mission unfulfilled.

Cutter blamed himself for these misses. He logged:

Although we knew the target's course and speed accurately at the time of firing, we should have held out for a more favorable firing position, knowing as we did that the target was maneuvering radically at

frequent intervals. All hands were exhausted after a
chase of eighty hours, and we were probably too
anxious to get it over with.

Slade Cutter was desperate to end this marathon
battle. Functioning on adrenaline mixed with a lot of
caffeine and Benzedrine, he knew he couldn't keep
this up much longer. He was afraid that he would
become impaired to the point of making an error in
judgment, which might cause the loss of his ship and
crew.

With only two Mark 18 electrics left in the stern
tubes, he decided on another change in tactics. He
moved to a position 10,000 yards ahead of the target,
dived, and waited for the freighter to come to him.
Tracking the enemy ship over these many hours, he
had observed that although she zigged frequently, she
never got farther than 800 yards from her track. It
would be a simple matter of waiting, and accepting
whatever track developed, then firing the torpedoes
when the range was short enough to prevent a miss.

At 0347, the freighter changed course to the left,
giving Cutter a beautiful shooting setup. With one of
the escorts only 800 yards away, *Seahorse* presented
her stern to the target. The time to fire was now, but
Cutter was having considerable trouble seeing the
target well enough through the periscope to get a
point of aim. As became his habit in these situations,
Cutter summoned Joe McGrievy. He explains why:

Chief Quartermaster Joseph L. McGrievy was the
ultimate in a chief of the boat. The top enlisted
man aboard any submarine and right behind the
exec in value to a skipper. McGrievy was tough as

nails, but fair. He brought things to me on a man-
to-man basis, yet was respectful. He was truly a
Naval professional petty officer and a top submariner.

McGrievy had the best night vision of anyone
on the boat. He was like a cat. I made several night
submerged attacks during the war so we could get
in closer and I didn't have to worry about the escorts. I put McGrievy on the periscope. I couldn't
see anything, but he could see those black hulks
through the scope. The way he did it was to move
the scope from a black blurb until he could see a
star, which meant he was ahead of it. Then he
would move it back to the hulk and say "fire!" He
then swung the periscope in the other direction
until he saw a star and moved it back and said
"fire!" He was inside the bow and inside the stern
and then he would fire one where he judged the
middle of the target to be. That's when he was an
enlisted man and that's why I made him an officer.

He was also my officer of the deck at night during battle stations, when we made night surface attacks. Mind you, this was as a petty officer! I would
be in the conning tower where I had the TDC. He
was feeding data to me such as the bearing and
the disposition of the target ships. He was invaluable and absolutely fearless. Nothing bothered
McGrievy.

At a range of 1,050 yards, McGrievy fired the first
torpedo inside the bow; twenty-four seconds later he
fired number two inside the stern.

All torpedoes were expended and Cutter had to
think about getting the hell out of there. The escort

was dangerously close on *Seahorse*'s starboard beam. He ordered, "Left full rudder, standard speed, take her deep." *Seahorse* started down to the security of deep water. She hadn't gotten far when two tremendous explosions rattled her and sent water rushing through the superstructure. All hands thought that depth charges had detonated close aboard, but soon realized that it was the sweet sound of their torpedoes hitting home, putting an end to this Japanese merchantman's career.

The depth charges came eight minutes after the torpedoes hit, but their noise didn't compare to what was occurring in the devastated freighter. Two thunderous blasts ripped the victim apart, followed by literally hundreds of light explosions which sounded like strings of firecrackers going off. These secondary explosions were ammunition and gasoline drums cooking off. A short time later, two much heavier explosions occurred in the dying ship.

Depth charges were also thundering, but none of them anywhere close to the submarine, so Captain Cutter brought his boat back to the surface to witness the aftermath of the crew's long, grueling labors. The hatches were cracked, and when the personnel came out onto the bridge, they witnessed an inferno raging on the ocean's surface around the freighter. Floating gasoline drums exploded continuously. This funeral pyre marked the grave of the 4,004-ton Navy-controlled transport *Toei Maru*. Silhouetted against the flames on the water, the escorts scurried from place to place trying to pick up survivors before they toasted.

Now barren of her primary means to wage war,

Seahorse put this hellish scene astern and set course for Pearl Harbor.

Commencing with the sighting of the convoy on 28 January 1944 and ending with the sinking of the last freighter on 2 February, this epic struggle lasted eighty-four hours. It was one of the longest sustained convoy battles by one submarine in World War II.

Slade Cutter fought the entire battle attired in his pajamas. The crew was mentally and physically drained. Captain Cutter ordered *Seahorse* down to 200 feet, where she would remain until the crew could rest and recuperate. Only a skeleton crew was kept on duty to keep the boat functioning.

Most of the sailors were asleep before their heads hit the pillow, but some, including the captain, couldn't sleep. Even though he was thoroughly exhausted and already in his pajamas, sleep refused to come to Slade Cutter. He left his cabin and went to the wardroom where he began a game of acey-deucy with Frank Fisher, but he felt terrible and couldn't concentrate. In search of relief, he called the pharmacist's mate to the wardroom. After hearing the skipper's problem, the pharmacist's mate left, but soon returned with a bottle of Old Crow whiskey, which was kept locked up for medicinal purposes. He gave the bottle to Cutter, who quickly ingested all of its contents, but it had no effect on him. Summoned once again, the pharmacist's mate gave Cutter some sleeping pills. Since the beginning of the convoy pursuit, Cutter had been living on coffee and Benzedrine, and the sleeping pills were not potent enough to counter their effects on him. Although little more than a zombie, Cutter remained wide awake. The pharmacist's mate again responded to his captain's call; this time, however, he refused to give him anything except advice, which was to return to his cabin and lie in his bunk until he went to sleep.

Cutter followed his doctor's order and in a short time fell into slumber. Less than two hours later, he was awakened by the worst headache he had ever experienced. He suffered in this manner for several days before his body returned to some semblance of normalcy.

The journey home was interrupted by a message from CornSubPac, ordering *Seahorse* to Wake Island. She was to perform lifeguard services during air strikes by B-24 Liberators from Midway. She remained on station off Wake for four days, but received no calls to rescue downed airmen. She was then released by Com-SubPac to return home.

Captain Cutter was always devising ways to keep the crew's morale up. On the journey home, he had each man write an essay on why he enlisted in the Navy. With Cutter as judge, the most interesting essay won a pint of rye whiskey, to be awarded to the winner upon his going on leave in Pearl. This was a prize any sailor going on leave would covet. The winning entry was submitted by Electrician's Mate Gerhard Nelson of Tucson, Arizona, who wrote:

Upon graduation from high school in 1942, a friend of mine and I went to work for a construction company building an ordnance plant in Wisconsin. Our first job was working on the cafeteria area.

Our supervisors—all women school teachers on summer break—took great pleasure in bossing my

friend and me around. After a month of this dicta-
torial treatment, we got to wondering if this is
what it would be like if the Japs won the war. Our
minds were soon made up. I enlisted in the Navy
and my friend signed up with the Army.

Not all of the problems which faced the commanding officer of a fighting submarine in wartime were
life and death matters. Incoming vessels to Midway
had a sunset deadline for entering the harbor. If a
ship arrived after sunset, she was required to remain
outside until sunrise. *Seahorse* would probably make
the deadline if she continued at four-engine speed;
however, there was a question as to whether or not
sufficient fuel remained to maintain that speed long
enough to arrive on time.

Early on the crucial day, Lieutenant Lindon provided Cutter with the distance to Midway and their
projected time of arrival at various engine speeds.
This information suggested that if speed were reduced
to avoid running out of fuel, as was recommended by
Chief Engineer "Les" Lessard, *Seahorse* might miss
the sunset deadline and have to suffer the humiliation
of waiting until morning to enter the harbor. Cutter
initially decided to accept Lessard's recommendation.
Later, however, Cutter changed his mind when a mid-
morning navigational check showed a real need for a
boost in speed to make the sunset ETA, which had
already been radioed to the harbor master at Midway. Cutter opted to return to four-engine speed. Lessard protested to his captain, pointing out the real
chance they were taking of running out of fuel and
suffering the embarrassment of having to be towed
into port. Cutter, with Solomon-like wisdom, calmed

Lessard's fears by pointing out that in addition to the fuel remaining in the tanks, *Seahorse* had a "full can" (a fully charged battery). That evening, just before sunset, *Seahorse* sailed into the harbor at Midway. When she tied up to her berth, her normal fuel tanks were bone dry; the clean fuel oil tanks had only the barest amount remaining.

After refueling and making minor repairs, *Seahorse* left Midway for Pearl Harbor, where she arrived on 16 February 1944. Triumphantly, a proud but weary crew was home. It had been a relatively short patrol, but officers and enlisted men alike were drained. They looked forward to a much needed period of rest and recreation. The eighty-four-hour convoy battle had taken its toll, but a happier bunch of submariners couldn't be found anywhere. They had one of the most successful boats in the fleet and were high on their accomplishments. Two consecutive outstanding patrols proved that *Seahorse*, under Slade Cutter, was no flash-in-the-pan. They were "hot."

Admiral Lockwood's endorsement to this patrol reads:

The third war patrol of the *Seahorse* was conducted in the Palau area. For the second time in succession, the *Seahorse* carried out an aggressive and successful patrol. All approaches were made after careful study of the situation and were followed by determined, extremely well planned and executed attacks. The percentage of torpedo hits, 54%, is highly commendable. This patrol is designated as successful for Combat Insignia Award.

CONVOY HUNTING
SOUTH OF THE EQUATOR

FROM *Wake of the Wahoo*

---

by Forest J. Sterling

*T*his next excerpt is from Forest J. Sterling (1911–
2002), who had already served a stint in the U.S.
Navy before World War II, but had been out of the
service for so long that by the time he wanted to reenlist during the war, they wouldn't take him at first. He
persevered, however, and signed back up in 1942, in
time to serve under one of the top submarine skippers in the Navy—Commander Dudley "Mushmouth"
Morton, on the USS *Wahoo*. Morton was to accomplish many firsts during his patrols, including the first
U.S. submarine to penetrate a Japanese-controlled
harbor, and the first submarine to successfully execute a "down-the-throat" attack on an enemy destroyer. Sterling served on the *Wahoo* until just before
its last patrol, when Captain Morton transferred him
off the boat forty-five minutes before it was set to
head out again. The *Wahoo* never returned to port,
presumed destroyed by depth charges from a Japanese airplane. After his tour, Sterling also served in
the Korean War as part of a secret communications

crew, then retired and worked in the San Diego Motor Vehicles Department, and as a motel night clerk. Fifteen years later, after a few English courses, Forest J. Sterling set down the five combat patrols of the *Wahoo* that he had participated in in his acclaimed memoir, *Wake of the Wahoo*. After the death of his wife, in 1989, Sterling was admitted to the Naval Home in 1991, where he passed away in 2002. His awards include the Presidential Unit Citation, Good Conduct Medal, and combat insignia with three bronze stars.

While many submarine books tell of the heroics of the officers on board, Sterling spends just as much time with the yeomen and sailors on the decks below. His firsthand knowledge permeates every page of his book, and brings to life what war was like when serving under a man who understood his men, his ship, and how to gain the maximum effort out of both to fight the enemy. But that doesn't mean that there isn't time for a bit of fun as well. Sterling shows that the men can also play as hard as they work when he also sheds light on the mysterious "shellback" ceremony that occurred when a submarine crossed the equator with sailors who had never been on the far side of the world before.

No land was discernible from the lookout station on the 1600–1800 watch. The watch was not wasted, however, as it produced an awe-inspiring tropical sunset. When the sun balanced itself precariously on the earth's horizon for that fraction of a second before the earth continued revolving eastward, it presented an enlarged blood-red, slightly distorted orb that could be viewed with the naked eye. The overhead sky took on chameleon changes from blue to a deep purple. In the east, a darkening band of gray widened, getting ready to push the colors out of the sky as soon as the sun would be swallowed up. A dim moon took shape, becoming a brighter silver in proportion to the evening's waning.

Gradually the sun flattened out and dissolved into nothingness. I had a tremendous struggle keeping my attention away from this awe-inspiring phenomenon and concentrating on other areas of the sea, for I knew that an enemy submarine, plane, or ship would like nothing better than to get *Wahoo* silhouetted against nature's footlights.

Wonderful, tantalizing, exotic tropical smells carried across the darkening greenish graylike ocean in an effort to seduce me into quiescence—lassitude that *Wahoo* could ill afford, since the safety of every man aboard depended on lookout's alertness. Appel was the other lookout.

This feeling of oneness with the universe lasted until Ater relieved me from my pleasant occupation.

I came below decks with a deep feeling of serenity upon me.

I had just managed to manufacture a Dagwood sandwich, several layers high with cheese, sardines, cold roast beef, pickles, and a few condiments made available by Rowls, who watched my handiwork with distaste, and was drawing a cup of coffee when Lane came in. He sat down across the table from me.

"They certainly do starve a guy on this boat," he observed sagely.

"You said it," I managed between bites. "I'm nothing but a mass of skin and bones."

"Bunch of belly-robbers," Lane added.

Rowls leaped up angrily. "If you bastards don't like the way I feed on this boat, why don'cha get yourselves transferred?" His eyes were flashing dangerously.

Lane said soothingly, "Take it easy, Cookie, we're only kidding. Besides, I've got some news you'll want to hear."

I picked up my big ears and flapped them, waiting while Rowls, now curious, calmed down to a simmer.

"Yeah, what is it?"

Lane lowered his voice and we unconsciously bunched our heads in conspiracy.

"Tomorrow we cross the equator. Now Pappy Rau has already learned that you two guys are shellbacks. We're going to have a meeting of the shellbacks in the messhall at 2000. Yeo, you go through the service records and get me a list of the qualified shellbacks, and Rowls, chase everybody out of here at 2000, okay?"

I answered eagerly, "You damn betcha I will only . . ."

"Only what?"

"Only will 'Mush' let us hold an initiation?"

"He's the one that suggested it. He told Pappy about it on your last run and gave him money to buy some shellback cards in Brisbane. We should cross the equator after noon chow sometime tomorrow, so Rowls, you get the noon mess squared as soon as you can."

Rowls was all enthusiasm now. "Boy, them guys will hardly get seated before I start yanking their plates away from them."

Lane got up and strolled away. I picked up the remnants of the sandwich, looked nonchalantly about, noticing that the card games were in their usual progress and that we had apparently not been heard, and sneaked secretively to the sink, disposed of the food in the garbage pail, set the cup down quietly on the sink, and crept secretively out.

0800 found shellbacks ensconced in the crew's messroom.

Pappy Rau said, "I crossed the equator in '22. Anybody cross before then?" He looked around at our negative head swings. "Okay, I nominate and elect myself as King Neptune by virtue of seniority." He made some notations on the list and then read them to us in a low tone.

"Lennox, you be Queen Neptune, Lane be Davy Jones. Yeo, you'll be Royal Scribe, Wilcox be Royal Prosecutor. There won't be any need for a defense counsel. Let's see—Rowls is about the fattest, so he can be the Royal Baby. Who is the youngest shellback, Yeo?"

I thought over the list. "I guess Krause is."

Rau said, "Okay, then, Krause will be the Royal

Princess. Lindhe can be the Royal Physician, Hunter the Royal Barber, O'Brien the Royal Electrician, and let's see— Oh, yeah, we'll make Muller the Royal Executioner, and Carr and Vidick the Royal Masters-at-Arms." He paused, studied the list, and said to Lane, "That ought to do it." Then to me, "You'd better get started making subpoenas."

O'Brien tapped me on the shoulder when the midwatch came around and I left the typewriter to go up on lookout.

After the watch ended, I finished doing the subpoenas and turned in. The monotonous clanging of the general alarm bell brought me upright. "Man your battle stations surface, man your battle stations surface" whipped out of the speakers as I hit the deck and slipped into my moccasins. Already dressed, I lost no time in running for the control, bumping into others as I ran. Rau was waiting with binoculars, which I grabbed as I sped by—up the two ladders onto the bridge, into dazzling sunlight, and on up to the starboard lookout platform, passing Gerlacher on his way down.

I quickly adjusted the binoculars to my eyesight after making a fast visual search. I could see nothing but water and clouds. Then bringing the horizon and distant waves into closer focus with the high-powered glasses, I began to scan the entire area closely. Now that my reflexes had stopped working, I began to wonder if this was a drill.

I took time to look below and saw men at their gunnery stations, some still moving agitatedly about. Captain Morton, Lieutenant O'Kane, and Lieutenant Paine were on the bridge. Reports came drifting up. "Twenty millimeters manned and ready, sir." "Deck gun manned and ready, sir." "All stations manned and ready, Captain."

"Very well, stand by."

I turned my attention back to my job but kept my ears tuned to what was going on below.

"There she is, Captain, two points off the port bow."

The sun was getting warm on my face and neck. I cursed myself for not stopping long enough to grab a blue-dyed hat, and made a mental note to have one handy the next time.

When it came time for me to search the ocean forward again, my curiosity got the better of my judgment, and I swung the glasses across the bow and two points the other side. I saw a long narrow native banca in the water with six men in it. Three were standing up with their arms raised above their heads. I swung the binoculars back into my allotted area of ocean and searched it thoroughly. There was still nothing on my side.

"All clear on the starboard quarter," I sang out.

Lieutenant Paine below answered automatically, "Very well."

Captain Morton's voice drifted upward, "Come left to three-two-oh."

"Left to three-two-oh, sir," the helmsman echoed.

"Steady on three-two-oh, all stop."

"All stop answered, Captain. Steadied on three-two-oh, sir."

"Very well, hold her there."

"Aye, aye, sir."

Wahoo's speed reduced and we coasted toward the banca.

"Roger, take Carr and Rau and go up on the bow.

See if any of the natives speak English and find out what they're doing away out here."

"Yes sir, Captain," Lieutenant Paine's voice answered.

"If they speak English, find out if any Japanese ships have been by this way recently."

"Yes sir." Paine's voice was fainter this time.

"Control, get Manalisay and Jayson on deck immediately."

Lieutenant Henderson's voice from the bridge speaker replied, "Yes sir, Captain, right away."

"Very well, Hank."

The captain must have turned to Lieutenant O'Kane. "When the messboys get here, send them down to Paine. See if they can speak these people's language, Dick!"

The executive officer's voice answered, "Yes sir, just as soon as they get here."

I took my eyes away from the binoculars for a quick look. *Wahoo* was moving in close to the boat. Carr, with forty-five in hand for ready use, and Carter, standing by with a Browning automatic rifle, were spaced along *Wahoo*'s bow. Pappy Rau and Lieutenant Paine had their heads close together apparently talking. Rau turned, pointing the length of the boat aft and then out toward the banca.

Quickly wiping the binocular lenses with lens paper I kept in a shirt pocket, I turned my attention back to sea. Then I glanced downward at another commotion beneath my feet and saw Manalisay and Jayson tumble out on deck, still in white orderly jackets.

O'Kane said, "Hey, you two . . ." I did not catch the rest as I was peeking at the sun between the narrowed slits of my fingers to keep the rays from scorching my eyeballs while I searched in that area of the sky to make certain that no Jap Zeros were sneaking in on us with the sun behind their backs.

When I was thoroughly satisfied that there was nothing of a hostile nature in my area, I reported again, "All clear on the starboard side, sir."

Lieutenant O'Kane's voice answered quickly, "Very well, starboard lookout."

The captain said, "Krause, go up forward and see if you can find out if they've learned anything yet."

"Yes sir, Captain." I heard Krause's running footsteps along the bridge deck.

After a little while I looked down on deck and then turned the binoculars on the banca, which was close by. The powerful glasses made it near enough to reach out and touch.

They had their arms down now and one of the three natives was making motions with his arms and hands in a sign language. I could see his mouth working. They all had strong Negroid features and had on loincloths. An old man with gray kinky hair and skinny arms, which were half raised in supplication, was staring with the blank, open-eyed fixity of a blind person. Another lay huddled in the stern of the boat taking no interest in what was going on. Still another figure sitting on his haunches got up stiffly while I was watching, and I could see that his skin was covered with scabs and sores. There were numerous spots where the dark skin had lost its pigmentation, leaving pink spaces to offset the natural color.

Having seen this much, I began searching my side of the ship again. I was not anxious to have a Jap submarine, plane, or destroyer catch us napping while *Wahoo* was dead in the water.

I heard Krause's voice as he came back on the bridge. "Mr. Paine says the messboys can't make out their dialect, but they've found out enough to know these people have been to sea for days and are out of water and food."

Captain Morton's voice replied, "Thank you, Krause. Get word below for the cooks to send up food and water. We can't stay around here too long." Shortly afterward he secured us from battle stations.

The sun was starting to blister me and my relief, the regular lookout, was late in getting topside. Finally I heard Gerlacher's voice below requesting permission to come on the bridge. I formulated a particularly scathing remark to greet him with. He pulled up alongside of me and I turned to him angrily. Whatever I had in mind I never said it, because he was dressed only in shorts, over which was thrown a blue Navy peacoat, and he was wearing leggings. A chic blue hat set the outfit off nicely. Below the peacoat he displayed bare knees and thighs, which had been anointed with tan lotion.

"Sorry, Yeo, I'd been up sooner, only Pappy made me go change into these," he said apologetically.

"A slimy no-good polliwog! Please move over to the leeward side," I answered condescendingly. "I don't care for that fishy stale smell that is polluting the air."

"Gee, Yeo . . ."

"Furthermore, don't you have some special orders? Come on, what are they?"

"I am to keep an extra sharp lookout for the equator, sir!"

"That's better. You can't miss it. It's a broad black belt and lays close to the surface of the water. Keep that in mind."

"Yes, sir!"

I left the lookout station and went below decks.

I picked up the subpoenas at the office and went into the crew's messroom. Carr was there, so I handed them to him for delivery.

I went back, washed up for noon chow, and rummaged about in my locker. Finding an old mattress cover, I took it back to the office. I got out a pair of scissors and cut a hole for my head and arms. Then I remembered a spool of red tape left over from prewar days and cut off a length sufficient to make a belt. Digging around, I found a green desk blotter from which I scissored a green-leaf Roman headband. I got out some rubber bands to hold it on with and began a mental search for something to symbolize my badge of office. Remembering a rusted and useless numbering stamp machine, I pulled it out of a lower drawer and tied it onto the red-tape belt. My costume was now complete. I was ready for the afternoon's business.

Rowls, true to his word, cleared the messhall in record time. The shellbacks met in the messhall while the polliwogs were sent to the forward torpedo room to wait and contemplate their sinful living.

Pappy had on Morton's old bathrobe, and a new swab was hanging down around his ears. He had a gold cardboard crown on his head and a set of long white false whiskers that he had bought in Brisbane. He carried a wooden broom-handle trident with tips electrically charged from dry-cell batteries in a box suspended by a shoulder strap.

Lennox had on a woman's gingham dress that displayed skinny hairy legs and black socks held up with men's supporters. He had a swab hairdo also.

A black patch fitted over one of Lane's eyes, and he

had a red bandanna about his head and gold earrings. Black Jack chewing gum gave him the appearance of missing teeth, and he wielded a mighty "bolivey" made of canvas and stuffed with water-soaked cotton, making a very effective, persuasive instrument.

Fat Rowls, stripped to bare skin, was wearing a gigantic diaper held together with a horse-blanket safety pin.

Krause had located a lipstick memento and painted luscious red lips on his mouth, sprayed himself liberally with a loud perfume, and was wearing a Hawaiian sarong.

Everybody had "boliveys" or paddles with holes in them except Rau, Lennox, Rowls, and myself.

When everything was ready, Pappy looked around at the eager assemblage. He had as motley a crew of bloodthirsty cutthroats as any Captain Kidd would be pleased with. "Let's go."

We single-filed into the control room and filled it with savage growls and threats. Lieutenant Henderson was the diving officer, and Jesser was handling the chief's duties.

Lieutenant Henderson called into the bridge speaker, "Captain, His Majesty King Neptune has come aboard and commands your presence in the control room."

Morton's voice came right back, "Very well, I will receive His Majesty immediately."

He came down from the bridge, followed by Lieutenant O'Kane. He saluted Pappy Rau mockingly and said, "Welcome aboard, Your Majesty. To what pleasure am I indebted for this visit?"

Davy Jones answered, "It has come to the attention of His Royal Highness that your ship is crawling with slimy, sneaky, leprous polliwogs. This is a disgrace that can only be remedied by a summons of these vermin to the Royal Court and the culprits being properly transformed into shellbacks."

Morton was shocked. "My ship crawling with stinky, low-down polliwogs? Will you ask His Majesty if it would be His Royal pleasure to hold court on the *Wahoo*?"

We all went into a huddle. When we came out, Davy Jones said, "His Royal Highness has been advised by His Court that this outrageous condition should be handled with all expediency. It is His Royal Highness' command that these—I hesitate to use the word—polliwogs be dragged out of the bilges and tried in court."

Morton answered, "I am deeply gratified that this is His Royal Highness' decision. Will he take over the ship now?"

"His Majesty will. It is his command that *Wahoo* be dived under the equator while court is in session."

"Very well, proceed with your plans."

Lane went over to the bridge speaker and spoke into it. "Officer of the Deck, His Royal Highness King Neptune orders you to dive ship."

"Very well." Then Lieutenant Paine's voice drifted down through the hatch, "Clear the bridge, clear the bridge." Two raucous blasts from the siren nearly deafened us. The duty section in the control room went into quick action. *Wahoo* tilted on her way down, and the Royal Court opened a passageway for the King and Royal Family to pass through. I heard Captain Morton laughing with loud guffaws and I looked to see what he found to be so funny. He was looking and pointing at Rowls, who waddled along behind with his thumb in his mouth.

I went with Carr, Muller, and a big portion of our piratical crew to the forward torpedo room.

"Will Polliwog Grider step forward?"

He moved away from the crowd and up the two steps to the door. Carr had a big pile of bandages waiting in the officers' pantry. He selected one and placed it over Grider's eyes. Grider's beard made a wonderful target under that and we eyed it enviously.

"Find your way to the messhall on your hands and knees," Carr ordered.

I worked my way through flailing paddles back into the crew's mess and found O'Brien, the Royal Electrician, with an ingenious electrical persuader. It was his job to help the victims through the door solicitously and then to check their vitality for run-down batteries. Laffin was on the other side of him, as Royal Traffic Cop, to direct the traffic into the crew's sleeping quarters with a handsomely made "bolivey."

Grider with half his beard and mustache missing had been through the cleansing process and was standing in the center of the messhall, still blind-folded, with Keeter and McGill holding on to his arms.

Wilcox was reading from a subpoena, "—and charged with being a polliwog and with failure to set the watch after it had run down."

"How do you plead?"

"Guilty."

Pappy Rau said, "I am inclined to be lenient with this misguided polliwog. Will you swear to be a good and faithful loyal subject for the rest of your natural-born days?"

"I do."

"Very well. Then, prove it by kissing the Royal Baby's bottom."

Lieutenant Grider was forced to his knees and his face was rubbed into Rowls' belly. He was yanked to his feet sputtering and laughing.

Pappy said, "What are you?"

Grider answered, "I am a lousy, no-good polliwog."

Paddles descended on his posterior and he waved his hands backward trying to ward them off.

Pappy repeated, "What are you?"

This time Lieutenant Grider got the idea. "I'm a full-fledged shellback."

I moved on into the sleeping quarters. Lindhe met me at the door with a shoe box filled with marble-size dough pills. "Would you like one, Yeo?"

"Hell, no," I rejected the offer. "What are they made of?"

"A little bread dough with some Tabasco sauce, red chili powder, a touch of iodine, slum, and castor oil, and I added some vinegar and a touch of soap powder for flavor."

I made a wry face and waited. Berg, Jimmie G., Fireman, from Washougal, Washington, came crawling uncertainly through the door.

Lindhe said, "This is the Royal Physician speaking. Stand up for your physical."

Berg said meekly, "Okay, Doc, sir!" He scrambled happily to his feet, glad to get off his hands and knees.

"Open your mouth wide, say ah-h-h, stick your tongue out, and keep your mouth open."

"A-h-h-h-ugh!!" Lindhe had reached over and deftly painted Berg's tongue a Mercurochrome crimson with a cotton-swathed stick.

"My, your tongue looks terrible," Lindhe commented professionally. "I prescribe one of Doctor Lindhe's cure-all pills for polliwogs. Open your mouth wider."

Berg complied and Lindhe tossed a pill into the back of his mouth. "Swallow that."

Berg gulped and screamed, "My Gawd, Doc, whatcha do to me?"

Lindhe said, "You pass the physical, move along."

I watched several more get physicals and rushed to Hunter's assistance, where he was having trouble getting Davison to sit in the Royal Barber's chair. I guided Davison back into the messroom.

Wilcox was reading a summons, ". . . failure to scuttle the scuttlebutt on the scuttle deck . . ."

Steadily we changed polliwogs into shellbacks, and late in the afternoon we came to the end of the initiating ceremony.

The evening meal of veal stew was seasoned with repartee.

"Hey, Yeo, howdaya get this crude oil outa your scalp afterward?"

"You don't. Just let nature take its course. You should be rid of it in three or four months. Besides, it's good for you. Grows new luxuriant hair and keeps the crabs away."

Hall said, "Old Pappy Rau appointed me Sir Diddle-de-doo, and when he touched me on the ear with that damn electrical stick, I liked tuh jumped through the overhead. Boy, did that thing sting!"

After the messroom had been cleaned, I joined O'Brien, Hunter, Carr, and Krause in a bull session in the corner.

"What gives on those natives in the boat this morning?"

"We made out there was originally nine of them. Three died. They'd evidently been trying to get away from one of the Jap-held islands. There was another real sick one lying in the boat."

I said, "I know, I saw him from lookout. Could they speak English?"

"Naw, the messboys couldn't understand but a few words. They was Polynesians or Micronesians or something like that. 'Mush' said they was Malayans. I don't know which."

Keeter, Dalton C., Machinist First, from Vickery, Texas, came over and said in a confidential tone in my ear, "Has the Old Man told yuh he rated me chief as of yesterday?"

I said, "No, it's news to me. How did this happen?" The others quieted down to listen.

"It was my atlas I bought in Brisbane. Lieutenant Grider enlarged a photo of a map that was in it and got a good map of Wewak Harbor from it. 'Mush' was so tickled he told O'Kane to make me chief. I thought you'd know about it by now."

"Well, all right, I'll get it squared away for you first thing in the morning. I'll see O'Kane myself."

"Thanks, Yeo." He sat near me as though fearful I might get away. Hunter was telling Carr, ". . . them Japs was really churning up the water with their gunfire around the periscope. I could hear the shells striking above and whizzing off. Whoever said them bastards can't shoot is a Goddam liar. Why, we was in such shallow water a snake couldn't a crawled between the keel and the bottom. I thought sure we was all headed for Davy Jones' locker for sure . . ."

I noticed that it was time for me to get ready to go on watch. I got up to go to the control for checkoff. Hunter was still talking when I left, ". . . we didn't have no time to turn around to use our stern tubes, and when that fifth fish left the tubes . . ." I was out of ear range leaving the messhall.

Wahoo made her morning trim dive and stayed submerged. Breakfast came and went without anyone calling me for the 0800–1200 watch. My subconscious kept warning me that something was afoot. Finally, after tossing restlessly for some minutes, I awoke and got out of my bunk.

Carter, Rowls, and Boutzale were the only ones in the messhall. Without asking, I knew that *Wahoo* was making another approach. I plopped two slices of bread into one of the electric toasters, got a knife and butter from a locker, drew a cup of coffee just as the browned toast popped up. I sat down and started buttering my breakfast.

"What is it this time?"

"The lookout spotted a streamer of smoke on the horizon just before we dived. We got close enough to see it's a convoy."

"Howsabout escorts?" I asked, trying not to show my anxiety.

"They ain't spotted any yet. The Old Man thinks maybe this one is unescorted. They might even be rendezvousing here, waiting for the destroyer we sunk at Wewak. I sure do hope so."

"Me, too," I said fervently and stirred condensed milk and sugar into my coffee.

I turned to Carter, who was manning the battle phones. "Anything new happen?"

"Only that we're up front of them. They gotta pass over to get by. They're making ready the bow and stem tubes now, opening the outer doors."

I nibbled on the toast, thinking about the situation. The only thing I could think of was that all hell was due to break loose soon. "Have they spotted any destroyers yet?"

"No, not yet. O'Kane reports that there's a couple of good-sized freighters and another ship looks like a troop transport."

There was nothing here that seemed dangerous. I guessed that I was just edgy from the other attacks. I was leaning with my back against the forward bulkhead when I fell to wondering if a depth charge transferring its shock wave through the hull of a submarine might not be powerful enough to break a man's back. The thought made me uneasy and I moved out to the end of the bench away from the partition.

Carter moved and the three of us leaned toward him waiting. "We're laying crossways between them. They're going to pass in front of and behind our bow and stem. Boy, what a setup!"

I felt myself becoming excited. Turning to Rowls, I exclaimed, "I hope we get the whole damn shootin' kaboodle."

"Me, too," Rowls and Boutzale answered simultaneously.

I looked at the clock. It was close to 1000.

Boutzale said, "Yeo, you made a mistake on my shellback card."

I said, "Let me see it," and then, "It looks all right to me."

"Today's the twenty-sixth of January, ain't it?"

"Yeah. Oh, I see, it's dated the fifteenth. That's a typographical error. The next time you catch me in the office remind me and I'll change it. Okay?"

"Okay."

Getting in late on the approach caused me to misjudge the moment of attack. It came suddenly in a fury that left me breathless.

Wahoo began spewing out fish in such quick succession, firing them from bow and stern tubes so quickly, that I lost track of the number fired. There must have been four or five. The internal noises increased in noticeable volume. Voices and commands activated men to feverishly concentrate on their individual tasks. As time condensed into seconds, we three nonparticipants put a heavy suction on coffee cups and smoked cigarettes in two or three puffs.

Wahoo began bucking in a renewed attack, lashing torpedoes out in venomous hate.

A loud explosion was lost in the mad scramble, and Carter's words were barely audible. "We hit one of the sons-a-bitches right in the bow."

Following this came another explosion. Then still another explosion rocked *Wahoo*.

"Damn if we didn't hit another one of the ships. Yippee!"

An aftermath of comparative silence reigned while we waited for a recapitulation of results. I began thinking of Lieutenant O'Kane and wondering what he must be seeing through the periscope. Not any destroyers pushing their bows toward us, I hoped.

The voice of Morton broke out of the loudspeaker. "We've crippled one ship and a transport is sinking. We may battle-stations-surface on them after we look around a bit. All men on gun crews get ready."

I jumped up and ran back to my bunk for the blue-dyed hat under my pillow. I was not going to get caught short this time. Back in the control room I yanked a submarine jacket from a locker and picked up a pair of binoculars. Next I filled one of the pockets with lens paper and stood waiting nervously out of the way of *Wahoo* men manning diving stations. I could hear locker doors and hatches to the ammunition lockers being banged open as gun-crew members grabbed off submarine jackets, weapons, and other paraphernalia needed to fight a surface battle.

Lindhe came into the control room with his first-aid kit and stuffed a wad of cotton in my hand. I picked out strands of it, wadding them into eardrum-size pellets, and pushed them into my ears. All sound became so deadened that I had to get close to hear Lindhe. Yanking out one cotton ball, I said, "What were you saying, Doc?"

He repeated excitedly, "Just before I left the conning tower, O'Kane reported that troop transport sank. It only took eight minutes for it to go down and there are hundreds of Jap soldiers in the water."

I nodded an answer, getting the mental picture. There was a buzzing of the periscope in the pump room beneath our feet. The general alarm bell began clanging, and Lieutenant O'Kane's voice came to us from the loudspeaker, "Battle stations surface, battle stations surface."

Vogeler, the other battle lookout, came alongside prepared as I was for the surfacing. Lindhe thrust a wad of cotton at him.

Gerlacher, Wesley L., Seaman, from Philadelphia, Pennsylvania, and Glinski, who had just been relieved from the stern planes, stood in the passageway leading to the messhall. They each had a container of twenty-millimeter ammunition and a gun barrel. Stooping, I looked through the oval framework of the watertight door and saw Carr moving up the ladder into the messhall access hatch. Below him stood other members of the deck-gun crew.

Captain Morton's voice vibrated the control room talker. "Surface bring her up quick, George."

Lieutenant Grider sprang into action as the words came down. "Lookouts to the tower."

As I scrambled up the ladder, I could hear a confusion of commands around me: "Blow bow buoyancy," "Blow negative," "Bow and stern planes three degrees up-angle," "Vent inboard," "Maneuvering get ready to shift from motors to diesels," "Ninety feet, eight-nine feet, eight-eight feet."

When I got into the conning tower the commands were different. Hunter was up the ladder with his hands on the steel hatch wheel. Lieutenant O'Kane was standing with his hands on the sides of the ladder and one foot on the second rung from the bottom. Captain Morton and Lieutenant Paine were back in the far corner. I stood next to the executive officer and Simmonetti, the helmsman, with Vogeler behind me. Buckley was sitting at the sound gear, Krause near him, and Gerlacher and Glinski were filling in space. On the ladder leading into the control room more of the gun crew were waiting. I glimpsed Carter with a Browning automatic at the foot of the ladder. I thought of the other wad of cotton and stuffed it quickly in my ear.

With the prospect of action upon me, I began to experience an emotional excitement. Adrenaline was pouring into my bloodstream and I felt a primitive instinct to do battle.

Faintly I heard Lieutenant O'Kane shouting, "Crack the hatch." Seconds later and even with the cotton in my ears, I felt the air pressure release on my eardrums. "Open the hatch." Salt water poured into the opening, drenching Hunter and the executive officer, wetting my upturned face and dungaree trouser legs at the same time that air escaping from the boat helped carry me up the ladder.

Lieutenant O'Kane was leaning over the bridge coaming, looking forward, and Hunter was sliding to a stop at the end of the cigarette deck, shading his eyes, looking astern.

I slipped on the wet deck, regained my balance, and clambered up to the starboard lookout platform. I could hear footsteps running, metal striking metal, and feel the quick movements of bodies below me. A rapid hand-shaded survey showed me that there was no immediate danger in the enameled blue of the seas or the paler blue, cloudless skies on the starboard side of *Wahoo*.

"Two ships on the starboard beam," I sang out loudly. "One is crippled with a starboard list and smoking badly. The other is standing by it, sir."

Captain Morton's voice below answered, "Very well."

Vogeler, whose back was to me, shouted excitedly, "Jap troops, boats, and debris in the water off our port bow, sir."

I looked over on the portside of the ship, unable to control my curiosity. The water was filled with heads sticking up from floating kapok life jackets. They were scattered roughly within a circle a hundred yards wide. Scattered among them were several lifeboats, a motor launch with an awning, a number of rafts loaded with sitting and standing Japanese fighting men, and groups of men floating in the water where they had drifted together. Others were hanging on to planks or other items of floating wreckage. A few isolated individuals were paddling back toward the center in search of some human solidarity.

I took in as much of the scene as I could grasp in a quick look and turned my attention back to starboard. I felt a crawling sensation along my backbone at the thought of so many of the enemy at my back.

"Permission to start the turboblow." Lieutenant Grider's voice through the deck speaker.

"Permission granted," Captain Morton's reply.

"Permission to charge batteries."

"Permission granted."

The distant rattle of machine-gun fire came to my ears.

"Damn him," Morton's voice roared. "Roger, have the gun crews knock that machine gun in the motor launch out of the water."

"Aye, aye, sir," Lieutenant Paine replied.

"Commence firing on the motor launch."

This was followed by several rounds from the deck gun and the rattle of the twenty-millimeters.

Whenever the deck gun went off, I flinched from the shock wave that followed. There would be a blinding flash of yellow, which I saw from the corners of my eyes against the binoculars, the shock jarring my whole body, followed by a cloud of acrid white with brownish tints and pale blue colors drifting into view on the starboard side of the ship.

A sharp explosion of a shell going off near the twenty-millimeters caused me to jump. I looked down and saw the barrel pointing in the air and Gerlacher staggering dazedly away from the gun. Glinski was sitting on deck and looking stupidly at his right foot. The shoe leather was brutally torn and I could see blood spurting from a wound onto the deck. I resolutely returned to scanning the ocean.

"Pharmacist's mate to the bridge on the double," Lieutenant O'Kane yelled down the voice tube.

A yell went up from the deck-gun crew. I gathered that the motor launch had been hit.

"Cease firing, cease firing."

Wahoo's diesels were racing to pump new electrical blood into her storage batteries.

Lindhe's voice carried up to my lookout station. "Somebody bear a hand here to help me get these guys down below."

I heard a commotion and recognized Krause and Hunter's voices as they assisted Gerlacher and Glinski down the hatch.

Morton, O'Kane, and Paine moved into a huddle below me.

"What do you think? They look like Marines to me," Lieutenant O'Kane said.

"Yuh damn right they are. They're part of Hirohito's crack Imperial Marine outfit. I run into some of them before the war at Shanghai," Captain Morton replied.

"There must be close to ten thousand of them in the water," said Roger Paine's voice.

"I figure about nine thousand five hundred of the sons-a-bitches," Morton calculated. "How's our batteries, Roger?"

Lieutenant Paine answered, "Pretty low, Captain, they need charging badly."

"All right, we'll circle these bastards several times while we charge batteries and look them over."

Lieutenant O'Kane said, "'Mush,' if those troops get rescued, we're going to lose a lot of American boys' lives digging them out of foxholes and shooting them out of palm trees."

"I know," Morton growled, "and it's a damn stinking shame to think of it when we've got them cold-turkey in the water."

"Do you think they had a chance to radio an SOS, Captain?"

"Probably, but even so there's still that oil tanker and cargo ship out there. We're going after those babies as soon as we get a battery charge."

Lieutenant O'Kane raised his voice. "Starboard lookout, are those ships still in sight?"

"Yes sir. I can still see smoke on the horizon and they are hull down."

"Very well."

Captain Morton commanded, "Secure from battle stations surface."

Lieutenant Paine picked up the word and passed it to the men on deck. "Secure from battle stations surface."

I undertook another quick look at the Japs in the water. Some had drifted in to about twenty-five yards of *Wahoo* and I could see the close-cropped skulls of those without campaign visors. They all stared without expression at *Wahoo*'s hull. The situation looked about the same except that the motor launch was missing and I saw one Jap standing on a raft waving a large piece of canvas in the air.

"I didn't think the Japs ever surrendered," I said over my shoulder to Vogeler.

"Me, too," he muttered, keeping his binoculars trained on the horizon. I turned back to my own job.

Shortly after the gun crews went below, I was relieved from lookout by the regular afternoon duty section lookout.

The messroom was a shambles. Men sat around with smoke-smeared faces, drinking coffee and eating sandwiches. Empty gun cartridges filled the passageway. Carr and Kemp were dipping twenty-millimeter ammunition into buckets of petrolatum, wiping the excess off, and reloading empty cartridge containers.

"Hows to help us, Yeo?" Kemp asked.

"Sure," I said, "just as soon as I get something to eat."

Rowls had set out two large dishpans of sandwiches. I selected a sandwich, got a cup of coffee, and went back into the sleeping compartment. The lights were on and I found Lindhe fussing over his two patients.

"How are they?" I asked, looking first at Glinski, who was wrapped in blankets with only his face showing. He looked terrible. His eyes were closed and he was whining softly.

"I had to operate," Lindhe said proudly. He pulled the blanket away from Glinski's feet, showing me a foot heavily bandaged in gauze and taped with adhesive strips. There was a strong smell of medication in the air. "He's under sedative now, but when I got him down here, three of his toes were hanging by skin and broken flesh."

"No fooling." I was impressed.

"Yeah, I knew they had to be amputated but I didn't have anything to operate with. So I bummed a pair of tin snips from Kohut and sterilized them and snipped his toes off."

My expression encouraged him to go on. "Well, after that I washed out the wound with antiseptic, tied off the blood vessels, and sutured the skin together. There was nothing to it."

Gerlacher was lying on his stomach in a bunk across. He was covered up to the waist and was resting his head on the backs of his hands. He grinned at me shyly.

"What happened to you?" I said gruffly. "Ain't you got no better sense than to get yourself laid up like this?" I noticed a square white piece of gauze taped with a white-cross adhesive band just under his left shoulder blade and over his heart.

"We had a hot shell, and after we changed barrels, we left it laying on deck. It went off," Gerlacher answered sheepishly.

Lindhe interrupted. "Yeah, you damn fools shoulda heaved it overboard." He pointed at the wound. "A piece of the brass cartridge went through his submarine jacket and was stuck in his skin. If it'd gone much deeper we'd a had a burial at sea. I've always wanted to see a burial at sea."

"What some gold-brickers won't do to get out of work," I remarked sagely.

Captain Morton came pushing into the sleeping quarters. "How're the patients coming, Doc?"

"Everything's under control, sir. Here take a look

at Glinski's foot." Lindhe drew back the blanket with justifiable pride.

I said, "Excuse me, sir," and edged around the captain's big form squatting on deck to see better.

"Sure, Yeo," Captain Morton answered absently and turned to Lindhe again. "O'Kane tells me you did a magnificent job on Glinski's toes. Tell me about it."

Lindhe filled out with egoism. "Well, you see, sir, when we got Glinski down here . . ."

I moved toward the door. ". . . nothing to operate with so I got these here tin snips from Kohut and . . ."

In the messroom I sat down to help Kemp and Carr. They were handling the shells rather roughly I thought, but not being a gunner's mate I hesitated to say anything. I picked up a cartridge and dipped it gingerly into the pail of thick grease.

"Aw, grab a handful," Carr invited, "they won't bite'cha." The record player began to play and I looked over my shoulder to see O'Brien standing near it. "Sock 'em down, Winsocki, sock 'em down." When that record played through, there was a brief silence while he changed records and then I heard the music of an unfamiliar ballad. I turned again to ask the name of the piece when it broke into lyrics with Bing Crosby singing "I'm dreaming of a White Christmas."

O'Brien said to all the messroom assemblage, "It's a new song came out in the States. My wife sent it to me at Brisbane."

Everybody knocked off what they were doing until the song finished. We just sat there meditating in silence.

O'Brien said, "Aw, to hell with it." He changed the record back to "Sock 'em down, Winsocki, sock 'em down."

We finished with the cartridges and I helped them clean up the crew's messroom. It was going on to 1400.

Wahoo was running on the surface. Hunter came in for coffee and told us that the officers were still plotting and tracking the other two ships and that he expected *Wahoo* would catch up with them around 1800. Some of the men off watch turned into their bunks. I was too keyed up to lie down for even a little while, so I waited in the crew's mess. Rowls did not attempt to cook an evening chow. He just filled three large dishpans with more sandwiches and kept the coffee urn filled.

Keeter came in and by way of greeting said, "Got me fixed up for chief yet?"

I answered, "Will you get to hell out of here? I ain't about to lay a finger on that typewriter until this attack is over."

"You don't have to be so sarcastic about it."

"If you're so all-hell-fired to make chief, why don't you see O'Kane yourself?"

"He's busy now or I would, but he would listen to you."

"Oh, bat feces. If you'll just keep your pants on until this is over, I'll get you squared away, but if you pester me again, those papers will get lost in the mail," I added ominously.

"Okay, Yeo, I won't bother you again, but hows to get on it as soon as you can, huh?"

I just looked at him sullenly, and he turned and went aft.

The 1600–1800 watch standers came in, ate, went out again. The men they relieved drifted in, ate, and drifted out. Finally only Carter with the talker set on and myself were left in the compartment. He was pre-occupied with a *Life* magazine and that left me with nothing to do except twiddle my thumbs, drink cup after cup of coffee, and smoke cigarettes.

It was getting close to the time for me to go up on lookout, and I was debating with myself whether to relieve early or not when things sprang into action again. There was a commotion topside, followed by quick movements in the control room, and the Klaxon gave warning that *Wahoo* was diving. Blasts from the horn were still echoing in the boat when Appel, Jesse L., Seaman Second, from Evansville, Indiana, burst into the crew's messroom and looked wildly around. He still had on a submarine jacket, and the binoculars he had been using on lookout dangled heavily from the strap about his neck.

Seeing me, he scurried over and huddled up close as though he thought I might be able to protect him from some wild terror. His teeth were chattering, his face pale under a lookout's tan, and his eyes were di-lated.

Wahoo was on her way down to put tons and tons of protective water around her.

I looked wonderingly toward the watertight door to see what could have scared Appel. As I looked, Tyler the other lookout came in out of breath.

"What happened?"

"Boy, did Appel ever clear that bridge!" Tyler said admiringly. "We got in too close to that Jap freighter and he started firing at us. One of the shells screamed right over us. Appel was down that hatch before Paine could push the diving button. I never saw anyone move so fast before."

Hunter came in. "Hey, Yeo, you shoulda seen Appel

come down that hatch. He was just a blur when he went through the conning tower."

"All right, you guys, take it easy." I turned to Appel. He was blubbering something I could not understand. I said soothingly, "Everything's all right now, Appel. There's nothing to be afraid of. They can't reach us here."

He said a little plainer, "They was shoo-shooting right at me. I c-c-c-could hear that s-s-shell going right over my head."

I said, "Hunter, get him a cup of coffee." Then to Appel, "The guys are real proud of you the way you cleared the bridge."

He said, "Yeo, I'm scared. I don't care what anybody thinks. I'm scared." I thought he was going to cry.

Everybody stopped whatever they were doing and listened. *Wahoo* was firing torpedoes again. A terrific explosion let us know that one of them was a hit.

Appel said, "I gotta get up to the forward torpedo room, they might need me there," and he left.

Carter announced into the silence that followed, "We got that oil tanker that was standing by the freighter. That damn freighter has got away again."

Hunter said, "The Old Man's raving about the flashless gunpowder the Japs are using. You can't see their gun flashes unless they're firing right at us, then it's a little late to do much dodging. It's darker'n hell up there too. Good thing we got radar to track with."

I asked, "How big were the ships, Hunter?"

"Well, the transport was about seventy-five hundred tons, the crippled freighter up there about a ten thousand tonner, and the other freighter and oil tanker are in the vicinity of about seven thousand . . ."

Krause had stuck his head through the door. "Hey, Hunter, the Old Man wantsya."

Hunter jumped up and went out.

Pruett, Ralph R., Electrician First, from Topeka, Kansas, came into the messhall with a checkoff list and a flashlight. "Better get some red goggles and wait in the control room, Yeo. We're going to surface in about ten minutes, and you've got the port lookout."

"I know, I know," I said, "I'm coming."

Pruett grinned at me and went on to the sleeping compartment.

I got up, stretched, and lit a cigarette—it would be my last for a while—and smoked it going into and while waiting in the control room.

Everything was red with the goggles on, but they were necessary in order to adapt my sight to the dark night when I got up on lookout.

I watched idly Stevens, George V., Fireman Second, from Springfield, Illinois, on the stern planes. He sat on a swivel seat without shirt or undershirt. Sweat made the muscles on his back glisten, the highlights rippling with his shoulder blades and neck muscles whenever he turned the large wheel in his hands from right to left or back again. His concentration was entirely on the dial in front of him. Moving the indicator up or down a few degrees made the rudders rise or fall, keeping *Wahoo*'s stern on an even keel and at the required depth.

His team mate, Berg, was operating the bow planes station. When either or both got off the required depth, even a foot, Lieutenant Grider was right behind them urging them to get back on depth. They would jockey the wheels quickly and then relax back on their seats waiting for a change to occur.

Pappy Rau was standing by the Christmas tree with all its green lights showing, sucking on his pipe and meditating about something probably far removed from the business at hand. Vidick was the eternal sentry, standing stolidly by the electrical switchboard.

A portable board table was placed on the master gyrocompass. This was covered with graph paper tacked down along the edges with thumbtacks. A parallel ruler, an Artgum eraser, and several sharpened pencils were neatly set in one corner. By looking close through the red goggles, I could see penciled lines that were terminated with X's and then going off on a tangent to change position at another X. Faintly penciled in by the X's would be a compass bearing, and every half inch or so were Naval chronological times. There were three separate trails of lines, one of which terminated with a circle around it.

Interpreted, this chart was showing the exact positions of three ships in a scale area of miles. One I knew was the *Wahoo*, the other the freighter we were having so much trouble with, and the line with the circle ending was where the tanker had sunk. This was a graphic picture of the late afternoon and evening battles.

Veder came in and donned red goggles. We stood quietly by nervously fingering the binoculars at the strap ends. I zippered down my submarine jacket, opened a button of my shirt, and stuffed the binoculars inside, zippering back over. This would keep salt spray off the lenses until I got them to my lookout station.

There began a stirring in the conning tower, and I noticed the watch standers in the control room tense with muscular expectation. I felt my own breathing quicken and my heart beating faster.

"Bring the masthead out of the water, George, and man the radar screen."

"Aye, aye, sir." Lieutenant Grider said to the planesman, "Bring her up to . . ." His voice was drowned out by the whine of the periscope motor. He turned to me and ordered, "Yeo, man the radar screen until we can get Cook in here to relieve you."

I moved over to the screen, flipped the toggle switch to "on," and waited for grass to appear. I could feel *Wahoo* slanting upward.

The grass came up suddenly and I spotted a constant sharper pip about two-thirds along the strip. "Pip contact at fifteen thousand yards," I sang out.

Lieutenant Grider was at the speaker mike. "Radar contact at one-five-oh-oh-oh, Captain."

"Very well. Prepare to surface."

Someone shouldered me aside. "You're relieved, Yeo." It was Cook.

"Lookouts to the conning tower."

I did not wait for Lieutenant Grider's command. Instead, I started up the ladder followed closely by Veder.

Krause said, "Lookouts in the conning tower, Captain."

Captain Morton's voice from the shadows in the corner replied, "Very well. Surface."

I followed Hunter and Lieutenant O'Kane out into a watery world, which was lighted only by the faint radiance of bright stars overhead. Water showered down from the radar mast, wetting my thin hat. I jerked the binoculars to my eyes and realized for the first time that I still had the red goggles on. Yanking them off with one hand and stuffing them into my jacket pocket, I bent forward with the glasses trying to bring the horizon in closer.

"Shift to all four diesels. All ahead standard." The tinkle of the annunciators in the conning tower, *Wahoo*'s four main engines roaring into being with loud blasts from the exhausts aft, sixty-four cylinders began urging the twin screws to dig in and push.

"Swing left and come to two-seven-oh."

"Swinging left to two-seven-oh, sir."

"Hunter, fix a pair of binoculars into the port TBT" (target bearing transmitter).

"Aye, aye, sir."

"All clear on the port lookout."

"Very well, keep a sharp lookout at about three-eight-oh. The target is too far away for you to see it yet."

"Aye, aye, sir."

"All clear on the starboard side, sir."

"Very well."

Wahoo pushed steadily into the night. From below, periodic reports of the lessening distance between the freighter and *Wahoo* kept coming up.

"See her yet, Yeo?"

"No, Captain, all's clear on the port bow."

"Very well. Let me know as soon as you spot her."

"Aye, aye, sir."

I strained my eyes into the darkness, willing the ship to materialize. I caught a glimpse of a darker object and waited a fractional moment to be sure my eyes were not deceiving me. Yes, it was still there.

"Ship ahoy, two points off the port bow."

"Very well."

I heard quick steps below and could just barely

make out the captain's form bent to the TBT. "Relative bearing . . ." The wind carried his voice away.

I searched hurriedly the rest of the ocean but kept coming back to the freighter. We got in close enough for me to see the dark hulk without the aid of the glasses.

My hair stood on end, and I felt an urge to drop off the lookout station and run as sharp cracks of gunfire reached me.

"He's firing off the other side," Captain Morton's reassuring voice came up.

"Probably spotted a whitecap on one of the waves. Bet the skipper is really anxious," Lieutenant O'Kane's voice replied.

"He's not taking any chances. Probably shooting at anything suspicious trying to scare us off. He's a nervy devil," Morton answered admiringly.

"Searchlight beam on the port beam," I screamed as loud as I could shout.

"Where away? I see it. It's flashing around the water."

"Whataya think, Captain? A destroyer or a cruiser?"

"That's hard to tell, he's too far away. Hey, I bet that freighter will stop zigging and head toward it for protection."

"We can't fight a warship with only two fish in the stern tubes, Captain."

"I know, but we're not going to let that freighter get away. Helmsman, come left to two-two-five. All ahead emergency."

The target moved right, past *Wahoo*'s bullnose, as *Wahoo* swung left. I lost sight of the freighter as it moved into Veder's area but I had a new interest now. The searchlight was having an almost hypnotic effect on me. I could hardly pull my eyes off it for quick looks at the rest of the ocean.

Morton called below to the fire-control party for information on the distance of the track, to intercept the freighter as it swung toward the searchlight beam.

I was watching the light search the ocean and get nearer when *Wahoo* changed course again and the light moved back to the port beam. I looked carefully forward but could not see the freighter, so it must still be on the starboard side.

"Come left, full rudder."

Wahoo began a circle. The searchlight seemed to be about ready to burst over the horizon and onto us. It started moving up toward the bow as *Wahoo* circled. I wondered what the hell the Old Man was up to now and remembered that our last two torpedoes were in the stern tubes.

The light disappeared as *Wahoo*'s bow swung around. Veder reported, "Searchlight on the starboard bow, sir."

"Check the rudder and steady on one-zero-zero! All stop. Back two-thirds on the starboard engines."

There were some more commands that I did not catch in my concentrated search for the freighter. I caught up with it on the port quarter.

"Ship three points abaft the port beam," I yelled.

"All stop," I heard again.

Wahoo settled down to watchful waiting.

"Fire nine!!" I jumped at the suddenness of the command. I swung around looking aft.

"Fire ten!!" *Wahoo* shuddered as number nine left the tube in a vicious hungry search for Oriental prey. *Wahoo* bucked again and number ten swished out of its tube.

I kept the binoculars glued to the freighter's silhouette. It seemed a long distance away and I wondered if the torpedoes would reach it.

"All ahead standard. We're heading for the barn." A thrill of pleasure and relief ran through me.

Wahoo stood still until her propellers caught footing in the water and then we began to move. I kept the binoculars pressed to my eyes until the metal eyepieces hurt the skin. I was just about to give up hope of a hit when a white and yellow flash spread out on the horizon like a heavy sheet of summer lightning. It grew in size and faded away.

"We got 'er, we got 'er!" officers and quartermasters on deck were shouting in jubilation.

The explosion, muffled by distance, swept by my ears as another flash lighted the ocean temporarily. "Two hits, two Goddam hits," Morton was screaming.

Still watching, I saw the searchlight beam sweep across the ocean and steady on the sinking ship. The second explosion roared by on vibration wings and was lost into history. The freighter turned slowly over and split into two dark sections before one end tilted up and then slid out of sight. The other end just faded into blackness.

The wind whistled a song of victory, using *Wahoo*'s radio antenna and the signal halyards for a musical instrument.

I was still watching the angry lashing of the searchlight beam, greatly diminished by distance, when Gerlacher relieved me.

"What in hell are you doing up here?"

"I relieve you. It's nearly midnight."

"I don't mean that. Why ain't you in bed with that shoulder?"

"Oh, it feels better now. It don't hurt much and I wanted to see what was going on."

"Does Rau or Lane know you're up here?"

"Yeah, I had a heck of a time convincing them I was all right. Lindhe said a little fresh air wouldn't hurt me."

"Suppose you have to clear the bridge?"

"I'll make it all right," he said convincingly.

"Look, kid, why don't you go below? It's just a little while until the midwatch comes on anyway."

"Naw, I'm all right I tell you." Then excitedly, "There's a searchlight astern of us, I just saw it."

"You're so right. At one time we was so close I leaned over and polished the lens on it."

"You're kidding?"

"Just ask the captain. I got news for you. We're headed for the barn."

"Gee . . ."

Ensign Misch's voice called up, "Anything wrong up there on port lookout?"

"Negative," I answered. "I've just been relieved. I'll be right down."

"Very well."

I moved to the blue-lighted hatch opening and went wearily below. The messroom was filled with jabbering idiots. I grabbed a cup of coffee and sank listlessly in the corner.

"They musta been a million Japs in the water this morning!"

"It was my torpedo tube that got that last bastard. I'm going to paint a Jap flag right on the . . ."

". . . and then Doc came runnin' up to me and said, 'Kohut, do you have something I can cut Glinski's toes off with . . .'"

"The Old Man said, 'We ought to shoot the sons-a-bitches.' Say that would make a good motto for the *Wahoo*, wouldn't . . ."

I looked up and saw Lindhe stirring a cup of coffee. "How's Glinski?"

"He's fine. I just come from there and he's sleeping like a baby. He will be all right if infection doesn't set in, but I dusted plenty of sulphate powder on the wound and . . ."

"We just wanted to know how he was doing, not his medical history."

Lindhe retorted, "I never saw a worse bunch of constipated guys in my life," and he went forward.

The group dwindled as rapidly as it grew. I found myself alone in the corner with Appel. I said, "Guess I'll turn in."

In the sleeping quarters all I could see of Glinski was a bundled form. I kicked off my moccasins and climbed into my sack. The last thing I remembered was the strong smell of antiseptic and my saying, "Thank you, dear Lord, for bringing us through safely."

At 0330 Hayes came in, laid a hand on my shoulder, and was about to squeeze softly and shake gently. My eyes came open and I raised my head. "Time to go on lookout, Yeo."

"Okay." I yawned and threw my legs over the edge of the bunk. He vanished quietly. A cup of coffee did not awaken me fully, and I groped my way sleepily into the control room.

Wilcox was checking off. "Take the first helm watch, Yeo."

"Okay," I answered sleepily and somehow crawled up the ladder to the conning tower.

"You're relieved."

Wach said, "Don't you want to know what course we're steering?"

"Oh, sure, whatsa course?"

"Zero-two-seven."

Delicious early-morning fresh air was pouring through the open hatch. Its oxygen content finally worked into the blood vessels of my brain and chased out the drowsiness. I stood in the darkness smoking and eyeing the gyrocompass indicator, deftly coming to course when *Wahoo* was inclined to seek a tangent. The darkness began to thin out near the open hatch. Details began to stand out on objects that were dark masses a moment before.

"Bridge," Wilcox's voice from below was saying, "we got a contact on the radar bearing three-three-oh, sir, range fifty thousand yards."

Ensign Griggs answered from above, "Very well, send a messenger to notify the captain and executive officer."

"That's already been done, sir."

"Very well."

A few seconds later there was a scurrying noise at the control room hatch opening, and the captain and Lieutenant O'Kane were beside me.

"Good morning, Yeo." It was Captain Morton's voice.

I threw him a sideways glance and said, "Good morning, sir," taking in his good-natured grin. He seemed to be always smiling or laughing about something. The executive officer gave me a sleepy nod, his mind apparently on the more serious business ahead.

"Captain coming on the bridge," I shouted.

"Very well."

Captain Morton trailed by the executive officer went topside. I could hear their footsteps moving about on the steel plating and slotted wooden decks.

Ensign Griggs' voice came down the speaker, "Control, keep the radar ranges coming. Wake up Ensign Misch and set up a plot."

"Aye, aye, sir."

"Helmsman, come left to zero-one-zero degrees."

"Coming left to zero-one-zero," I repeated. I threw the helm over two degrees left rudder and waited for *Wahoo* to respond. The gyro indicator jumped and began jerkily swinging to the right as *Wahoo* swung left. About ten degrees before it reached zero-one-zero, I eased up on the rudder, and just before it passed the mark brought the rudder three degrees right, checking *Wahoo*'s swing and bringing the rudder back to zero. "Steady on zero-one-zero, sir."

"Very well, hold her there until further orders."

Krause came into the conning tower. We exchanged good mornings. Hunter showed up and went onto the bridge. The light streaming through the hatch announced it to be nearly daybreak. I was on the wheel an hour and a half while the contact was being investigated.

"There's two or three pips on the radar now, bridge. It looks like it might be a convoy." This was Lieutenant Jackson's voice. He was evidently checking the operation of the radar.

"Very well, Jack." There was a silence and then, "Control, call the battle stations submerged watch."

"Aye, aye, sir." Another long silence and presently I heard sounds below that informed me men were moving quietly to their stations. Lieutenant Paine came into the tower and played with the TDC.

Simmonetti came up with a cup of coffee in hand and relieved me. I went below.

Janicek and Robertson, the two messcooks, had the tables set for breakfast. They and Rowls were sitting in the corner, Rowls with a facial expression of deep disgust and disappointment. Carter was manning the battle phones. I looked over the neat arrangement of dishes, knives, forks, coffee cups, and bowls.

"What's doin' up there, Yeo?" It was Rowls inquiring.

"You got me. We spotted a convoy. Only with no fish left to fight with, I guess we'll just look 'em over and let 'em go by. Maybe radio their position to Pearl."

Carter said, "They've spotted the masts and stacks. Radar reports four ships. I wish we had some fish left."

Hunter came in full of suppressed excitement. "You know what, fellows? The Old Man's going to make an attack!"

"What?" we ejaculated in surprised unison.

"He's going stark raving maniac crazy," Janicek added.

Hunter put two slices of bread into the toaster and waited, keeping us in suspense. When the toast was ejected, he went on, "'Mush' says we're going to get up ahead of them and submerge. When they come over, we're going to surface and fire the guns at them."

"My Gawd," I groaned and asked the inevitable question, "Howsabout escorts?"

"They haven't spotted any. Looks like this convoy is unescorted, too."

Rowls jumped up and said to the messcooks, "Better clear these tables over the ammo locker. Stack the dishes on the other tables. They'll be wantin' to get into the locker soon."

I ducked into the sleeping compartment to get an extra package of cigarettes.

Glinski looked weakly up at me. "What's going on, Yeo?"

I said, "Hiya, kid. There's another convoy out there."

Lindhe raised up in bed. "What's that? Another convoy? What's 'Mush' going to do?"

"We're going to surface in the middle of it and go to battle stations surface."

"You're kidding?"

"Wish to hell I was."

Lindhe slipped out of his bunk. "Wonder why I wasn't called?"

"We just spotted 'em a little while ago. I had the watch is the reason I'm up. We'll probably be diving shortly."

Kohut raised up, stretched, and slid out of his bunk. Two or three others got up. O'Brien in an after corner lit up a cigarette and lay smoking it. I went out as Lindhe walked over to Glinski's bunk.

Rowls handed me a heaping plate of scrambled eggs. "Anybody else want anything to eat?" I was just finishing eating when *Wahoo* dived. She leveled off and Lane came through the boat. "Any of you guys got battle station surface better get ready for it." And he went aft.

Carr came in, pushed back the mess tables, unlocked the big brass padlock on the ammunition locker, and threw open the trap door. Members of the deck-gun crew came in, and soon there was a stack of fixed cartridges in the passageway. It was getting crowded so I moved into the control room and picked up a pair of binoculars. Veder was already there waiting.

After a long wait, we began to feel the presence of ships overhead. Excitement built up to equal the air pressure in the boat. The beat of propeller screws grew out of nothing and became loud all around *Wahoo*.

Wahoo eased up her depth controls and came to periscope depth. She poked up an artificial eye for a quick looksee, and then Morton pushed the button to the general alarm bell. The Klaxon let loose with three loud blasts. "Battle stations surface, battle stations surface"—fighting words that tightened the glands in the small of my back even as I raced out of the ship and onto the starboard lookout station.

Wahoo had burst from the depths and was rolling lazily on the surface with a great expanse of aerated salt-water bubbles to show from what part of the ocean she had erupted. Below me, voices were screaming.

"Decks are awash, sir!"

"Twenty millimeters manned and ready, sir!"

"Get that deck hatch open."

"Two ships on the portside, sir!"

"Full left rudder. All ahead standard on the diesels."

I added my voice to the others. "Two ships on the starboard side, sir. Both veering away."

"Get that ammunition on deck on the double."

"Deck gun manned and ready, sir."

"Close in on that small oil tanker. It is slower than the rest. Roger, have the men aim at the pilothouse and the rudder first."

I could see the sterns of two large ships as they headed away from *Wahoo* on divergent tangents. I almost missed the mast and stack of another ship just over the horizon. I swung the glasses back and saw smoke come boiling furiously out of its stack.

"Another ship abaft the starboard beam." I put everything I had into the shout.

Lieutenant O'Kane's voice, "Repeat that again, starboard lookout. Whereaway?"

"Another ship abaft the starboard beam, sir."

A rush of feet to the starboard side acknowledged my report.

"What is it? Dick! Can you make it out?"

"Looks like a destroyer, Captain, moving up fast."

"Gun crews secure from battle stations surface."

New noises below, stampeding feet.

"Leave your guns and ammo topside. Clear the top decks. Never mind the gun, Carr! Get your tail down below."

I kept my glasses on the destroyer. The smoke volume seemed to grow. Her superstructure was beginning to break the rim of the horizon.

I pushed the binoculars inside the jacket, grabbed the rail with both hands, and bent my knees. Looking below, I saw Captain Morton face upward cupping his hands to his mouth. At that moment I moved out into space, hit the deck with a jarring thud, regained my equilibrium, and skated on the slippery deck past the captain. I never heard him call, "Clear the bridge."

The next thing I remember I was standing in the messhall, braced against *Wahoo*'s steep down-angle dive.

Veder came in and began to shake my hand. "Congratulations, Yeo, you not only beat me down, you set a new record getting here."

Wahoo was searching frantically for the bottom,

piling tons and tons of protective water over her back. "Rig for depth charge, rig for depth charge."

I felt *Wahoo*'s decks level off and at that instant Pandora's box opened and all hell broke loose. Three depth charges went off in succession, seemingly right on deck over the crew's messroom. We were plunged into complete darkness, and a loose piece of metal shooting through the void struck my left ear, causing it to sting sharply. Dishes stacked on the table were lifted and thrown about. Loose knives and forks flew about at random, their screaming lost in the blasts of the depth charges. Patches of cork showered down, followed by a ventilationless room full of choking dust.

Carter coolly turned on the blue emergency light.

I waited in terror-stricken silence holding on to the table with a death grip. It could not have been much longer than a sharp circle turn before the approaching screws warned us to brace for the next depth charges. There was a repetition of the previous inferno, and then we settled down to a long period of peaceful quiet running.

Carter was the first one to break the silence. "The sonarman reports that the screws of the DE are going away."

I sat fearfully waiting for them to come back. Five, ten, fifteen minutes went dragging by.

Carter said into the phones, "The lights are out in the galley. We got the emergency lights on. From what I can see there are no leaks in the messhall or the sleeping compartment."

I got up and walked unsteadily into the sleeping compartment and looked for leaks. I could not smell chlorine gas so I figured the batteries were all right.

Glinski was asleep and I guessed that Lindhe had given him a sedative. I came back to the messroom feeling better. "Everything's okay in the sleeping compartment." Carter nodded his thanks to me. Sitting down, I felt the weight of the binoculars bump against my legs. I had forgotten completely about having them. We huddled in the messroom for nearly an hour. Finally *Wahoo* sneaked back to the surface.

"Everything is clear topside," Carter reported. "The Old Man seems to think that destroyer was only interested in keeping us down until he could collect his ships and get out of there."

"Secure from depth charge, secure from depth charge."

I got up slowly, got a cup of coffee, and sat down again. I lit a cigarette off the stub of one I had in my mouth. I wondered stupidly when I had lighted the first cigarette or was it the second or third. I could not remember.

Electricians came and replaced the light bulbs. The messroom by the brilliance of the white lights was a shambles. Rowls and the messcooks began cleaning up. The messroom began to fill with sailors and their experiences. Lindhe came through delivering a ration of "depth-charge" medicine. "You all right, Yeo? Your ear's bleeding."

I felt woodenly of my ear and stared dazedly at the slight blood smear on my hand. "It's just a scratch. I'll be okay after I drink this."

He turned away as I swallowed the contents of the bottle in two gulps.

I returned the binoculars to the control room and crawled into my bunk.

About 1630 I awoke suddenly with a guilty feeling

that I was doing something wrong. I got up and went through the messroom, noting the time and the fact that the messcooks were starting to clean up after evening chow.

In the control room Pappy Rau and Lane were chuckling over something one of them had said to the other. I said, "Gee, Pappy, I'm sorry I overslept for the watch but I don't remember being called."

They looked at each other and laughed again. "Don't worry about it, Yeo. We didn't call you. The exec left orders to take you off the watch list until we get in. They're going to start getting out the War Patrol Report."

"Gee, thanks." I went into the officers' country. The curtains were drawn on every officer's stateroom. Behind one or two I could hear gentle snores. I saw Manalisay in the pantry and asked, "What time are the officers going to eat tonight?"

He said, "Nobody eat tonight, everybody sleep but duty officer."

The action basket had some preliminary details to be rough-typed concerning the attack on the destroyer at Wewak Harbor. It hardly seemed possible that only five days had elapsed. I fell to studying the handwriting preliminary to the typing. Lieutenant O'Kane came to the door all business. "Good evening, Yeo. Ready to go to work?"

"Yes sir," I replied eagerly.

"I see you're studying those roughs. There will be more as fast as we can keep them coming."

"Yes sir."

He started to leave. "Oh, Mr. O'Kane, Keeter was telling me . . ."

I worked on into the afternoon, subconsciously

interpreting the sounds around me. Sometime in the afternoon we dived. I tried to continue the work but could not. Finally I got up and went into the messroom.

I found Hunter, O'Brien, Krause, and Rowls in our reserved corner.

"What gives with the dive?"

"We're going in close to Fais Island and take some pictures through the scope of the phosphate works."

O'Brien said, "I hear you beat Veder off the bridge finally, Yeo."

I said hotly, "I had an incentive. I could see that destroyer coming and he couldn't. They say it was shooting at us but I didn't wait to find out."

One afternoon Captain Morton came by and drove me into the typewriter with a slap of his massive hand, and after laughing at my frustration asked, "Have you made out the papers on Keeter's rating yet?"

"Yessir."

"Good, that atlas of his was a real find. Also, I rated Hall for spotting that first convoy while on lookout."

"The papers are all made out waiting for Mr. O'Kane's signature." I handed them to him. He went through them. "Good men, all of these." Seeing Gerlacher's name, he said, "I'm making a recommendation before we get in to get Gerlacher and Glinski Purple Hearts. There will be a recommendation for a Navy Cross for O'Kane, a Silver Star for Lindhe, a Bronze Star for . . . I guess I'd better see O'Kane about this now and get something started on it." He hurried away.

The next morning found *Wahoo* approaching the

island of Oahu, and it did not take much coaxing from Lane to get the crew to turn out for reveille. The blessedness of being alive was on us all, and the prospect of two weeks at the Royal Hawaiian Hotel was so motivating that we polished our shoes and had our sea bags packed before the island ever came into sight.

Krause caught me at breakfast and handed me a slip of paper. "Will you do me a favor and type up a requisition for this item? I'll get the Old Man to sign it."

I glanced at the paper. Scribbled in Krause's neat handwriting were the words, "Ten gallons of grain alcohol. Purpose: to be used for cleaning periscope lenses."

I looked up at him and he gave me a broad wink. I replied, "I'll give it number one, triple A priority."

JACKPOT AT MONTE CARLO

FROM *Submariner*

by Captain John Coote

*O*ne of the most impressive books on the life of a submarine crewman is the relatively slim (239-page) volume *Submariner*, written by Captain John Coote, which covered his life in the Royal Navy from 1939 to 1960. Transferred into the submarine service to avoid being conscripted into the Fleet Air Arm, Coote spent most of his war service fighting in the Mediterranean. Along with the traditional destroyer attacks and counterstrikes, Coote also depicts the life of a submarine crew outside the ship, particularly on the barren outpost at La Maddelena, off Sardinia. After the war, he served on various other submarines, including the *Amphion* and the *Totem*, which he commanded. After the USS *Nautilus* was launched, Coote tried to convince the Royal Navy to invest in nuclear-powered submarines, but their decision to go with Strike Carriers relegated submarines to the back burner, and led Coote to retire in 1960, when he began a second career in journalism. Along with his memoir, he also wrote or cowrote several books on the sea, including *The Shell Guide to Navigation*, *The Sea*, *Yacht Navigation: My Way*, and covered the rest of his life in a book entitled *Altering Course: A Submariner in Fleet Street*.

Of all the missions a submarine could take on, a harbor shoot had to be one of the most hair-raising. Sneaking past mines and anti-torpedo nets into relatively shallow water, always wondering if they were going to be detected, to take a shot at a sitting duck of a ship without the torpedo hitting the bottom of the harbor. And that was only half the fun, as they still had to make their escape afterward. Come with the crew of the HMS *Untiring* on just such a mission, followed by a bit of hide-and-seek with a convoy escort destroyer, all written by a master storyteller.

For our fifth patrol we were sent back to the area off Nice again.

A signal from S.10 warned us of a ship due to pass through our area at night, but, even though we lay stopped on the surface within a mile of Cap Ferrat for much of the night, we never saw it, even with a bright moon to seaward of us, which made us vulnerable to anyone looking out from ashore. At 0100 it was flat calm and the captain decided our target was behind schedule. Fifteen minutes later we were in the grip of our first mistral, a vicious wind we endured four days a week throughout the winter. The same gales dissipated the thermal layers which protected us against Asdic pings in summer.

Next day keeping periscope depth was awkward, with vision frequently obscured by steep waves. The captain took the boat close in to Monte Carlo for the day to get under the lee of the land.

During the afternoon Gus sighted a mast coming from the direction of Nice. The captain looked at it for a long time.

"Looks as though it might be a medium-sized coaster—tall single funnel and two masts. Start the plot."

For the next hour and a half we waited for the enemy to reach us. The plot gave the unlikely target speed of 2 knots. She was steering an erratic course, possibly due to the bad weather. Abreast of the headland of Monaco she turned sharply to port and scuttled into Monte Carlo harbour. The captain followed the enemy towards the harbour entrance where she was seen to berth alongside the northern jetty.

"That'll be the *Quai de Plaisance*," Gus said, looking up from the chart. "It used to be the straight coming out of the tunnel during the Monaco Grand Prix." I leaned over his shoulder and saw that the harbour was in the form of a square, entered through the breakwater forming its eastern side. It was plain that only a vessel berthed against the western wall would present a clear target from the harbour mouth. The captain had other ideas.

"How much water is there two cables outside the breakwater?"

"Fifteen fathoms, sir."

"Can do. Now, what's the least depth of water between the target and the harbour entrance?"

"Twenty-one feet."

"Well, Coote, so long as the fish is fired far enough outside the breakwater to allow it to find its true running depth, there should be no question of it exploding on the bottom."

After another long look at the target the captain then headed out to seaward.

He has decided it's an impossible shot, I thought, along with everyone else in the control room. Then the captain came over to the chart-table and placed the parallel rulers through the harbour entrance to a point halfway along the *Quai de Plaisance*.

"Now let's see. There are probably nets across the harbour mouth. So we'll have to fire one to blow them open and then another to go through and hit the target. We'll let him have it nearer dusk at 1700, so that we'll be able to get away on the surface. By the way, where's *Jane's Fighting Ships*?"

The captain opened it up at the French section and started working through.

"It's flying a Nazi ensign, but the funnel cowling looks French to me. Besides, the Germans can't send ships this size by rail, and I'm damn sure this one didn't slip through the Straits."

He paused at one picture. "Quite like that, only more old-fashioned, and it's got a whale-back ramp over its counter as if it were a . . . that's it! A mine-layer!"

"Of course," Gus said, "that is why it was steering that crazy course at such a slow speed along from Cap Ferrat. It was on a lay."

"At least we know not to go back along that way tomorrow. This picture is the one, I think, 'One thousand tons, length 275 feet, draught 12 feet—carries at least one hundred mines. Also employed on net-laying duties.'"

A pencilled track of a torpedo through the entrance of the breakwater on an oblique shot showed that we needed half a degree accuracy from the torpedo's gyroscope.

"The nearer we fire from, the wider the margin of permissible torpedo error—but if we get too close the kipper will hit the bottom in shallow water before it has recovered its depth. Besides, we've got to allow room for ourselves to turn away after firing. We'll squirt off the first one here"—he marked a point five hundred yards outside the harbour—"and the second one, if necessary, here. That's three hundred yards off. If one of those two runs off its course and hits the breakwater it will sound mighty loud in here. Number One, go to Watch Diving now and go to Diving Station at quarter to five." He turned to me. "You're

officer of the watch now, aren't you? Keep on out on
140° till quarter to four, then turn back on to 320°
and call me. Don't use too much periscope and don't
spend your time goofing at the pretty girls on the
promenade."

It was odd looking through the periscope at the
peaceful Sunday afternoon scene which we were to
interrupt so rudely at five o'clock. The long grey ship
was lying alongside with some washing billowing
from a jackstay on her fo'c'sle. Seen against the background of plane trees along the quayside and white
buildings rising up the steep hill behind, she looked
more like a pleasure steamer than a warship. The
only other boats in the harbour were yachts laid up
for the duration.

At teatime we started back towards the harbour
again, our course once again being plotted through
an area marked as "Mined" on the chart. One worry
was whether the Germans had laid a controlled minefield off the harbour, linked to hydrophones or Asdics
ashore which could trigger off the whole minefield on
hearing a submarine's screws.

By the time the ship's company went to Diving Stations the boat was approaching its firing position.

"Yes, everything seems much the same as before.
Set the torpedoes to six feet. Take down this fix."

He swung the periscope round, taking bearings of
the breakwater light, the Musée Océanographique
and cathedral spire.

"Three hundred yards to go for the first one, sir."

I quickly thought of all the things which could go
wrong with the torpedo. The balance chamber might
be flooded, in which case it would plunge straight to
the bottom. Or the relay valve of the gyroscope might

be seized up, causing the torpedo to swerve off course and blow up on the breakwater. Worse still, the propeller clamps might still be on, or the air vessel stop-valves shut, but I was confident we had followed the correct drill before the rear doors were shut after loading.

"Now, gunlayer, this is up to you," the captain said to the helmsman. "If you go so much as a quarter of a degree off your course I'll break your neck. Steady as you go on 321 degrees. Remember you're the chap who decides which way the kipper will run."

Len, the gunlayer, scratched his beard and grabbed the wheel tighter. All eyes were on the compass repeater tape in front of him. 321½ . . . it jerked back to port, 321 . . . 321½ . . . Len gave the wheel half a turn . . . 321 . . . the tape was steady.

"Fire one!"

Again that shudder as the torpedo was blown out through the tube.

"There's one to knock down the door," the captain said, still looking through the periscope. "I do wish all those people sunning themselves on the quay would get away from that minelayer. If they only knew. There's a woman with a pram just near the bows . . . Jesus!"

A violent thunderclap explosion rocked the boat as though we'd been straddled by a pattern of depth charges. "Controlled minefield" flashed through my mind, but no water was coming in.

"Quick, Number One, your camera."

The captain stood aside from the periscope as Number One held up his camera to the eyepiece and snapped the mushroom of smoke that was rising out of the water where the minelayer had been.

"I think we can save the other torpedo," the captain remarked. "It looked as though that chap still had most of his eggs on board. One torpedo would never make a bang like that. Any damage, Number One?"

"No, sir, just a few lights."

"I expect most of the blast was contained inside the harbour. That *Quai de Plaisance* doesn't look too pleasant now. Half the trees are down and there are bits of wreckage all over the place. Hullo, I see the buildings round about have lost most of their windows, too. Hope we didn't upset the wheel in the Casino."

He let us each have a quick look through the periscope as we hurried away from the harbour. Through the narrow gap in the breakwater, I could just see a tangled heap of metal sticking up above the water. The line of trees along the quay was interrupted by gaps where the force of the mines counter-exploding had uprooted them. The branches of those still standing were covered in clothing and debris. People were running down the hillside to the harbour.

When I first revisited the Côte d'Azur in the early fifties the little man running the newspaper kiosk at the end of the quayside remembered it well. He had nipped off to a Bar Tabac for a pastis and returned to find his stall had been wiped out. Bowing to commercial and political pressures, the Monegasques have renamed the beautiful quayside avenue in turn after the Liberation, John F. Kennedy, Charles de Gaulle and now des Etats Unis. On Grand Prix day you pay £1000 for a place on one of the motor yachts berthed stern to the wall where we blew up the minelayer, then the *Quai le Plaisance*. Before being commandeered by the Nazis and renamed *UJ2213* she had been FS *Heureux*. The archives in Monaco insist she was a minesweeper, which would not account for the force of the explosion.

The news would have been flashed along the lines to Nice. All available destroyers and E-boats would soon be raising steam for full speed to come after us. The captain thought so too, for he took the boat deep and increased speed. During the hour that was left till it would be dark enough to surface he presided over our usual post-mortem in the wardroom.

"There's just a chance they didn't see the track of the fish, in which case the whole thing might be put down to sabotage or an accident. Just the same, we mustn't take any chances. We'll get out of this area to-night and go round towards Genoa. How about your photograph, Number One?"

"Should be a good one. The light wasn't too bad." It turned out to be a clear snap of some officers standing on the balcony of the mess at Lazaretto with a vague blur of smoke and houses superimposed. Evidently he had forgotten to wind on the film.

In the torpedo stowage compartment the lads had cleared away everything in readiness for reloading. The signalman was busy cutting a piece off the tail of a red shirt belonging to the gunlayer. It was to make the red bar on our Jolly Roger, to indicate a warship sunk. The gunlayer took full credit for having pointed the submarine accurately at the target and was reminding the tubes' crews that it took a gunnery rating to aim their torpedoes for them.

"Mind you all bring your tots round when we're back in 'arbour to show your appreciation."

The new torpedo was loaded in with a very rude message to A. Hitler chalked on it.

We surfaced five miles off Menton, expecting to spend an uncomfortable night dodging angry E-boats and being put down by hunting aircraft. But the weather took a hand. Within an hour it was blowing a gale once more, with driving sleet reducing visibility to a few cables. Unpleasant it may have been for those on the bridge, but there was a comfortable feeling that no hunting craft could find us in that weather. All night we steered what we hoped was a course parallel to the coast. By dead reckoning we should be to the north-east of Cape Noli at dawn—just short of the large minefield protecting Genoa itself.

The weather moderated slightly during my watch, and when I came down at 0430 it was choppy with occasional rain squalls. I could make out the snow-covered peaks of the Alpes-Maritimes, without being able to identify any one single point. Just after I turned in, the night alarm sounded.

An attack quickly developed. From the information passed down it sounded like a fast-moving ship coast-crawling northeastwards. In a break in the visibility the captain recognized it as a destroyer moving at over 20 knots. It was too far away to attack, and soon crossed our bows and disappeared. As we would be diving soon, Gus and I sat down to a cup of cocoa and a game of crib in the wardroom instead of turning in for the short remaining period of darkness. The charge had been broken and the boat was proceeding dead slow in towards the beach on its motors. Suddenly there was a shout from the control room:

"For Christ's sake, torpedoes approaching!"

Gus and I shot over to the Asdic where a shaken operator was holding out his earphones at arm's length.

"Torpedoes! Green 110, sir!" He pointed wildly out across the control room, as if he expected something to come bursting in through the boat's hull at any second. No mistaking the torpedoes. The noise coming from those earphones sounded like a tube train approaching a station.

"Hard a-port. Tell the bridge torpedoes approaching on the starboard beam."

The operator put his earphones on again and picked up the noise of the torpedoes.

"Very loud; bearing Green 85, sir," he stammered and took off the earphones again. The bearing was growing for'ard, so they were going to miss ahead if they ran straight.

There was a series of clatters and bumps as the look-outs came tumbling off the bridge, followed by Number One.

"There's a bloody great destroyer lying stopped beam on to us with her tubes trained outboard. Range about fifteen hundred yards. We've seen the tracks of his fish. They've missed ahead," he told us breathlessly.

The Asdic operator soon confirmed that, but they still sounded right on top of us. For a moment I wondered if they might be the new acoustic torpedoes, which would home in on the noise of our propellers. I was badly rattled.

"Why the hell doesn't he dive?" I asked.

The answer came down the voicepipe. The captain sounded as calm as though he was still in Inchmarnock Water.

"Bring all tubes to the ready."

I wondered if the captain had taken leave of his senses. He had sent the look-outs and the officer of the watch down below, and now he was staying on the surface to argue the point with a destroyer, which had a surfaced submarine in its sights, having just fired three kippers at us. Now it would turn in and ram us.

"Set all tubes to eight feet," he ordered calmly.

The HSD had taken over the Asdics now and could hear the torpedoes still running faintly in the distance. He swept round on the bearing where even Charlie on the radar set had an echo the size of a house at 500 yards.

"Turbine HE increasing," he reported.

That would be the destroyer speeding up as it came in towards us. The faint patch of light under the conning-tower hatch was blotted out as the captain stepped down off the bridge. Urr . . . urr. The Klaxon sounded like an air-raid siren. No one needed any urging to get the boat under. By the time the captain had got down below we were already passing twenty feet.

"Ninety feet, shut off for depth-charging. Silent routine . . . And hold on to something," he added quietly.

"Transmissions on Green 30, sir. In contact," the HSD reported. "HE increasing."

We were at seventy feet when the destroyer passed straight over the top of us, the thrash of her propellers plainly audible throughout the submarine. You could see it written on everyone's face: This is it, here it comes. A straddle first time. Ten feet a second to sink. That's ten seconds for a pattern set to a hundred feet. Seven . . . eight . . . nine . . . ten . . . counting too fast . . . probably only five seconds so far . . . seven . . . eight . . . nine . . . ten.

"Vessel lost contact, sir. He's sweeping on Red Y10. Transmission interval 2,500 yards."

What had happened? There was no earsplitting crash . . . nothing. The signalman rose to the occasion.

"Maybe those depth charges were made at the Skoda works and filled with sand."

"Or M and V," the gunlayer put in.

We squatted on the deck, waiting for the destroyer to pick us up again. The captain was wearing a head-set plugged into our Asdic and could hear the enemy's transmissions as he swept round to pick us up again. It wasn't long coming.

"In contact, sir," the HSD said casually. "Red 90."

We listened while he reported that the destroyer was coming in again, speeding up and cutting down its transmission intervals as it closed on us unerringly. Perhaps that first run had only been a sighter. This time we were for it. Once again the thrash of propellers overhead. The noise died away and the counting started again. But nothing broke the suspense.

For an hour the destroyer hung about, making fewer and less accurate runs over us as time went on. Then the HE faded altogether. We waited another half an hour and then came cautiously up to periscope depth. Just because the noise of his screws faded, it did not necessarily mean that the enemy had departed. He might easily be sitting somewhere near, waiting for us to make the next move. The captain searched swiftly round with the aft periscope.

"Not a sausage. Well, I wonder what all that was about. Now we've got to find out where we are."

He identified a cliff against the barren line of hills as Cape Noli and gave Gus a fix which put us four

miles off the beach. When we had fallen out from
Diving Stations and were seated round the wardroom
table having our breakfast, the captain produced his
theory.

"I didn't like to say this in front of the troops, but I
think they may have been using depth-charges with
contact pistols. Not the usual ones set to go off hydro-
statically, but maybe a large pattern of small charges
with graze fuses like our hedgehogs. It wouldn't take
more than one direct hit by a very small charge to
blow a hole in our pressure-hull. Nice chaps. Now,
what's Jane up to today?" He picked up the *Good
Morning* newspaper and settled back to enjoy the
strip cartoons with his coffee.

The thought of those small contact bombs sinking
all round us without exploding like any decent depth-
charge was creepy.

"Give me an honest-to-God pattern of 450-pounders
any day," Number One said. "At least you know after
the explosion where you stand, or if you do."

If we thought we were to be left on our own for a
quiet day patrolling at Watch Diving we were mis-
taken. The lights in the wardroom had only been out
a few minutes and we had barely settled in our bunks
when Gus, who was on the watch, came in and shook
the captain.

"There are some masts and some smoke coming
down from the north, sir."

"Oh dear. I suppose that destroyer has rustled up a
few of his chums to continue the good work."

He went to the periscope and tried to make out
what went with the masts. But it was still blowing
hard, with spray continually clouding over the upper
window. It was some time before the captain could see.

"Just as I thought. Three of the bastards, sweeping in line abreast. Heard anything, Asdics?"

"Yes, sir," the operator replied, "I can just hear transmissions sweeping."

Wearily the ship's company went to Diving Stations as we went deep and waited. At least this time the enemy could only hunt for in a general area. He hadn't seen us dive, as he had earlier in the morning and been able to go straight for the patch of bubbles where our main ballast tanks had vented themselves. They might miss us altogether.

"In contact, sir."

They had us again. It was a repeat of the earlier performance, with three sources of HE and pinging, making their attacks in turn, though not with the deadly accuracy of our old friend. In all they kept us deep for a further two hours. Everyone's nerves were a little on edge. The coxswain, squatting in front of his after-hydroplane handwheel, could stand it no longer.

"If those Wops want an A/S exercise, why don't they use their own bleedin' submarines? We didn't come all the way out from U.K. to be a clockwork mouse for training their Asdic ratings," he muttered to the second coxswain.

When we came up again, the captain was able to identify one of the three hunting craft as it went away to the south.

"They look like those sketches we have of UJ-boats: converted coasters, with a big gun for'ard, a tall single funnel and a pronounced sheer."

"UJ" stood for *Unterseebotjaeger*. We had recently been warned they were nasty customers. They were more efficient as anti-submarine vessels than destroyers and carried large quantities of depth-charges. The patrol report of the first British submarine to encounter one told how it surfaced to gun down what was taken to be an unescorted coasting-vessel; she was quickly put down again by heavy and accurate gunfire. "They carry at least 84 depth-charges," the report ended laconically. We were glad to see the last of them.

At last it really did seem as though they had given up. We had lunch in peace and I took over the afternoon watch. Quickly the lights went out for'ard as all hands turned in to catch up with their sleep. The captain decided it was not worthwhile trying to get away from the area, even if it was compromised. Better to lie in towards the land till dark, and then shift patrol elsewhere on the surface. There was not very much chance of the Germans sending any shipping past Cape Noli for a while, when they knew there was an enemy submarine off there.

I looked across the troughs of the waves at little villages each with their prominent church towers spaced at intervals along the coast. I was wondering vaguely how Napoleon ever coaxed his armies across those peaks when I saw what at first I took to be a stick on the water. There was another mast near it. The boat pumped up to 24 feet with the swell and I saw that there were two squat vessels plunging in our direction, not very far away. With difficulty I awoke the captain, who took over the periscope, threatening a horrible end to the next Wop who disturbed his afternoon's sleep.

"More UJ-boats, I suppose."

He stared at them for a while and went on: "These look like a couple of dressed-up canal barges. Might be UJ-boats though. Wait a minute. What have we here? A couple of R-boats or chasseurs on either bow. Good enough—Diving Stations."

When the order was given to get all tubes ready, the crew knew we were no longer on the defensive and were going to hit back for having been kept on the hop all day.

The targets were two cargo vessels, with their engines and superstructure aft, very like the little Dutch coasters in the English Channel. These two were on their way towards the war front, so they were for it, and their escort of chasseurs were not going to stop us, especially after the way we had eluded the much more formidable UJ-boats. The captain fired a full salvo from eight hundred yards. He was still looking through the periscope when the bang came. It was followed by a succession of small explosions like a string of Chinese crackers going off.

"No doubt about what those two were carrying. There are shells still bursting all round the spot where that chap blew up. Looks as if we've missed the other one."

He was not in the slightest perturbed by the presence of the two chasseurs. Instead of going deep he stayed up to watch the fun.

"They're not much more than motor boats, and they're making heavy weather of this sea. Get one tube reloaded as quickly as possible, I'm going to trail this other fellow—I think we can keep up with him."

The plot showed the target to be making good not more than seven knots against the head sea, so we would be able to keep pace submerged whilst our batteries lasted.

In under a quarter of an hour I was able to report
to the captain that we had one torpedo ready. We had
managed to overhaul the target, so were able to turn
and fire at our leisure. The captain watched the torpedo's track cut across the waves to its mark.

"Damn! Missed ahead," he said savagely.

"A series of small explosions all round, sir," came
from the HSD.

"Lord, yes, someone's firing at our periscope. Is there
an aircraft about?" Another look round at the periscope. "Well, I'm buggered. It's the chasseurs. Both of
them are firing every gun they've got at our periscope.
There's a chap manning an Oerlikon on the bows of
that one who is getting very wet indeed. They've got
the wind-up properly. The target's turned away and is
heading in towards the beach."

He watched as the ammunition ship bolted like a
scared rabbit for the shore. The two chasseurs must
have fired every round of Oerlikon they carried before they too went in after their charge. The captain
was now determined to dispose of the remainder of
the ammunition convoy. We loaded in our last three
torpedoes and then nosed into the shallow water. The
ship had beached itself stern on to us, so it would
only be possible to get in an oblique shot set to run
on the surface from farther up the coast. The first
torpedo blew up on the bottom just under the stern
of the target.

"That's shaken them. They're all jumping over the
side and wading up the beach."

The second torpedo hit it fair and square. There
was another sharp explosion, and once again bursting shells and rockets put up a Guy Fawkes show.
This was too much for the chasseurs. With one ac-

cord they both turned and ran. Judging from the direction they headed, it seemed as if they were making for the little village marked on the chart, appropriately enough, as "Finali."

Disposing of those two ships had cost us six torpedoes, but as they were carrying well over a thousand tons of ammunition between them, it had been taxpayers' money well spent.

We made best speed to get away from the area. It did not take much imagination to foresee what the local German naval commander's orders for that night would be. All shore leave for destroyers and UJ-boats based in Genoa would be cancelled. I wished them a pleasant night flogging backwards and forwards off Cape Noli in a gale. By then we should be well on our way back to Maddalena. A signal was sent telling Captain (S) that we only had one torpedo remaining and were accordingly leaving patrol. It was then just under twenty-four hours since we had fired through the breakwater into Monaco harbour.

POW RESCUE

FROM *USS Pampanito: Killer-Angel*

---

by Gregory F. Michno

When historians turn their hand to writing about military history, the result can be both entertaining and educational, as in Gregory F. Michno's book *USS Pampanito: Killer-Angel*. Known primarily for his nonfiction Western writing, Michno is the author of *Lakota Noon: The Indian Narrative of Custer's Defeat, The Mystery of E Troop: Custer's Gray Horse Company at the Little Bighorn,* and *Battle at Sand Creek: The Military Perspective*. He has also written numerous articles in *Montana: The Magazine of Western History, Journal of the West, Wild West,* and other Western history publications, as well as another naval book, **Death on the Hellships**. A member of the Western History Association, Order of the Indian Wars, Little Big Horn Associates, and several other organizations, Michno holds a master's degree in history from the University of Northern Colorado. He lives in Longmont, Colorado.

Unfortunately, many casualties of war didn't come from combat, but from prisoners of war being trans-

ported by enemy cargo ships, which were then torpedoed by Allied submarines. Even more terrible is
the idea of a submarine coming upon the scene
afterward, with hundreds of soldiers floating in the
water, and the captain and his crew knowing that
they can't possibly save every man. With a discerning
eye, Michno sets the stage with a discussion of the
average casualty count from torpedoed ships, then
delves into the horrific details of the *Pampanito*'s
encounter with the men it had just put into the ocean
less than an hour earlier.

The destruction of Japanese ships ferrying POWs was not unique to HI 72. Early in the war the Japanese took a rather cavalier attitude about transporting POWs by sea, often routing lone ships across waters that American submarines had not yet made especially dangerous. During the course of the war, 120,000 POWs were moved by sea—at the appalling shipboard space of less than one square yard per man. Eventually, American submarines began hitting them. The first deaths in great quantity came in July 1942, when the 7,266-ton *Montevideo Maru* out of Rabaul was sunk off Luzon by USS *Sturgeon* (SS 187). It was carrying 160 civilians and 1,053 Australian soldiers, the majority from the 2/22 Battalion. They all died. Off Shanghai on 1 October, the 7,053-ton transport *Lisbon Maru* was torpedoed by *Grouper*. About 850 out of 1,800 British POWs were killed. The rescue ships used the swimming prisoners for target practice.

The worst year for a POW to be at sea was 1944. On 24 June, the 6,780-ton freighter *Tamahoko Maru* almost made it to Nagasaki when it was jumped by the ULTRA-directed *Tang*. *Tamahoko Maru* went down with a loss of 560 out of 772 POWs, including 15 Americans.

The worst month to be a POW at sea was September 1944. On 7 September the 2,634-ton *Shinyo Maru* was taking 675 American prisoners from Mindanao to Luzon. Two torpedoes from USS *Paddle* (SS 263) sent it to the bottom. Only 85 Americans made it to shore. On 18 September the British submarine HMS *Tradewind* sank the 5,065-ton cargo ship *Junyo Maru* off Sumatra. Over 5,000 men died, including over 1,400 Dutch, British, and Australians and a handful of Americans. On 21 September, *Hofuku Maru,* en route from Manila to Japan, was found by American carrier torpedo planes. They sank it within three minutes and over 1,000 British and Dutch POWs were lost. The destruction of HI 72 killed another 1,500.

On 24 October 1944, *Arisan Maru* sailed from Manila. About 225 miles from Hong Kong, the 6,886-ton cargo ship was torpedoed by USS *Shark II* (SS 314). The Japanese shut the hatches and abandoned ship. Of the 1,802 prisoners aboard, only 8 survived. The last POW convoy out of Manila left on 13 December. The 7,000-ton *Oryoko Maru* carried 1,619 prisoners. American carrier planes damaged it near Subic Bay, Luzon. *Oryoko Maru* pulled into the bay, but the planes returned the next day and finished it off. About 1,350 of the prisoners made shore. Within two weeks they were split up and loaded on *Brazil Maru* and *Enoura Maru.* In January 1945, at Takao, Formosa, *Enoura Maru* was bombed and another 270 were killed and 250 wounded. The survivors were moved to *Brazil Maru.* During the remainder of the two-week voyage, another half of them died in the holds. Only about 400 made it to Moji alive.

In a March 1945 memorandum, Captain Harry L. Pence listed fourteen Japanese ships sunk by Allied forces while carrying POWs. Japanese records indicated that about twenty-five ships carrying POWs were bombed or torpedoed during the war. Admiral Lockwood said, "The sinkings of Japanese

merchant ships resulting from Communication Intelligence ran into hundreds of ships and probably
amounted to fifty percent of the total of all merchantmen sunk by submarines." If anyone could give an accurate assessment of ULTRA's success, it was Charles
Lockwood.

Should one be surprised that so many POWs went
to their doom on HI 72? Probably not. We are not
here to debate the morality of war. If HI 72 had been
left unmolested, the ships, personnel, and cargo that
would have reached Japan would have had the potential to do more harm in the future. America and
Japan were in a bloody death-struggle, and any means
taken to gain victory were justifiable at the time. Both
sides had been dehumanized. The psychological dis-
tancing that facilitates killing was in evidence not
only on the battlefields but also in the plans of the
strategists and tacticians. The Pacific war was a Man-
ichaean struggle between completely incompatible
antagonists. It was a war without mercy. If any inno-
cent parties got in the way, they would have to suffer.
It is harsh, and indubitably heartless, especially when
looked at through a fifty-year cushion of time. But
such is war. In the grand scheme of things, ships
carrying tons of gasoline, oil, and bauxite had to be
destroyed, regardless of the possibility that Allied
lives would be lost in the process. The fatal ULTRA
was sent.

These events were unknown to the POWs. If they
realized anything at all, it might have been the ironic
fact that they had become free men—but at what
price? They were free to drown in the middle of the
South China Sea. Some had resigned themselves to
their fate and faced the end stoically, but most, K. C.

Renton said, "began to go a bit dippy." Two men in his party had just drunk seawater and had thrown themselves off the rafts in despair only a few hours earlier.

On one raft, former schoolteacher Frank Farmer and Curly Martin had been discussing their likely fate. They were interrupted by a raftmate who had been delirious and kept claiming that he saw masts on the horizon. They ignored him. Finally his persistent interruptions caused them to strain their oil-blinded eyes. Martin heard the sound of engines. A ship was coming, and she appeared to be a submarine. At first she went by, and Martin thought she was a U-boat. Farmer stood up and waved his hat, and the submarine closed in. She swept past again, and Farmer could see armed men on the deck. Finally they turned back. Martin waved, too. "I, fortunately," said Martin, "had a lot of fair, curly hair at the time, and they knew I wasn't Japanese and they came back to have another look."

Ken Williams had the same explanation. "One of our men, Curly Martin, had a hat, and when he waved it they could see fair hair, so they reckoned he couldn't be a Nip." K. C. Renton was about to give up when, about five in the afternoon, "a marvelous and wonderful thing happened, a submarine was making straight for us. We did not know whose it was. My eyes were in pain from the oil and I could not see clearly, but when it was right opposite us, I saw a couple of men with machine guns pointing them at us. I did not care because it would have been a quicker way out—and believe me, those men looked tough."

Another man on the raft noticed the guns that

were trained on them. Not as ready to meet his maker, he called out to the submarine in defiance.

Gordon Hopper was still grasping the trigger of the 20-mm gun, waiting, not knowing what to do if the order came to fire. *Pampanito* had approached the first group of men on a makeshift collection of hatch covers and timbers. There were about fifteen of them, scantily clad and covered in crude oil. Some had Australian "Digger" hats, and a few wore Japanese-style caps. They were waving frantically and shouting all at once so that no words could be distinguished. Most of the crew on deck were startled when they heard an obviously English voice angrily call out: "First you bloody Yanks sink us. Now you're bloody well going to shoot us." Bob Bennett remembered the exchange as: "You sink us, then you save us, you bloody Yanks." On the bullnose, Tony Hauptman lowered his shotgun and called back: "Who are you?"

"Prisoners of war," one yelled. "Australians. British. Prisoners of war. Pick us up, please."

Several men moved to assist them, but Summers was not yet sure. Just one, he cautioned, then yelled out, "Get the one that speaks English."

"You dumb bastards," came the defiant reply, "we all speak English."

Hauptman put down his shotgun, held up one finger, and said, "One man. One man only." A rope was thrown across, and several men broke for it or jumped into the water and began swimming for the submarine. Hauptman shouted for them to stay put, while Jim Behney raised his machine gun.

Frank Farmer was the first to reach out. "I grasped

the rope," he said, "and was hauled across the intervening water to the sub's side, up which I was assisted by two crewmen. When I thanked them in English, they were incredulous." He was escorted to the conning tower, where he met Lieutenant Commander Davis. Farmer's brief story about the POWs' being on the convoy greatly distressed the exec, but the officers were finally convinced that they were not Japanese.

"Take them aboard!" Summers ordered, and Frank Farmer became the first survivor of the "Railway of Death" to return to Allied control. Harold Martin and Ken Williams followed close behind. "They threw us a line," said Williams, "and the three of us were soon on board. After hearing our story, they immediately started searching for more."

Word passed through *Pampanito* like a flash, and almost everyone not on duty tried to come up to help. Fireman Andy Currier was one of the first in the water to help pull the rafts closer to the sub, followed by Bennett, Hauptman, and Behney. Yagemann stopped repairing the TBT and climbed down on the side of the hull. He saw that the men were so weak they couldn't even grab the lines; they'd reach out and fall off the rafts. They were almost impossible to haul up. "It was like trying to capture a greased pig," Yagemann said. Crouched on the side tanks, he cut his knees on barnacles and had his back wrenched by someone using his leg as a ladder. Hopper breathed a great sigh of relief, slid down from the 20-mm gun, and jumped into the water. On deck and along the tanks they were assisted by Mike Carmody, Ed Stockslader, Don Ferguson, John Madaras, Seaman First Class Jack J. Evans, and Motor Machinist's Mate Third Class Richard E. Elliott.

Jeff Davis climbed down and tried to get in the water to help a survivor on board. "I had to call him back to the bridge," Summers said. There was some decorum to be maintained. Besides, if a plane appeared, he might have to leave some of his own crew behind.

More men came topside and helped strip the remnants of clothing off the survivors, while others took rags to swab off the oil and lower them inside. In the forward torpedo room, Clyde Markham had some rags soaked in "pink lady." He was trying to be helpful, but "one POW screamed when it got into his open sores," Markham said. "After that we used soap and water."

Red McGuire was below when he heard the order, "Stand by to pick up prisoners." One survivor climbed down the ladder under his own power. McGuire saw a short, oil-covered man who barely came up to his chin and thought he was Japanese. Coming from behind, McGuire grabbed him in a headlock and banged his head into the ladder.

"Blimey!" the fellow yelled out. McGuire wiped some oil off his face with a rag and asked, "Who the hell are you?"

"I'm a British prisoner of His Imperial Majesty, the Emperor of Japan," the man smartly answered.

"No you're not," McGuire countered. "Now you're a free man on a United States submarine." The man's eyes lit up, and McGuire, rather embarrassed, said, "I'm sorry. Does your head hurt?"

"Oh, no," the man answered. "I'm just fine." And he walked away, McGuire said, "as happy as a lark."

Not everyone could stand seeing the conditions the poor survivors were in. Frank Fives tried to help, but he said, "My stomach couldn't take it. It was terrible." It was the first time he had seen the bloody side of war, and he didn't like it. It was why he had chosen submarines. Fives went back up to the bridge.

Pampanito combed her way through more wreckage. The first group of fifteen men was all aboard by 1634. In the patrol report Summers recorded: "A pitiful sight none of us will ever forget."

Heading for a second raft, *Pampanito* broke radio silence and sent out a message to *Sealion II* asking for help. About twenty-eight miles to the northeast, Reich got the word and swung his boat back to the scene at four-engine speed.

Cliff Farlow was having hallucinations from heat and thirst. "I looked out and saw my mother and father milking cows under palm trees in the South China Sea," he said. "Obviously I was getting pretty delirious." One of his mates saw something that looked like a submarine, then they heard the thunder of the engines, but they figured it was "a bloody Jap sub." When it neared, Farlow saw "blokes come out on the deck with machine guns and we thought we were going to be done over." However, one of them called out, "They're Australians!" Two sailors jumped over the side and swam over. As they helped Farlow and his mates aboard, one of them kept saying, "For Chrissake hurry up—we gotta get down!"

About 1720, *Pampanito* had cleared the second raft, and bearings were taken on three others in sight. The second had nine men aboard, and they were less covered in oil, making their boarding a bit easier. While heading for the third raft, the sub passed a small piece of floating debris that appeared to have a single man aboard. Upon closer inspection the crew found the occupant to be dead—with part of his head gone.

The raft Bob Farrands was on was thoroughly waterlogged, and he sat in water up to his chest. He was "thirst crazy," he said. "I would shut my eyes and see the soda fountain running in a shop back in my home town, but no one would give me a drink. We always had a water bag on the verandah at my home. Water was running out of it, but still I could not drink." He was going a bit balmy when he heard an engine and saw what appeared to be "a Yank sub."

"A sailor dived in and put a rope around my chest," Bob said. "I was pulled and assisted onto the deck. There I stood stark naked, covered in emulsified oil. A sailor said, 'Are you all right, Aussie?' and I said, 'As good as gold.' Then he let go of me and I fell flat on my face." Farrands was given a water-soaked cloth to suck on and hauled below.

The third and fourth rafts, carrying six men each, were picked up by 1730. Then another small raft was seen with one man lying motionless on his back. A sailor dived in with a line and swam out to him. When he reached him, the survivor sat bolt upright and tried to jump off, perhaps thinking that the Japanese had found him again. He was nearly blind. This was John Campbell, Second Battalion, Gordon Highlanders. He collapsed while being hauled on deck and remained in a semiconscious state.

Roy Cornford saw what appeared to be a small ship in the distance. "It seemed like hours," Roy said, "watching this black looking dot going to the rafts, when we realized it was a submarine." Finally she closed in, and a sailor dived in with a rope and pulled them aboard. "I can remember lifting my hands up, but pleading with the sailors not to grab my arms because they were just blisters and sores." When Cornford got on deck he was surprised he could still walk.

Paul Pappas was topside with his camera and was given the ship's 16-mm movie camera to record the action. He shot all the film and used all three of his own rolls. At 1753 they found another large raft with eleven men. While they were hauling this group aboard, there were about fifty men on deck.

Scanning the horizon were Harry S. Lynch and Clarence Williams, both electrician's mates third class. Williams, who had joined up in Miami, Florida, in March 1943, was a novice at lookout. This was his first patrol on *Pampanito*, and he was diligently searching his sector when suddenly he saw aircraft.

"A flight of low-flying Jap planes!" Williams called out.

Summers shouted to clear the deck. It had happened. The Japanese had found them, and at the most vulnerable time. In moments, crewmen, as well as survivors who could hardly walk, somehow came to life and dashed for the open hatches. Then almost immediately the crisis passed. Williams shouted: "Never mind. It's a bird!" A flight of frigate birds hovered almost motionless on the air currents. Williams felt a bit foolish when he realized his mistake. Summers recorded: "Fortunately one of the planes was seen to flap its wings, proving the formation to be large birds gliding in perfect order."

Chief Clarence Smith strapped on a sidearm when he heard the call about men in the water. But by the time he got ready to go topside, the survivors were coming down. It was hard to carry them, and they

couldn't easily be lowered, because they were still too
slippery. Smith stood below the after battery hatch
and caught the POWs as they were dropped down.
Roy Cornford was one of the men given the heave-
ho. He had just taken off his clothes to get the oil
swabbed off when he heard a shout, "Planes, planes!"
A sailor grabbed him, lifted him, and dropped him,
Roy said, "down the hatch onto a big plump sailor's
stomach." Chief Smith had finally found a use for his
belly.

At 1835, *Pampanito* sent a message to ComSubPac
notifying them of the situation. Five minutes later, a
second minor panic swept topside when a patrol boat
was sighted through the high periscope. A closer look
showed that the craft appeared to be a submarine,
but with a gun aft. *Sealion II* did not have an after
four-inch gun, and since the craft did not answer a
challenge, *Pampanito* dove. One of the survivors said
that there was a German sub in the area, and Summers tracked the mysterious boat for half an hour. By
1940 they were close enough to see the submarine
dead in the water. She was *Sealion*. The "gun" on the
after deck was a cluster of rescuers hauling survivors
aboard. Summers surfaced, but they had lost valuable
rescue time.

In the approaching darkness, they spotted what
looked like a man waving a white flag. They moved
closer to find the "flag" was really his hand, bleached
white from the salt water. He was hauled aboard, and
they headed in the direction of where they had seen
another raft before they dove. It was 2005 and almost
totally dark. Chances were they would never find anyone, but incredibly, looming up out of the black sea
was another group of about one dozen men. After

taking them aboard, the crew made a cursory head count. They had rescued over seventy men, which almost doubled *Pampanito*'s crew of seventy-nine men and ten officers. Being "cramped for living space," and unable to sight anyone else in the tropical night, Summers broke off the operation.

One of the last men brought aboard was Harry Pickett. He had been on his own for quite a while. "It was darkish," he said. "I could feel the regular pulse of a motor through the water. Then I saw a sort of shape." Pickett heard what he called "a good old American accent" call out to him: "Can you catch a rope, buddy?" It was the Floridian, Jim Behney. He tossed Pickett a line and lifted him bodily in his strong but gentle arms. Behney's name, said Pickett, "I will never forget. He carried me below."

Gordon Hopper didn't return to man the 20-mm gun. "All the rest of my life," he said, "I have thanked God that I didn't have to make the decision to fire or not to fire. All the rest of my life I have treasured the memory of helping save lives rather than terminate them."

Three days earlier, *Pampanito* had bared her teeth, sending her first ships to the bottom of the sea and killing hundreds of men. During the past four hours she had plucked seventy-three men from the sea, more than were rescued by any other American submarine during the entire war. A boat of steel with men of flesh and blood can serve two masters. *Pampanito* had become a killer-angel.

The wounded, burned, emaciated survivors were carried down the hatches, and Maurice "Doc" Demers got his chance to prove his mettle. Crew members volunteered to be nurses, helping to wash off the oil,

administering medicines, feeding, and donating clothing. It was a most moving experience: hardened soldiers and sailors weeping together in sorrow and joy.

The first thing to do was to find a place to put everyone. The crew thought they should quarantine the survivors all aft, but that proved impossible. "There was
no way you could fit seventy-three men in the after
torpedo room," Hubie Brown said. Many were bunked
there, but some went to the crew's quarters and others
went to the forward torpedo room. While some of his
mates had to give up their bunks, Brown never did,
because his was on the top level in the forward torpedo room, and the weakened men couldn't climb up.
Some of them were so skinny, however, they could fit
two to a bunk.

Torpedoman's Mate Third Class Peder A. Granum
was making his first patrol on *Pampanito*. He had
been born in Mohall, North Dakota, in 1913. Being
thirty-one years old and only five and one-half feet
tall, Peder was called "Grandpa" Granum by the
crew. He had made one patrol on *Gudgeon* but had
broken an ankle while jumping down the hatch. After
getting his leg in a cast and going to the States, he was
eventually sent back to Midway, where he was assigned to *Pampanito*. Granum was good with electric
torpedoes. "The guys thought I was a spy for the
Naval Bureau, the way I got quickly added to the
boat."

Granum had been in the boat's rubber raft, helping
pull in the drifting survivors. He swabbed them off,
helped them down the hatch, and heard more than
one man thank God for being rescued. Granum used
"pink lady" to clean off the oil, carefully avoiding the
open tropical ulcers. Demers broke out the rubbing

alcohol to wash down the survivors. The sailors approved; there was no sense in using up good torpedo juice when rubbing alcohol would do the trick.

Summers appointed Lieutenant Swain to oversee placement and care of the survivors. Lieutenant Fulton made a head count. Forty-seven of the men were Australians, and twenty-six were British. Among them were Wally Winter and Alf Winter. Alf thought it was remarkable that two Winters were rescued by a Summers.

Ted Swain had not needed his .45. He had put the weapon away, helped lower men down the hatches, and wished they could have picked up every man on the ocean. When Summers told him, "No more," he felt like disobeying. Swain helped weave rope lines in the torpedo racks to construct makeshift hammocks, then laid blankets on them, and they became fairly decent bunks. The worst cases stayed in the crew's quarters. "They smelled terrible," Swain said.

Still delirious, John Campbell was carried down and placed in Van Atta's bunk, starboard and aft of the galley. Al didn't mind. He also helped clothe Campbell from his own wardrobe.

Demers quickly found himself worked to the limit. He checked his supply locker: atabrine for malaria, aspirin, merthiolate, mineral oil, castor oil, gentian violet, glucose, bismuth, sulfa powder, burn ointment, tincture of benzoate, boric acid, morphine, vitamins, plasma, syringes, gauze, and bandages. Unfortunately, the survivors had numerous maladies that a lone pharmacist's mate was not equipped to deal with.

Most of them were in shock, and they looked like they would pass out or die any minute. He gave fifteen of them morphine shots. Their eyes were gray from vitamin deficiencies. He worked on their eyes, cleaning out the oil and dirt, then moved to the ears, nose, and mouth. Some had globs of oil in their mouths like chaws of tobacco, but they were too weak to even spit them out.

After treating the most obvious physical symptoms, Demers retreated for a few minutes to his medical books, with which he diagnosed a few of the diseases such as beriberi and pellagra. The survivors should have been quarantined, but the crew resigned themselves to the situation and went about their jobs as nurses with a passion. "You didn't have to ask anybody to help," Demers said. "They just did it."

The survivors were first given moist cloths to suck on, then cups of water. Very soon they were asking for something more substantial. Cooks Joe Eichner and Bill Morrow and Ship's Cook Second Class Daniel E. Hayes had their work cut out for them. Dan Hayes in particular, newly arrived on the boat, became a full-time assistant to Demers, serving tea, cocoa, bouillon, and soup. Harry Jones was overcome by the kindness he received. He got a large mug of hot vegetable soup, and even though his lips and tongue were cracked and swollen, he was happy that he could still taste the wonderful brew—"something good and wholesome, the like of which I had not partaken of for the last two and a half years." Jones and some of the more fit ones just sipped their soup in silence, sometimes unable to restrain the tears of joy that came to their eyes.

K. C. Renton thought he was going to be machine-gunned, but "instead of lead," he said, "we got a rope and were taken aboard. Can you imagine the shock? We got water and tomato soup and crackers for our first dinner, something that we never had for two and a half years." He added, "And since then we lived like lords."

Bob Farrands was quartered in the after torpedo room. He perked up rapidly. "The poor bloke that looked after me must have got sick of my voice," he said, "as I never shut up." Farrands was given plenty of hot soup and tea, he said, "but the best meal was a slice of bread and butter, it was beautiful."

Almost everyone but John Campbell responded well. Try as he might, Demers was unable to find a vein substantial enough to give him a glucose injection. It was as if the man didn't have any blood. In one foot there was a hole the size of a silver dollar, going clean through. They speculated that fish had been gnawing on him.

Even so, Campbell became lucid for short intervals. McGuire had the job of going to every man and getting his name, rank, service number, and name of next of kin. When he got to the Scotsman, however, he had a tough time. "I had to ask him his name about twenty times," McGuire said. "He had a burr about a mile long." Finally, McGuire deciphered his name as "Jack" or "Jock," and found out he was with the Gordon Highlanders. Attending Campbell was twenty-year-old Seaman First Class George W. Strother. Strother learned that Campbell had been a cook on the Burma Railway. He had a wife and three kids, but he had never seen his youngest child. Strother thought Campbell had a beautiful personality. The man's acceptance of his situation and his thoughts regarding his family made the young seaman think about his own mortality. "I was just a kid then," he said. "I grew up pretty fast."

Back among the rafts, *Sealion II* also had a busy evening 15 September. Reich conned his boat through the waters until 2200. He picked up fifty-four men: twenty-three Australians and thirty-one British. Reich believed no more could be safely taken aboard, and even with others close by and calling for help, he pulled away. "It was heartbreaking to leave so many dying men behind," Reich wrote. Some of his crew who were still on deck in the darkness had recurrent memories of the scene for years afterwards, especially of the plaintive cry of "Over here! Over here!" fading out in the night.

Sealion also radioed Pearl, and Lockwood gave both subs permission to head for Saipan, about eighteen hundred miles away. Since Reich reported that many men were still in the water, Admiral Lockwood, at 0300 on 16 September, ordered *Barb* and *Queenfish* to head immediately to the scene of the rescue. On *Barb*, Gene Fluckey, still complaining that the "Busters" had not informed him about the convoy, was irked again because he had to retrace another 450 miles back to the site he had left a couple of days before.

However, about 150 miles from the scene, Fluckey happened across something that would quickly change his disposition: a convoy. *Queenfish* found it first, and *Barb* picked it up minutes later. It was big, and the rescue of any remaining POWs would have to wait.

This convoy, HI 74, had left Singapore on 11 September. It consisted of the *Harima Maru, Omuroyama Maru, Otowayama Maru, Hakko Mara*, and the big tanker *Azusa Maru*, filled with 100,600 barrels of oil. It was escorted by the frigate *Chiburi*, the training cruiser *Kashii*, and *Coast Defense Vessels Nos.*

13, 19, 21, and *27.* Guarding them all was the twenty-thousand-ton escort carrier *Unyo.* On 12 September, while moving north in the wake of HI 72, HI 74 received word of an attack on its sister convoy. The convoy commander, Rear Admiral Yoshitomi Eizo, ordered them to swing about sixty miles to the east to bypass the attack area. They succeeded in avoiding the "Busters," but late on 16 September they ran smack into the "Eradicators."

Swinburne ordered the boats in, and *Barb*'s torpedoes sent down *Azusa Maru* and *Unyo.* When the carrier finally sank at about 0700 on 17 September, again the codebreakers knew. Back at Pearl Harbor, Captain Wilfred J. Holmes, a liaison officer between the Submarine Force and the cryptographers, was looking through a batch of the latest Japanese naval messages. He picked up a garbled one about a vice admiral shifting his flag from one ship to another and a second one that commented about the safety of the imperial portrait. Holmes knew that vice admirals rode on carriers, and he knew a carrier had gone down even before the men on the submarine that sank it. *Barb* and *Queenfish,* however, had lost a few more hours in their race to pick up the last survivors.

The POWs had been in the water for five days, and they were in terrible shape. After noon on 17 September, *Barb and Queenfish* found them. Now, however, the barometer had dropped and the seas had risen; a typhoon was approaching. Submarines and men were tossed about in the heavy waves. Scenes played on *Pampanito* and *Sealion* were re-enacted on *Barb* and *Queenfish* as the dazed, incredulous survivors were hauled below and kindly cared for by men of war suddenly become angels of mercy.

The two subs combed the area. Charles Loughlin picked up eighteen men. Fluckey, having rescued fourteen men, contended that he would have forgone the pleasure of an attack on a Japanese task force to rescue any one of them. "There is little room for sentiment in submarine warfare," he wrote, "but the measure of saving one Allied life against sinking a Japanese ship is one that leaves no question once experienced." By dawn, with winds the two captains estimated at between sixty and one hundred knots and "skyscraper waves," the rescue was over. All that remained were dead, bloated bodies bobbing grotesquely in the seas. If any man was left alive by that time, Nature would soon eliminate him. *Barb* and *Queenfish* broke off and headed for Saipan.

While Fluckey and Loughlin were attacking HI 74 on the evening of 16 September, Summers was already two hundred miles to the east, approaching Balintang Channel. Most of the men had made remarkable comebacks in the twenty-four hours they had been aboard *Pampanito*. Try as Demers might to ease them back into a regular diet, many of them overdid it. Wally Winters decided he wanted a good old American hamburger and a Coke, and he sneaked into the galley to look for some. Not seeing the harm in it, Joe Eichner fried him a big burger, complete with onions, relish, and ketchup. Winters wolfed it down and about an hour later was as sick as a dog. Demers could only say, "I told you so."

A similar incident occurred while Hauptman was looking after John Campbell. The Scotsman seemed to take a turn for the worse, and Hauptman called Demers. Demers didn't know what to do but tried again, unsuccessfully, to shoot some glucose into the man. Meanwhile, Tony left and went to see McGuire.

"I think I killed him," a shaken Hauptman confessed. "He looked hungry and I fed him a big piece of bread and butter." Naturally the word got back to Demers, and the order went out absolutely no one was to feed the survivors without the permission of Doc Demers or Lieutenant Swain.

The unfamiliar food caused havoc with their systems. Within twenty-four hours all of them who did not already have dysentery had diarrhea. Many were berthed in the after torpedo room, and that compartment was serviced by only one head (toilet), which had to be discharged to the sea after each use. Said Ken Williams: "A bit of panic occurred when one of our chaps pushed the button on the toilet when we were submerged—of course we had been told not to."

A sailor was detailed to assist them. Woody Weaver explained: "The poor guys were lining up to use the one head, and we had to have a man on watch to operate the discharge valves for them. The poor sailor on that watch had quite a job. As fast as he took care of one man, there was another ready to sit on the commode."

As daylight waned on 16 September, so did the life signs of John Campbell. He never came out of his latest lapse into unconsciousness and about 1830 he died, his head supported in George Strother's arms. It was a deeply moving moment, for everyone had tried so hard to save him, and no one had ever died on *Pampanito* before. In the discussion of plans for his burial, a small argument ensued as to how to weigh him down.

"We compromised," said Carmody, "and placed a

four-inch shell and a connecting rod with him. We figured 'Jock' deserved the best we could give. We sewed him into a double mattress cover and took him topside." Van Atta knew he would be getting his bunk back when he saw them hauling the bag up the access hatch. "What a way to go," Van Atta thought, "being dumped alone into the South China Sea."

On the after deck a burial ceremony was conducted in the gathering darkness under a beautiful star-filled sky. The ship was rolling smartly in the swells. A layer of thick, black crude oil remained on the deck, making the footing hazardous. Because the men considered Pappas the cleanest-living crewman, he read a short service by the light of a red flashlight shielded by a sailor's cap. Bill Yagemann remembered that he, Tony Hauptman, Peder Granum, and Lieutenant Swain were in the burial party, but he couldn't see the other faces in the darkness. McGuire watched from above while on lookout. They had draped the bag with an American flag, and they apologized to the British that they had no Union Jack with which to cover him. When the prayers were over, Campbell's body was committed to the deep. But there was one last glitch, for the ship rolled, and the men holding the bag slipped on the oily deck. Campbell's body slid along the ballast tank and hung up on the hull. Carmody observed: "'Jock' didn't want to leave us!" A sailor stretched over the side and kicked the bag free. Campbell's body sank to the depths.

Two days later, one of the men *Queenfish* had rescued and who had been in a coma the entire time finally died. Since they were riding out rough weather, they committed his body to the deep by blowing him out of a torpedo tube.

Pampanito cleared Balintang Channel and headed east through the Philippine Sea. The survivors were improving in health by the hour and many were able to move freely about the boat. Roy Cornford, however, was still bed-ridden. He lay in his bunk for days with nothing to do but listen to the record player. He heard the Al Dexter song "Pistol Packin' Mama" so many times he memorized it.

Private William Cray was in the Sixteenth Advance Regiment, Royal Artillery. The gunner from Hull, England, took up with Bob Bennett, sharing stories and correspondence. Bennett seemed to have a knack for making friends, for he and Frank Farmer also became close, exchanging letters for another fifty years. Dagger Ward, of Nottingham, England, later wrote a letter to Hubie Brown, closing it with a little verse:

When you're sailing on the deep
And the sun begins to set
When others you are thinking of
Won't you sometimes think of me?

The kindness shown by the submariners needed no repayment. All the survivors had to give was a heart-felt thanks. They were completely destitute, almost to a man. Only Frank Coombes had managed to come through with more than just a few scraps of clothing, but he still had his hidden diamonds.

Motor Machinist's Mate First Class Wendell T. Smith, Jr., of Portland, Maine, had served on USS *Jenkins* (DD 447) before coming to *Pampanito*. Smith was on duty in the forward engine room when the survivors came aboard. The first few were so thin and oil-covered, he thought they were Japanese. When he realized they were British and Australian, he selected the next one through as his personal charge and thus became quick friends with Frank Coombes.

As they nearerd Saipan, Coombes wondered how he could repay Smith's kindness. He reached down for the money belt he still had under his shorts and produced the diamond earrings.

"I have a gift for you," Coombes said to Smith, and he handed him three diamonds that he had extracted from one of the earrings. He told Smith he had "liberated" them from a store in Singapore just before the Japanese had marched in. Coombes also gave some diamonds to two other sailors who had looked after him. After the war, Smith took the diamonds to a jeweler, who pronounced them excellent stones and mounted them in a ring that Smith's wife, Virginia, still wears.

A. John Cocking, a private in the 2/4 Machine Gun Battalion AIF, was from Perth. He recuperated quickly and got to know several of the crew. Cocking told them that back home he owned some horses for racing and for stud service, and that if they ever got to Australia he'd show them the racing business. He also became friends with Woody Weaver, and the torpedoman gave him a little black book with the crew's names and addresses. Weaver was destined to cross paths with Cocking's son twenty-five years later.

Pampanito had been on patrol for a month, and the food was rapidly being consumed. The crew subsisted on sandwiches. The last hot meats, said cook Dan Hayes, were hot dogs and beans, but everyone enjoyed them nevertheless. Ed Stockslader remembered that the pantry was down to mustard and bread.

After noon on 18 September, *Sealion II* caught up

with *Pampanito*, and they both made rendezvous with USS *Case* (DD 370). Aboard *Pampanito* came medical officer Lieutenant Commander Paul V. H. Waldo and Chief Pharmacist's Mate Lynn T. Wilcox. Demers had been up for three days; he had lost weight, and his legs had swollen. Summers gave him a shot of brandy and ordered him to go to bed.

They discussed transferring all the POWs to the *Case*, but Reich and Summers decided they had brought them this far, and they might as well take them the rest of the way. The POWs had a say in the matter also. When they were told of a possible transfer to an American destroyer, Curly Martin said they resisted. "We said, 'No way! The captain picked us up on his sub and we want to stay here.' And I believe he [Summers] grew about ten foot at this statement."

The survivors stayed aboard the subs. Unfortunately, the new doctor never examined one man. Ted Swain was tired and not in a diplomatic mood. Lieutenant Commander Waldo asked what he had been feeding the POWs.

"Liquids, soft eggs, and toast," Swain answered.

"Why not citrus?" the doctor asked.

"We haven't seen citrus ourselves in thirty days," Swam answered. When Waldo asked for Swain's records, he snapped back, "What records? We been working, not keeping records!"

Summers directed the doctor and corpsman to remain in the wardroom, then woke Demers. Still groggy, the pharmacist's mate went back to work. Soon he diagnosed another serious problem. Being down in a submarine with air conditioning blowing on them, the survivors had begun to develop coughs, colds, and pneumonia.

Hospital records later indicated that the survivors were an average of sixteen pounds underweight; 95 percent had malaria, 67 percent had dysentery, and 61 percent had tropical ulcers. All had vitamin deficiencies and malnutrition. All had skin lesions, five had scarred corneas from the oil, 20 percent had acute bronchitis, nine had pneumonia, and one had tuberculosis.

The after torpedo room began to smell so bad that Lieutenant Swain called for a field day to clean it. The sailors and the most fit of the POWs lent a hand. The British were a "little uppity" at first, said Swain, but they eventually pitched in. Soon enough, the torpedo room was cleaned up and disinfected like a hospital room. At sunup on 20 September, *Pampanito* met USS *Dunlap*, and the destroyer escorted her the rest of the way. About 0900 a pilot came aboard and guided her through the torpedo nets and into Tanapag Harbor, Saipan, where she moored next to the tender USS *Fulton* (AS 11).

All but the most seriously ill were allowed topside to witness the docking. They stood on the decks, dressed in submariner's clothes, looking almost part of the crew. Six could still not walk, and basket stretchers were used to haul the last of them topside. Demers was proud of his work. He believed most of the former POWs looked better than the majority of the crew. Lighters came alongside to ferry them to shore. While they were waiting, ice cream and fresh oranges were brought aboard, giving both the crew and the former POWs quite a treat.

As the submarine emptied, Joe Eichner, still in the galley, thought about giving one of the survivors a memento. "I noticed the oblong plate on the hot water heater in the crew's mess next to the sink," he said. "The idea came to me to unscrew the plate, which read, 'USS *Pampanito*, Hot Water Heater, Crew's Mess.'" Joe grabbed one of the exiting Australians and handed him the plate for a keepsake. He never knew whom he had given it to.

Although most of the survivors appeared relatively fit, one sailor who didn't look so well for wear was Dan Hayes. The cook, thin to begin with and now appearing haggard, stumbled along with the POWs as they were loaded onto a small boat. He was grabbed by a Marine and helped aboard.

"Hey, I'm an American!" Hayes protested. The Marine wouldn't listen, especially when prompted by the laughing sailors still on deck. "No he isn't," they yelled down. "Take him ashore." Eventually the former POWs admitted to the joke, and Hayes was released to climb back on board *Pampanito* to the guffaws of his mates. The boats took the survivors ashore. Summers wrote that they "shoved off with cheers, thumbs up, and a mutual feeling of friendliness that will be hard to exceed anywhere."

Of the British POWs on *Kachidoki Maru*, about 520 were eventually rescued by the Japanese and sent on their journey to Japan. About 157 British and Australians from *Rakuyo Maru* were picked up by the Japanese. Submarines rescued 159 men: *Pampanito*, 73 (one died); *Sealion II*, 54 (four died); *Queenfish*, 18 (two died); and *Barb*, 14.

The British survivors sailed to Hawaii on the liberty ship *Cape Douglas*. From there another ship took them to San Francisco, a train carried them to New York, and another vessel took them to England. The Aussies sailed on the liberty ship *Alcoa Polaris* to

Guadalcanal, and from there on the minelayer *Monadnock* to Brisbane. Six of them, including Roy Cornford and Reginald H. Hart, were too sick to leave and spent six weeks in "an American tent hospital where we," said Cornford, "were cared for by lots of American doctors and lovely American nurses." Eventually the liberated men spread the word of the atrocities they had experienced while slaving on the Burma Railway and told of their torpedoing and miraculous rescue by the same men who had sunk them.

The transfer ashore of the former POWs was completed by 1100, 20 September. Ten minutes later, *Sealion II* came in, moored outboard of *Pampanito*, and unloaded her POWs. Demers watched them come up the hatches and was startled. The POWs' heads were shaved, perhaps to counter problems with lice. They hardly had any clothing; some simply wore blankets draped around their shoulders. They looked like walking skeletons. Demers thought *Pampanito*'s POWs looked much better.

The rival crews began ribbing each other. Demers thought that Red McGuire was the loudest yeoman in the navy. If that was true, then he believed *Sealion* had the second loudest, a man he remembered by the name of O'Neill. The two verbally sparred across the decks.

"You glory-hunting sons-a-bitches," McGuire began. "You shot your torpedoes all over the damn ocean and just missed us. You jumped in when we were going to fire and took our ships. You hogged the damn convoy for yourselves." O'Neill jabbered right back that it was a dog-eat-dog world, and that if *Pampanito* couldn't keep up with the big boys, she had better stay on shore. Reich and Summers were on their respective bridges and could hear the shouting. The same thoughts were probably on their own minds. Finally, the captain *of Fulton*, towering several decks above both subs, sent down a message for them all to shut up. The incident ended, but there were still hard feelings between the crews.

Demers went to see a doctor on *Fulton* about his own condition. His feet and legs looked like balloons, and the doctor told him to stay off his feet. He took a hot shower, then marched back to the sub. Summers gave him more brandy and ordered him to go to bed. He slept for thirty-six hours.

OFF TO CONVOY COLLEGE

FROM *Nothing Friendly in the Vicinity*

---

by Claude C. Connor

*O*f all the authors in this volume, the one that seems to have sunk into obscurity the most is Claude C. Connor. My research found very little on him, save that he served during four patrols on the USS *Guardfish*, the submarine that was responsible for a terrible friendly-fire accident (which is hinted at in the title) when it torpedoed and sank the USS *Extractor* while on patrol. This book was critically acclaimed when it was first published, winning raves by authors such as Clay Blair, author of **Silent Victory** and **Hitler's U-Boat War.** (His quote about the book: "I can attest to the authenticity and soundness of Claude Connor's **Nothing Friendly in the Vicinity.** It is an excellent firsthand account of the Pacific submarine war, and I heartily recommend it." High praise indeed.) There is no evidence that Mr. Connor wrote anything else during the rest of his life, but it is very possible that with the publication of this memoir, he'd said everything he had to say about his wartime experiences.

By 1943, the Allies had borrowed a few tactics from the enemy, and the submarine "wolf pack" was one of them. Connor takes us on patrol from resupplying at a still-battered and rebuilding Pearl Harbor to stalking convoys off the Philippines, and does it all with deceptive ease. His accounts of everyday life aboard a submarine are as engrossing as the tense minutes of a depth-charge attack, and equally informative for both.

We wound our way through the entrance to Pearl Harbor about noon on June 1, seven days after leaving San Francisco. The devastation from the surprise December 7, 1941, attack was still visible more than two years after it was delivered. Everywhere I looked, twisted hulks of warships protruded from the water. I admit seeing the wreckage in that matter was rather unnerving.

There was no visible damage at the Submarine Base. Fresh supplies poured aboard *Guardfish* for the first four days following our arrival, including food, fuel, fresh water, deck gun ammunition, and torpedoes. The flurry of activities impressed me; there were men scurrying everywhere. An officer with a clipboard in hand documented food storage locations, as his team stuffed packaged and canned items into every nook and cranny, into every pigeonhole throughout the boat. Base personnel, with their fuel and water tanker-trucks on the dock, draped large hoses over to the boat. The main deck was covered with those snake-like hoses and the smell of diesel fuel was everywhere. Another loading crew carried live ammunition by hand across the deck to topside watertight lockers and down the after-battery hatch into the ship's magazine.

Torpedo loading was the most impressive of all. Transfixed on the pier, I watched as the crane lifted a torpedo from a carrier vehicle on the dock and swung it into the air over *Guardfish*. The 2,000-pound underwater missile had a warhead containing 600 pounds of high explosive. The crane operator slowly lowered the fish toward the submarine's main deck, as a torpedoman guided it down onto the sloping skids that led through the loading hatch. For the torpedo crews, loading twenty-four torpedoes into the boat was a time consuming, backbreaking, nerve-racking job.

We faced ten days of sea trials and training before *Guardfish* left for her eighth war patrol, so there was no time for liberties. Everything was strictly business. Well, almost everything. The pending reentry into the war arena by such a famous submarine as *Guardfish* did not go unnoticed in the social circles of Pearl Harbor. A couple of days before our departure, the entire ship's company received an invitation to a party to be held in our honor.

The gathering took place in a large white Colonial mansion on a hill overlooking the harbor. It was a glittering gala with officers in their dress whites and ladies in their jeweled finery dancing and toasting and eating. I felt completely out of my element and I don't think I was the only enlisted man who felt that way. However, this celebration was an indication of the democratization that was infiltrating the navy, albeit little by little.

Our departure day, June 14, 1944, finally arrived. Shortly after we reached the open sea, the captain told us over the speaker system that our patrol area was to be north and west of the Philippine Islands, from the Straits of Luzon into the South China Sea. He also announced that our mission was "unrestricted warfare against the enemy." We were to be part of a coordinated attack group, or "wolf pack" (as similar German operations in the Atlantic were known), with United

States submarines *Thresher*, *Piranha*, and *Apogon*. The commander of the group's operations, Captain William Vincent O'Regan, was aboard *Guardfish*. O'Regan's nickname was "Mickey," so he named his wolf pack "Mickey Finns." Our patrol area was the eastern sector of "Convoy College," bounded by the coasts of northern Luzon, southern Formosa (Taiwan), and China.

Four days after leaving Pearl we made an eight-hour refueling stop at those small mounds of coral sand known as Midway Islands. A number of submarines and other vessels went aground on the reefs adjacent to Sand Island's very narrow channel, and the wreckage served to remind skippers of the danger of entry. In addition to the remains of vessels, the islands of Midway were a home for thousands of "Gooney Birds," large, seagoing albatrosses that patrol much of the Pacific Ocean.

We left Midway and resumed our westward voyage toward our patrol area, staying on the surface most of the time. We were in company with the other submarines, though we rarely saw them. The nearest boats were usually over the horizon, but we occasionally picked up their radar indications. After finishing our watch, those of us in the conning tower often got permission, one at a time, to go topside for a quick smoke on the cigarette deck. The weather, sea, and sky were beautiful. A couple of Midway's "Gooney Birds" flew behind us for days. Flying fish and porpoises were our constant companions. It was a beautiful, and often breathtaking, scene.

The war front was no longer around the Solomon Islands. American forces had captured the Gilbert and Marshall Islands during and after *Guardfish*'s seventh war patrol. The fighting for control of New Guinea by Allied forces began during the boat's overhaul in San Francisco and continued during the entire eighth run. The American invasion of Saipan, the first island in the strategically important Marianas group, began as *Guardfish* set out on patrol number eight. The critically important island chain was only 1,500 miles east of the Japanese-controlled Philippines, and 1,400 miles south of Tokyo, Japan. Violent land, sea, and air battles for control of Saipan were in full swing as we passed about 800 miles north, on our way to "Convoy College." It was only then that we got our first inkling that a war was in progress.

Twice on June 28 we were attacked by planes, each of which forced us to dive to escape destruction. The second plane triggered our IFF transponder several times as it made a bombing run on us, which indicated that the aircraft was a friendly plane checking us out. Nevertheless, it continued its hostile approach as our boat labored to get under the water.

The boat's slow submergence probably had something to do with a sticking vent valve on one of the ballast tanks, but the captain was not certain. He made a submerged periscopic examination of the boat's topside to see if he could spot anything else. I remember hearing him comment to the officer of the deck, in a matter-of-fact voice, "There are air leaks all over the place." I did not realize the seriousness of the situation at the time.

Our lives changed radically just four days later when we reached our patrol area. Each morning at dawn we submerged as normal, not merely for a trim dive but to stay down all day. A pall of quiet slumber fell over the boat. The deck was motionless, and all

we heard was the quiet background hum of electric
motors and muted speech. We manned the underwater sound equipment continuously, both submerged
and on the surface. Our submerged patrol depth was
usually around 100 to 120 feet. Every fifteen minutes
the officer of the deck in the conning tower called
down the hatch to the diving officer to have him bring
the boat to periscope depth. When we reached 60 feet,
the officer of the deck raised the search periscope,
made a quick spin around to look for airplanes, then
slowly and methodically scanned the horizon for
smoke from enemy ships. After he was satisfied that all
was clear, we returned to 120 feet.

Wolf pack leader O'Regan's instructions called for
all boats in the pack to listen for coded radio transmissions from the others during the first few minutes
of each hour. We did that by sticking our periscopic
SD radar masts out of the water with our radio communication equipment connected to the mast, using it
as a radio antenna. Thus, any of the boats could report enemy contacts to the others even though we
were all submerged.

The Straits between the northern tip of Luzon and
the southern end are relatively shallow and filled with
small islands. There are two major east-west deep water channels between those islands. Bashi Channel, the
northernmost one, was our first patrol assignment.
The boats in the pack, spaced about twenty miles
apart, patrolled below surface, north and south, across
the channel. *Guardfish* spent the Fourth of July dodging twenty fishing sampans. O'Regan did not want to
reveal the presence of a pack of American submarines,
so the pack skippers were ordered to avoid contact
with and not attack the sampans.

Very early the next morning our sound operator picked up sonar pinging from our first ship contact, an anti-submarine patrol boat. Our radar detected her forty minutes later at a range of about six miles. We tracked and avoided her for a couple of hours. Then, after we submerged at dawn, we changed course and headed for the nearby southern tip of Formosa. Nevertheless, the patrol boat's pinging stayed with us. We heard distant, mysterious underwater explosions shortly before I came on watch at 8:00 A.M.

My radioman friend Anthony (Tony) Ubriaco relieved me at the end of my watch on the sonar, and I moved to the stool at the inactive SJ radar. As the officer of the deck, Lieutenant Donald C. Bowman raised the periscope to make an observation. At that moment an earsplitting, bone-rattling explosion rocked our starboard side. Another explosion followed immediately on our port side. The source of the explosions became quickly apparent: An unseen airplane had straddled us with bombs.

"Take her down, flood negative!" the officer of the deck shouted to the control room. "Rudder amidship, all ahead full!" he ordered the helmsman.

"Rudder's amidship, all answered ahead full, sir," came the reply.

"Make the depth two hundred feet. Check for damage," Bowman ordered.

The bow and stern plane operators in the control room had their planes at full dive. Normally, full speed would take us to about seven knots, submerged, but not this time. Our stern probably broke out of the water because the boat took on a steep downward angle and we were slow to get down. I had to hold on to the radar cabinet and brace my feet against the inclined deck. Seconds after the explosions I looked down and saw Captain Ward climbing into the conning tower through the lower hatch. He surprised me when he laughed and had a big grin on his face as he spoke to Lieutenant Bowman. "Those SOBs caught me in the head. I stumbled and hopped my way into the control room trying to pull my pants up." A third bomb exploded overhead as we went down, but it was not as close as the first two.

The captain took the conn and had us reverse course to evade the attacking airplane. A short while later I heard him lecture the diving officer about broaching the stern, which caused us to lose propulsion during submergence. After a couple of hours at 200 feet, we went up to periscope depth and found the sky clear. The captain left the conning tower and the officer of the deck resumed normal patrol duties.

After finishing my turn on the sound gear, I was back at the inactive radar, killing time. When I remembered that I had not finished filling out my radar maintenance log, I asked the officer of the deck for permission to go down to the radio shack to complete it. I promised to come right back to take over the sound watch at the appropriate time. When he agreed, I climbed down to the control room, walked aft to the shack, and sat down at the ECM. The seat that we used was the metal spare-parts box for the SJ radar. It had a thick, green cushion on top. I sat there, straddling the box with the logbook and pencil in my hands. Suddenly, I heard another bomb splitting through the water directly overhead: swishshshshsh . . . BOOM! The boat rolled violently, almost throwing me off the box. The sharp vibration from the depth charge caused the hull, piping, and bulkheads to crash together loudly for several seconds before merging into discordant musical tones. Cork particles from the hull coating showered the deck. My ears rang, my pulse raced, and I felt like running—but there was no place to hide. The airplane had found us again, even though we were 120 feet below the surface. For years I thought that the pilot must have seen us through the crystal clear water. It was not until recently, when I read the patrol report, that I realized he must have seen our track of leaking air bubbles Captain Ward had commented on several days earlier.

After hurriedly completing my logbook entries, I went back to the conning tower to take over the sound watch. Captain Ward was there and he had us going deeper. As we passed 230 feet, another bomb exploded, but it was far away and barely rocked the boat. Back at the sound gear, I had only been listening on the QB for a few minutes when I heard the rapid screws of a patrol boat. She was coming directly at us from the south, probably in response to a call from an airplane. I reported the sound contact to Captain Ward. He immediately ordered, "Sound battle stations." The helmsman reached to his right and actuated the battle stations alarm contactor: bong, bong, bong . . . went the alarm, softly, seventeen times.

"Rig for depth charge," the captain said calmly. "Rig for silent running." He also called down the hatch to the diving officer, "Close all vents." Closing the vents prevented air that was leaking into our ballast tanks from marking our location on the surface.

Brink Brinkley, whose battle station was QB/QC sound gear, quickly relieved me and I ran to the forward torpedo room. My station was with the torpedo reloading crew—about which I knew absolutely nothing. I sat on one of the torpedo racks and watched Ojay across the room. He had the JP sound operator station at the after end, starboard side of the room, regularly reporting the patrol boat's bearing over the chest-mounted battle telephone hanging around his neck. After noting the bearing, he cranked the sound head 360 degrees to look for other possible targets. When he got back to the patrol boat, he again reported her bearing, then continued his search. Operating on silent running (with fans and air conditioning off) was really stifling. Ojay stripped his clothes off down to his undershorts. Cranking the sound head was a strenuous job and rivulets of sweat poured off him, soaking his shorts.

Eight minutes after we detected the patrol boat, the first depth charge exploded far astern. First we heard a "thud," as if someone outside hit the hull with a ten-pound sledge hammer (not a "click," as is often heard in the movies), followed a few seconds later by the explosion. Then we heard swishing and gurgling sounds, as water rushed through the superstructure supporting the boat's main deck. The time interval between the "thud" and the explosion, swishes, and gurgles became shorter and shorter as the depth charges got closer: Thud. . . . boom! Thud . . . boom! Thud . . boom! ThudBOOM! I quickly learned that if no thud was heard, the depth charge was disastrously close to the boat. As the explosions became more violent, the ship's piping and other structures vibrated and clattered together for several seconds. No submarine movie I have seen has accurately protrayed the cacophonous racket brought about by a depth charge explosion.

The patrol boat stalking us dropped thirteen charges over a three- or four-minute period. Luckily, none of them was close enough to cause serious physical damage, but the strain on the nerves was real enough. Eventually the patrol boat left, but we stayed deep for the rest of the day. The damage control party found that either the aerial bomb or the deep dive had caused some flooding of several electrical circuits leading up to the bridge. One of the boat's three air banks was found to be leaking. Damage Control spent the following day attempting repairs, and ended up bleeding all the air out of the damaged air bank, thereby preventing its use to surface the boat for the rest of the patrol.

The next five days were relatively uneventful. All I could think of was the oppressive heat and humidity in the conning tower while we were on the surface at night. I discovered why they called an experienced sailor an "old salt." The salt-laden air caused salt crystals to encrust on my bare neck, back, arms, and chest. Boy, did I long for my weekly shower. The monotony was broken one day by a couple of enemy aircraft. One of them closed for an attack and forced us to make a quick dive to safety. We found out much later that the ferocious battle for American control of Saipan successfully came to an end that week.

One of the submarines in our patrol group broke radio silence on July 11 at 10:41 p.m., waking the Mickey Finns from almost a week-long slumber. *Thresher*, the westward boat, had made a radar contact twelve miles west of her position, as the pack was in the process of moving on the surface to new hunting grounds about ninety miles to the south. The target was soon determined to be a convoy of nine large ships steaming in three columns. It was surrounded by five escort vessels. *Guardfish* changed course and went to full speed on four main engines to assist *Thresher*. We picked up the convoy on our radar at a range of about fifteen miles. Our fire-control party tracked the convoy on radar while we tried to get into an attack position on the port side of the Japanese ships. Visual contact was made around midnight, when our starboard lookout spotted the convoy ahead of us in the bright moonlight.

Captain O'Regan, the commander of the group's operations and stationed aboard *Guardfish*, was pleased with the way the situation was developing. "The attack doctrine at this time was working beautifully," he later explored in his report of the action. "The situation resolved itself into this: The *Thresher* was trailing astern and reporting movements of convoy. The *Apogon* was working up the starboard flank and the *Guardfish* the port flank. The *Piranha* was kept informed of the convoy's movements and was closing from the northwest at four engine speed."

O'Regan directed the *Apogon* to open the attack. At 2:30 A.M., she made a submerged radar approach (that is, with only her radar antenna out of the water). Shortly after 3:00 A.M., we heard ten sharp explosions. The blasts caused a ripple of speculation in *Guardfish*. Some of us thought that two of the explosions had been torpedoes, and the rest depth charges, while others were unsure of their origin. *Guardfish*, meanwhile, soon reached a position about nine miles ahead of the convoy, at which point we were ordered to battle stations and dived for a radar approach.

Fire-control party personnel packed the conning tower. Captain Ward was working the periscope, while Ensign Curtis, with red flashlight in hand, stood on the opposite side of the scope reading its bearings and operating the lifting motor. Lieutenant Schnepp was on the TDC at the after end (port side) of the room. Lawrence F. (Larry) Teder, the enlisted fire controlman, stood behind him as relief TDC operator, with his back to Brinkley, who sat at the sonar or the starboard side. The SJ radar operators, Chief Dudrey and Lieutenant Howarth, sat on the port side with their backs to the captain and Ensign Curts. The executive officer, Lieutenant Commander Alexander K. Tyree, was there as well, as a backup for the captain. Two enlisted men manned the ship's log and helm positions. I was a relief radar operator, but since I had no deck to stand on, I straddled the lip of the lower hatch—and waited.

The dark room glowed softly with a low intensity red lighting. The two radar screens illuminated the faces of the operators with an eerie radiance: green light from the A-scope, yellow from the PPI. We were tracking the leading ship in the convoy, trying to obtain firing solutions on the TDC. It wasn't working, however, because we were too far away. Closing the distance meant we had to get past the convoy's two forward escorts without being detected by their sonar. It was a dangerous proposition because of the bright moon, and Captain Ward was concerned the enemy lookouts might see our radar antenna and the sizable phosphorescent wake stirred up by it and our periscope shears. Instead, he decided to go deep to avoid the escorts.

"Make the depth one hundred feet," Ward said.

"One hundred feet, aye."

"Right full rudder, steady on course zero one six."

"Zero one six, aye."

"All ahead one-third."

"All answered ahead one-third, sir."

"Q33 sound, keep a sharp watch," Ward intoned coolly. "Tell me if either escort switches to short-scale pinging [which indicates that the enemy may have a sonar contact at short range]. Keep the escort bearings coming to me. Tell JP sound to maintain a continuous 360-degree search."

We were barely creeping through the water at about two and a half knots, but the convoy's closing speed was nearly thirteen knots. We all held our breath while the first escort passed down our starboard side to the east of us. One down and one to go.

"QB, now give me continuous bearings to the escort on the port side," Ward ordered.

Ward's gamble paid off. After we passed the second escort undetected, the captain resumed the submerged radar attack.

"Make the depth sixty feet."

"Make ready all bow tubes."

"Up scope."

"Plane up to forty-two feet."

"All ahead two-thirds."

"We have ready lights on all bow tubes, sir."

"Radar, give me a range to the nearest ship in the convoy."

"3,800 yards, sir."

"Stand by to mark the bearing," said the captain, as he trained the periscope on the target. "Mark!" The tension mounted with each passing exchange.

"Three five nine."

"TDC, how does that check out?"

"We've lost our solution light, Captain."

"Very well, keep radar ranges coming."

"Stand by to mark scope. Mark!"

"Zero zero two."

"Captain, it looks like they've changed course."

The convoy had made a radical course change to the southeast shortly before dawn. We went to standard speed (about six knots) and changed course, but submerged there was no way we could keep up. A short while later we secured from battle stations, surfaced in the dawning daylight, and fired up four main engines. Although we gave it everything we had and tried to again overtake the convoy as it steamed westward toward the Babuyan Channel, our effort was to no avail. By this time the convoy was covered by air as well as naval escorts. On six separate occasions we were driven down by Japanese airplanes, and we lost contact with the ships. The disappointment in the conning tower was palpable.

The probable course of the enemy ships was plotted as we traveled on the surface, over the horizon from the convoy, until dead reckoning placed us ahead of it. The captain repeatedly sent messages to the engine room to reduce the smoke produced by our diesel engines so we would not give away our position. In the early afternoon we turned back for what we hoped would be an intercept course—but the ships were not there. We discontinued the search at 6:30 P.M., July 12, reversed course, and resumed the voyage to our new patrol area. *Piranha* and *Thresher* reported by radio that they were also heading to the new station.

We repeatedly tried to contact *Apogon*, but our efforts proved futile. A chilling fear spread throughout the boat that *Apogon* had been lost. Had the enemy gotten the better of our group? The faces of the crew showed few smiles, just tightly set jaws and grim determination.

We received good news on the night of July 14 as we plied westward through Balintang Channel toward a new station: *Apogon* was safe, although she had sustained serious battle damage. A ship in the enemy convoy she was attacking had rammed her periscope shears, destroyed her periscopes and radar antennas, and flooded her conning tower. Fortuately, no lives were lost, but it had been a close call. She informed the pack commander, O'Regan, of her abort as she blindly limped back to base. The news that *Apogon* was safe raced through *Guardfish*'s narrow hull, and some of the men even woke their sleeping buddies to share the good news.

I was on my July 14th night watch when a series of problems disabled the SJ radar. The first problem involved a serious component breakdown. Dudrey and I worked on it for over seven hours before we got it back in commission, after which I went back on an uneventful watch. Shortly after I was relieved, the radar's power source, a DC-to-AC motor generator set, went out of control. The set's finicky amplidyne motor needed frequent adjustment. After a couple of shutdowns, Dudrey left instructions for the conning tower watch to call me to make further adjustments. Unfortunately for me, this piece of equipment was located below the control room deck in the auxiliary room. I spent much of my off-watch time down in that oily, steamy tightly crammed "hell hole" over the next two days. The motor generator refused to cooperate. Every time I wanted to get some sleep, it broke down again. To this day I remember the exhaustion and frustration I experienced dealing with it.

We reached our new panel area about midday on July 15, surfaced, and fired up all four of our diesel engines. Excitement coursed through the boat, because the roaring engines usually signaled to the crew that we were out to chase an enemy ship. According to a radio message we received, a convoy was somewhere in our general vicinity, northwest of Luzon. O'Regan had the three boats left in the pack (*Piranha*, *Thresher*, and *Guardfish*) make a coordinated search spaced twenty miles apart. *Thresher* received the order for a course charge, but *Piranha* somehow missed the message and continued searching to the northeast. The mistake was our good fortune, for it was *Piranha* that made contact early in the morning of July 16. She reported a convoy of twelve ships traveling in three columns about 100 miles directly north of the northwestern tip of Luzon. She reported she was traveling on the surface trying to get into position for a submerged attack. While the news was welcomed by all of us, *Guardfish* and *Thresher* were out of position about 110 miles to the west of the convoy's location. O'Regan ordered full speed on the surface and we moved as fast as we could to join *Piranha*.

Near the middle of my morning watch Lieutenant Bowman, the officer of the deck, sighted smoke on the horizon off our starboard bow. It turned out to be a new convoy heading south, a different one than that reported by *Piranha*. Our lookouts quickly determined that this convoy had at least two airplanes overhead acting as escorts. Bowman called Captain Ward to the bridge. The skipper immediately ordered what we referred to as an "end around," a change of course roughly to the convoy's heading in order to stay over the horizon as we pulled ahead to an attack position. Simultaneously, the captain directed Lieutenant Howarth, the communications officer, to compose a contact report and radio it to the other two boats. Twenty minutes later, one of the convoy's air escorts spotted us and banked in our direction, zeroing in for the kill. We dove for cover as fast as possible. While submerged, we heard two of *Piranha*'s torpedoes explode against one of the enemy ships. *Piranha*'s attack, of course, revealed her presence to the Japanese and she quickly became the quarry. Her pair of torpedo blasts were soon followed by a series of forty-eight explosions. *Piranha* was taking a depth-charge beating from the escorts. Knowing your fellow submariners were going through such hell without being able to assist them is an awful feeling.

We surfaced several times and tried to move ahead of our convoy, but the air cover kept driving us down, causing us to drop behind the ships. During our submerged runs we heard over twenty more underwater explosions, which meant that *Piranha* was still under attack. At 5:00 P.M. we received a message from *Thresher*. She was tracking yet a third convoy comprised of four ships and two escorts, all traveling in a westward direction. "Convoy College" (a gathering of convoys) was certainly a good code name for this place.

In spite of harassment from their planes, under cover of darkness Ward finally managed to work *Guardfish* into position ahead of our convoy. When my round of watch rolled along, I took my normal first watch position at the radar. For some unknown reason, our ra-

dar's motor generator held steady. I fervently hoped it
would not decide to go out while we were tracking
the enemy. The convoy was still beyond the horizon
when unusual radar indications, coming from the direction of the ships we were tracking, appeared on
our screen. I could tell from the width and shape of
the radar pulses on the A-scope that the strange emanations were not from an American radar transmitter.
I immediately reported this to the captain, who was
on the bridge with the officer of the deck, Lieutenant
Bowman.

The enemy's radar antenna, high atop his mast,
was apparently high enough to peek over the horizon.
This was one of the earliest inklings we had in the war
that the Japanese had microwave radar capability.
Somehow they had succeeded in copying our "secret
weapon," the microwave magnetron. Captain Ward
directed Lieutenant Howarth to come to the conning
tower and examine the radar interference. Howarth
reached the conclusion that the Japanese were attempting to jam our radar screen to make it more difficult for us to detect their ships. Actually, their signal
led us right to them, and within a short time we detected the convoy on our radar screen at a range of
about eleven miles.

"Battle stations torpedo," the captain ordered.

Immediately the man at the chart desk broadcast the
announcement to all compartments over the 1MC and
the helmsman actuated the general alarm. Men went
scurrying to their battle stations throughout the boat.
Dudrey climbed briskly up into the darkened conning
tower and took the stool at the radar's A-scope. Lieutenant Howarth relieved me at the PPI position. Although we were on the surface, the executive officer,

Alex Tyree, took over the search periscope. The night was clear, but there was no moon. The exec coordinated all the activities in the conning tower. Enlisted man Larry Teder was on the TDC. Brinkley sat at the sonar with the equipment in standby condition. Ensign Curtis, the gunnery and torpedo officer, was periscope bearing reader. I stood aside until everyone was in position, then got out of their way by taking up my familiar position straddling the lower hatch. I craned my neck to watch the emerging picture of the convoy on the PPI screen. Lieutenant Schnepp was in the control room plotting the target course on the Dead Reckoning board.

"Keep the radar rotating constantly," the captain instructed.

Initially, the radar picture of the convoy was merely a single big blob of light, but soon we were able to distinguish pips representing the individual ships. Eventually we were able to make everything out. There were ten ships in the convoy arranged in two columns of five each. Four escort vessels encircled the convoy, two ahead, port and starboard, and two spread behind on the flanks. The group was traveling southwest, less than fifty miles off Luzon's northwest coast.

"Lookouts, keep a sharp watch in your sector," I heard the captain repeatedly call to the men topside. "Do not get distracted by the action ahead."

When we closed range to about five miles, the captain was able to vaguely discern the enemy ships. The phosphorescent sea was relatively calm, rolling with long, glowing swells. He decided that we would attack on the surface and that our best approach was to let the ships pass us so we could attack the port flank. That gave us the advantage of having a dark background of clouds and rain squalls behind us, making it more difficult for the Japanese to spot us. He decided on that course of action even though "the most desirable target was leading the starboard column." Later, one of his superiors described Ward's approach as "masterful." The captain began to carry out his plan as we crept up on the lead escort.

"Make ready all torpedo tubes, fore and aft. Open outer doors forward. Set depth at eight feet," Ward instructed.

"We have ready lights all tubes forward, Captain."

"We have some big babies up here. A tanker leads the starboard column, and a large AK [cargo ship] leads the port column. We will target the lead ship in the starboard column with a spread."

Firing "a spread" of torpedoes meant that they fanned out, each one aimed slightly differently, to compensate for measurement errors and uncontrollable variations as they traveled toward the target.

The exec leaned over and studied the radar PPI. He discussed the situation with Howarth for a bit and then pointed to the pip on the radar that was our target. Each time the radar antenna swept over that pip, Dudrey and Howarth called out the target's range and bearing, which Teder then entered into the TDC. The coffee-grinder-sounding mechanical computer noisily worked away, until its "solution light" finally came on. As Teder fed in more data, however, the light suddenly blinked off. Something was wrong.

Although the radar range measurements were very precise, the bearing readings, under the best of conditions, were not as good as optical readings. The best radar bearing accuracy could be obtained by stopping the antenna rotation and activating a bearing improvement device, called the "lobing motor." But the captain's instruction to keep the antenna rotating meant that we could not do that. The bearings had to be taken directly from the inaccurate PPI screen. A further complication was that for each measurement, Howarth had to mentally add two and a half degreees to correct the PPI observation before he called out the bearing. The exec repeatedly tried to use his periscope to get accurate bearings on the target, but there was not enough light. He reported the situation to the captain over the intercom. Ward immediately responded with a command: "Lieutenant Howarth to the bridge."

Howarth was being called topside to take optical bearings using the Target Bearing Transmitter, the TBT, a binocular-equipped target sighting device that electronically transmitted the bearings to the conning tower. The recently installed TBT system had much better light gathering power than the periscope.

As Howarth was leading, he turned to me and said, "Conner, take over the PPI." My head swam as I tried to read the target bearing from the PPI, add two and a half degrees, and call out the corrected number to the waiting TDC operator. I stumbled and stammered and missed some observations as the antenna whizzed by the target. My mind seemed numb; I could not think straight. The exec said, "Keep those bearings coming." I stammered out additional corrected readings. The TDC solution light came on briefly, then went dark a second time.

The exec yelled at me in exasperation, "KEEP

THOSE BEARINGS COMING, DAMN IT." Finally, I just called out the uncorrected readings. That kept the exec off my back until Howarth was ready.

Howarth got the TBT binoculars focused on the target ship in short order. The exec read the bearings from the TBT indicator that was mounted on the starboard side, between the periscope lift motors and the sonar. Teder fed several more sets of ranges and bearings into the TDC before jubilantly announcing, "I have a solution; it's a good one!"

The exec relayed that word to the captain. Ward responded, "Very well, fire when ready. Make a two-degree spread." By fanning out the torpedoes as they went toward the target on the starboard column, the captain hoped that some of them might hit ships in the closer port column, as well.

The exec told Ensign Curtis, the mustang torpedo and gunnery officer who had been an enlisted torpedoman, to fire the torpedoes. That order elated Curtis, who had never fired a torpedo in battle. The firing panel, located on the port side over the radar's A-scope, had switches representing each of the torpedo tubes. Dim orange lights above each indicated all forward tubes were ready to be launched.

"Fire one!" called out the exec, who had a stopwatch in his hand to time the torpedo's journey to the target.

Curtis switched tube number one to the "Fire" position and pushed the two-inch-diameter red firing key above the panel with the palm of his hand.

Fifteen seconds passed.

"Fire two!"

Fifteen seconds more.

"Fire three!"

The voice of the captain interrupted our thoughts. "New target. Second ship in the starboard column." New TBT bearings and radar ranges went into the computer.

"We have a solution," Teder called.

Tyree responded quickly. "Fire four!" . . . "Fire five!" . . . "Fire six!"

The captain could see the faint phosphorescent glow of the wakeless electric torpedoes as they shot out of the tubes and angled off to intercept the unsuspecting targets. At the moment of firing, Ward's attack plan came to fruition. The images of five ships in the port and starboard columns merged, forming a continuous line of vessels. It was almost impossible to miss. That is, it was impossible if the ships did not see the ghostly torpedoes coming toward them and make radical course changes to escape.

Three minutes after fixing, the slow electrically powered fish found their marks. The first hit struck a large tanker loaded with fuel. Ward's patrol report described the resulting cataclysm:

The Tanker was loaded with gas and blew up immediately sending flames thousands of feet high. The large AK was also loaded with combustibles, commencing [sic] to burn aft and later blew up. The third ship in line, an AK, broke in two in the middle and sank, and the fourth ship in line went down bow first. The scene was lit up as bright as day by the explosions and burning ship.

The horrendous explosions and flames awed even Captain Ward, who invited each man from the fire-control party to come to the bridge, one at a time, to view the spectacle. To this day I still get a chill when I think of the sight I saw that night.

Radar interference from the convoy disappeared from our screens when the first ship exploded. As the port and starboard columns of ships erupted, the forward Japanese escort sped away at top speed. She careened into the space between the baling columns and dropped depth charge after depth charge. The escort commander had no idea where we were. Meanwhile, we veered right and increased speed in an attempt to get set up on the next group of ships with our stern tubes. Unfortunately, we were not fast enough and the small convoy broke up, the ships scattering in all directions.

Just past midnight on July 17, we found ourselves surrounded by the remnants of the convoy. With depth charges exploding in the distance, the captain isolated his efforts against a large cargo ship and we started to track her. I remember wondering, each time a depth charge exploded in the distance, how many Japanese were killed in the water that night by their escorts.

When we reached our attack position we could see only two ships on our radar screen: an AK (cargo ship) and a small escort. Tracking went without a hitch. We turned right to bring our stern tubes to bear, as we were on the cargo vessel's starboard bow. Ensign Curtis fired tubes seven, eight, and nine at ten-second intervals. The exec counted off the minutes and seconds with his stopwatch. BOOM! . . . BOOM! Two hits engulfed the big ship, which erupted in explosions and flames from stem to stern. We were dangerously close to the escort vessel at this time, and

wisely pulled away when the fish hit the target. Our
torpedomen worked frantically to reload the torpedo
tubes while the captain continued to hunt for the
residue of the convoy. The burning ship turned over
on her starboard side, about four miles from us. After
one last explosion, she disappeared under the water.

We searched for a little over half an hour and
found another ship from the splintered convoy. The
fire-control party tracked the new target as *Guardfish*
moved ahead to get into firing position. The target
ship had an escort and was zigzagging radically every
four or five minutes. It took us about an hour and a
half to get into position. The captain ordered two
stern tubes fired. Just as Ensign Curtis hit the firing
key the target zigged, and as a result both torpedoes
passed ahead of the ship's bow.

In an effort to obtain another attack position,
Ward ordered *Guardfish* "ahead flank, swing left and
make two bow tubes ready." When the boat was
within 1,250 yards, tubes three and four fired. Both
shots struck the cargo ship. According to the captain,
the "proximity of [the] escort and rising moon in-
duced [him] to head out fast," especially since he was
"sure this ship would sink immediately." The stricken
merchant freighter, however, continued steaming at
about three knots although she was visibly settling by
stern. According to Captain Ward's patrol report, the
ship . . .

disappeared from the radar screen at 13,000 yards
with escort seen at 12,500 yards at same time.
Numerous lights and much activity was seen on
the target as we hauled clear. It is believed this ship
sank, but only damage is claimed. Did not con-

sider it possible to make another attack on any of the widely scattered targets, so secured from battle stations and pulled clear to northwest on four engines. Everyone in the control party was beginning to show fatigue after six hours at battle stations under constant tension; the commanding officer had not enjoyed any rest for over fifty hours. Under these conditions it was considered best to let the others go.

The captain was right. I was thoroughly exhausted and, like him, had been up for almost fifty hours because of repeated radar problems and the torpedo action. We secured from battle stations around 3:30 A.M., May 17. "Amazing," I thought, "the radar didn't go out while we were at battle stations. I hope it doesn't crap out again soon." I was scheduled to go back on watch in less than five hours, so I dragged myself to the crew's quarters, climbed to my top bunk, and crashed into it with my clothes on. Sleep immediately enveloped me as the boat submerged and peace returned once again.

"Rig for depth charge! Rig for depth charge!"

The announcement blasted out through the loudspeaker directly above me. As the patrol boat headed toward us, the boat dove to a depth of 350 feet. I was too tired to move, and I did not know what I was supposed to do. Although it may seem odd today, I fell back asleep. The exploding depth charges, however, threw me wide awake.

Thud. . . . boom! Thud. . . . boom!

The explosions were far off the mark.

Thud. . . . Boom!

I turned over and closed my eyes again.

Thud . . BOOM!

That one was closer! Back to a fitful drowse. Hour after hour the attack continued, with over forty depth charges being dropped around us. Only a few were close enough to raise eyebrows, but each one woke me up with a start. Finally, the patrol boat gave up his search. Our loudspeakers blared, "Secure from depth charge!" A few seconds later the below decks watchman shook me twice to get me to wake up. "Conner, get up, it's time to go on watch."

We soon learned *Thresher* had been busy as well. She had sunk her convoy of four cargo ships, expended all of her torpedoes, and was on her way back home. Now the Mickey Finn wolf pack consisted of only *Piranha* and *Guardfish*.

WOLFPACK

FROM *War in the Boats: My WWII Submarine Battles*

---

by Captain William J. Ruhe

*O*ur next sailor-turned-author is Captain William
James Ruhe, a decorated veteran of three wars
who wrote extensively about his World War II experiences in submarines for both literature and film. A
1939 graduate of the U.S. Naval Academy, Ruhe
served in World War II aboard the submarines USS
Crevalle and USS *Sturgeon*, and received three Silver
Stars for his heroism. The tours later became the subject of dozens of stories about the boats' war patrols.
In the 1960s, Ruhe translated his war experiences to
the screen as a scriptwriter and consultant for the
television series *The Silent Service*. During the Korean War, Ruhe was given his first command aboard
the USS *Sea Devil*, and his last command was the USS
Topeka, a guided-missile cruiser that he served on at
Vietnam in 1964. Following his retirement from the
Navy, he became the corporate director of marine
programs for submarine manufacturer General Dy-
namics, managing the New Products division. During
this time he also became the editor of *The Submarine
Review* and began writing about his war experiences.
In 1994 Ruhe published his first book, *War in the*

Boats, a memoir about submarine warfare, followed by the novel *Slow Dance to Pearl Harbor*, about a young naval ensign in the days before the attack on Pearl Harbor.

Submarine patrols often epitomize the maxim "hours of utter boredom interspersed with minutes of sheer terror." Ruhe's account of this patrol late in the war off the north coast of Australia has plenty of both, from the early days of their mission, when they sight nothing but fishing vessels, to the target-rich environment later on when they find more vessels than they almost know what to do with. But the men of the *Crevalle* do their duty, with very successful results.

Departure for the *Crevalle*'s fourth war patrol was set for the afternoon of June 21, 1944. Her patrol was going to be coordinated with two other submarines, the *Flasher* and the *Angler*. The three submarines had been directed to operate as a *wolf-pack*, the first such utilization of Fremantle-based boats.

Three-boat wolfpacks had operated out of Midway and Pearl for the past six months. They differed, however, in one essential way from the wolfpack the *Crevalle* would be a part of. Instead of having a division commander aboard one of the boats for tactical coordination of the wolfpack, an on-scene submarine skipper would be in charge. Hence, Lieutenant Commander Reuben Whitaker, the captain of the *Flasher* and senior skipper, was named "Tactical Commander of Whitaker's Wolves."

A short meeting of the skippers and the execs of the three boats was therefore convened on board the *Flasher* on the morning of departure, to finalize the tactics and communications for the pack's operations as a coordinated unit.

Whitaker, a short, aloof, elegant, and supremely confident man with a blond, wispy mustache and lots of flair, made the meeting brief. He wanted to leave Fremantle as quickly as possible. He emphasized simplicity in communications and said in effect that "the skippers should use their good judgment as to when to use plain-language communications and how to disguise what they were saying, if necessary." He also said that he did not "contemplate having to encipher any of the communications," nor was he demanding precise radio circuit procedures.

"I'm using the call sign 'Dumbo.' Walker will be 'Patsy,'" and then Whitaker paused, giving Frank Walker a knowing suggestion of a smile. He had undoubtedly heard more than once how Walker had called himself a Patsy when he was fooled by the Japanese. Whitaker added, "Hess, you'll be 'Goatfish.'" Hess cringed at the sound of his call sign.

Whitaker looked at the other two skippers for their approval. They merely shook their heads in amusement while rolling the call signs around on their thirsty tongues. They were testing how such names might sound to the Japanese out in the South China Sea where "Whitaker's Wolves" would operate.

"Just do what's necessary relative to the information passed between the boats. And play everything by ear," Whitaker counseled with finality. The plan of action for his wolfpack had apparently been decided upon in his mind and nothing more he felt need be said.

However, Ray Dubois, his scrappy, aggressive exec, insisted upon discussing details. "Captain, we haven't talked about submerged communications as yet." But Whitaker with an impatient wave of his hand cut Dubois off. Jake Bowell, the exec of the *Angler*, and I remained silent. So Whitaker turned to Captain Walker and Frank Hess and suggested that all three of them go to the Officers' Club for a farewell drink. This left Dubois, Jake Bowell, and me to discuss what concerned us about Whitaker's far too brief instructions. But none of us had much of an idea how best to operate in a three-boat wolfpack so the subsequent discussion bogged down into some foolish solutions to unlikely situations.

I'd read a few newspaper articles about what the Germans over the past two years were doing with their large wolfpacks of seven to eleven U-boats against Atlantic convoys. But the U-boat wolfpack tactical problems were markedly different from those confronting Whitaker's Wolves. Tactical command of a German group of U-boats was effected by a submarine commander at a shore command-center back in Europe. Thus, there was a large volume of communications flowing from the U-boats far at sea to the tactical commander ashore. Then his tactical instructions were radioed back to the German wolfpacks in encoded messages. By comparison, Whitaker's concept of wolfpack operations against Japanese convoys was so simple that I felt we were dealing with kindergarten stuff and trying to learn how to crawl before being able to walk. For Whitaker's Wolves, details weren't important.

After returning to the *Crevalle* and just before lunch, two shore patrolmen brought three *Crevalle* torpedomen on board, having picked them up at the train station in Perth where they'd drunkenly staggered off a train from Kalgoorlie. They'd missed muster on board at 0800 and were thus over leave. Hence, the shore patrolmen, unceremoniously and without delivering a shore patrol report telling of the men's offenses, dumped the men along with their duffel bags onto the *Crevalle*'s main deck and departed. Langfeldt, Locktov, and Niemczyk had many bottles of gin and whiskey in their duffel bags, that I felt could be destroyed. But with Langfeldt on his knees and blubbering, "Please, Mr. Ruhe, don't do that.

Save our booze so we can celebrate after the patrol," I had second thoughts. Tears were in the three men's eyes and Langfeldt's drunken appeal was with pure anguish. So I relented and had the liquor secretly stowed in a locker with a padlock on it and had the men led to their bunks "to sleep it off."

At the end of this incident, Walt Mazzone, who had become the engineering officer when Luke Bowdler had been transferred after the end of the third patrol, in a conspiratorial whisper suggested that he had something to show me. He then led me back to the after engine room and told me to look into the bilges outboard of the port engine, There, Walt had stowed a portable, electric sump pump! To my questioning look, he explained that he and an engineman had stolen it from the *Jack* two days previously. "We used a punt to go alongside the outboard side of the *Jack*. Then, the engineman went down the engine-room hatch and stole it. Unfortunately, the *Jack*'s below decks watch saw him briefly and asked why he was in the *Jack*'s engine room. The reply given was, 'I'm checking the damage *Jack* sustained on her last patrol.' " But this didn't sound very credible.

This could cause a good deal of trouble, I felt, yet I gave Walt a well-deserved "Attaboy." It was also hoped that the *Crevalle* would get under way before Miles Refo, the *Jack*'s exec, discovered the sump pump's loss. He was a tough man to deal with.

Then just after lunch the messenger poked his head into the wardroom to say that the *Flasher* had gotten under way and was leaving early. Evidently, Whitaker was so eager to get on patrol that he couldn't wait until Walker and Hess returned to their boats.

When the three skippers had gone to the Officers'

Club, they had tentatively set 1500 as departure time. By 1445 I was sufficiently worried about Captain Walker and his timely return to the *Crevalle* that I called the Officers' Club. The person who answered said that Walker, Hess, and Selby, of the *Puffer*, were having a last round of drinks and that they were preparing to leave. Was this last round a round before another last round? We waited.

Then at 1635, down the dock came Captain Walker, followed by Hess and Selby strung out across the dock. They were baying at each other like wolves. Selby with his silver-white hair was easily distinguished from a mob of workmen going off their jobs at the end of the day and who had paused to watch the *Crevalle* and the *Angler* leave. Selby kept waving and baying at his two pals as they staggered and teetered across the temporary wooden planks thrown across the bows of the boats. The two skippers refused proffered helping hands from deck watch personnel as they made their way to their boats, which were singled up with all hands chomping at the bit to get going. When Captain Walker arrived on the *Crevalle*'s bow, I pulled her clear using full speed on the batteries. Then, rapidly shifting to the diesels, the *Crevalle* at flank speed sped past Rottnest Island making up for lost time. Nobody looked back to see if Frank Hess had made it to his *Angler* without falling overboard.

The first day out was one of recuperation rather than training. Later, with the *Angler* in company, night radar attacks were conducted against her until midnight. The *Crevalle*'s gray paint job made her so invisible at night that Captain Walker decided to keep the submarines at least three thousand yards apart at all times.

After midnight, I broke out two mail bags full of newspapers. There were about ninety daily editions of *The Morning Call*. At sea, the newspapers were eagerly read by the entire crew. The procedure was to dole out the twenty latest papers to the officers and the rest went to the forward room where Chief Howard had his torpedomen clip out the comic strips and paste them into scrapbooks. These were routed to the crew. What remained of the papers were well scrutinized for baseball scores and football results. As for the war in Europe and the Atlantic, the officers seemed more interested than the crew in such news. The campaigns in Europe were well covered and the new things being developed by the Germans were lengthily described, but news of the Pacific War was almost nonexistent. By the end of a patrol the newspapers would be in shreds, but there were still some men trying to read the pieces of the papers remaining.

Wednesday, June 23, was a calm, bright sunny day at sea. More training dives and a few periscope approaches on the *Angler* were held. The *Crevalle* would race ahead, submerge, then the captain would try to get a good firing set-up as the *Angler* passed by on the surface.

I observed that in between the simulated torpedo attacks on the *Angler*, all of the officers including the captain were busy writing letters to their wives to make up for their failure to produce many letters during the time in port. Moreover, it was discovered that George Morin was bilging all the other officers by writing one-a-day letters to his wife. Unfortunately, the wives back home when getting together had swapped notes as to letters received. They complained about their poor treatment as to numbers of letters from "their husbands." Hence, their husbands did some back-dating of their hastily written letters to make it appear that a good many letters had been written during rest leave. The mailing of all accumulated letters from Exmouth Gulf, where the *Crevalle* would refuel, should fool the wives, it was felt, into thinking they were being remembered just as often as the insidious George Morin's daily letters to his wife, Hope.

For the first two days, better meals were being served, thanks to Chief Emme, the new commissaryman. This indicated that the crew would put on some weight during the patrol instead of always arriving at the rest camps at the end of a patrol in a scrawnier condition. For lunch, however, Chief Emme served mashed potatoes made from dehydrated potato flakes and powdered milk. I ordered the chief to stop that and first expend all the potatoes stored in the after battery trunk leading to the main deck. Emme had also brought tins of powdered onions, carrots, and eggs aboard so he wouldn't run out of food by the end of a long patrol. But sampling the reconstituted carrots and onions and tasting an ersatz omelet forced me to order Emme to leave those items off the menu until there was a severe food shortage.

The *Angler* was the first to enter Exmouth Gulf on May 24, and promptly bent one of her screws on a bottom obstruction near the fuel barge. Consequently, Jake Bowell, the round-faced, snaggle-toothed exec of the *Angler*, and I in a small boat, sounded the area round the fuel barge. But we failed to find anything shallow enough to cause trouble with submarines using Exmouth Gulf to top-off with fuel before going further on patrol. In addition, our hands were badly blistered by the sounding-line we used.

The *Angler* left before noon on one screw to return to Fremantle and have her propeller replaced; so there would be no opportunity to form the three-sub wolfpack very soon.

The *Crevalle*'s fuelling was completed by 1600. Then, while she was heading out to sea, it was discovered that the SJ surface search radar was out of commission and needed a part that couldn't be found on board. Thus, *Crevalle* was forced to return to Exmouth Gulf to wait there until the part was flown up from Perth. In the meantime, Manny Kimmel's *Robalo* and Charlie Henderson's *Bluefish* arrived and tied up alongside the *Crevalle*. They were en route north for patrols.

On the following day at 1400 a spare part for the SJ radar, plus a radar technician, arrived by plane from Perth. The radar technician was certainly not needed since the *Crevalle*'s masterful radarman, Biehl, could readily fix the radar by himself.

By 1535 the *Crevalle* was under way and headed back out to sea. On the way and at flank speed, the four-inch gun crew fired ten rounds at a derelict freighter that was aground on Northwest Cape near the entrance to the Gulf. Four brightly flashing hits at 4,200 yards range on the old hulk indicated that the *Crevalle*'s 1919 vintage gun was well aligned for long-range engagements. The *Crevalle* was finally on her way to see some action.

In the next three days, the *Crevalle* raced towards The Barrier. Then the *Crevalle* shut down both her radars as she entered Lombok Strait. Two small enemy patrol craft were sighted in the moonless blackness, but they completely ignored the *Crevalle* as she

eased past them and moved into the Bali Sea without
incident.

Just after dawn and south of Sakala Island in the
Bali Sea, the *Crevalle* was forced to dive when another patrol boat was sighted. This was in the same
spot where the *Crevalle* had been bombed on her
first patrol. The *Crevalle* remained submerged and
moved northwest into the Java Sea where the captain sighted through the periscope a motor sampan
with a red meatball on the side of her pilot house. A
similar Japanese flag was painted on the sampan's
deck house and a tall radio antenna extended above
the pilot house. The *Crevalle* was then quickly surfaced and eighteen four-inch shells were fired into the
eighty-ton vessel. Many devastating hits sank her. But
the sampan had remained on the surface sufficiently
long to be able to transmit an emergency radio message before she went under. Within minutes, and not
unexpectedly, out came a plane that forced the *Crevalle*
to submerge.

June 30 was one of those on-edge, tense days of
waiting-for-something-to-happen. The green-blue waters of the Java Sea were so shallow and crystal clear
that it was a miserable place to encounter any of the
Japanese first-string warships. Yet, in the morning,
as the *Crevalle* was heading west on the surface
across the shallow Java Sea, a "flash" contact message was received from a U.S. Black Cat flying boat
on reconnaissance out of Darwin. It told of sighting
a Tenryu-class cruiser and two escorting destroyers
heading east across the Java Sea. The *Crevalle*, as she
hurried towards Karimata Strait, was in the path of
this deadly force of enemy warships. She'd meet them

shortly along her track, which showed depths varying from nineteen to twenty-five fathoms.

My heart sank. The *Crevalle* was in the wrong place to encounter such a lethal force of ships. I dolefully had the thought, "If we tackle these ships, they'll beat us to death. It's been a good war so far—so why does it have to end this way?" Then I timidly decided that the smart thing to do was to submerge and sneak out of the path of the oncoming ships.

The captain, as he read the message, muttered, "Oh, shit." His clenched jaw and squinted sad eyes showed that he was just as concerned as I was about the situation.

Then, radar emanations were detected that indicated a closing aircraft. Even before it was sighted, the *Crevalle* was dived. Remaining undetected was the essence of survival in such brightly lit shallow waters. After a short period of running submerged, the *Crevalle* was surfaced and resumed her dash across the Java Sea. But within an hour, the *Crevalle* was again driven down by an enemy aircraft that first used its radar to locate the sub and then shut it off for the final run-in for an attack. But no bombs were dropped. George suggested that the plane was on a sweep out ahead of the warships and that they would be sighted shortly. This sent a cold chill down my spine and the adrenaline started flowing.

Just before surfacing again, the captain spotted several hair-like masts jutting above the horizon out to the west. The *Crevalle* was planed up to fifty feet to examine the contacts with the scope extended fifteen feet above the water. As the captain studied the topworks below the masts there was another growled "Oh, shit." Then, "The ships seem to have sharp starboard angles-on-the-bow and are headed for us." The moment of truth had arrived. Shaking his head sadly, he muttered, as he lowered the scope, "We can't be chicken. Let's go get 'em."

I watched the captain's face closely. His knit brows and pensive stare at the conning tower deck showed little determination to do battle with the warships but also that he was puzzled by what he had observed. He kept the *Crevalle* at sixty-five feet for the next thirty minutes, periodically poking up the scope for quick looks. But he saw nothing on the bearing of the warships. They weren't arriving as fast as expected. Meanwhile, sweat poured from my bare chest, soaking my shorts.

When the *Crevalle* was planed up to fifty feet for another extended periscope look, what he saw caused another "Oh, shit." But this was uttered with a note of self-flagellating disgust. "Those ships are only harmless sailing craft—a big one and two small ones. Christ! What a Patsy I am." He had let the Black Cat's message fool him into believing that what he vaguely saw out on the horizon had to be the threatening warships.

A heavy weight seemed to have been lifted from my shoulders as the *Crevalle* regained the surface and continued westward. And I was proud of the captain for not chickening out when he thought that a deadly battle was imminent.

For the next three days, the *Crevalle* uneventfully picked her way across the Java Sea, up through the shallow waters of Karimata Strait, and on into the South China Sea. But during the third day, the *Crevalle* was forced to dive away three times from sighted planes. She was running radar-silent. Yet on each dive there was radar interference on the *Crevalle*'s SD scope while no visual sightings were made, except at short ranges. Jim Blind had rigged the SD for a receive-only mode.

The *Crevalle* had moved into monsoon weather. The skies were leaden gray and mottled with swiftly moving storm clouds that produced occasional drizzling rain. Visibility was cut to less than three miles. The captain no longer worried about enemy aircraft spotting the *Crevalle*'s wake on the frothy seas churned up by gusty winds. Hence he pushed the *Crevalle* north at high speed. He was eager to join Whitaker and start operating as a partial wolfpack of two boats until Hess in the *Angler* could join up.

Then, another secret "burn message" was received. It told of the departure of several warships from Singapore that were headed northeast through the South China Sea. A second "burn message" which was received just before twilight gave the 2400 geographical position of the warships—a few miles north of the equator. The captain was understandably excited about the prospects of tangling in deep water with some of the best warships of the Japanese fleet. So he called on me to get a good "fix" to verify the *Crevalle*'s position and give him a good chance of intercepting the ships at their midnight position.

But getting a fix using star sights seemed quite hopeless. The rain-dimmed horizon and scudding black clouds sweeping across occasional patches of open sky allowed only fleeting sextant sights to be taken on stars that were not clearly identified. Four sights were finally "shot" and seemed good enough to calculate their lines of position. But the "fix" generated by the four lines of position produced a thirty-five-mile triangle.

The captain said that such a position was next to useless. So the *Crevalle* had to be conned towards the 2400 warship position using the dead reckoning device, the "DRT." It was a "by guess and by God" method of getting there.

At midnight, a few short radar sweeps were made but no ships were detected. No wonder, because when I finally got a radar fix on a well-identified small island on the Fourth of July, I was dumbfounded to realize that the *Crevalle*'s position, as shown by the DRT, was forty miles north of where the *Crevalle* actually was. It was thus apparent that the star sights taken on the third were calculated for the *Crevalle* being north of the equator, not south of the equator, where she actually had been. All the lines of positions were wrong because the tables in the Celestial Navigation Book were different for north latitudes and south latitudes. I didn't admit this error to the captain but it certainly humbled me—"the compleat Navigator."

The Fourth passed without fireworks. Navy holiday food was served at supper time: turkey and minced pie. To help the holiday mood, I wandered around the boat and chatted with many of the crew, inviting their comments and feelings about serving on the *Crevalle*. To my great alarm, more than a few of the men said they wanted to get off the *Crevalle* and have shore duty in Perth, rather than being transferred back to the States for new construction. It was evident that some of the crew had become "Perth-happy" lovers. So I loudly observed that if being great lovers of Aussie women affected their onboard performance, I'd have them detached and sent to the boats in the Aleutians. And I emphasized "the Aleutians!"

For the next eight days, the *Crevalle* was on station, patrolling on the surface across the Saigon-Takao-Formosa sea route and waiting for the *Flasher* to come up from the south and join the *Crevalle*. The *Angler*, meanwhile, had arrived on station to the east of the *Crevalle*.

On one surfacing into heavy seas, the OOD failed to put his foot on the upper hatch to shut it as a huge wave piled over the bridge. The resulting flood of water down through the hatch soaked much of the electrical gear in the control room and in the pump room below with salt water. The mess caused, plus no targets, drove the captain into moving the *Crevalle* over to the Indochina coast south of Cape Varella.

The day of the twelfth, the *Crevalle* conducted a submerged patrol off Hon Doi Island where the seas were even worse than out in the middle of the ocean. Deep swells bounced the boat around when at periscope depth and made periscope looks very dicey. Even with five feet of scope extended, the mountainous waves sloshed over the periscope's window, blanking it. And then the spray off the top of the waves would douse the upper window and cause a blurring of images out beyond the scope. Predictably, when a two-thousand-ton steamer that was hugging the coast passed inboard of the *Crevalle*, she was not sighted until she was abeam. Her dark gray camouflage made the ship blend well with the jungle beyond. Moreover, a chase was rejected since the depth keeping performance of the Mk-14s in such violent seas seemed questionable.

When the *Crevalle* was surfaced at night after the seas had abated somewhat, the long swells churned up the waters, making them glow brightly as a result of the high density of phosphorescent sea life near the surface. Large jellyfish littered the main deck showing spots of light and silvery streamers. Unfortunately, this marine life rotted and stuck to the *Crevalle*'s topsides, making the stink on the bridge decidedly unpleasant.

Between the thirteenth and the eighteenth of July, all-day patrols were conducted. But uselessly. First, a five-hundred-ton motor vessel too small for a torpedo was sighted on the fifteenth. Then a Dave-type aircraft spent a few hours flying back and forth across the *Crevalle* as though the pilot knew the *Crevalle*'s location quite accurately but wasn't able to spot her periscope. Again, the seas were so rough that the hull could not be seen when just under the waves. Then a "burn message" was received that said that a Japanese sub was hunting for an enemy submarine in the vicinity of Cape Varella. That wasn't close enough to the *Crevalle*'s actual position to cause even a slight chill down my spine. Then, on the seventeenth a small motor ship passed within two thousand yards. But she was no torpedo target, considering the high waves' effect on torpedoes.

Because of this lack of action all the men were in foul moods. The officers were no exception. George Morin had started sulking and was not speaking to anyone except members of his watch. Jim Blind was ignoring Mazzone, who was now in a bad humor at all times. And Ronnie Loveland, a newcomer, had refused to play cribbage with Dick Bowe. The captain inscrutably played solitaire in the wardroom. But that was OK because nobody was talking to anybody else while in the wardroom.

Only two full meals were being served with breakfast at 0700 and supper at 1900. Lunch was skipped and only soup was served if someone needed some sort of sustenance. The crew showed a lack of interest in eating, and their waistlines were getting slimmer.

Then on July 19 a message from Whitaker was received that said the *Flasher* had put two torpedoes into a Kuma-type light cruiser of 5,100 tons and that Whitaker had seen her mainmast topple after one of the hits. The cruiser got away, but Whitaker felt that she was badly damaged and would probably sink before she reached port. Whitaker's message also said the *Flasher* had six torpedoes remaining, having sunk two cargo ships and a tanker before she joined the *Crevalle* in the South China Sea. Whitaker requested the *Crevalle*'s patrol results to date.

That was easy to answer, "Nothing."

Whitaker also wanted Walker to cover the possible escape route of the Kuma cruiser in the direction of Camranh Bay where the cruiser might go to effect repairs.

Thus, the captain and me, using the position of Whitaker's attack on the cruiser, designed a retiring search curve for optimizing the *Crevalle*'s chances of finding the cruiser if she was limping in the general direction of the *Crevalle*. But after a day of futile search, Whitaker sent another message directing "Patsy" to discontinue his hunt for the cruiser and to begin patrol across the possible track of a fifteen-ship convoy of merchant ships that was headed down the coast towards Singapore. The message was vague and didn't promise much of a chance to locate the convoy. But all day of the twentieth was spent patrolling rapidly back and forth across the convoy's possible line of advance. Yet, as before, nothing materialized.

In the morning, while I was taking a sun sight to

check the *Crevalle*'s position, I was amazed to find the sun in its first phase of an eclipse. I still had my childhood enthusiasm for this phenomenon, remembering how, many years ago, I'd watched the sun go through a total eclipse through a smoke-blackened piece of glass.

With only ten days left for wolfpack action, Whitaker asked headquarters in Perth for a change of station for all three of his submarines. Shortly, a ComSubs 212002 dispatch directed Whitaker's Wolves to head for Cape Bolinao on the west coast of Luzon above Manila. Another message received at about the same time told of Hank Munson taking command of the *Rasher* and taking the *Rasher* back to Pearl for an overhaul at the end of his patrol.

On the afternoon of the twenty-fourth, the *Angler* hove into view and radar interference on the *Crevalle*'s SJ scope indicated that the *Flasher* was nearby. So all three of the boats were finally on station off Cape Bolinao and the wolfpack was ready to function as a coordinated attack group.

Then another burn message was decoded. It detailed the route of a Japanese submarine that was making seventeen knots and proceeding on the surface to Japan, having left Germany several months earlier. She was transporting a shipload of the latest German technology and her ballast tanks carried mercury, which was in short supply in Japan and necessary for their gyros and other instruments. The message emphasized that at all costs the Japanese submarine had to be intercepted and sunk. There was too much at stake. The Japanese war effort, rejuvenated by the latest German inventions, could prolong a war, thought to be won at this point, for many additional months.

The message also gave a geographic position through which the Japanese submarine would pass at 0700 on July 25.

This time I felt that the burn dope was reliable. Thus, as I drifted around the boat to see if the men were ready for the impending action, several members of the crew cautiously asked, "Mr. Ruhe, when are we going to sink something?" My emphatic answer was, "Now!" Even George and Walt Mazzone began to be pleasant once more.

At 1700 a *Flasher* message ordered the three subs to form a search line at 0500 on the twenty-fifth, 252° True from the *Flasher* and with eleven-mile spacing between subs, with *Angler* in the middle and the *Crevalle* on the western end of the line. After forming the line on the surface, the three subs would then submerge just before 0700. The *Angler*'s position was at 15° 03.5' North latitude and 117° 11' East longitude. It was the position of the Japanese submarine at 0700 and where she should pass over the *Angler*.

Before dawn on the morning of the twenty-fifth Whitaker's Wolves took station across the path of the Japanese sub, which was closing from the southwest. Blinker identification signals had been exchanged with the *Angler* and the *Flasher* before the *Crevalle* fanned out towards her westerly position relative to the other two subs.

As dawn began to break, with the *Crevalle* on the surface and her bow pointed towards the oncoming Japanese submarine, the number two high periscope was raised to carefully study the seas to the southwest, hoping to make a first sighting of the very important Japanese submarine.

At 0653, however, a plain-language voice transmission from the *Angler* said, "Goatfish has just sighted the masts of a large number of ships bearing 115° True from me, at about ten miles from my present position."

I swung the high periscope with its four feet of additional length over that of the number one scope, away from the bearing of the expected enemy sub and around to the eastward. After much slow scrutiny of the horizon, I was able to discern many tiny masts bristling just above the horizon. Their bearing was 105° True. This sighting was immediately sent to Dumbo.

He replied, "I've got the ships in view bearing 215° True."

Whitaker had a tough decision to make: keep waiting for the Japanese sub and ignore the convoy, or go with the bird-in-a-hand option. It was almost 0700 and there was no sign of the Jap sub. If the enemy submarine was late but still on her predicted track, she could get mixed in with the convoy and be difficult to sort out from the mass of ships and escorts. Moreover, Whitaker had mentioned in one of his messages that other American subs were being taken off their patrol stations to congregate along the Japanese sub's route to Japan, a defense-in-depth to back-stop Whitaker's Wolves. There were plenty of U.S. subs in reserve to make sure the enemy sub never got to Japan.

Consequently, Dumbo sent orders to Patsy and Goatfish by voice radio. "Leave your present stations and go after the big convoy you have in sight. I'll trail the convoy and give you information on its makeup and actions. I've only got six torpedoes left, so you fellows get in your licks first."

Whitaker's decision hadn't been easy to make. If the sub carrying the German technology got to Japan, Whitaker knew he'd be fried for not carrying out the orders he had received to have his wolfpack intercept the enemy sub and sink it. Even a lot of ships sunk from the convoy at hand would not be mitigating. But Whitaker, I knew, would brook no questioning of his decision. Nor would Ray Dubois, like a good exec, risk counseling Whitaker about the risk he was taking relative to his future career in the Navy.

Whitaker's use of plain language in wolfpack broadcasts seemed very cavalier. It invited the Japanese convoy commanders to intercept the wolfpack's radio transmissions and be alerted to the imminent attack of at least three U.S. submarines. Dumbo evidently hoped that such knowledge would so confuse and panic those who ran the convoy that they'd do dumb things and be easy prey to the attacks of his Wolves.

Shortly, Dumbo sent another voice broadcast to Patsy and Goatfish. "There are two outer columns each with five big ships and the center column has four even bigger ships. They've got many destroyer-type escorts in some sort of circular perimeter defense. All are valuable ships. Go get 'em."

Meanwhile, Frank Hess's *Angler* had bent on four engines to speed ahead of the convoy—paralleling the advancing ships twelve miles away to prevent being sighted while moving into a position where she could dive for a submerged approach. Frank Hess, a short, heavy-set, broad-shouldered man with wavy, sandy hair and a broad face, promised a good start for the wolf-pack's attacks.

Within minutes both the *Angler* and the *Flasher*

reported that a four-engine seaplane was making sweeps out from the convoy in cloverleaf patterns. No attempt was made to authenticate their broadcasts. However, spurious and deceptive broadcasts might be heard on our voice radio frequency, originated by a clever, wily Japanese officer trying to fool and disrupt the communications of Whitaker's Wolves. Without authentication he could get away with such a ploy.

Goatfish reported: "The convoy is heading north on courses between 305° True and 010° True and seems headed for Formosa. The marus are all making eleven knots and zigzagging frequently."

Then at 0752 Goatfish reported that his *Angler* was twelve miles ahead of the convoy and diving for an attack.

Three minutes later there was a frantic call from Dumbo. "I'm being forced down by a closing aircraft. But at the earliest I'll resurface and continue reporting the convoy's disposition. Good luck."

The *Crevalle*, in pursuit of the convoy, began her end-around on a slightly northeasterly course on the assumption that the convoy was actually heading for Japan and within hours would change her present base course to the right. Like Hess, Captain Walker conned the *Crevalle* to remain about twelve miles from the nearest ship in the convoy. Speeding to get ahead of the mass of ships, the *Crevalle* had three diesels pounding away with a heavy roar while the fourth was on battery charge to ensure a full battery at the start of the *Crevalle*'s submerged attack.

Of first concern was the seaplane hovering over the convoy. It eventually swung towards the *Crevalle*, having evidently spotted "a stranger" that it had to investigate. When the range to the aircraft had dropped below six miles, the captain pulled the plug and down the *Crevalle* went. No bombs were dropped.

After half an hour of staying deep, the captain brought the *Crevalle* to periscope depth, ascertained that there was no plane nearby, and after surfacing resumed the chase, keeping the convoy's masts in sight.

Two planes were now hovering over the convoy. A second anti-submarine aircraft had joined the seaplane.

There was an exhilarating feeling of excitement on the bridge as the *Crevalle* raced once more up the port flank of the convoy.

The day was one of a brilliant sun that beamed on a scarcely ruffled, silvery blue sea. Occasional large masses of low, dark clouds drifted across the sky, blanking the sun for a few minutes as they passed. When the sun was shut off from the surface of the ocean, strong breezes were generated that whipped the sea into a choppiness that caused the *Crevalle* to bounce along as though on a rough road. Some of the clouds were so black and full of moisture that it was only a matter of time until one of them dumped its rain on the ocean.

Before arriving at the planned diving position to commence an attack on the convoy, the *Crevalle* ran through a heavy downpour that fell too suddenly to get rain clothes up to the bridge watch. Hence, those on the bridge, including the captain and myself, were quickly soaked by the tropical rain. But we felt pleasantly warmed as the rain took the chill out of our bodies—the fear that the two patrolling aircraft might spoil the *Crevalle*'s hunting day.

Prior to diving at 1340, Patsy had received reports

from Goatfish and Dumbo. Dumbo broadcast that the ships were "on a base course of 350° True and making zigs of up to 60° every half hour." Goatfish had sent a discouraging report. "After I went in for my attack the convoy had a big zig to the eastward which left me out in left field. The closest I got to a ship, an escort, was four thousand yards." Then Dumbo explained that the big zig that frustrated Goatfish "caused convoy to head directly at me. Two destroyers passed directly over me. They held contact on the *Flasher* and kept her deep. There was no opportunity to shoot at anything."

When the *Crevalle* dove for her attack she was dead ahead of the first ship in the center column of ships which, according to Captain Walker, looked like a cruiser; a good target to take on first. Thus, when the range to the warship was fourteen thousand yards "Battle Stations, Torpedo Attack" was called away. But there was no sense of urgency since the closing rate on a wildly zigging bunch of ships making only eleven knots was only about a thousand yards every three minutes, making for a long, drawn-out approach.

The mood in the conning tower was upbeat. Good things were about to happen. Although the patrol so far had been long and depressing with no successes after great hopes had been raised, now with the torpedoes operating reliably, perhaps all of the *Crevalle*'s torpedoes would be fired and she'd go home with a goodly bag of ships.

George, the assistant approach officer, was buzzing around the conning tower making tactical suggestions in a friendly, low-pitched, confidential manner to everyone in the conning tower. Below, Walt Mazzone stood by as battle diving officer and didn't have to suffer from this change in George's attitude—one that exuded such friendliness towards all that it was down-right sickening.

When a 5,500-yard range to the nearest ship was obtained by the ST radar in number one scope, the captain complained that he'd lost sight of the ships. Heavy rainfall had drawn a curtain over them. The only hope then of getting off torpedoes was to lock the listening sound head on the noise of the heaviest approaching screws. There was a sound-bearing dial over the chart desk that indicated the bearing on which the sound head was oriented, while a loudspeaker beside the sound dial broadcast the noises being picked up by the sound head. A 360-degree sweep of the sound head moreover showed where the heavy propeller beats of convoy ships were located. The bearings of the escorts' light screws were also discernible.

One pair of light, high-speed screw sounds grew rapidly in intensity and their bearing moved swiftly to the right. This indicated that an escort was passing the *Crevalle* close aboard. The captain swung the scope to the bearing of the escort's screws and vaguely saw through the heavy downpour a Japanese fleet destroyer. One of their first string. She was passing about one hundred yards off the stern, according to the captain's estimate. The periscope's radar scope unfortunately was a blanket of white light making the radar return from the destroyer impossible to distinguish. The range was also too short for a stern tube shot, although all fish in both rooms were ready in their tubes.

A target with very heavy propeller beats was spotted by the captain. He could barely see it but identi-

fied it as a tanker. The stadimeter range taken through
the periscope read 2,200 yards. The tanker was definitely closing the *Crevalle*'s position. But a check-
swing of the scope revealed two freighters close to the
Crevalle with one of them about to run over the top
of the *Crevalle*'s stern. The captain watched the threatening maru closely and had standard speed rung up to
pull the stern clear. But he'd wasted too much time
worrying about clearing the freighter. As he started to
swing the scope back to the tanker, a four goal-post
cargo ship hove into sight with a small angle-on-the-
bow. She was followed by another big cargo ship.

With the ST's scope blanketed by the surrounding
rain, the captain was forced to guess at the ranges to
the ships moving by. He couldn't take the time for individual stadimeter readings. Moreover, the captain's
guesses as to range all seemed bad. The bearing rates—
evident on each ship on which the captain steadied the
scope—were much higher than they should have been
for the ranges he estimated.

Unquestionably, the situation was too complex for
the captain to both do the periscope job and at the
same time try to make difficult tactical decisions. It
was assumed that George as assistant approach officer would be doing the same job Captain Munson
did in the earlier patrols. Yet George didn't have the
years of submarine training that it took for this sort
of capability and hence was of little help.

"Let's go after the four-goal-post ship," I begged
the captain.

"What's her bearing?" he asked, indicating that
he'd lost track of what seemed like the only good target to shoot at.

"160° relative, Captain."

At this he ordered, "Left full rudder. We'll get her with the stern fish." Then he forgot that the *Crevalle* was still swinging rapidly to port when he took his next look at the big freighter.

"Steady on a course," I pleaded. The solution on the TDC was going all haywire.

"Steady as you go," the captain snapped to the quartermaster on the wheel. Then, "Here's the set-up." He called out, "Mark the bearing. The range is about nine hundred yards."

"The range is much closer," I cautioned.

But the captain ordered, "Fire all four torpedoes at the target." The gyro angles being fed into the torpedoes aft were over 90° right when the first torpedo left the tubes and the final and fourth torpedo went out with a 122° right gyro angle.

All four torpedoes missed, their wakes passing far astern of the big ship. I heard a mumbled "Oh, shit."

While the four torpedoes aft were being fired, the soundman shouted over the loudspeaker that there were very loud screws close aboard.

The captain swung the scope to the bearing shown by the pointer on the sound head's direction dial. With an almost unintelligible shout, the captain excitedly said, "Get this set-up. It's an aircraft carrier with a forty-degree port angle-on-the-bow. And use a range of: one thousand yards." But this range was too optimistic. It was also noted that there was nothing quiet or coolly efficient about the *Crevalle*'s fire-control team at this point in the attack. As the saying goes, "Everything had gone to hell in a basket."

Then the captain rotated the scope to see if the *Crevalle* was about to be run down by another ship.

"Here's an escort passing to port." . . . "That's the stern of a big ship." . . . "Here's another destroyer. But he's closing us with a big angle-on-the-bow." The captain was getting diverted again from his main target, the carrier.

"Get back on the carrier. Get back on the carrier," I muttered.

As the captain swung the scope towards the carrier's bearing, he cried out with anguish, "Bring me up. Bring me up." And then down to Mazzone, and much louder, "Bring me up. You've ducked the periscope."

Mazzone called back up through the hatch, "I can't hold the boat up. I'm using four degrees up-angle but the boat's getting heavy aft."

Then an agitated voice over the loudspeaker tremulously reported, "The after room is flooding."

As I was picturing the carrier tearing off the *Crevalle*'s conning tower, the captain ordered Mazzone to flood negative and go deep. And disgustedly he snorted, "Break off the attack. That's it."

Next he called the after room: "Can you control the flooding? How bad is it?"

An apologetic voice answered, "A poppet valve jammed open on number nine tube, but we've got it closed and the flooding is stopped."

"Christ," the captain growled.

In a matter of seconds a depth charge crashed overhead. It was lucky that the *Crevalle* was taken deep so rapidly. Somebody's guardian angel was working real hard. An escort had undoubtedly sighted the periscope and charged in for the kill without anyone being aware of her attack.

The next fifty-seven depth charges that exploded close to the *Crevalle* were not a great worry and there was little "sweating-it-out" for the next hour. The *Crevalle* remained in good shape to resume the chase after the convoy. No glass or instruments were shattered.

At one point while the *Crevalle* was at deep submergence listening to the screws of attacking destroyers weaving patterns of depth charge runs over or near the *Crevalle,* the soundman reported, "I hold light, fast screws passing close aboard. It sounds like a submarine making 280 rpm."

A Japanese submarine making about seventeen knots would have just about that number of revolutions per minute on her screws. "There goes our Jap sub loaded with the German technology," I concluded.

By 1900 the *Crevalle* was free of searching destroyers and was surfaced to take another crack at the convoy. With three diesels bent on the screws, the *Crevalle* headed north once more to get ahead of the mass of ships that seemed unscathed.

When Captain Walker called Dumbo on voice radio to report that he'd failed to get any ships, he also asked, "How are we doing?"

"So far we've struck out," was Dumbo's pained reply.

Wolves? Whitaker's Wolves were more like a bunch of Lapdogs.

Dumbo then advised Patsy to start the *Crevalle* on another end around up the port side of the convoy. Dumbo said he would stay on the surface and shadow the convoy from well astern of the ships. "I'll keep giving you the course and speed of the main body of ships," Whitaker emphasized.

The convey was sufficiently fast and the *Crevalle* was so far behind it that it would take several hours to get to a position ahead of the convoy for a night surface attack. One of the escorting destroyers had done her job well by forcing the *Crevalle* to run deep until nightfall.

The waning moon was not due to rise until after 0200. Thus, the dense blackness all around the *Crevalle* for the next seven hours promised little interference from Japanese anti-submarine aircraft. The surface search radar had to be used at infrequent intervals only and then for momentary single sweeps.

For the next several hours the occasional radar sweeps indicated that the escorting destroyers on the port side of the convoy were using a clever and disturbing tactic. Their circular screen had been expanded so that the destroyers patrolled their stations at about six miles from the mass of ships they were protecting. The destroyers in the van were pinging away with their active sonars searching for submerged submarines that tried to sift their way into the formation of ships. On the other hand, the destroyers on the flanks of the convoy remained quiet and crept at the speed of the convoy, so as to ensure long sonar listening ranges against loud submarines making high speed on the surface. Thus, with the *Crevalle* making 17.5 knots on three engines, her noisy movement was being detected by a screening destroyer that would peel off from the formation and head to intercept the *Crevalle*. This forced Captain Walker to slow the *Crevalle* so that her screws were no longer detectable at long range. Then the destroyer would start pinging to find the *Crevalle*. After about five minutes of futile searching, the destroyer would turn around and return at high speed to her station in the circular screen.

So much time was wasted avoiding the screening destroyers on the port side of the convoy that hope for a night attack slowly faded. Captain Walker, when he climbed down into the conning tower from the bridge, moved wearily as he studied the red-lit radar plot. With a sagged face, narrowed eyes and a slow shaking of his head from side to side, he regarded the *Crevalle*'s position pessimistically.

Yet earlier in the night he had scrambled up and down the ladder with much vigor and his voice had been eager and high-pitched. The imminence of battle had pepped him up. But the frequent delays eventually sapped his normally ebullient vitality.

Then, about 0100 on July 26, Dumbo called to say, "There's a large hole in the convoy's screen and I'm heading on in at high speed for a surface attack. Here's for luck!"

How Whitaker's *Flasher* had moved ahead of the *Crevalle* up the port flank of the convoy was a mystery. But hopefully, at that moment, the *Flasher*'s attack could change the whole complexion of the situation. Discreet radar sweeps shortly showed the *Flasher* going east through the circular screen of destroyers then moving northward to get to the bow of the convoy before heading directly towards the port column of ships for a discharge of her remaining six torpedoes.

At 0214, two explosions were heard from the direction of the convoy, out to the east. Then there was a much heavier explosion from the same general direction. This was spectacularly followed by a massive sheet of flame that rose skyward from a torpedoed tanker in the center column of ships.

At this point Captain Walker called me to the bridge

to see the fireworks. The sky was so brightly lit by the erupting flames that the ships in the port column were easily seen in dark silhouette against the raging oil fires on the damaged tanker. One of the big ships in the port column was well down by the stern. Moreover, the *Flasher* was startlingly visible and looked like a tiny, gray mouse in the center of a large number of ferocious black cats. She was scurrying north to go back through the screen just astern of the lead destroyer. But suddenly every ship in the convoy started wildly blowing whistles as gunfire erupted on all of the ships. Big guns boomed, red tracer shells crisscrossed the skies and some of the tracers were directed at the *Flasher*. So not unexpectedly, she suddenly dove, like a mouse disappearing into a hole in the floor. In short order, a few sporadic depth charge explosions were heard that indicated a nuisance anti-submarine counterattack to ensure that the *Flasher* went deep and stayed there until the convoy was well clear of the area.

The captain chuckled quietly and began humming a tune as he studied the scene of destruction through his binoculars. He was delighted that Whitaker had gotten in his licks. More to the point, he should have been concerned with the *Crevalle*'s precarious position, because the *Crevalle* had started in for an attack and was passing through the destroyer screen on the port side of the convoy. The bright fires rising from the burning tanker's deck at that instant made the *Crevalle* more visible to the destroyers than the *Flasher* had been. Yet all of the escort interest was focused on the disappearing *Flasher* and the sinking ships.

Unfortunately, as a result of the *Flasher*'s attack,

the convoy had zigged to the east leaving the *Crevalle* astern of the convoy and "out in left field."

At 0405, shortly before dawn, distant explosions were heard coming from the eastern side of the convoy. Then the muffled booms of big guns drifted across the waters while red streaks from small caliber tracer shells rose from the horizon like Fourth of July sky-rockets. The *Angler* was finally helping the wolfpack strategy.

A sliver of waning moon had risen, but the cloud cover allowed only a faint amount of light to filter through and make ships distinguishable. The *Crevalle* remained relatively invisible in the light from a rising moon. Only her bow wake seemed enhanced in its whiteness. Thus she remained unseen by the destroyers of the protective screen.

Then, there was good news from Jim Blind, the radar officer. "All the ships have come to a dead stop."

The information on the convoy galvanized the very exhausted fire-control team into renewed optimism and alertness. Getting overly tired, it was feared, would dull Captain Walker's capability to calculate the risks involved, just as the *Dragon*'s skipper Pete Ferrall had seemingly neglected to recognize the dangers involved in his attacks on Christmas day of '42. And like the *Dragon*'s experience, the officers would also tend to get sloppy in their performance of their battle duties. But being pooped out and mentally dulled had a good side to it. It pushed fear far into the back of a man's mind, with risk to one's life scarcely thought about. The great bravery shown by men in many battles could be explained by their utter weariness.

It was reassuring to hear the bright firmness in

George's voice as he called out bearings on the escorts in sight. Dick Bowe, the battle officer of the deck, could also be heard cheerfully laughing about the way the situation was developing. Even the captain showed an unusual amount of vigor as he scrambled down into the conning tower to check Jim's radar plot to ascertain where he could best get at the ships in the port column.

Then, Jim observed that the convoy was once again under way but had zigged to the north, making the *Crevalle*'s attack on the surface a piece of cake.

At 0422, with only ten minutes remaining until the first light of dawn, the captain put all four engines on the line and rang up flank speed. The *Crevalle* then raced through the screen and at the port column of ships. The captain's last words as he left the conning tower and climbed to the bridge were, "We're not going to have enough time to bore in and get the carrier. We'll just have to settle for the freighters close at hand."

The tubes forward and aft were made ready with six feet running depth set on each torpedo. It still wasn't certain that the depth problem of the torpedoes had been corrected.

When the radar range to the lead ship of the near column was 2,200 yards the captain ordered "commence firing the forward tubes." George had been instructed to lay his TBT on the two lead ships so as to get two hits in the first, put the third torpedo between the two ships in the hope of getting a stray hit in a ship in the second column a la the *Flasher,* and then ensure two hits in the second ship—while saving the sixth torpedo for a threatening escort.

With five torpedoes launched the captain ordered

hard right rudder and swung the *Crevalle* around for stern tube shots.

Just before the first of the stern torpedoes was launched, George reported seeing three flashing hits, two in the first ship and one in the second.

George aimed the stern torpedoes so that two would hit in the second ship and two in its following ship. These were very big cargo ships and there wasn't enough time to get piggish and try to get single hits in a couple more ships. The range was 2,900 yards when the stern torpedoes were fired but the setup on the TDC looked excellent. Soon, two more explosions were clearly heard in the conning tower that coincided with the time of run for the after torpedoes.

On the bridge it was reported that a huge column of smoke had risen from the second ship and that the lead ship had taken a large up-angle and was about to sink. This ship was later identified as the *Aku Maru* of 11,409 tons. The second ship, identified as the *Amigasan Maru* of 7,600 tons, had fires break out all along her main deck. Then with a big explosion, she seemed to disintegrate and disappeared from view. Meanwhile, gunfire had erupted on many ships. An escort swung a bright searchlight over the waters trying to pick up the fleeing *Crevalle*. The captain, without slowing, had headed her south, trying to escape on the surface so rapidly that the convoy protectors could not catch up. The inside of the conning tower resonated with the big bangs of large caliber gunfire. That was par for the course but hard on the ears.

Then George spotted a huge splash close to the *Crevalle*. That did it. It convinced the captain that the *Crevalle* was in the sights of one of the ships. So he lost interest in trying to make a clean getaway and dove the *Crevalle*. Dick reported after he'd dropped into the conning tower that a last look had showed the lead ship with only her bow out of water. Then at 0447 there was a heavy explosion that swished water through the *Crevalle*'s superstructure, indicating that the shock wave produced by the exploding ship was so great that its force extended over a mile in the direction of the *Crevalle*. The ship had blown up as she sank.

The *Crevalle* by that time had sped down through isothermal water to 350 feet, where a thermal layer was discovered that produced a six-degree change in water temperature in the next one hundred feet of depth. That was what the captain felt would hid the *Crevalle* from the pursuing destroyers as it prevented both their active and passive search sonars from holding contact on a submarine hiding within such a cold layer. The captain also ordered the *Crevalle* headed at five knots towards the scene of where the *Flasher* had attacked the convoy. He felt that there might be a ship in that location that still needed to be sunk by one of Whitaker's Wolves. And so sure was the captain of the *Crevalle*'s immunity, because of the density of the thermal layer in which the *Crevalle* coasted, that he announced he was going to his cabin for about two hours of sleep. "Wake me when your dead reckoning track shows the *Crevalle* to be about seven miles from where the *Flasher* hit the big tanker."

As soon as the captain left the conning tower the men were secured from the battle stations, even though a destroyer had peeled off from the convoy and was following the *Crevalle* as though she divined her intent to return to the scene of the first crime. The destroyer pinged away, conducting an active sonar search. At frequent intervals the destroyer would stop to listen carefully for any noise that the sub she was chasing might make. It was like a hunter in a forest steadily calling out to get an answering cry from a nearby hunter. But failing to hear a reply he would stop to pick up the faintest noise that might pinpoint a threat to his safety.

At 0700 the captain was called back to the conning tower and the *Crevalle* was brought up to periscope depth. All noise from the pursuing destroyer had disappeared. A quick look, however, showed a Fubuki-type destroyer lying dead in the water at about two thousand yards range. The crew was called back to their battle stations and all tubes forward were made ready to fire. Though the *Crevalle* was at dead quiet and the captain showing only a foot of scope, the Fubuki cranked up her engines and headed for the *Crevalle* at full speed while pinging in the short-scale attack mode. Back down to four hundred feet went the *Crevalle* and no depth charge explosions followed her down.

For the next hour and a half the *Crevalle* edged towards the position where the *Flasher*'s tanker had burned up. Reports by the soundman indicated that there were now two destroyers circling out ahead of the *Crevalle* at a considerable distance. So at 0850 the captain eased the *Crevalle* up to periscope depth once more. With only six inches of scope showing he determined that the two destroyers were patrolling clockwise around a large stopped ship that was about twelve thousand yards distant. He studied the big freighter which looked brand new and didn't show any signs of being damaged. "Perhaps she had engine trouble and might start up in a moment," he guessed. Then rapidly, he decided his tactics to get four torpedoes into this valuable target that was being so closely guarded by the best of the Japanese ASW warships. "We'll go back down to four hundred feet, head for the target at five knots for about an hour, and then if we can pick a hole between the two circling destroyers, we'll pop up fast and fire at the ship as soon as I get a bearing. Then we'll go back deep and under the target so the destroyers will be picked off our back by the sinking ship. Hopefully, she won't sink on the *Crevalle*." It was a really nice plan. And down the *Crevalle* went to four hundred feet to start the approach.

After an hour of numb, no-talk waiting with the *Crevalle* churning in towards the freighter, the soundman reported that he held a single set of screws off the *Crevalle*'s port beam. She was then on her way through the circle being patrolled by the two destroyers. So the captain brought the *Crevalle* up smartly to periscope depth. He pushed the scope out of the water, got a range to the target ship with the periscope radar of "two thousand yards," and marked the bearing with, "I'm on the center of the target." At this, and with a good fire-control solution, four torpedoes were fired, spread along three-quarters of the estimated target length.

All of the torpedoes were heard to hit. The captain observed the first torpedo striking the center of the maru and said that a large sheet of billowing flames covered her bridge. The second threw a vast cloud of debris into the air. And then a bomb hit close to the *Crevalle*'s periscope. The captain had failed to look into the air for aircraft. "Down express," the captain shouted. The attack had progressed far too easily.

When the bomb blast shook the conning tower it knocked the ship's movie camera off the number one periscope where the quartermaster was about to record the sinking of the big freighter. It landed on Jim Blind's feet making him cry out as though mortally wounded. "You lucky devil," Dick Bowe smirked. "That will earn you a Purple Heart."

On the way to deep submergence the sonar's loud-speaker broadcast the wrenching, screeching and wailing of a ship being torn apart. Some of the sounds also came from overhead as the *Crevalle* ducked under the sinking ship. At the same time there were fourteen depth charge explosions well astern of the *Crevalle*. The attacking destroyer was not risking ploughing through the ship's wreckage. But out on the other side of the disintegrating ship, the *Crevalle* took a string of twelve more depth charges that were close but shallower than the *Crevalle*, which was quietly cruising at four hundred feet.

The captain decided that the ship sunk was the 8,800-ton *Aobasan Maru*.

All afternoon there were sporadic depth-charge attacks by the two destroyers that refused to give up and rejoin their convoy. Initially, the charges exploded overhead, apparently with a one-hundred-meter depth setting. But successive attacks were increasingly far astern of the escaping *Crevalle*. And when one of the destroyers speeded up and her sonar could be dimly heard yelping on short scale, the string of ten charges she laid produced explosions that were several miles astern of the *Crevalle*. It was guessed that the sub had been leaking oil and it was on this trail that the destroyers had made their attacks.

After dark, the destroyers abandoned the chase.

Their screw noises faded out. I was asleep on my feet after thirty-seven hours of no-sleep, tension-packed, but satisfying submarine action.

When back on the surface, Captain Walker called Dumbo on voice radio and gave him the results of the *Crevalle*'s attacks on the convoy. When he "Rogered" Patsy's message, Captain Whitaker sounded genuinely pleased at the results.

Whitaker then told of his night attack eighteen hours earlier. He said that the *Flasher* was headed home and that Captain Walker should take command of what was left of the wolfpack and get some more ships. A wolfpack of two submarines?

Whitaker's follow-up explanation of his attack at 0211 of the twenty-sixth indicated that he'd seen two hits in the first ship he fired at and one hit in the second and that a stray torpedo had gone through the port column of ships and hit a tanker that burned up and sank. He felt certain that he'd sunk a big freighter, and the tanker that lit up the skies so brightly. And that he'd possibly damaged a second very large cargo ship. His voice shook as he recalled how the *Flasher* tried to escape on the surface but then the gunfire had gotten so close that he was forced to dive.

An hour after Whitaker's voice transmission, Frank Hess of the *Angler* came on the air and reported that his attack at 0401 of the twenty-sixth had netted him only one hit although he shot ten of his torpedoes. He added that a half hour later he'd heard several distant explosions and then his soundman had reported hearing the noises of ships breaking up. The *Crevalle*'s targets going down? He also mentioned that at 1029 he heard four explosions far to the west of the *Angler*.

This checked with the *Crevalle*'s attack on the stopped freighter.

Before midnight a most welcome message was decoded that told of Alan Banister in the *Sawfish* sinking the Japanese submarine I-29, the one carrying the German equipment. *Sawfish* was part of a wolfpack with *Tilefish* and *Rock* that was back-stopping Whitaker's Wolves if the Jap sub slipped through Whitaker's three-sub formation. The loss of this sub in Bashi Channel was crippling to the Japanese war effort and was possibly the most important contribution made by a U.S. submarine in the Pacific War.

On July 28 (my birthday), Captain Walker directed the *Angler* to form a scouting line with the *Crevalle* and move quietly, without any quack-quacking on voice radio, towards Cape Bolinao. And this paid off.

At 0905, Mazzone, the OOD, spotted through the periscope the tops of merchant ships heading north towards the *Crevalle*. Within a few minutes an eight-ship convoy with four escorts hove into view. The lead escort was a Chidori. And that was bad news from our past experience with this type of ASW warship.

The captain selected as the best target a large maru with cage masts and a canopy of steel latticework that ran up over the bridge, then aft over the stack and from there down to a break in the well deck. The captain guessed that the ship's cage-like mantle was some sort of protection from objects falling out of the sky. But what? His description checked exactly with the picture of the 8,800-ton *Hakubasan Maru* shown in the Japanese Merchant Ships book. Her gray paint-job also indicated she was a naval auxiliary, an important ship.

The convoy was making only seven knots with its course taking the group of ships close to Piedra Point Light on Cape Bolinao. Thus the *Crevalle*'s submerged approach on the convoy's starboard bow seemed perfect, until a periscope look showed all of the ships zigging directly towards the *Crevalle* with the Chidori showing a large broad bow wake and charging at the *Crevalle*'s scope. The captain muttered, "This guy looks like a mad pit-bull with a helluva big bone in his teeth." So the firing of torpedoes was a bit frantic.

The *Hakubasan Maru* showed a zero angle-on-the-bow as the captain ordered, "Commence fire." He said that there was a big ship which fit the description of the *Aden Maru* that was astern and just off the port side of the *Hakubasan Maru*. And that a half-degree spread on the torpedoes should favor the port side of the target ship so that one or two torpedoes might miss the *Hakubasan Maru* and go on to hit the *Aden Maru*. What optimism.

On the Chidori rushed, and down sped the *Crevalle* to 450 feet while six torpedoes raced at the naval auxiliary. On the way deep there were two convincing torpedo explosions properly timed for hits in the *Hakubasan Maru*. With her bow torn off she would nose under shortly. Soon there were four, very close bone-rattling depth charges from the Chidori that shook the *Crevalle* violently, throwing men against equipment and starting jet-spraying leaks through hull packing glands. All rooms were called over the sound-powered telephone to report their damage. But none had anything serious that couldn't be fixed by the men in the room.

The bathythermograph had shown an isotherm—no change in temperature of the water—all the way down to 450 feet and the captain was reminded that, if the Japanese were using a 150-meter depth setting on their charges, the *Crevalle* was at the wrong depth. So the captain eased the *Crevalle* down to five hundred feet with ultra quiet conditions set. Then when there were eleven close explosions followed by eight more very close ones, he ordered, "550 feet." That was 138 feet deeper than the *Crevalle*'s test depth. But there were no looks of grave concern on anyone in the conning tower. No one even bent his head and cocked his ears to listen for the creaks or groans that would indicate that the hull was being over-stressed by the great pressure of the sea at that depth.

At 550 feet and dead quiet, and with the gyros and lighting motor generator secured, the Chidori still hung on to her submarine contact. This was a birthday party? Back and forth the Chidori directed her sound gear, pinging first to one side of the *Crevalle*, then the other and periodically laying more depth charges close overhead. Finally, the captain got tired of using large turns to throw off the aim of the Chidori. So he just put the *Crevalle* on a steady course at two knots and said, "To hell with it." Anything above "dead slow" and the *Crevalle* was rattling like a Model T Ford.

The conning tower had become a shambles of pieces of glass, chunks of insulation corking, and on the deck a pile of soggy papers dumped off the chart desk.

Mazzone reported from his diving station that the *Crevalle* was getting heavier and heavier from water leaking into the boat and that he would have to come up to four hundred feet in order to control her if dead slow was continued. The expansion of the hull at the shallower depth would lighten the *Crevalle* some-what, and add an hour or so of dead-slow running at ultra quiet. Then, wonder of wonders, the pinging slowly died out so that by 1630 the captain felt it was safe to start up the ventilation blowers and the light-ing generator and head the *Crevalle* south. She was headed home.

Miraculously, all of the *Crevalle*'s equipment seemed to be working OK.

After dark, she was surfaced and on three engines with the fourth on battery charge, she hurried to-wards the Sulu Sea and Lombok Pass. At the first op-portunity Captain Walker called the *Angler* and told her skipper that "you are now the commander of a single-sub wolfpack" and "good luck." Then he turned to me and said, "Now Ruhe . . . break out all that li-quor you have stashed away and we'll celebrate." So I passed the word over the loud speaker system that the crew could "splice the main brace" (à la Hank Mun-son) and that "the liquor will be in the mess hall, courtesy of Rocky Langfeldt and his pals." Then I told Dick Bowe and George to go to the mess hall and be sociable but to make sure nobody imbibed too much of the stuff. Shortly, as expected, Langfeldt ran to me with tears in his eyes and begged that I not give his liquor away. But I kept a stony-faced blank expres-sion. After hearing some moaning pleas, I smilingly said, "Langfeldt, you'll earn a lot of bucks with the crew from this generous gesture of yours." Then I turned away.

We weren't home yet. After dawn I was out on the *Crevalle*'s main deck looking for the source of the many rattles that were heard when she was running fast submerged. Much of the decking and iron framing had been torn loose by the shock of many close depth charges. However, using a couple of men, the topside damage was temporarily repaired by tieing down everything that was loose with white line.

The trip back to Fremantle was without event. When the *Crevalle* raced through Laparan Pass there were no spying small craft. The same was true for transiting Sibutu Passage and Makassar Strait. Only at Lombok Strait was there potential action. But a Chidori that the captain spotted several miles off was easily avoided.

On August 6, the *Crevalle* moored beside a fuel barge in Exmouth Gulf and topped of with fuel oil; then in three days she was near Fremantle Harbor. En route, the *Crevalle*'s radar picked up interference that seemed to be coming from U.S. submarines on their way north to patrol areas. But unlike Munson, Captain Walker gave the submarines a wide berth and didn't feel compelled to advise the other skippers about how to conduct their patrols to get a good bag of ships.

The three days also gave me a good chance to summarize lessons from this successful patrol. As to the efficiency of wolfpacks, it would appear that enemy anti-submarine warfare efforts to pin down and destroy one U.S. submarine gave the other submarines in a wolfpack a better chance to exploit weaknesses in the enemy's protective screen. So the wolfpack was a big plus when attacking a Japanese convoy. On the other hand, a single submarine encountering the same convoy would likely be frustrated in her attack by the level of efficiency shown by enemy ASW escorts. Perhaps some of the efficiency exhibited by our specific convoy's escorts was due to their understanding of what our subs were up to by their DFing and monitoring of "Whitaker's Wolves" plain-language voice transmissions. Fewer, shorter and more secure communications were certainly indicated. It wasn't evident that the quack-quack of our submarines had created confusion and dumb decisions on the part of the convoy commanders. Moreover, there was plenty of time in most cases for encryption and decryption of wolfpack messages. Again, being a Silent Service made sense.

In fact, it was the continuous submarine attacks on the convoy by the three submarines, over a twenty-four-hour period, that caused radical changes in convoy course and a slowdown in the convoy's advance. This allowed Whitaker's Wolves to regain attack positions after being pinned down by ASW warships and falling far astern of the convoy. Importantly, persistent attacks when ships are within striking distance net additional sinkings. An eleven-knot convoy was speedy enough to cause our submarines long delays in regaining an attack position. A fourteen-knot convoy would probably make only a single attack possible by each submarine. Thus, for higher speed convoys, a three-sub pack might not be appropriate. Against a high speed twenty-knot fleet of warships, many subs would have to be staggered along the fleet's path in order to achieve a few significant sinkings.

The newly installed bathythermograph proved invaluable on this patrol. The increased efficiency of Japanese ASW ships, described in the material that was read at the start of this patrol, was evident in their sonar searches and their precision of depth-charge drops. Only the protection of a thermal layer offered

the *Crevalle* a good degree of safety from lethal depth
charges. But although the ASW ships frequently placed
their depth charges well, the great inefficiency of this
weapon rarely gave satisfactory results. One depth
charge in a hundred might create serious submarine
damage. What the Japanese seemed to need were ship-
launched acoustic homing torpedoes, like the Germans
were using in the Atlantic and the technology for
which was probably carried in the I-29 that was sunk
by the *Sawfish* on her way to Japan.

If ever I doubted that a guardian angel had been
assigned to hover over my shoulder at all times, this
patrol convinced me that being a Christian was the
best insurance one could have for getting back home
at the end of the war.

Significantly, the *Crevalle*'s torpedoes functioned
well. Finally. Eleven devastating hits out of twenty-
three torpedoes fired had bottomed over thirty-four
thousand tons of Japanese shipping. It was a great
boost to the U.S. war effort. Whitaker's additional six
ships sunk, including a cruiser, made his Wolves about
the most productive of all wolfpacks. One marked failure of the *Crevalle*'s fire-control team was its lack of
capability to fire torpedoes when the periscope and its
radar were blanketed by a dense sheet of rain. Using
only sound bearings (which were available) for a firing
solution was possible and should have been trained for.

By mid-morning of August 9, the *Crevalle* was tied
up in Fremantle Harbor. The welcoming party on the
dock consisted of the admiral, a few of the refit crew
who used this as an excuse to loaf for a few minutes,
and Miles Refo with three of his sailors from the
Jack. The sailors were menacingly carrying baseball
bats. Refo's intent was clear. He wanted his portable,

electric sump pump back and no stalling. So after Admiral Christie went below to talk to the captain, I didn't beat around the bush. Friendly like, I yelled over to Miles that I'd have his pump brought topside and we'd be delighted to deliver it back to the *Jack*. "It was only borrowed for this tough patrol," I apologetically told Refo.

Miles acted very friendly but insisted that his men would carry it back to the *Jack* by themselves. He wasn't going to let it get out of his sight. So I gave in easily. He didn't trust a *Crevalle* man?

Later, when back at Lucknow, Miles and I joked about the theft of his sump pump, while I shared some of my ration of twenty-four quarts of Bulimba beer with him. The *Jack*, under Art Krapf, had just sunk four ships so Miles was in a good mood and let bygones be bygones. There was lots to drink about.

The *Crevalle* had steamed 11,727 miles in fifty days and had used 132,000 gallons of fuel oil. Although severely depth-charged, the portable sump pump had never been put to use, probably because it was there ready to be used. And there were no serious discrepancies that would delay the *Crevalle* from getting back to sea in three weeks.

The admiral's words of wisdom appended to the *Crevalle*'s war patrol report were:

"It is felt that the effectiveness of wolfpacks in areas of concentrated shipping increases in geometric proportion to the number of submarines utilized."

The admiral also cited the *Crevalle* as "a sturdy ship with a stout-hearted crew," in his comments on the *Crevalle*'s fourth war patrol. And that was true. But was "concentrated shipping" still possible?

A footnote to this patrol was supplied by Bing

Gillette of the *Lapon*, who was at Lucknow on my arrival there. He said that the *Lapon* along with the *Raton* were stationed to intercept the Jap sub I-29, the one carrying the German technology, and that by some sort of confusion the *Lapon* was submerged and saw a submarine rushing past on the surface. The *Lapon*'s skipper, certain that it was the I-29 buzzing by on schedule, let go two torpedoes and then checked fire—unsure that the submarine was Japanese. *Raton* people reported feeling and hearing a dull thud that they thought was a dud torpedo hitting their targeted sub. But Gillette reassured me that both of the torpedoes the *Lapon* fired had missed.

PIERCING THE POLE

FROM *Nautilus 90 North*

---

by Commander William R. Anderson
with Clay Blair, Jr.

*O*ur next selection is distinguished by both of its authors having served aboard submarines. Commander William R. Anderson (1921–2007) set several records during his military service, and continued serving his country after retiring from the U.S. Navy. His time in World War II was distinguished, as he received the Bronze Star and several other combat decorations from his participation in eleven combat submarine patrols. He was selected by Admiral Hyman G. Rickover to be the skipper of the first working nuclear submarine to be placed into service, the USS *Nautilus*, and was its commander from 1957 to 1959. Anderson and his crew received international notice when the *Nautilus* became the first submarine to sail successfully under the polar ice cap surrounding the North Pole. He wrote his book about his experience, *Nautilus 90 North*, in 1959 with Clay Blair. Upon retiring from the Navy, Anderson entered politics, serving four terms as a U.S. congressman. After losing his fifth bid for reelection when the districts of Tennessee were redrawn following the 1970 census, Anderson retired from public life. He served as an officer with the Public Office Corporation, and lived in Alexandria, Virginia, until his death in February 2007.

Clay Blair, Jr. (1925–1998), grew up in Georgia, Mississippi, and Washington, D.C. During December 1943, he enlisted in the U.S. Navy, volunteering for submarine duty. Blair served on the submarine USS *Guardfish* during his Navy career, on two long war patrols for which he was awarded the Submarine Combat Insignia. After the war he attended Tulane University and Columbia University's School of Journalism. During the 1950s Blair was a correspondent for *Time-Life* before becoming a staff writer and Washington editor for *The Saturday Evening Post*. He served as managing editor and editor in chief of the *Post* during the early 1960s and also served as editor in chief of Curtis Publishing Company, which published the *Post* as well as *Ladies' Home Journal*, *American Home*, and *Jack and Jill* magazines. In 1965, he left Curtis Publishing to become a freelance author, specializing in military history, including a number of books about submarines and the Korean War. He also wrote several novels and a biography of James Earl Ray. Along with his wife, Joan, he wrote a book about the early life of John F. Kennedy, and his most recent work was a two-volume study of German U-boats during World War II, *Hitler's U-Boat War*.

When two great submarine sailors come together to write a book, the results are often amazing. Instead of the trials of World War II, Anderson chose to write about the new chapter in submarine history he had been a part of, the dawning of the nuclear age, and the ultimate adventure he played a part in as his boat and crew went after one of the ultimate prizes—reaching the North Pole underwater.

Peary describes the polar pack near the North Pole as a "trackless, colorless chaos of broken and heaved-up ice." Sir John Ross had this to say: "But let them remember that sea ice is stone, a floating rock in the stream, a promontory or an island when aground, not less solid than if it were a land of granite." They were right. But little did they dream of *Nautilus*, U.S. Navy, nuclear power, 1958.

Saturday morning, August 2, found 116 people running along at four hundred feet at cruising speed on course 000 true, just about forty-four hours short of culminating the most thrilling and adventurous cruise any sailor ever embarked upon. Overhead the ice was almost solid and incredibly rough, projecting downward as much as sixty-five feet from the surface, but averaging ten to fifteen feet thick. It would be less than honest to say that one can submarine under it with total abandon.

At first Frank Adams and I stood "watch and watch," which meant that one of us was up and about at all times. When my co-skipper took over, I could turn in for a few hours of sleep, knowing that the ship was in experienced and capable hands.

As we plunged deeper under the pack, I thought: *Where is the point of no return? Here? A hundred miles from here? A day's journey away? At the Pole itself, perhaps?* Frankly, I did not know. But I had computed it to be at the "Pole of Inaccessibility," the geographic center of the ice pack, about four hundred miles below the true Pole. But who cared? We were safe, warm, and comfortable in our home beneath the sea.

Morale was high and excitement at fever pitch. Once we had reached deep water beneath the pack, all hands felt that from then on out it was a run for "home." Although our ship's log read eighteen knots, Chief Machinist's Mate Stuart Nelson, who by then was nicknamed "Stop Leak," scampered forward from the engine room to ask if the engineers couldn't make "just a couple more going-home turns." I ordered twenty knots. The whole ship seemed to purr along contentedly.

"Boy, this is the way to explore," remarked Robert N. Jarvis, Hospitalman First Class. Pipe in hand, a cup of coffee beside him, he took his ease between atmosphere analyses. "Pinging up and down and all around at twenty knots, fresh air all day long, a warm boat, and good hot food—we sure have the situation in hand. I'd hate to walk across these ice fields up there to the Pole the way Admiral Peary did it."

Though most of us considered the North Pole a desirable objective, our primary mission was to cross from the Pacific Ocean to the Atlantic Ocean, blazing a new northwest passage. Actually, from the standpoint of compass performance, it might have been preferable to avoid the Pole, to ease around it at lower latitude. However, the route across the Pole was the shortest and fastest. Besides, who could resist the temptation to cross the North Pole when it was so close at hand?

Dr. Lyon remained glued to his sonar equipment hour after hour, watching the recording pens trace the contour of the underside of the ice. His new instruments displayed the ice in far greater detail, and with much greater accuracy, than the machines we had used in 1957. In fact, it was at this point that we discovered that the ice pack was far thicker than we had estimated in 1957, and that pressure ridges (ice forced downward when two massive floes press against one another) projected down to 100 or 125 feet. As we sped along, Dr. Lyon's instruments collected in each hour more precise data on the ice and the Arctic Basin floor than have been assembled in all history. When he finally left the ship, he had accumulated two trunkfuls of data.

And what of peaks rising abruptly from the uncharted ocean floor? Our detection equipment kept a sharp "eye" on these obstacles. We found several. At latitude 76 degrees 22 minutes north, in a region where there are no charted soundings, our fathometer, which had been running along fairly steadily at about 2,100 fathoms, suddenly spiked up to 1,500 fathoms, and then, to my concern, to less than 500.

I camped alongside the fathometer for several hours, intently watching the rugged terrain as it unfolded beneath us. I saw incredibly steep cliffs—undersea ranges—rise thousands of feet above the ocean floor. Several times I ordered speed slackened, then resumed, as a promontory leveled off or descended as rapidly as it had risen. The shape of these undersea mountains appeared phenomenally rugged, and as grotesque as the craters of the moon.

As I paced from instrument to instrument, Chief Hospitalman Aberle arrived with the latest atmosphere analysis. He reported our air vitalization machines were working well enough to maintain an atmosphere averaging 20 to 30 parts per million carbon monoxide, 1.0 to 1.5 per cent carbon dioxide, and between 20 and 21.5 per cent oxygen. These figures were all within, or below, safe limits.

At latitude 83 degrees 20 minutes north we passed abeam of the geographical center of the ice pack, the "Ice Pole" or "Pole of Inaccessibility." Before the day of nuclear-powered submarines, the name was probably fitting. It may now have to be changed.

It has been reported that for the crew *Nautilus* "hung motionless in time and space." Nothing could be further from the truth. Every man aboard was acutely aware of our rapid and inexorable movement north. As the hours passed, each watch squad gasped at our astounding progress. Men remained transfixed at the electronic machines clocking our track mile by mile, or before the television set on which they could watch the ice passing overhead like beautiful moving clouds. A mixture of suspense, anticipation, and hope was discernible throughout the ship. Few could sleep. Many of us had been praying for the successful attainment of our goal, and now, God willing, it appeared within our reach. Our psychiatrist, Dr. Kinsey, went about his work methodically and mysteriously, probing for, I suppose, those men who were afraid. Each day, to a random group of volunteers, he distributed cards containing a series of questions, such as "Do you feel happy?" If a man did not feel happy, he was supposed to indicate by writing a single "V" on the card. If he felt slightly happy, he wrote "VV." Three V's meant that he was in fine spirits, and four V's signified total enchantment. Personally, it made no sense to me. I was not one of the select volunteers.

The main fear within me was that which we all shared: a materiel failure, such as that which occurred in 1957, which would force us to turn back.

Every man on board examined and reexamined his instruments and equipment. Vigilance, they all knew, would prevent a small fault from becoming a casualty that would terminate the voyage or leave us stranded beneath the ice.

I did not—could not—sleep. I wandered restlessly about the ship, occasionally taking a peek through the periscope. I was surprised on these observations to see phosphorescent streaks in the water. This is a phenomenon common in tropic waters. It seemed unusual to me to find these streaks in water so cold that the outside of our engine room sea-water pipes was covered with thick layers of rime ice.

As I walked about the ship, taking the measure of the crew, I listened as the men spun tales and cracked jokes.

One crewman, recalling the time when *Nautilus* paid a memorable visit to New Orleans, captivated his shipmates with this story:

"I was headed back for the ship early in the morning. We'd spent most of the evening in the Monkey Bar in the French Quarter. Well, it's about dawn, and I'm walking down this deserted street. Suddenly, out of the corner of my eye, I saw a panhandler crossing the street headed full speed in my direction. He stopped me and asked for a quarter. I looked this bird in the eye and said, 'Look, bud. I'm working this side of the street. You stay on your own side.' Well, I wish you could have seen his face. He was really shook."

In another compartment, two crewmen on watch were talking.

"Joe, do you know who man's best friend is?" Bill asked.

"Well, I always heard it was a dog," Joe said.

"That's not so," Bill said.

"Well, if the dog isn't, then who is?" Joe asked.

"Lady alligators," Bill explained. "You see, every year these lady alligators come up on the beach and they lay about 1,000 eggs. Then, they tell me, the lady alligator turns around and devours about 999 of the eggs she laid."

"How does that make her man's best friend?" asked Joe.

"Well, Joe, it's like this. If that lady alligator didn't eat those 999 eggs, we'd be up to our neck in alligators."

In spite of this lighthearted talk, every man was alert for an emergency. The leads or polynyas were infrequent, but the position of each was carefully plotted, so that if it became necessary to surface, we would know where to find an opening. James H. Prater stood watch in the torpedo room, carefully bleeding just the right amount of oxygen into the hull. Nearby was Richard M. Jackman, prepared to make all torpedo tubes ready on an instant's notice, if it became necessary to blast a hole through the ice. We were ready, but the possibility of a casualty seemed remote. Indeed, I had never seen the ship's machinery function so perfectly. Our "out of commission" list reached a new low. It was as if *Nautilus* herself had found peace and contentment beneath the ice. If she could have filled out one of Dr. Kinsey's cards, it would have contained four V's, or five, or six, for every question.

Shortly after midnight, August 3, we passed latitude 84 degrees north. Since we had entered compass-baffling waters, we made preparations to guard against longitude roulette. At that time we placed our auxiliary gyrocompass in a directional gyro mode so that instead of seeking north, it would tend to seek the line we were following, a Great Circle course up the Western Hemisphere, across the Pole, and south again to the Eastern Hemisphere. This was the track I intended to cruise. When our master gyrocompass began to lose its north-seeking ability, as it would when we approached the northernmost point on earth, then we intended to shift to the auxiliary. Thus we would have something to steer by in the darkness below— something to lead us out on our track south.

In order to insure that all of the gyrocompasses remained properly oriented, we made all course, speed, and depth changes extremely slowly. For example, when we came near the surface to decrease water pressure on the hull (this is desirable in operating the garbage ejector), we rose with an angle of one or two degrees, instead of the usual twenty to thirty degrees. Once we changed course twenty-two degrees. So gradual was the shift that six minutes elapsed before we had settled on the new heading. Some wag had suggested that when we neared the Pole we might put the rudder hard over and make twenty-five tight circles, thus becoming the first ship in history to circle the earth nonstop twenty-five times. Any such maneuver was, of course, out of the question.

As we rapidly closed in on the North Pole, Tom Curtis, manning the inertial navigator, which constantly plotted our position by electronics, made minute adjustments to insure that his complex instrument was operating properly. At 1000 we crossed latitude 87 degrees north, breaking our record of last year, and with the passing of each new mile we moved farther north than any other ship in history.

Two hours south of the Pole, a wave of unchecked excitement swept through *Nautilus*. Every man was up and about, and unabashedly proud to be aboard. Frank Adams, staring intently at the electronic gear, uttered a word often employed by *Nautilus* men who have exhausted all ordinary expressions to sum up their reaction to the never-ending *Nautilus* triumphs: "Fan-damn-tastic."

When we crossed the Pole, of course, no bells would ring, nor would we feel a bump. Only our instruments could tell us how close we had come. Since we had made the decision to cross the Pole, we were determined to hit it precisely on the nose. Along with Navigator Shep Jenks and his assistant, Chief Petty Officer Lyle B. Rayl, I had stationed myself in the attack center, and although we were almost as far north as man can go on this planet, we were literally sweating over the charts and electronic position-indicators, making minute, half-degree adjustments at the helm. The hour by *Nautilus* clocks, which were still set on Seattle time, was 1900, or seven o'clock in the evening. Our nuclear engine, which up to then had pushed *Nautilus* more than 124,000 miles, was purring smoothly. Our electronic log, or speedometer needle, was hovering above twenty knots, the depth gauge needle about four hundred feet. Our sensitive sonar indicated that the endless polar ice pack was running between eight and eighty feet thick. Above the ice, we imagined, the polar wind was howling across its trackless, barren stamping ground, grinding massive floes one upon the other.

By then we had been under ice for sixty-two hours. Obviously, it was not possible to take the usual fix on heavenly bodies to determine our position, so we were

navigating primarily by dead reckoning. This means
that we were spacing our speed and course on the
chart and plotting our position every half-hour or so,
accordingly. Our bottom soundings, sometimes useful in submerged navigating, did not help, of course,
in this uncharted, unsounded area. Our precision
fathometer had indicated differences of as much as
eight thousand feet at those rare points where soundings were made, so we could not rely on it. Our only
check on our navigating was the inertial navigator. At
the exact moment we crossed the Pole, we knew, the
instrument would give a positive indication. Tom
Curtis moved closer to his dials and scopes as we
drew near.

A mile south of the Pole, I told Jenks to inform me
when we were four-tenths of a mile from the Pole as
indicated by the electronic log. The mileage indicator
was moving rapidly. It was only a matter of seconds.
Nautilus crewmen had gathered in the attack center
and the crew's mess.

On Jenks' mark, I stepped up to the mike of the
ship's public-address system:

"All hands—this is the captain speaking . . . In a
few moments *Nautilus* will realize a goal long a
dream of mankind—the attainment by ship of the
North Geographic Pole. With continued Godspeed,
in less than two days we will record an even more
significant historic first: the completion of a rapid
transpolar voyage from the Pacific to the Atlantic
Ocean.

"The distance to the Pole is now precisely four-
tenths of a mile. As we approach, let us pause in silence dedicated with our thanks for the blessings that
have been ours during this remarkable voyage—our

prayers for lasting world peace, and in solemn tribute to those who have preceded us, whether in victory or defeat."

The juke box was shut off, and at that moment a hush literally fell over the ship. The only sound to be heard was the steady staccato of pinging from our sonars steadily watching the bottom, the ice, and the dark waters ahead.

I glanced again at the distance indicator, and gave a brief countdown to the crew. "Stand by. Ten . . . eight . . . six . . . four . . . three . . . two . . . one. MARK! August 3, 1958. Time, 2315 (11:15 P.M. Eastern Daylight Saving Time). For the United States and the United States Navy, the North Pole." I could hear cheers in the crew's mess.

I looked anxiously at Tom Curtis. He was smiling. The inertial navigator had switched precisely as expected, positively confirming that we had crossed the exact North Pole. Curtis sang out: "As a matter of fact, Captain, you might say we came so close we pierced the Pole."

I stood for a moment in silence, awestruck at what *Nautilus* had achieved. She had blazed a new submerged northwest passage, vastly decreasing the sea-travel time for nuclear submarines from the Pacific to the Atlantic, one that could be used even if the Panama Canal were closed. When and if nuclear-powered cargo submarines are built, the new route would cut 4,900 miles and thirteen days off the route from Japan to Europe. *Nautilus* had opened a new era, completely conquered the vast, inhospitable Arctic. Our instruments were, for the first time, compiling an accurate and broad picture of the Arctic Basin and its approaches. *Nautilus*' achievement was dramatic proof of United States leadership in at least one important branch of science; and it would soon rank alongside or above the Russian Sputnik in the minds of millions. Lastly, for the first time in history a ship had actually reached the North Pole. And never had so many men—116—been gathered at the Pole at one time.

I was proud of what *Nautilus* had done, yet I felt no sense of personal triumph or achievement. That we had reached the Pole was due to the work and support of many people. My reaction, frankly, was an overwhelming feeling of relief that after months and months of preparation and two unsuccessful probes we had finally made it.

Precisely at the Pole, for the record, I made note of some statistics which may or may not prove useful. The water temperature was 32.4 degrees Fahrenheit. The depth of the sea was 13,410 feet, exactly 1,927 feet deeper than reported by Ivan Papanin, a Russian who landed there, he claims, in an airplane in 1937. (In 1909 Admiral Peary had found the depth "greater than 9,000 feet.") At the exact Pole our ice detectors noted a pressure ridge extending twenty-five feet down.

After crossing the Pole, I made my way forward to join in the "North Pole Party" in the crew's mess. My first act was to pay modest tribute to the man who, more than any other, had made our historic voyage possible: the President of the United States. A few minutes before, I had written him a message. It concluded: "I hope, sir, that you will accept this letter as a memento of a voyage of importance to the United States." In the mess, before seventy crew members of *Nautilus*, I signed this letter, and one to Mrs. Eisenhower, who had christened the ship.

Other events followed. A "North Pole" cake, pre-pared especially by leading Commissaryman Jack L. Baird, was cut, distributed, and wolfed down. Electri-cian's Mate First Class James Sordelet raised his right hand and became the first man in history to reenlist at the North Pole. In a special North Pole ceremony eleven other men, having passed the rigid written and oral examinations, were "qualified in nuclear subma-rines." The prize-winning title to correspond to Shell-backs and Bluenoses was announced: Panopo, short for "Pacific to the Atlantic via the North Pole." A "North Pole" postcard, stamped with the special North Pole cachet, was distributed to all hands. On the reverse side was a cartoon by McNally showing a sailor in a bathing suit standing on a small block of ice leaning against a striped "North Pole." The card read: "Greetings from Sunny Panama." All during these pro-ceedings, movie and still cameras whirred and clicked.

Then a distinguished citizen "came aboard." It was our talented McNally, dressed as Santa Claus. What a sight he made! Red vegetable coloring was splattered on his face. His whiskers were made of medical cot-ton, and a pillow was stuffed inside his Santa Claus suit, made of flag bunting.

Santa berated us for entering his private domain during the vacation season. He chided us particularly for our failure to abide by his restriction on the use of garbage disposal units by submerged transiting sub-marines! I pleaded ignorance and promised on behalf of all the ship's company children to abide by all his rules henceforth.

That done, Santa Claus relaxed and became his usual jovial self. He listened very patiently as one of the fathers in the crew, Chief Engineman Hercules H.

Nicholas, argued that the behavior of our children was absolutely beyond reproach. Santa promised, in light of our personal visit to the North Pole, that the coming Christmas season would be merry and lucrative for all our children.

Perspiring heavily, Santa finally said, "Well, I've got to go back to the Pole to make sure the elves are working." And with that our extraordinary party ended. The juke box was turned back on; men drifted to their bunks for a little rest.

An "extra" edition of the ship's newspaper was published that day, entitled "Nautilus Express—North Pole Edition." It was unusually mild in tone and contained nothing libelous, which is an indication, I believe, that all hands were deeply moved by *Nautilus*' triumph. The feeling of the crew was summed up in an article by the paper's editor, John H. Michaud. He wrote:

At NAUTILUS' Greatest Moment

The crew of the USS Nautilus (SS(N)571) have at this time accomplished one of the greatest feats that is possible for a peaceful nation composed of average citizens. We have reached a point that has never been attained before this time. Many courageous men have tried, few succeeded. Of all those men that have tried we humbly ask their forgiveness. They had courage and fortitude that many of us never had, never will have in our lifetime. To those men this is dedicated. We have arrived at the North Pole. The very last region of the earth that has never been explored. True we came to this region in a habitat that is not normal for man. We came with the best equipment, the best men, and a relative new form of power. Without this power we would have never attained the goal we set out for, now that we have reached that goal this same power will take us home to our loved ones, who have endured many hardships that will never be told to us. They bid us good-bye, some with tears, others with a strained look and always a question in their eyes. Is it this time? They know the goal that we have been striving for, since our return of last year, but the time and place we cannot say. We have left our loved ones not unlike the explorers of other times, with prayers to bring us Godspeed and a safe return. We are on that return now with much rejoicing and many happy thoughts for those we left behind. To my fellow shipmates this has been one of the most enjoyable trips I have ever been on, and without a doubt the most important. May God be with you on all other voyages that you make.

THE BELLS OF HELL

FROM *One Hundred Days:*
The Memoirs of the Falklands Battle Group Commander

by Admiral Sandy Woodward
with Patrick Robinson

*O*ur next pair of authors is led by Admiral Sir John
Forster "Sandy" Woodward, GBE, KCB, who is,
quite simply, a sailor's sailor. Born in 1932, he joined
the Royal Navy at age thirteen, right after World War
II. He became a submariner, and received his first command, the Valiant-class nuclear hunter-killer submarine *Warspite*, in 1969. In 1978 he was appointed to
the Ministry of Defence. Promoted to Rear Admiral,
in 1981 he was appointed Flag Officer First Flotilla.
In 1982 he commanded the South Atlantic Task
Groups in the Falklands War. Woodward was later
knighted for his efforts during the war. In 1983 Woodward was appointed Flag Officer Submarines and
NATO Commander Submarines Eastern Atlantic. In
1984 he was promoted to Vice Admiral, and in 1985
he was a Deputy Chief of the Defence Staff. Before
retirement in 1989 he also served as Commander-in-
Chief Naval Home Command and Flag Aide-de-
Camp to the Queen. Along the way, he also showed
an amazing knack for strategy and tactics, as in the

time he defeated the aircraft carrier USS *Coral Sea* during war games by disguising his destroyer as an Indian cruise liner and sneaking up to within range of his anti-ship Exocet missiles and simulating a launch, destroying the other ship and winning the exercise. Retired from the Royal Navy, he currently lives in England.

Patrick Robinson is a British novelist and former newspaper columnist. His recent books are naval thrillers *Hunter Killer* and *Ghost Force*, each about a crisis facing the world at the start of the twenty-first century. His earlier works include four nonfiction books about thoroughbred horses; *True Blue*, the story of the 1987 Oxford Boat Race mutiny for which he and coauthor Dan Topolski won the inaugural William Hill Sports Book of the Year in 1989; and of course *One Hundred Days*, the biography of Admiral Sandy Woodward.

One Hundred Days, describing Admiral Woodward's Falklands experiences, is possibly the most candid account ever of the pressures of high command in wartime and the impact on an individual commander. Told completely from his point of view, it is a masterly look inside the mind of a superb strategist as he embarks on his campaign. The following excerpt is from the beginning of the hostilities, when the two forces are about to meet for the first time, and what follows is the careful circle, feint, and thrust only when the attacker is as sure as he can be of achieving victory.

We established, I believe, several thousand miles back, that while truth is generally recognized to be the first casualty of war, the second is almost certainly politeness. After just one day in battle, I now know the third. Sleep. A commodity rapidly becoming as rare as the first two. I replaced it, largely, with adrenaline. Having retired to bed in the small hours of 2 May—the first night of my second half-century on this earth—I was awakened about one hour later at 0320 with the message: "Possible Arg Tracker (recce aircraft) to the north. Harrier despatched to investigate."

I got up, went to the ops room, asked a few questions, and returned to bed, preoccupied with the careful advance of their surface fleet, and wondering how to deal with it. Sleep was just about impossible and anyway, within the hour, they called me again, when one of our probing Harriers reported several surface contacts on his radar out to the northwest, range two hundred miles. My feet hit the floor before they had finished telling me.

As I walked quickly along the short corridor to the ops room it was becoming all too clear what we were up against. The contacts were just about where we expected them to be—northwest of the Battle Group and north of the islands. They represented, almost certainly, the Argentinian Carrier Battle Group: the 20,000-ton *Veinticinco de Mayo,* pride of Admiral Anaya's Fleet, and her escort of perhaps five ships. Two of them, I suspected, might be the Type 42 antiaircraft destroyers *Santisima Trinidad* and *Hercules*, sister ships to *Coventry*, *Glasgow*, and *Sheffield*.

The moment I entered the ops room this was confirmed in my mind. The Harrier pilot's report said he had been "illuminated" by a Type 909 Sea Dart tracking radar—and that had to be from one of the Args' Type 42s. It took only a very short meeting with my staff to assess the situation and to conclude that they were about to attempt a dawn strike, launched against us from the deck of the carrier. Since she could carry ten A-4Q Skyhawks, each armed with three five-hundred-pound bombs, we could expect a swift thirty-bomb attack on *Hermes* and *Invincible* at first light—around 1100Z for us. She might also have Exocet-armed Super Etendards to add to our problems.

And in the middle of that rather sombre night, out near the edge of the British Total Exclusion Zone, we prepared to "form Line of Battle" for the first set piece of the war, the Royal Navy versus the naval and air forces of Argentina. Actually this entails anything but a "Line of Battle," since modern tactics require formations which look completely haphazard at first sight, and anything but a "set piece." The commander who so indulges himself makes it altogether too easy for his opponent.

I elected to finalize my arrangements two hours from that staff meeting, at around 0700, when the *Glamorgan* and *Brilliant* groups returned. For the moment we had a great deal more thinking to do, because *Veinticinco de Mayo* represented exactly one half of our problem. The other was situated two hundred miles to the southwest of me and to the south of the islands—the *General Belgrano* and her two destroyers. In addition to all of the above Argentinian ships, there were three frigates in the area, plus their only tanker.

Rear Admiral Gualter Allara, their Commander at Sea, was in the carrier, and it all looked to me very like a classic pincer movement attack on the British Battle Group. To take the worst possible case, *Belgrano* and her escorts could now set off towards us and, steaming through the dark, launch an Exocet attack on us from one direction just as we were preparing to receive a missile and bomb strike from the other. Our choices of action were varied, but limited.

We could of course take immediate evasive action and head away from our position to the southeast, making it more difficult for the bombers to find us, and possibly placing ourselves beyond their effective range, for lack of fuel or useful weapon load. But we had worked specifically towards bringing their fleet to action, and I did not want to be squeezed out of our own Total Exclusion Zone like a pip from an orange. That would have given added complications to the ROE, it would scarcely have been in the traditions of the Royal Navy, and anyway I had work to do inshore tomorrow night too. No, I could not allow that. But equally I could not just stay there and do nothing. I had to make a move, and since we were in contact with the *Belgrano* group, but no longer so with the carrier group, my thoughts began to center on the cruiser.

The *Belgrano*, on her own, was not that big a threat, but neither was she likely to be a push-over. A cruiser of 13,500 tons, and over six hundred feet long, she carried fifteen six-inch guns, and eight five-inch guns—all bigger than any guns in my entire Force. She was old, built in the United States in the mid-1930s as the "Brooklyn" Class light cruiser *Phoenix*, and had seen active service in the Pacific during the Second World War, having survived the Japanese attack on Pearl Harbor in December 1941. In the American naval archives there is a picture of her coming out of the Harbor under her own steam, past the enormous wreck of the *Arizona*. A year later she became the flagship of General MacArthur's navy commander Admiral Thomas C. Kinkaid, and for extended periods MacArthur himself was on board, conducting the Pacific campaign. *Phoenix* saw service in exalted company for many months as MacArthur and Kinkaid drove the Japanese back, all through the southern islands. She was purchased by the Argentine Navy in 1951 and, five years later, re-named the *General Belgrano*, immediately after the overthrow of President Perón.

Now she was ranged against us and, in a sense, against America, whose total support we now had. Commanded in this war by Captain Hector Bonzo, she was an historic ship with a thousand tales to tell. But I was rather afraid this venerable armoured veteran was approaching the end of her journey. I simply could not risk her group launching an attack on us with ship-to-ship guided missiles—the same Exocets with which we in *Glamorgan* could so very easily have eliminated the USS *Coral Sea* six months ago. And should it come to the point where I considered ourselves in danger of attack, when it may be us or them, my choice was simple enough—*them*.

So now I and my team, gathered high in the "Island" of *Hermes,* had to "Appreciate the Situation," that rather grand military colloquialism for "thinking it through," in short order. Both of the Argentinian surface groups could now be less than two hundred miles away, north and south of the Falklands, outside the TEZ. The aircraft of the one, and the Exocet-carrying destroyers of the other, could both get in close to us very quickly in the present calm weather. The long southern nights gave them fifteen hours of darkness, and between now and first light there was still six hours, during which either *Belgrano* or *Veinticinco de Mayo*, or both, could have moved comfortably within range for a decisive battle which would give them, tactically, all the advantages. We assessed that we could probably shoot down five or six of the incoming Skyhawks—but that it would be very bad news if sixteen Exocets arrived from the southeast at more or less the same time. Also we wished fervently we knew a little more about the strength of the Argentinian warships in the inshore waters around East Falkland, which might have been waiting their chance to slip out and join in with the other attacks.

It was clear enough that unless we were extraordinarily lucky we could find ourselves in major trouble here, attacked from different directions, by different weapons requiring different responses, all in the half-light of a dawn which would be silhouetting us. At the very least, it was going to be a two-pronged strike, a straightforward pincer movement on us, from the southwest and the northwest. *Coral Sea* had failed to deal with a much lesser threat, with a far greater capability.

There was but one fast solution. I had to take out one claw of the pincer. It could not be the carrier, because our SSNs *Spartan* and *Superb* up there were still not in contact with her. So it would have to be the *Belgrano* and her destroyers. I am obliged to say that if *Spartan* had still been in touch with *Veinticinco de Mayo* I would have recommended in the strongest possible terms to the C-in-C that we take them both out this night. But as things were I had no right hand, just a left, and the best I could do would be to use it with as much force as I could manage.

The situation in the southwest was fairly clear. *Conqueror*, commanded by Commander Christopher Wreford-Brown, had been tracking *Belgrano* throughout the night, having picked up her tanker more or less by accident late on Friday afternoon, and had stayed close until *Belgrano* turned up to refuel. Christopher, a thirty-six-year-old former pupil of Rugby School, was married with three children and had served as my correspondence officer in *Warspite*. I knew him quite well and took some pride in the fact that I may have influenced his career in one or two minor ways during our time together. In manner he was rather shy and very restrained even in his delivery of important information. But he was very steady in controlling a situation, thoughtful, and correct. There was, I always thought, rather more to him than his obvious intelligence and courteous, rather droll manner. I could be sure enough that in battle, should it ever come to that, he would be coolly effective, even though he had only taken command of *Conqueror* a few weeks ago.

On this night, as we conferred in *Hermes,* he had come to precisely the same conclusions as we had. Remarkable, you may think, given our vastly different perspectives. But remember, we both had the same picture of what was going on, we both had the same

training, and we both had the same operational doctrine. So it's hardly surprising that Commander
Wreford-Brown was accurately tuned in to the mind
of his old boss. I may be an ex-submariner but in spirit
I am always a member of that strange brotherhood
which fights its battles from underwater. Having already put in an enormous amount of work in finding
and tracking *Belgrano* this far, Christopher privately
considered it would be a bit of a waste to do absolutely nothing. Thus he was hoping for a signal changing his Rules of Engagement, giving him permission to
attack, *outside* the Total Exclusion Zone but inside the
general warning area announced back in April, giving
him permission to attack *any* Argentinian warship,
giving him permission to sink the *General Belgrano*
and her Exocet-carrying destroyers.

He also had to ponder the intricacies of torpedoes.
He had two types, the first being the old Mark 8** of
Second World War vintage, with a fairly accurate and
very reliable close-range capability, plus a sizeable
warhead, amply powerful to penetrate the hull of the
big Argentinian cruiser and do great damage. This is
a pretty basic torpedo which travels at a pre-set depth
and on a pre-set course with no "ears" or "eyes" in
the front. Basically, it is dead stupid and runs straight
until it either hits something or runs out of fuel. It is
nothing more intelligent or subtle than a large, mo-
torized lump of TNT, which will do about forty knots
in whatever direction you fire it. It is called a "salvo"
weapon because we usually fire at least two and possibly as many as six at a go. This is done because, although it is necessary to aim as correctly as possible,
all sorts of errors can creep in to ruin your "solution"
to the torpedo attack problem: you may have mis-

judged the target's course or speed or range marginally; the target may alter course or speed after the torpedoes have left the submarine; the torpedoes themselves may not run entirely accurately. The "salvo" is also used because you may want *more* than one torpedo to hit the target, particularly if you are trying to sink a large warship, and submariners do not relish having to go back for a second attempt against heavily armed and now alert opponents. *Conqueror* also carried the wire-guided Tigerfish torpedo, a "single-shot" weapon with a longer range and the ability to be guided from the submarine all the way to the target, but which had become a cause for concern due to its rather doubtful reliability at the time. To use the Mark 8** Christopher was going to have to get in close, to less than a mile. If the attention of the two destroyers and their depth charges should be too great, he would have to give it a shot with the Tigerfish from farther out. The trick was to stay undetected, as I had taught so many of my "Perishers."

Back in *Hermes* my own view of the situation was more simple: The relatively heavy armour plating on the cruiser was such that I had only two weapons that could put her out of action—thousand-pound bombs, which would be nearly impossible to deliver, or Christopher's torpedoes. The decision was obvious. However, we had to face the added problem of the Burdwood Bank, a large area of fairly shallow water which sits on the edge of the South American continental shelf. It runs over two hundred miles from east to west, passing some hundred miles to the south of East Falkland, at which point it is about sixty miles across, north to south. Farther south, the Atlantic is more than two miles deep, but around the

Falkland Islands and inshore to the continent, the sea-bed slopes up to the continental shelf, giving a general depth of about three hundred feet. On the Bank, however, the bottom rises to shallows just one hundred and fifty feet below the surface. These shoals are quite well charted, but they can be a lethal place for a submerged submarine trying to stay with a cruiser making more than twenty-five knots through the water. To do that speed in a nuclear-powered submarine, it is necessary to run at a minimum depth of two hundred feet to avoid leaving a clear wake of disturbed water on the surface. At one hundred feet, which is where they would have to be as they crossed the shoals, they would leave a marked wake which would be fairly obvious to the hurrying surface ships.

There is then of course the additional problem of tracking an enemy: At high speed you cannot hear or see because the sonar is drowned out by the noise of the water rushing past your hull, which means you have to slow right down to listen, or come up to periscope depth to look every so often, to check your quarry has not altered course. It's a sort of Grandmother's Footsteps, with lethal consequences if you're caught. The additional problem here is time: the moment you head to the surface and your periscope breaks clear of the water, like a big broomstick, you are immediately vulnerable to detection, either by the look-outs who are trained to spot a submarine or by the enemy's radar. Thus you put a periscope up for the shortest possible time for a very quick look, and a few seconds' gulp of information. The man who looks through the periscope needs a photographic memory, and he needs to use every bit of his training

in the Perisher. Each time the submarine conducts this
time-pressured manoeuvre she loses precious speed
and distance. Thus the submariner's rule of thumb is
that you need a thirty per cent speed advantage to
trail an enemy successfully, because you have to keep
stopping. Under calm-surface conditions *Belgrano*
could probably outrun a submerged *Conqueror* without working up too much of a sweat. In a race across
the Bank I was afraid the Argentinian would be a
heavy favourite.

If the three Argentinian captains were clever they
might decide to split up and rendezvous later, closer to
the Falkland Islands, in which case we would have little chance of locating them accurately. Perhaps more
likely was the possibility of all three of them making a
dash for it, across the Bank, deep into the TEZ, knowing the near-impossibility of a submarine tracking
them among the shoals. (And remember, when we
caught the USS *Coral Sea* in *Glamorgan*, we achieved
it by means of a high-speed run, at night, from outside
her TEZ—even if we were wearing turbans.)

My conclusion: I cannot let that cruiser even stay
where she is, regardless of her present course or
speed. Whether she is inside or outside the TEZ is irrelevant. She will have to go.

Even now, in the hours before dawn, both the
General Belgrano and her escorts are heading east-
wards at about thirteen knots, which may not sound
very much, but it is a speed which would give her a
lead of well over a mile on any of the upwind legs in
the old America's Cup races for twelve-metre yachts.
She is staying about twenty or thirty miles outside
the TEZ, moving, apparently, around the perimeter,

towards us. Even at her present low speed, she and her escorts could turn up right behind us, at a range of about fifty miles, some fifteen hours from now. And under my present Rules of Engagement I can do nothing about it. As they say in New York, thanks, but no thanks.

However, deep down, I believe she would continue to creep along the back of the Bank, and then when she is informed that the carrier is ready to launch her air strike, she will angle in, on a northeasterly course, and make straight for us, the Exocets on her destroyers trained on us as soon as they are within striking range. I badly need *Conqueror* to sink her before she turns away from her present course, because if we wait for her to enter the Zone, we may well lose her, very quickly.

As we all sat in the ops room of *Hermes* that morning, I knew I had to find a way of getting the Rules of Engagement changed in order to allow Christopher Wreford-Brown to attack the *Belgrano* group as soon as possible. This, actually, was a bit of problem because the proper procedures were inclined to be rather slow and, in theory, *Belgrano* could already have changed course without my yet knowing, and five hours from now, still just before dawn, she would be in a position to attack us. The correct, formal process for any commander to alter his ROE is as follows: sit down and draft a written signal, in hard copy, which says, at length, "Here is my tactical and strategic situation. I wish to do this and that, and I am faced with this, that, and the other. My conclusion is that I need a change in my Rules of Engagement, namely permission to attack *Belgrano* group before she enters the Exclusion Zone. That is, as soon as possible. Like, now." And preferably an hour ago. Actually three hours ago by the time you get this. And eight hours ago by the time *Conqueror* gets your answer.

Of course, it all takes time: time to write, carefully and lucidly, and then, because it would be rather better if no one else heard it, the signal must go in encrypted code on to the satellite to Northwood. It will then be read by the duty officer on this quiet Sunday morning in the western suburbs of London. He will then inform the Chief of Staff, who will take it to the C-in-C, who will ring up the Ministry, and they will brief the Chief of Defence Staff, Admiral of the Fleet Sir Terence Lewin. When they have all read it, all understood it, and are all quite clear why Woodward wants to proceed with this major change in the plan, Sir Terence will then take it to the War Cabinet, for Mrs. Thatcher's final approval. Only then can the process of sending the reply start. And that can take just as long again. And *then* it might not be the reply I wanted and needed. All of which was largely hopeless from my point of view, since it could not take much less than the best part of five or six hours, by which time (unless I blatantly exceeded my ROE), we could all be swimming around in the South Atlantic, getting a bit cold, and wondering where the hell those sixteen Exocets just came from.

I thus clearly have no time to hang about writing a formal assessment. Nor yet can I risk getting the "wrong" answer. As far as I know, *Belgrano* and her escorts may already be on their way to us and, if they are, *Conqueror* is going to be so busy trying to chase her over the Bank, there is never going to be time for him to slow down, come to periscope depth, whistle up the satellite, and start exchanging formal messages to Northwood. The general drift of such a signal would have to be something like this: "*Belgrano* has changed course to the northeast. Am attempting to maintain contact. Does the change of course affect my ROE? Am I permitted to attack? Urgent advice needed." All of which would have been quite hopeless. With such a delay *Conqueror* would probably lose the cruiser altogether, just while sending the signal. Therefore the question is: How can I startle everyone at home into the required and early action? I have to get those ROEs changed exceedingly fast and to do so I instituted the formal process by getting Jeremy Sanders to get on to DSSS and spell out to the Duty Officer at Northwood precisely what my feelings were. Meanwhile I immediately put on to the satellite my permission to *Conqueror* to attack immediately. The signal read: "From CTG [Commander Task Group] 317.8, to *Conqueror*, text priority *flash*—attack *Belgrano* group."

Now, I knew that the captain of *Conqueror* would know that I was not empowered to give him that order—you will recall that the submarines were being run from London (against my advice). Thus I could expect a very definite set of circumstances to break out upon receipt of my signal. For a start Northwood would read it. Having then seen what I had done, the flag officer submarines, Admiral Sir Peter Herbert, my old boss in *Valiant*, would know beyond any shadow of a doubt that I must be deadly serious. It would serve as the strongest possible reinforcement of the formal request being prepared now by Jeremy Sanders in readiness for his phone call home. What is more, my signal will be in London in the next twenty minutes, which should provide them all with an interesting jolt at six o'clock in the morning.

As it happened Peter Herbert's staff read my signal and immediately took it off the satellite, in order that *Conqueror* should not receive it, which indeed she didn't. I had quite clearly exceeded my authority by altering the ROE of a British submarine to allow it to attack an Argentinian ship well *outside* the TEZ. Such a breach of naval discipline can imply only two things—either Woodward has gone off his head, or Woodward knows exactly what he is doing and is in a very great hurry. I rather hoped they would trust my sanity, particularly because there is always another aspect to such a set of circumstances—that is, should the politicians consider it impossible for the international community to approve the sinking of a big cruiser, with possible subsequent great loss of life, I had given them the opportunity to let it run and then blame me, should that prove convenient. I quite understood it might be extremely difficult for them to give what some were bound to see as a ruthless order. Indeed I am keenly aware that there are some things politicians simply cannot do, no matter what the extenuating circumstances may be. But now they could do it. And if it went wrong, I was there to be blamed. But if it went right, they could take the credit.

Actually I had intended the signal to get as far as the Commander-in-Chief, Sir John Fieldhouse, and I had rather expected he would personally recommend that it should run, given the urgency of my message. FOSM had pre-empted me a bit, by pulling the order off the satellite. Nonetheless I imagine they immediately went to the C-in-C and said: "Look what Woodward's done." This, I am quite sure, would have gingered him up, and caused him to go to Admiral Lewin and tell him, "Look, Woodward means this. They need a change in the Rules of Engagement out there. Fast."

Whatever the true process back home actually turned out to be, this was how I saw it happening. Suffice it to say, by the time the War Cabinet met at ten o'clock in the morning at Chequers everyone was apprised of the situation. After quick but careful consideration of the military advice, the Prime Minister and the War Cabinet authorized changes to the ROE which would permit *Conqueror* to attack the *Belgrano* group. I do not suppose it occurred to Mrs. Thatcher for one moment, certainly it did not occur to me, that in a very few months from then a certain section of the House of Commons would endeavour to prove that this was a decision which could only have been perpetrated by a callous warmonger, or at least a group of callous warmongers, of which I was very much one. But political thinking and military thinking are often diverse, even when both sets of executives are on the same side, with overwhelming public support. And, by necessity, the military commander under the threat of missile attack is required to be more crisp than someone thinking the matter over some weeks later in front of the fire in a country house in the south of Scotland.

My own case is simply stated, because it comes from the same folklore as that followed by Admiral Nelson, Admiral Jervis, Admiral Hood, Admiral Jellicoe, and Admiral Cunningham. The speed and direction of an enemy ship can be irrelevant, because both can *change* quickly. What counts is his position, his capability, and what I believe to be his intention.

At O745Z on 2 May my signal had gone and Jer-

emy Sanders had talked very succinctly to the duty
officer at Northwood. There was little more to be
done about the *Belgrano* except await the outcome.
By now the anti-submarine group were back, as were
Glamorgan and her group. I felt we were a bit less
exposed, but I was still irked by the fact that the other
submarines—not *Conqueror*—were somehow unable
to find the Argentinian carrier.

We were positioned some eighty miles east of Port
Stanley and as prepared as we could be to receive a
dawn strike by the aircraft from the deck of the *Veinticinco de Mayo*. I deployed the three Type 42s *Sheffield*, *Coventry*, and *Glasgow* some thirty miles
up-threat as our front-line defence, the picket line.
Much, I thought, would depend on the speed of the
reactions of their ops rooms. The bigger "County"
Class destroyer *Glamorgan*, her guns only just cooled
from the night bombardment, was positioned in an
inner anti-aircraft screen—and if necessary, an anti-
submarine screen—with the frigates *Yarmouth*, *Alac-
rity*, and *Arrow*. They would form the second line of
defence in front of the two Royal Fleet Auxiliaries *Ol-
meda* and *Resource*, which would take up a position
near *Hermes* and *Invincible*. Each of the carriers
would operate in company with a "goalkeeper," one of
the Type 22 frigates. Ours would be Captain Bill Can-
ning's *Broadsword*, while *Invincible* would operate
with John Coward's *Brilliant*. The latter combination
packed enormous punch, because Coward was likely
to be extremely quick off the mark with his Sea Wolf
missile system, and *Invincible* carried a Sea Dart system. We did not have any airborne early warning radars to assist the pickets, which meant our maximum
radar range against low-fliers, from the Type 42s, was

about forty-five miles out from *Hermes*. We would of course fly constant combat air patrols from the decks of both carriers, but with the Skyhawks coming in very fast, at wave-top height, I thought we might have our work cut out to down all ten of them.

And so we waited, all of us very much alert for a coordinated air and sea attack from almost any direction. But, to our surprise and relief, it never materialized. Sea Harrier probes to the northwest found nothing.

Out here in the notoriously windswept South Atlantic, what we had not even considered had happened: with winter approaching, the air was absolutely still. And the Args could not get their fully laden aircraft off the deck without at least some natural wind, regardless of their own speed through the water into the breeze. With daylight approaching, the constant threat of our SSNs finally catching up with them and the slowly growing realization that we were not in fact about to put the Royal Marines on the beach at Port Stanley, they wisely turned for home and safety, though of course, we did not know it.

By 1130, however, we were fairly sure the carrier group had in some way withdrawn, simply because no air attack had arrived. We regrouped after a quick lunch to decide what time we should once more head west towards the islands for our second night of recce insertion, and at that time the scene switched very decisively to *Conqueror*. I should mention here that I knew nothing more about the subsequent activities of the submarine for many hours. In the ensuing months and years since the war, I have pieced together from the people most closely concerned what happened on that chill but windless Sunday afternoon.

I cannot, as a submariner myself, resist providing some detail of one of the more riveting days in the history of the submarine service.

We now know that at 0810Z *Belgrano* and her escorts reversed course, and were in fact on their way home. But they headed back to the west on a gentle zigzag, not apparently in any great hurry or with any obvious purpose. When I became aware of their westerly course that afternoon, I still had no reliable evidence as to their intentions. For all I knew they might have received a signal telling them to return to base; but perhaps they had only been told to wait and come back tonight; perhaps they hadn't been told anything. But if I had been told to return to base, I wouldn't hang about, that was for sure. I'd get on with it, PDQ. Either way, *Conqueror* trailed her all morning. At 1330Z, she accessed the satellite and received the signal from Northwood changing her Rules of Engagement. Commander Wreford-Brown had, apart from self-defence, thus far been permitted to attack the Argentinian aircraft carrier and, within the TEZ only, other Argentine combat ships. The change said quite clearly he may now attack the *Belgrano*, outside the TEZ.

Actually the significance of this change was clear to all the British ships *except* poor old *Conqueror*, the only one that really needed to know it. They had, unfortunately, a very dicky radio mast that kept going wrong, and they could not make sense of the signal. Neither could they hang around indefinitely, at slow speed with masts up, trying to re-access the satellite. The danger of losing the *Belgrano* was too great. Commander Wreford-Brown went deep and fast again to continue the pursuit and all afternoon they tried to fix the mast, as they trailed the Argentinians, furtively, through the depths of those grey seas, south of the Burdwood Bank. At 1730 *Conqueror* came up again, accessed the satellite once more to get a re-run of their signal, and this time they could read it.

The captain took a careful look at the *Belgrano* and the two destroyers before going deep to try to catch them up from his position some seven miles astern of the cruiser and her escorts. The Argentinians were steaming in a V-formation, *Belgrano* to the south, with one destroyer positioned about half a mile off her starboard bow, the other one a mile off her starboard beam. As an anti-submarine formation the British captain considered it "pretty pathetic, especially as the ships were largely obsolete, and the crews were displaying a fairly minimal amount of skill." They did not, in fact, even have their sonars switched on.

In retrospect I am inclined to go along with Christopher's assessment: had I been the captain of the *General Belgrano*, I would have been doing many things differently at this time. For a start I would have had my two escorts positioned on my port and starboard quarters using intermittent active sonar, rather than have them both, passively, to my north. Also I would never have been dawdling along at thirteen knots for hours on end, if my fuel state remotely allowed it. Rather I would have been zigzagging determinedly and varying my speed quite dramatically, occasionally speeding up to twenty-five or more knots, making it much more difficult for a shadowing submarine to stay with me. At other times I would have slowed right down, making it equally hard for a shadowing submarine to hear me, but allowing me perhaps to hear *him* charging along in the rear making a noise like an express train. Finally, I would have edged up towards the Burdwood Bank, thereby making it less likely that an SSN would approach from that direction and enabling me to put my escorts in a better place.

Captain Hector Bonzo was doing none of this. He was no submariner, nor had he any experience of what SSNs could or could not do. He had not thought it through, and all the while, right on his stern, there was *Conqueror*, following in a standard sprint-and-drift pursuit—running deep at eighteen knots for fifteen or twenty minutes, then coming up for a few minutes to get another visual setup to update the operations plot for the fire-control officer. Every time they came up, they reduced speed to five knots or so, which of course lost them ground as they "drifted," but they made it up again in the eighteen-knot "sprint."

It was approaching 1830 when the British submarine captain judged they were close enough for the final approach, at a range of just over two miles. He went deep at high speed to take a long left-hand swing so as to come up on the port side of the Argentinian cruiser. He wanted to fire his torpedoes from a position just forward of her beam, at a range of about two thousand yards. Having had plenty of time for solid thought, Christopher had decided to use the Mark 8** direct, straight-running torpedoes. The tubes were loaded with three of them, but he had also taken the precaution of loading three Tigerfish just in case it should prove impossible to get in close enough.

By 1857, *Conqueror*'s captain estimated he could

turn in for the firing position, and come to periscope depth for the final fire-control setup. Up forward, in the torpedo space, they were making ready to fire three Mark 8** torpedoes in the standard fan formation, with each of them aimed off, ahead of the *Belgrano* sufficiently to ensure that torpedo and ship would meet in the identical patch of water.

The tension throughout the submarine was high, as the sonar operators listened carefully to the continuing steady beat of *Belgrano*'s three-bladed propellers . . . "*Chuff*-chuff-chuff . . . *chuff*-chuff-chuff" . . . rising and falling in the long Atlantic swells, slightly fainter as the stern ploughed deeper. In the control room, Commander Wreford-Brown ordered *Conqueror* to periscope depth—and, as the "eyes" of the submarine came up out of the floor with that familiar "Whoosh!," his hands grabbed for the handles before they reached knee level, ducking down to use every precious second of sight. (Remember the manhole in Piccadilly Circus I told you about during the Perisher Course? Commander Wreford-Brown was now in it.) Time was running out for the big, grey, American-built veteran of Pearl Harbor.

He called out bearing, then the range—"Three-three-five . . . Thirteen-eighty yards"—then under his breath he said, "Damn. Too close." But there was no time to correct that. He hesitated for a few more seconds, as *Conqueror* slid forward, now on a perfect ninety-degree angle to the Argentinian ship. Then he called out the final order to his fire controller: "Shoot."

The sonar recorded the double-thump as the first torpedo was discharged from its tube and then the high-pitched whine as the torpedo's engine started up and it accelerated away at forty knots. *Conqueror* shuddered. Seven seconds later there was another, then another. As the whine of the third torpedo died away there was again silence, save for the "*Chuff*-chuff-chuff . . . *chuff*-chuff-chuff" which had been with the British sonar operators for so long.

The seconds ticked by, and the big cruiser steamed on, still at thirteen knots, moving ever closer to the fatal patch of water the British captain had selected. Fifty-five seconds after the first launch, number one Mark 8** smashed into the port bow of the *General Belgrano*, aft of the anchor but forward of her first gun turret. Very nearly blew the entire bow of the ship off. Through the periscope, Christopher Wreford-Brown was astonished to see a big flash light up the sky.

Conqueror's sonar operator matter-of-factly reported in the same tone of voice you might count sheep, "Explosion . . ." Then came, ". . . Second explosion . . ." Three more reverberating explosions combined the sound of the "echoes" with the two torpedoes which struck home, the second one hitting below the after superstructure. The last of the explosions sounded different, more distant, more metallic, lighter. One of the escorts, the destroyer *Bouchard*, said later that she had been hit a glancing blow by a torpedo which had not gone off.

It had been, by any standards, a textbook operation by Christopher Wreford-Brown and his team, which is probably why it all sounds so simple, almost as if anyone could have done it. The best military actions always do. As the young commander said rather dryly some months later, "The Royal Navy spent thirteen years preparing me for such an occasion. It would have been regarded as extremely dreary if I had fouled it up."

Back in *Conqueror* they all heard the unforgettable impact of the strike and knew their torpedoes had hit something. Then, as the noise subsided, for the first time for twenty-four hours the "*Chuff*-chuff-chuff" of the enemy's propellers had gone. There was only silence, save for an eerie tinkling sound on the sonar, like breaking glass or metal, echoing back through the water, like the far-lost chiming of the bells of hell. So sounds the noise of a big ship breaking apart on a modern sonar.

Every Argentinian account since has reported a "fireball" rushing through the ship, in which three hundred and twenty-one men were lost. Which suggests the cruiser was ill-prepared for war. If the blast did travel so quickly in this way it must have been because too many bulkhead doors and hatches had been left open, rather than kept tight shut, with their clips on, in readiness to hold back both fire and water. Keeping hatches and doors properly shut is domestically inconvenient because it can then take about fifteen minutes to get from one end of the ship to the other, unlocking, unclipping every door to get through, then clipping up behind you. Captain Hector Bonzo learned to his cost that if you are in the process of invading another country's islands, and they are, in turn, not pleased with you, it is probably best to remain in a fairly efficient defensive position. But he was acting in a way which suggested he believed he was in no real danger, despite receiving a warning a few days before, from the British government, that Argentinian ships posing any threat to the business of the British Fleet would be sunk, provided only that they chose to go outside the mainland twelve-mile limit. Here, perhaps, was a man who had not yet quite accepted the reality of the situation we were now all in, and of course he was not alone in his attitude.

On board *Belgrano* the flames, the heat, and the damage were merciless, beyond control, and totally ill-contained. Sea water flooding in quickly shut down all power, a combination of fire and water shut down the auxiliary generators, which in sequence shut down the anti-flooding pumps and the fire-fighting emergency equipment. All the lights failed, and the communications systems crashed simultaneously. The captain and eight hundred and seventy-nine of his company managed to abandon the now darkened ship, and it took half an hour for them all to find their way into the inflatable life rafts. A quarter of an hour after Captain Bonzo left the deck, the *General Belgrano* rolled over on her port side and her stern rose high into the air as she pitched forward and sank. Packed into the surrounding life rafts, almost nine hundred of her crew, some of whom would not survive this freezing night, sang the Argentinian National Anthem as she went. I am always startled by the emotions the Malvinas can stir in the breast of an Argentinian. For us this campaign was a tough and demanding job on behalf of our government. For them it was something close to a holy war.

Commander Wreford-Brown, whose nearest experience to such an event had been on exercises from Faslane, was almost overcome by an immediate instinct to wipe the sweat from his brow, pack up, and have a cup of tea, before setting about collecting all the copious records required to establish whether his "attack" had been successful or not. But that lasted for all of a split second, as reality returned. There were a few urgent tasks to accomplish: first, avoid the destroyers, get clear—fast. That means deep, too. Rudder hard over, down they went and away to the southeast, away from the chaos that always surrounds a stricken warship, away from the retribution the surviving ships will hope to exact.

Within a few minutes the sonar operators heard three explosions which the captain assessed to be depth charges from the Argentinian destroyers. They sounded fairly close. Your first one always does. But this was no time to be curious, so he ran on, still deep, for four or five more miles until the Argentinians faded astern. He wondered, perhaps warming to his new task, whether to go back and have another shot, perhaps sink the other two. However, discretion proved the better part of valour and he elected to ensure that *Conqueror* stayed in one piece rather than engage in further heroics on this particular day. In the intervening years he has refined that view yet further. "In retrospect," he told me recently, "I do not suppose Mrs. Thatcher would have thanked me all that much if I had reloaded and hit the other two ships." An opinion I would have assessed as more or less faultless because, as far as I knew, he only had permission to fire at the *Belgrano* anyway. I have to add that Christopher is equally sure that he had received permission to attack *any* Argentinian warship anywhere up to the twelve-mile limit of her shores. I am always amazed at how two trained observers can harbour totally opposed views on a "simple fact"! And even more so if it turns out that I am the one who is wrong.

Indeed Commander Wreford-Brown did return on the following day and saw the two destroyers, quite a way southeast by now, because of the wind and current, helping with the search and rescue of the many Argentinian survivors. But they were engaged on a mission of mercy now, not war, and Christopher Wreford-Brown turned *Conqueror* away, and left them to their unenviable task.

From my own perspective, it was rather a disjointed sort of day. Of course we were unaware of the activities of *Conqueror*, just as they knew nothing of our preoccupation with the possible attack from the Argentinian carrier. In turn neither of us knew, at that time, what was in the minds of the Argentinian High Command. In fact, by 0900 Argentinian time it was clear to them that the wind would not return in the next few hours and the dawn strike against us, which was very definitely planned, was called off. *Veinticinco de Mayo* and her escorts were ordered back to the mainland. At more or less the same time, the *General Belgrano* was also ordered to return to base. She was already steaming west and she was merely ordered to keep on going. Admiral Anaya, faced with the nonfunctioning of one of his "pincers," quite reasonably decided to cancel the whole operation.

We of course knew nothing of this. Thus, as that Sunday morning wore on, we continued to search to the north and northwest for signs of an incoming attack, trusting that *Conqueror* would deal with the threat from the south. I kept the Group in a high state of anti–air warfare readiness, at least until the afternoon when we began to head west in preparation for the recce insertion that night. At 2200 I once more detached *Glamorgan* and her group to bombard the Argentinian positions around Port Stanley, with the intention of maintaining their belief that we were about to land in the Port Stanley area and still in hopes of defeating their Fleet, now on the following day.

It was not until 2245 that we received a signal from Northwood to tell us that HMS *Conqueror* had sunk the *General Belgrano*. We received the news without excitement. There was only temporary relief that the threat from the southwest had, for the moment, diminished. I did, however, realize that this news would make all kinds of headlines back home and that it would be immensely good for morale. Not wishing to rain on this particular parade, Northwood recommended that I recall *Glamorgan* and the two frigates, in case one of them should be lost. I agreed. Probably just as well too. On the face of it, it had been another moderately successful day for us: we were still more or less intact, and we had reduced the sea threat to the Battle Group by one cruiser. We were not to know for weeks that the effects of *Belgrano*'s sinking would be so all-embracing. Even as we planned our next activities, late that night, the entire Argentinian fleet was on the move. The two destroyers in the south were on their way back to Porto Belgrano, the carrier and her Type 42s were heading back towards the River Plate, and the three other frigates had also made an about-turn and were heading west for home.

What no one knew then was that Christopher Wreford-Brown's old Mark 8** torpedoes, appropriately as old in design as the *Belgrano* herself, had sent the navy of Argentina home for good. Unwittingly we had achieved at least half of what we had set out to do from those days at Ascension: we had made the Argentinians send out their fleet and a single sinking by a British SSN had then defeated it. We would never see any of their big warships again.

ACCIDENT ON *K-219*

FROM *Hostile Waters*

**by Captain Peter Huchthausen,
Captain First Rank Igor Kurdin, Russian Navy,
and R. Alan White**

A trio of sailors and writers combined to create the gripping narrative *Hostile Waters*, one of the most thrilling accounts of submarines and superpowers during the Cold War. Captain Peter Huchthausen, U.S. Navy (Ret.), has had a distinguished career serving at sea and on land as a Soviet naval analyst and as a naval attaché in Yugoslavia, Romania, and the Soviet Union. During the Vietnam conflict, he rescued a badly injured Vietnamese child in the Mekong Delta, only to lose her during the Tet Offensive. They were reunited years later, when he was able to sponsor her immigration to the United States, and the entire incredible story is chronicled in his book *Echoes of the Mekong*. He is now a consultant and writer, and is the author of the bestselling *Hostile Waters*, along with his nonfiction books *October Fury*, *Shadow Voyage*, *America's Splendid Little Wars*, and *K-19: The Widowmaker*, among others.

Captain First Rank Igor Kurdin saw the ill-fated *K-219* off from the dock on its last voyage. A Russian submarine officer who had served aboard the outdated nuclear submarine, Kurdin later provided hours of interviews with various crew members, myriad photographs, and other factual material, which Peter Huchthausen translated for their book *Hostile Waters*. Currently he is the chairman of the St. Petersburg Submariners Club, founded to honor the valiant men aboard the *Kursk* and their families.

In addition to his work on *Hostile Waters*, R. Alan White has written five thrillers, including *Siberian Light*, *Typhoon*, and *The Ice Curtain*. He currently lives with his wife near Monterey, California.

Like any other piece of modern equipment, a nuclear submarine is a vast, complicated, self-contained environment made up of dozens of interlocking systems that all must work perfectly in order for the vessel and its crew to perform their duties. When an obsolete, decrepit Yankee-class submarine puts out to sea staffed with new submariners on their first patrol and faulty systems, the results can be catastrophic. In the following pages, the first major problem with *K-219*'s weapons systems reaches critical mass, putting everyone on board in danger, and bringing the U.S. and the U.S.S.R. one step closer to all out war in the deep freeze of the Cold War of the 1980s.

In compartment four, Weapons Officer Petrachkov felt the sudden onset of the Crazy Ivan and grabbed at the catwalk railing.

Voroblev said, "What's he—"

An instant later the water-level alarm shrieked. Petrachkov stood there for a moment, stunned, then looked at the gauge for silo six.

It showed forty liters. Full.

"Pump it!" Voroblev shouted.

He screamed to the missilemen below, "Pump silo six now!" Then he vaulted down the ladder to help line up the valves and pumps. He landed on his knees and frantically spun the valves on the suction line, then slammed his fist into the black rubber start button on the pump. It started to whir.

He jumped to cut off the alarm. As he did, he saw the chemical-fume detector at full deflection, red-lined. A new alarm began to sound.

Seawater and missile fuel had found one another. Nitric acid was the result. Acid that even now could be eating into the pressurized vitals of the RSM-25 rocket. An explosion could happen any second.

Only venting the missile tube to the sea could save them.

Petrachkov grabbed the intercom microphone. "Control! This is Petrachkov in four! We have a major seawater leak in tube six! There's gas! I have to vent it! Give us fifty meters! I'm disengaging the hatch cover!" He threw the *kashtan* down. He threw open the panel on the missile tube control board, flipped open the red switch cover marked Six, and turned the red handle inside.

Outside on the pressure hull, high-pressure air began to turn the missile-hatch cover mechanism to the unlocked position. The chemical-fume alarm was blaring. Petrachkov listened for the rumble of air escaping the open hatch. It didn't come. "All of you!" he shouted to the stunned missilemen. "Put on your masks now! Get them on!"

From the bottom level smoking cubicle, the executive officer sprinted forward to his battle station in the central command post. Markov, the communications officer, lingered slightly too long. He didn't make it to the hatch before all watertight hatches were sealed. It clanged shut in his face. The two lounging cooks vanished back aft to compartment five. Voroblev, the damage-control specialist, stood by silo six at the upper level, his hand on the cold steel.

The process of opening the silo's muzzle hatch was automatic. Once begun it could not be stopped. But it took five minutes to complete. It was 0532, Moscow time.

"General Alarm!" Britanov shouted, all thoughts of the American submarine gone now. "Make depth for fifty meters!"

The planesman pulled his joystick back, heading the submarine up as sharply as she'd dived not a few moments ago. The hull creaked, her bulkheads groaned as the crushing pressures shifted.

———

Political Officer Sergiyenko was holding on to the hatch coaming leading into the mess area for dear life as the submarine planed steeply up. He could hear the engines laboring, the propellers speeding. He could hear the alarm from somewhere forward.

Forward was compartment four, the missile room.

The deck slanted up alarmingly. Suddenly, on the far side of the mess deck, the hatch to the missile room slammed open and Weapons Officer Petrachkov appeared along with Lieutenant Markov.

"Gas! Everyone clear out of here now!" He dived back into compartment four. Markov remained in the mess area.

After a stunned second, the sleepy men bolted from the mess, heading aft, away from the missiles, nearly trampling the political officer as they ran. Sergiyenko knew he should do something, that he should somehow take command. He was a representative of the Party, after all. But the words wouldn't come, nor would his feet obey him. He was frozen, panicked.

Captain Britanov's voice exploded over the intercom. His tone was completely different from the one he used in drills. It terrified Sergiyenko.

"Battle stations! Battle stations! Toxic gas in silo six! This is not a drill!"

The submarine was still pointed uphill when a massive detonation boomed through the hull. The lights blinked out at once. The battle lanterns flickered and once again went black. The deck fell away beneath Sergiyenko's feet as the boat stopped her rise and began, instead, to dive. As he held on to the edge of the hatch, he could hear water rushing in someplace nearby, flooding this dark, doomed pipe plunging out of control to the bottom of the sea.

The rolling detonation blasted the partially open missile hatch open and reverberated like thunder through the wounded submarine. The command post battle lamps remained lit.

Britanov had to hold on to a steel handle to keep his feet beneath him; the deck was plunging at an acute angle.

"Planes full up!" he ordered.

"Depth one hundred meters." The planesman had the joysticks full back, trying to arrest the dive. "My planes are full up. No response."

"Engines!" barked Britanov. "Turns for twenty knots! No. Make that all ahead full, both engines."

"All ahead full!"

Navigator Aznabaev heard the shouts, the alarms. He felt the steepness of the dive, the creaks and groans of steel squeezed by the increasing water pressure.

"Two hundred meters, Captain," said the planesman. "Still diving."

"Get ready to blow all tanks—"

"Depth two hundred and forty meters!"

How deep would they go before they pulled out—

"Three hundred meters, Captain!"

The navigator's hands shook as he plotted their position from the inertial navigation system: four hundred fifty miles northeast of Bermuda.

It was 0538 Moscow time, and *K-219*, oldest member of the NAVAGA class of ballistic-missile submarines still in operation, had just hours to live.

The chemical explosion inside silo six ejected the
smashed remains of the RSM-25 rocket and its two
warheads into the sea. Some of the high explosive
surrounding the warheads' plutonium cores also detonated, scattering radioactive debris both into the ocean
and down the shattered silo. The blast caused the silo's
thick steel skin to split like an overripe banana. A cata-
ract of seawater, plutonium fragments, and spilled
missile fuel roared through the fissure. Its thunder
drowned the screams of men and the groans of the
hull as *K-219* plunged out of control. The bottom of
the Hatteras Abyss lay three and a half miles below
her keel.

The battle lamps in compartment four came on
automatically at the loss of main power. But almost at
once they began to dim.

Two missilemen from the mid-deck scrambled
down the ladder to the lower level to get away from
the site of the explosion and the high-pressure stream
of water. But down at the bottom near the officers'
smoking cubicle, the water was already to their knees.
Above it swirled an acrid brown vapor. The two missilemen started to cough, then retch. Both men
snatched at their waist pouches and pulled out their
masks. They managed to get them on and plugged into
the central oxygen manifold as the water rose around
their legs. Clean oxygen began to blow, but they had
breathed too much of the strange brown mist. Their
lungs began to fill with mucus, the wet tissues seared
by nitric acid. A green foam flecked with red blood
rose up their throats. First one, then the other, fell
unconscious to the deck.

———

"Helm!" Britanov shouted. "Full speed on both engines!"

"Sir! Engines are both full! We're only making fifteen knots!"

"Depth now three hundred fifty meters!"

Fifteen knots? Why so slow? They needed speed to energize the diving planes. Something was slowing them down. Drag? A propeller problem? There were too many possibilities and no time to figure it out. "Blow the bow tanks."

"Blowing bow ballast!"

A *whoosh* came from the forward ballast tanks as high-pressure air forced out seawater. In theory, it would raise the bow and permit the engines to pull the sub out of her dive. Britanov swayed as he held on to a steel handle. The submarine was shuddering violently as engine rpm surged. Steam from one reactor was driving both screws.

The planesman had the joystick that controlled the planes full back. The depth gauge raced in reverse. "No response!" *K-219* still had her bow pointed at the bottom.

"Gennady!" Britanov shouted to the propulsion engineer. "I need the port reactor on-line!"

"I'm already working on it," said the unflappable Kapitulsky. The blast had spun the propulsion engineer in his swivel chair away from the main reactor control panel. It left him facing a depth gauge which did not contain good news. The starboard reactor was feeding maximum steam pressure to both turbines. But he could double the amount of power by bringing the port reactor on-line. It was a process that normally took five hours, but that was only if you wanted to do it safely. He was cutting corners with every switch, every button, every valve he operated.

Kapitulsky knew the port reactor's power might be needed, and very soon.

He continued the sequence, his hands flying over the panel even before his brain knew what it was he was pushing, pulling, and switching. He activated the primary and secondary coolant heaters, then before the necessary temperature rise, he punched the button that started the reactor's electric circulator pumps.

An alarm went oft. The coolant was still too cold. Thermal shock had split more than one reactor and had killed more than one Soviet sailor. But that was theoretical. *K-219* had more immediate concerns.

"What's wrong, Gennady?" Britanov called.

"Don't worry about it!" It was just a reactor alarm, a sound that would have sent men running anywhere but here. He selected the first bank of reactor quench baffles, the control rods used to smother the nuclear fires, and commanded them to retract.

Glowing in the light of the battle lamps, a beautiful woman in an ad for French lingerie gazed down on him like an angel. Did angels really look like that? As he raised the second bank of quench baffles, he realized that he might just have an opportunity to find out.

Alarms were being triggered in the central command post too fast to respond to them; the port reactor was too cold, there were fumes invading compartment four. The newest one warned of radiation in the missile room. That meant the blast had destroyed at least one of the RSM-25 rockets, and its plutonium warheads were scattered in pieces inside the submarine. Plutonium was the most deadly poison known to man, though at the moment Britanov doubted they'd live long enough to die from it.

"Depth three hundred eighty meters!"

Britanov's brain was mired, the images came too fast, his reactions too slow. He sensed the first tendrils of surrender. The feeling those lost in the snow sometimes had, when the endless white is like a warm feather bed, beckoning you down to rest, to sleep, to give in. It wasn't going to work. They were sinking deeper and deeper; the flood of water he could hear from where he stood would get worse as the outside pressures on the hull increased. At some point, the sea would simply crush them.

Britanov looked up at the small framed plaque that had caused so much consternation to the boat's political officer. *Submarine Life Is Not a Service, But a Religion.* No. He could not surrender. Not yet. This was his command. These men were his responsibility. He'd vowed to bring them home alive.

The dive made Britanov light on his feet in just the same way a dropping elevator gave the illusion of no gravity. It was like floating, floating upward even as ten thousand tons of low-magnetic steel and 119 men plunged deeper into the lightless deep.

"She's still going down!"

"Captain!" called the planesman, panic in his voice. Britanov looked up. The CCP watch all stared at him. Sonar, the planesman, Helm. Everyone. "All right," he said. "Blow the tanks."

"Which tanks do you—"

"Everything!" he ordered. *"Blow all tanks! Emergency surface!"*

Britanov didn't know how much water she had
taken in through compartment four. He didn't know
whether blowing all ballast would be enough to offset
the damage. It might take every liter of high-pressure
air they had. For all he knew the lines themselves were
ruptured and all he would accomplish was pumping
precious air into the sea. But he had to try. He would
not surrender. He would fight.

All that was left for him, for his crew, was to wait
and see if it would be enough.

In compartment four, Missile Officer Petrachkov
fought his way through a torrent of cascading water
to the mid-deck intercom station to report the damage
from the explosion. He was soaked to the waist and
breathing heavily. At some point he must have noticed
the strange smell: a sharp, acid odor mixed with the
sickly sweet scent of bitter almonds. In the dim light
cast by the few working battle lamps, swirling brown
mist hung low to the decks, curling evil tendrils up
and into the main air vents.

He began to cough. Petrachkov didn't need the
damage control officer to tell him what had happened.
The brown mist was spilled missile fuel reacting with
seawater. He was splashing through an appalling cock-
tail of flammable poison. And the scent of bitter almonds was nitric acid. Petrachkov pulled a rubber
mask from his waist pouch and put it on. He tried to
plug the end of the hose into the central manifold, but
for some reason he was having trouble seeing it.

The coughing became worse. He yanked the hose
out and tried to screw the fitting onto his OBA canister. He gasped, then retched. First it was dry heaves,

then wet, then burning, then agony. He staggered against a bulkhead as an evil green foam rose from his lungs and filled his throat with fire. He opened his mouth and the green bubbles flowed into his mask. He was drowning, drowning, not from the sea but from the foam filling his lungs, his throat, his nostrils. He spat it out but more came. Petrachkov couldn't breathe. He sank to his knees below the intercom as the last dim battle lamp winked dark.

In compartment five, immediately aft of the flooding missile room, Dr. Igor Kochergin picked himself up off the deck. The explosion had tossed him out of his bunk and thrown him against the ceiling of sick bay. He ended up huddled against the forward bulkhead, the one separating his cabin from whatever was happening in the missile room.

For ten seconds the deck dropped from under him. He could hear the loud creaks and groans as the submarine's skin and bulkheads were squeezed by building water pressure. The lights were out, the battle lamps dead.

The twenty-eight-year-old lieutenant from Leningrad pushed away from the bulkhead. He hunted in the dark for his slippers, feeling the strange way the deck plates were now no longer flat, but buckled upward. He could still hear the roar of water flooding into compartment four as well as the clank and thud of the engines from astern.

He found his slippers and put them on, then sat back against his bunk in the darkness, his brain mired in shock at the nearness of death. Miraculously, the sick bay battle lamp switched itself on.

Although it was the doctor's first submarine cruise since graduating from Naval Medical School, he could tell from the strange sensation of falling that the submarine was diving more steeply than he had ever felt her dive before. He knew from training that the water would crush them eventually, perhaps at a depth sufficient to compress the remaining air pockets and ignite them in a flash of fire. To be incinerated at the bottom of the sea, that was surely a curious way to die. He stared dumbly, his eyes hollow. Only after a few moments did his brain register what he was looking at.

His desk drawer hung open, pulled out by the submarine's acute dive. But on top of the desk stood a small glass dish with a sprig of evergreens in it, unmoved by blast or the steep deck angle. His eight-month-old son had given him the tiny branch the day they'd sailed from Gadzhievo and he'd kept it fresh for nearly a month. He could hear his son's voice, see his wife, Galina, their apartment in a gray concrete complex that overlooked the harbor, and from which you could sometimes see the mouth of the fjord itself. All from this tiny piece of green. In some way he did not understand, it gave him courage.

He stood, sliding on the angled, buckled deck, and started putting sick bay back together. The cabin was the size of a dentist's operating room. He closed his desk and locked it shut, opened his medical kit, found his supply of OBA canisters and rubber fume masks, and spread all the equipment he thought he might need out on his bunk. When his assistant, a conscript with barely six months' training, came in looking pale, Dr. Igor Kochergin was ready for customers.

"Captain! Helm is answering!"

"Depth now three hundred fifty meters."

"Mother of God," someone whispered. "*We're going up!*"

A cheer went up in the central command post. But Britanov knew it was premature. New alarms were still going off. The precise nature of the explosion was not yet identified, and they were still taking on water. But it was no small victory that the bow continued to rise under the influence of the pounding screws and the fully deflected diving planes.

"Where's Voroblev?" Britanov demanded. He needed his damage-control specialist at his side.

"Compartment four, Comrade Captain," said someone. "Petrachkov called for him."

Compartment four. Was Voroblev even alive? Was Petrachkov? What had happened to his submarine? The fume alarm meant a chemical explosion had taken place. The radioactivity alarm meant the blast had damaged at least one of *K-219*'s fifteen missiles. The water meant a hull breach. Fumes, plutonium, and flooding. If even one of those was true it was too soon for cheering.

With one hand holding on to the steel handle to keep his balance, Britanov grabbed the *kashtan* microphone and tried to calm his breathing and his voice before he spoke. He took a long, deep breath, then let it out.

"This is the captain. All compartments report! Set the emergency damage-control bill! Report from compartment four!" The words came automatically, without any thinking, the result of years and years of practice and drilling, all against a moment like this. But those were drills.

"Compartment one is manned and ready," came the quick reply from the forwardmost space. "No damage, no casualties."

"Two is manned and ready and very busy just now," said Propulsion Engineer Kapitulsky. "You'll have more power soon if we don't blow up or sink first."

"Helm?"

"Depth two hundred meters, Captain. Still rising. Speed eighteen knots."

The CCP watch team was beginning to function again. "Keep us heading up. All the way." Not that he could stop them. With her ballast tanks filled with air, nothing could keep them from bobbing to the surface now. It was the end of the patrol for certain. The only thing that remained to be seen was whether they could save the boat, and to see what the butcher's bill already totaled.

"Compartment four, report," he said.

There was no reply.

"Compartment four, answer."

"They must have evacuated it," said someone.

Britanov nodded, but he was thinking of the blast, the flooding. There could be twenty men inside compartment four. More if some off-duty crew were caught in there. How many of them were—

"One hundred meters depth, Captain."

The bulkheads creaked and groaned as the sea's fist slowly relaxed. Dust rose into the air, and loose gear not already knocked to the deck by the blast and the dive slid off in a clatter. The battle lamps blinked.

Chief Engineer Krasilnikov swore as his hands flew over the main power distribution panel. The lights faded, then brightened, then faded, as though trying to decide whether to fail.

Please, thought Britanov. *Not now. Don't die.*

"There!" said Krasilnikov as he lined up his switches. He threw a final one and the CCP's main lights came on strongly. The battle lamps winked out.

"Well done, Grandfather!" Britanov clapped him on the back.

"Depth fifty meters."

Almost periscope depth. Why wasn't he getting damage reports from aft? Had he lost communication with the rest of the submarine? Were they all dead? Why—

The rising submarine broached the surface like a missile fired from underwater. The bow rose, rose, then in a huge wave of white water, the ten-thousand-ton vessel stopped, and slowly slid backward.

The world seemed to tumble inside the CCP. If Britanov had let go of the handle he would have been dashed against first the overhead, then the rear bulkhead. He rode the violent rocking and rolling, feeling each motion slightly less than the one before.

"Engines all stop!"

"All stop!"

The lights flickered once again, but came back burning more brightly.

K-219 was on the surface under the stars, rolling in the low seas, her weather deck nearly awash, a black, smoking shape darker than the moonlit waves.

"I need damage reports. Someone go aft and find out what's happened," said Britanov. "And stop those damned bells!"

The alarms went off one by one. Then it was strangely quiet except for the normal hum of machinery.

It was 0540 Moscow time, just two minutes since

the explosion. Two minutes for *K-219* to die, and to be reborn.

Britanov was about to go back into compartment four to see for himself what had happened when the squawk of a man speaking through a heavy rubber mask came in over the *kashtan*.

"Compartment four . . . heavy fumes. Heavy fumes in here!"

"Who's reporting?" Britanov demanded. "Petrachkov?"

"Petrachkov is . . . there's fumes. He's . . . he's unconscious."

The intercom went dead for a moment, then another voice came on.

"Compartment five manned and ready," said Dr. Kochergin. "I can go forward into four if you want, sir. I have no communication with anyone in there, though."

The first voice came back. "We're in here! It's hot! It's hot in here. Water . . . there's smoke and fumes everywhere! Request permission to evacuate compartment four!"

Smoke, heat, and fumes. A missile-fuel accident for certain, and perhaps a fire, thought Britanov. Petrachkov was unconscious, but Dr. Kochergin was ready to treat casualties. Britanov put the mike to his lips. "This is Britanov. All compartments don life-support masks. We'll vent compartment four from here. Doctor, is Yoroblev with you?"

"No, sir."

"Then you'll have to do it. When I give the word,

I want you to go into four and report to me at once. Make sure everyone's on their OBA. Understood?"

"Understood."

Kochergin slipped on his rubber mask, checked to make sure the air bladder was inflated, then joined Security Officer Valery Pshenichny at the sealed hatch leading into the stricken missile compartment. A gauge mounted on the bulkhead showed the pressure differential between four and five was high, but coming down slowly. Tons of air pressure locked the watertight hatch in place. The seal could not be broken until pressures inside the two compartments were roughly equal. The door would not operate.

The doctor felt the need to do something. He found the *kashtan* hanging by the hatch and dialed Kapitulsky. "This is Kochergin in five. Are there any casualties forward?"

"We're all right," said the busy propulsion engineer. "But I'm getting some strange readings from four."

"Strange?"

"Radiation. Make sure you're protected before you go in."

The doctor hung the mike back up and looked at the security officer. There were no antiradiation suits in compartment five.

"Where's Voroblev? We need him. What do we do?" the doctor asked the security officer.

"Take your pulse, Doctor, and calm down. There are procedures for this. We'll follow them." Pshenichny was the senior officer in compartment five; maybe, depending on who was still alive, the ranking officer in the entire rear half of the boat. Even though he was a

KGB man, Pshenichny had completed submarine
training and earned the honor of being a qualified
watch officer. He'd served aboard several Gadzhievo
submarines and the crew respected him in a way it
did not respect *Zampolit* Sergiyenko. That he shared
their disdain for him and made no attempt to hide it
only left Pshenichny more popular with the crew.

"There's radiation," said Kochergin.

"We'll follow procedures, but we'll follow them
fast. Agreed?"

The doctor swallowed. "Agreed."

The gauge on the bulkhead now showed zero. Britanov's calming voice boomed over the intercom.
"Pressures in four and five are equalized. Open the
hatch and evacuate those inside to sick bay. Look for
Petrachkov."

"You're ready?" asked Pshenichny. "What's your
pulse?"

"Offscale," said Kochergin. He reached for the bar
that would unlock the hatch. He noticed the silver
glint from the security officer's open collar. A chain.
From that chain dangled one of the three keys necessary to launch *K-219*'s missiles. Britanov had one and
so did Sergiyenko. Nuclear missiles meant to destroy
people Kochergin didn't know, men and women he
didn't have anything against, really. Those overaged,
obsolete, dangerous damned missiles. They were why
they were here. Why, the doctor was now quite sure,
men on the other side of the steel barrier were dead
and dying. He swung the lock bar down and opened
the hatch.

Sergei Voroblev, the damage-control officer, nearly
fell through the opening. He was staggering under

the weight of a body in his arms. He was wearing his OBA, at least. The doctor only gradually recognized the body as Markov, the sub's communications officer. Markov was not wearing any protective gear at all. His face and uniform were flecked with green foam. Five more men of the missile crew followed them, all of them wearing masks.

"Take Markov to sick bay!" Kochergin shouted through his OBA mask.

Beyond the open hatch, compartment four was dim, filled with a thick brown mist and eerie with the sound of dripping water. There was a sizzling hiss Kochergin could not quite identify. Like meat frying in a cast-iron pan. He turned to Pshenichny. "I'll take the mid-deck. You go up. Petrachkov is there someplace."

Together they gingerly stepped inside the damaged space. Kochergin was first. Not two steps in he stumbled against something soft on the deck. He looked down, shining his explosion-proof lamp to see what it was.

He'd stepped on a sailor lying on his back, his fingers clutched tightly against his throat as though he were trying to rip away the skin. His mask was partly on, but all around it oozed a flood of bright green foam. It dripped onto the deck. Kochergin had slipped in it and his own shoe was now covered.

The sailor was drowning in green foam. "It's Kharchenko!" he said to a warrant officer who had just come in the hatch. Kharchenko was on the missile crew. "Help me get him out!"

The sailor's eyes were white, his mouth open. He gasped for breath and foam pumped from his mouth and nostrils. As Kochergin pulled him up from the deck, a huge quantity of it bubbled up and spilled down his chest. Despite his training, the doctor looked away, the bile rising in his own throat. When he looked back down, the sailor was no longer breathing.

They hauled Kharchenko out of compartment four and put him down on the deck just inside five. Kochergin attempted first aid, even injecting adrenaline straight into the heart. But without air there could be no life, and there was no forcing air down the injured man's clogged throat.

Nitric acid poisoning, the doctor knew. The acid had been strong enough to eat away the metal fuel tank of the blasted missile. What would such an acid do to mere lungs? The green foam was a mucus response from inhaling nitric oxide vapor; the vapor, when combined with wet tissue, formed acid. The brown mist. Kochergin looked back into the hatch. He could see tendrils of it snaking their way into compartment five. Even through his mask he could taste the telltale flavor of burnt almonds on his tongue. He let Kharchenko fall limp to the steel deck.

"Doctor! There are more men in here!" the security officer yelled back from the brown, murky space.

He left the dead sailor behind and began to grope his way deeper into the stricken compartment, looking for men he might still be able to save.

It was a war zone in compartment four. Acrid smoke billowed up from the bilges below. It was hot, far too hot for safety. The sizzling sound came from below. Water still dripped from above. Bodies were everywhere. Kochergin counted twelve; it was impossible to know who was dead and who was alive. When the tiny sick bay cabin could hold no more, he ordered

the rest laid out like cordwood in the narrow passageway.

Missile Officer Petrachkov was not among them.

Dr. Kochergin's own breathing was becoming
labored. He checked his air canister and saw the rubber bag almost deflated. He had little oxygen left, and
he had ample proof that the air beyond his mask was
lethal. But he couldn't stop. He knew that men might
be alive somewhere in the big dark missile room.
Men who would die if he didn't find them.

He reentered four and found the ladder leading
down to the smoking, hot bilges. His light lanced
through clouds of thick brown vapor. There he spotted two more men face down on the deck. He hoisted
one to his shoulder and called out above for help. For
some reason he looked at his watch. It was 0745.

Someone shouted back a name: "*I have Petrachkov!*"

The missile officer! The doctor hurried up the
ladder, or at least he hurried to the extent that carrying a heavy, unconscious man permitted. Kochergin
was slightly built; the men joked that his arms were
too thin for an injection—the needle would come
through. Yet he found the strength to accomplish
things his rational mind would have scoffed at as impossible.

Kochergin slid the injured man through the open
hatch to compartment five, then turned back as a warrant officer carried Petrachkov by. Like the others, his
face was covered in green foam.

Behind them was Pshenichny. He was staggering as
he weaved in the direction of the open hatch.

As the doctor watched, Pshenichny collapsed to
the deck and began groping at his rubber mask. The

bladder feeding it oxygen had collapsed, the canister empty.

Not him, too. Pshenichny had to survive. He was senior officer aft. Kochergin ripped off his own mask and strapped it over the security officer's face. "Breathe!"

Pshenichny's eyes lolled.

"Breathe!" Kochergin grabbed him under the arms and lifted him to his feet. He tried to hold his breath as he dragged him back to the hatch. He nearly made it before his lungs screamed for air, and despite what he knew, despite everything he'd seen, Kochergin opened his mouth and sucked down a gulp of pure poison.

"Port reactor is now on-line, sir," said Kapitulsky.

Britanov took the *kashtan* and said, "Compartment four, I need a report!"

A warrant officer surveying the damage reported improved visibility, a large rupture in the top of silo six, and poisonous fumes rising from the bilges.

"What about Petrachkov?"

"We just found him. He didn't look good."

"What about the rest?"

"There are many injured. Two dead, I think. I don't know how many. Kochergin has been moving them back to five."

"Where is Kochergin?"

A pause, then, "I don't see him."

"Keep looking. I want everyone moved out and silo six purged. Can you operate the silo flush controls?"

"I don't know . . . I've never done it. I'm not assigned to the missiles, Comrade Captain."

"You are now." The ones who did know how to

ACCIDENT ON K-219   411

flush silo six were either dead or incapacitated. He
needed to get that poison out of his ship before it
killed anyone else.

"I'll go back myself," said Chief Engineer
Krasilnikov.

"No. I need you here." Britanov gave Krasilnikov
the *kashtan*. "The engineer will talk you through the
procedure. In the meantime, rig some fans to blow
the fumes away from the hatch to compartment five.
Panyatno?"

"*Da, yest,*" the warrant officer replied. "Understood."

Britanov paused, then turned to Zhenya Aznabaev,
the boat's navigator. "Markov is back there, maybe
dead. I need a radio officer more than a navigator."

"I can do it, Captain."

"Good. We have to send a report to fleet headquarters. Request emergency assistance from all units. The
preset codes don't cover what's happened. You'll have
to send it in the clear."

The young executive officer Vladmirov piped in.
"It's against regulations, sir. If we break radio silence
with an uncoded message, the Americans will know
everything."

"It's against regulations to sink, too," said Britanov. He looked at Aznabaev. "Send it."

As Krasilnikov talked the men in compartment four
through the procedure to flush silo six, the situation
aboard *K-219* seemed to stabilize. At least there were
no new catastrophes demanding Britanov's attention.
After four attempts to attract Moscow's attention
to their plight, Navigator Aznabaev finally received a

terse, noncommittal acknowledgment from Northern Fleet headquarters in Severmorsk; five minutes later a second reply carne from Naval High Command in Moscow.

But fifteen minutes after the warrant officers turned the last valve and then switched on the purging pumps to clear the poisonous brew seething inside the shattered missile silo, it became clear that conditions were far from stable. Gas was once more forming in the flooded bilges below the lower deck in compartment four, awash in both seawater and oxidizer, and the temperature inside had risen to one hundred twenty degrees Fahrenheit. The fourteen other missiles, although apparently undamaged by the blast, could explode if the temperature continued to rise.

"Do you want us to purge the silo again?" asked one of the warrant officers.

"No," said Britanov. "Get out of there and make sure there's no one left behind. We'll try to vent the space to atmosphere."

"There's something burning in there," growled Engineer Krasilnikov. He wanted nothing so much as to go aft and get his hands dirty solving the problem. He knew Britanov was relying on him here in central command, but he didn't like telling others how to do things that he could do better and faster himself. Getting back there wouldn't be so easy though. Maybe over the deck and down the hatch in ten?

"What about the other rockets?" asked Britanov.

"Who knows?" Krasilnikov answered testily. "We've lost all remote readings from them. But I can feel it. We've got a fire someplace. Most likely it's electrical."

Britanov trusted the engineer's feelings. He was

about to order a thorough search of the bilge areas for any sign of flame when the *kashtan* buzzed. It was Pshenichny, the KGB officer.

"Everyone's out of four, Captain. I'm ready to seal the hatch."

"Proceed."

The security officer counted noses a third time—it was too easy to miss someone when everybody wore identical rubber masks—then slammed the heavy metal hatch shut. He spun the locking wheel, then stepped back. At least there was no way the poison could come through solid—

"Look!" said one of the warrant officers. He was pointing at the hatch.

From around the perimeter came a thin stream of brown mist. "It didn't seal."

They opened it, then closed it more carefully, pulling the locking wheel tighter. The brown mist still seeped around the edges.

When they opened the hatch a third time, Pshenichny took a close look at the rubber seals. They were curled like old, dried meat. The nitric acid from the spilled missile fuel had attacked them. He shut the hatch a final time, then retreated with the other men aft to compartment six. There he reported.

"Fumes now in compartment five, Captain."

"Five? Is the hatch closed?"

"It's coming right through. It's the acid. The seals are damaged." Britanov unfolded the greaseboard outline of *K-219*. He put a big black X across compartments four and five. His command had been cut in two, with no way to send help aft through the missile room, and no way to evacuate the injured forward.

Like a train with locked doors, he thought. "What about water? Will it hold?"

"I don't know if the hatch will stop it."

Poison gas, rocket fuel, and seawater. They were eating away at the vitals of his submarine. It was then, at this very moment, that Britanov thought for the first time the problems in compartment four might not be stopped before they consumed the whole boat. If the acid was destroying hatch seals so far from the explosion, what must it be doing to all the cables and controls that pass right by it? Cables that controlled the engines, the missiles, even the reactors. "Pshenichny?"

"Sir."

"There's no way you can move men forward through all that gas. Move everyone back into compartment eight. When you get everyone there, report in. Is Voroblev there?"

"I'm still in compartment six, Captain," said the damage-control specialist. "I was in four when it went off."

"What's your best guess of the damage?"

"It was a leaking muzzle hatch. The explosion ripped the silo apart. There's flooding, fire, gas. It's spreading through the hatches, all right. I'm surveying now for gas."

"You heard about the seals?"

"I heard."

"Make your survey and head to eight with Pshenichny." Britanov hung the *kashtan* back up and saw the other men in central command looking at him. "Helm. Make your course zero four five degrees. Gennady!" he shouted at the propulsion engineer. "How much speed can you give me?"

"No more than fourteen knots. If we go any faster we'll take waves over the missile deck. The water will start pouring in again and those seals might—"

"Turns for fourteen knots." He looked at Grandfather Krasilnikov. "We have to isolate four somehow."

"I can repressurize the boat and vent four out to the atmosphere. It might slow the fumes down."

"Do it." Then, into the *kashtan* again, he said, "This is Britanov. Seal all intercompartment hatches now. We're going to pressurize the boat to isolate compartment four."

Krasilnikov set the air controls and looked at Britanov for a signal to activate them.

"Wait," said the captain, "I want to see for myself what we're fighting." He grabbed his oilskins from the hook beside the small framed plaque with the saying that had so upset *Zampolit* Sergiyenko. He went to the ladder leading up to the main hatch. "I'm going to have a look. Interested?"

Krasilnikov was on his feet in an instant. Together they ascended the ladder into the closed bridge, climbed a second ladder, then undogged the main escape trunk hatch.

The sound of the sea echoed down through the open hatch. For the first time since diving off Gadzhievo, Britanov breathed the sweet, salty smell of fresh ocean air. The sky was filled with the first gray light of the new day.

Single file, the two climbed out into the exposed bridge, turned aft, and switched on their portable lamps.

Water sloshed over the missile deck. As each wave cleared, it parted like a curtain around the place where silo six's hatch should be. "Mother of God."

The hatch was gone and a shiny streak of gouged metal ran aft from it. Something heavy and sharp had cut the rubber coating that plated the missile deck, ripping away the hatch and exposing the underlying metal.

"Captain," said the chief engineer. "It doesn't look so much like a simple explosion."

"What are you saying?"

"It looks like we hit something. Or perhaps something hit us. I've seen damage like this before, but only after a collision."

Britanov swept the dark sea with his lamp. There was nothing out here to hit. Nothing, he thought, except for another submarine.

"Captain!" called up Aznabaev. "New message from Fleet."

"Let's go below," he said to Krasilnikov. "We'll have Pshenichny photograph this when it gets lighter."

Back in the close confines of central command, Britanov read the newly decoded message from Northern Fleet headquarters. Three merchant ships were changing course to render assistance to *K-219*.

Help from a freighter. He was about to comment on how quickly the situation had changed when the damage-control officer called in on the intercom.

"I've just completed the damage survey, Captain," said Voroblev. "I started in four and worked all the way aft to ten. There are traces of gas as far as seven."

"Gas is in *seven*? You're sure?"

"Yes, sir. It's bad in four and five, but it's spreading through the boat. There's an electrical problem in four as well. We may have lost some wire bundles in the explosion."

"Which bundles, Voroblev?"

"It's too hot to go down and see. But the reactor control cables run right through the worst area."

"All right. We're going to close everything up and pump some air into four."

"Understood, Captain."

Britanov was about to tell him to check again when the planesman shouted. Everyone in central command stopped and looked at him as he pointed at the overhead ventilator grille.

A thin wisp of brown mist emerged from it, carrying the sweet smell of almonds, of fuming nitrogen tetroxide, of death.

Britanov ordered the pressure increased inside central command. The flow of poison through the ventilator grille slowed to a thin stream, a wisp, and then finally stopped. But flushing silo six only made the situation worse in the missile room. Britanov had no choice but to order the space abandoned. When Security Officer Pshenichny reported fumes coming right through the dogged hatch leading to compartment five, he ordered that space evacuated, too.

Now, four hours after the initial explosion, as the sun broke the flat, gray horizon, dense brown smoke had found its way back to the hatch leading into compartment six, a tightly packed space filled with reactor controls, steam pipes, and storage lockers. The fumes were briefly stopped by the steel door, but the nitric acid had lost none of its potency. Gas and smoke began to seep through the ruined hatch seals. A seaman wearing an OBA was standing watch. He tried to close the hatch tighter, but when he tightened the locking bars the seals crumbled to powder. Smoke began to pour through, filling the passageway. And something more: seawater was coming over the lower lip of the hatch, flowing unimpeded through the same faulty seals.

"Captain! Smoke . . . smoke and water now in six!" he said into the *kashtan* mounted by the hatch. He'd seen the bodies carried out covered in brown rocket-fuel slime and green foam. Before waiting for an answer, he dropped the microphone and splashed aft. As he ran, he thought for an instant that it was the first time in his young life that he'd ever run *toward* a pair of nuclear reactors in order to feel safe.

Smoke and water in six. Britanov ran his hand over his cheek, feeling the unshaved stubble. How long had he been fighting this battle? It felt like days.

Engineer Krasilnikov was watching him. "Captain? Are you all right?"

He rubbed his eyes to clear away the fatigue. To think. Britanov was trying to save his boat without knowing enough about what was happening to it. He took the greaseboard outline of *K-219* and placed another black *X* on it. That made three uninhabitable spaces: Compartment four had blast damage, water, poison gas, radiation, and fire. Five had smoke so there was fire there, too. Now lethal smoke and water were spilling into six.

Three compartments, three deaths. So far. Another dozen or more of his crew were unconscious and some of them would almost certainly die without proper medical care. Kochergin, the boat's only qualified doctor, was one of the casualties. So was his communications specialist, Markov. Where would that medical care come from?

"I'm going up top," he told the chief engineer. He grabbed his oilskin coat and climbed the ladder up to the enclosed bridge. From there he climbed a second ladder, opened the main trunk, and pulled himself wearily up into the clean air.

The morning light was clear and penetrating. Purple-brown smoke billowed up in distinct puffs from the shattered missile silo like the exhaust from an old locomotive. He wondered, Why puffs? Then he saw the reason.

Low seas washed over the missing muzzle hatch in *K-219*'s missile deck. Every time water flowed down into compartment four, the column of smoke stopped. When the silo drained, smoke poured out once more.

Every wave meant more water, more water meant more reacting missile fuel, more weight, less habitable space, and less chance of saving his boat.

The clean air sharpened his thinking, blowing away the mental fog. An alteration began to take hold in Britanov, from trying to save his command at any cost to saving his men and to hell with the submarine. It was a subtle change, something like the way the waves in the fjord at Gadzhievo had become more serious out in the open Barents Sea.

Britanov had always thought of his crew's welfare. Some said he thought too much about it to be an effective commander. Well, perhaps they'd been right. His thinking now was different from what it had been when they first dived off Gadzhievo. Like the waves, it had become more serious.

He took a last breath of clean air, a last look at the light of the new day, and went back below.

"Yevgeny!" he shouted to the senior navigator, and now radio operator as well. "Find out which of those freighters is closest. I want an estimated time of arrival from all three. And let Moscow know we're still on fire with smoke and flooding now in compartment six."

"You want that sent in the clear, Captain?"

"I don't care if you use a semaphore."

His boat had been cut into two and the crew was being cornered, forced aft to escape the spreading damage radiating from the ruined missile room. At some point they would have to stop running. At some point there was nowhere else to go.

Compartment seven contained *K-219*'s reactors. Compartment eight her engines. Nine and ten housed machinery spaces as well as sonar and steering gear. At the submarine's farthest point aft in ten was another escape trunk for the crew.

The poison was herding them to it. "Damage-control crews forward to six, I need a report."

A seaman in a full-body protective suit, breathing from his self-contained OBA canister, fought his way through the dim, smoky passageways and reported electrical insulation burning in five and the bulkhead to four black with charred paint and nearly glowing with heat. The deck was awash with brown missile fuel and seawater. His OBA had two cartridges each good for ten minutes of normal breathing. Under the heat and stress the rubber bladder began to collapse after only eight. Britanov ordered him aft to compartment eight to join the rest of the crew.

Britanov took stock. A fire raging unchallenged on

the bottom level of the missile room. Progressive flooding spreading through acid-eaten seals. A bulkhead black with burning paint. All remote readings of the fourteen remaining RSM-25 rockets lost with temperatures surely approaching the critical point. At some point the rockets would detonate, cooking off in the heat. When they did there was no way to predict the extent of the blast. Each rocket carried two six-hundred-kiloton thermonuclear warheads.

Engineer-Seaman Sergei Preminin sat at the blinking reactor control console at the aft end of compartment six. The console duplicated the gauges and controls that Kapitulsky had in compartment two. The indicators monitored the health and status of *K-219*'s twin VM-4 reactors.

Right beyond the gray bulkhead, both ninety-megawatt power plants were putting out a sizable portion of their rated energy. A sphere of uranium nuclear fuel initiated a chain reaction, the fission generated heat, and the heat turned water into steam. This steam drove the engines as well as the generators needed to keep the submarine afloat, lit, and supplied with air.

Beside Preminin was his superior, Reactor Officer Belikov. They both wore masks plugged into the boat's central oxygen system. They were the only two nuclear-qualified men in the aft section of the sub.

The sound of pounding feet came from beyond the control space. Preminin's protective mask afforded limited forward vision and no peripheral view at all. He had to turn to see a silver-suited figure dash by, heading aft. The fleeing sailor stopped, turned back, and stuck his head into the reactor control space. "Smoke's coming through from five! There's a big fire forward! You'd better move it!" he yelled, then ran off again.

The twenty-one-year-old sat in silence, wondering why a *fireman* was running and *he* was sitting here. He wanted to run, too. But he had to wait until Belikov gave the word.

It was just his second operational cruise since graduating from engineering school. Sergei Preminin came from a tiny, landlocked village that had only recently seen the advent of electricity. He and his brother had escaped its medieval life by joining the Navy. Preminin worked hard to remain a part of the elite submarine service. He knew what kind of a life waited for him back home. He took his duty very seriously.

He watched the status board, waiting for Belikov to give the order to evacuate. All hell had broken loose inside *K-219*, and the situation was getting harder to understand. Why was gas seeping through closed hatches? Had panicky sailors fled and forgotten to shut them? All Preminin knew for certain was that compartment five was empty and that he and Belikov were now alone in compartment six. After so many days of crowded living conditions, the sudden emptiness was more than a little unnerving.

Lieutenant Belikov reached for his *kashtan*. "Captain. Lieutenant Belikov at station sixty-five. There's smoke reported now in compartment six and a fire, too."

"I heard," said Britanov wearily. "You're on ship's oxygen?"

"Yes, sir. Do you need us to remain here?"

"If it's unsafe you should evacuate to eight. The air's still good back there. Kapitulsky can control the reactors from here. It's your call, Lieutenant. Don't take any chances."

Belikov thought about it for a second, then said, "We're leaving." He hung the mike back up and nodded to Seaman Preminin. "Let's get out of here."

Together they shut down their console, leaving it on automatic status. Belikov took a last look at the gauges; coolant flow was fluctuating more than it should, but then power was being drawn from the reactors for damage control. It wasn't a matter of steady steaming.

They plugged their masks into their OBAs and made their way out into the passageway. A rivulet of seawater was already running aft along the deck. They splashed through it back to the hatch leading into compartment seven, the heart of the submarine. The reactor room.

The compartment was lit only by the dim glow of battle lamps. A minor steam line had ruptured in the initial explosion and it was still venting. Thank God it wasn't part of the primary or secondary reactor steam loops or they'd all be glowing. But it was enough of a leak to fill the air with a mist made even more eerie by the weak orange light given off by the dying lamps.

"It's hot in here," said Preminin as they passed the locked hatches leading to the reactors themselves. He could feel the sweat begin to flow almost at once. It was like stepping into a steam bath.

Belikov put his mask close to one of the remote temperature gauges. His lenses kept fogging. With poison nitric acid gas and smoke from the fires reported, he didn't dare take it off. "Preminin. Come over here. What does this say?"

Preminin came close. Why was it so hot in here? Maybe it had something to do with how the captain had pressurized the boat? It couldn't be fire, could it?

Preminin peered at the round instrument. Like the ones on Kapitulsky's console, like those back at his own station in compartment six, it looked as if it had been made for a locomotive. He read the needle, then blinked.

"Well?"

"It says—"

Before he could finish his sentence, the first reactor overheat alarm went off. Its terrifying screech echoed throughout the boat, through the burning, ruined spaces flickering with fire and through the increasingly crowded passageways where men huddled. But here, right next to the reactors themselves, it was deafening.

The screech of the reactor alarm paralyzed the command post watch. For an instant, Britanov thought this could not be happening. It was one of those drills conducted by a sadistic trainer back at submarine school, one who delighted in taking you to the very edge, then giving you a good, hard shove.

He grabbed the mike and switched the intercom to Kapitulsky's station in compartment two. "Gennady! Report!"

"I've lost all remote readings to the reactors. The wires must have burned through in compartment four. I don't know what's happening, but if the overheat is real, we have to shut them down. I can't . . . there's no response from my controls. They're running away!"

Britanov heard the thin blade of panic in Kapitul-sky's normally unflappable demeanor. Shutting down a reactor was normally accomplished from Kapitul-sky's station. But he was no longer connected to his power plants. It was why he sounded so brittle, so near to breaking. If Kapitulsky could lose control, then anyone could. Even Britanov. "Gennady. Listen to me. Belikov is back there. Have him revert the re-actors to manual control and scram them if he has to."

"I should do it—"

"No. Talk him through it. I'll stand by."

A pause, then, "Belikov?" said Kapitulsky.

The sound of the alarm doubled as the screech was fed over the intercom. "We're both still in compart-ment seven," said Belikov. "The readings are all going crazy back here and it's hot."

"Read me all the temperatures. Start with primary coolant."

Belikov wiped away the steam from his mask and read them off just the way he'd been taught in reactor disaster drills. "Primary temperature on number one is—" He stopped. "It's too high. It's way too high. Same with, number two!"

"Coolant flow?"

"Low and dropping."

Kapitulsky thought there was a good chance the readings were inaccurate. After all, a moment before all seemed to be well with the VM-4s. What could have caused them to suddenly run away like this? On the other hand, if the readings were true, they were moments away from a real meltdown, one that would eat right through the reactor vessel, burn through the bottom of the submarine, and then, when the mass of glowing hot slag hit cold water, explode in a fireball of radioactive steam. "Captain," he said, "if we shut one down we won't be able to make fourteen knots. We may lose all power except for the diesels."

"Do it," Britanov said to the propulsion engineer. "Start the diesels. Shut both reactors down. Start with the hottest one and scram it."

As he listened to Kapitulsky tell Belikov what to do, Britanov realized the crew was not the only one getting backed into a corner.

"Unlock the gravity release for quench baffles one through four," said Kapitulsky. "Did you hear, Belikov?"

"Yes . . ."

"That should do it," Kapitulsky finished. The baffles would absorb the runaway fission reaction, dousing the nuclear fires. There was a pause. The reactor alarm was still screeching horribly. "Well?"

"Sir!" said Belikov. "I can't!"

"What do you mean you can't?"

"Something . . . something's gone wrong with the gravity release. The quench baffles won't drop. The springs . . . they aren't forcing them down. It must be the heat. The metal's binding."

Kapitulsky grew pale. The quench baffles were designed to drop automatically when reactor temperatures got too high. If they failed to drop automatically, they could be commanded to drop by a sequence of steps Belikov had just taken; if they did not drop *then*, they still could be forced down, but by hand, from *inside* the reactors, by a man wielding a specially made oversized wrench.

"Captain?" said Kapitulsky. "Scram was unsuccessful. We have to go in there and crank them down."

Grandfather Krasilnikov stepped up beside the captain. "I can go back and do it," said the chief engineer. "I can walk out topside and drop back down through the escape hatch in ten. I'm old and I have all the children I want. Let me do it, Captain."

And lose his chief engineer when he might have need for him? Britanov shook his head. "I still need you here, Igor. What about protective gear?"

"There are two antiradiation suits back in eight," said Krasilnikov, "but they're designed for steam leaks in the coolant circuit. Not for going into the reactors. It's never done."

Britanov knew why. "Gennady? Tell Belikov about the suits. Tell him they may not shield him enough to be safe."

"He knows that, Captain."

"Belikov. Can you hear me? This is Captain Britanov."

"I hear you, Captain."

"We have to scram the reactors. You'll have to go in. There are some protective suits in eight but they—"

"I know, Captain," said the young reactor officer. "I'll shut them down myself. But my OBA canister is almost empty." In fact, Belikov was beginning to feel light-headed as his portable supply gave out.

"Go back to compartment eight. Pshenichny will get you equipped."

"We're leaving seven for eight."

Security Officer Pshenichny listened to the intercom speaker as he and sixty men sat huddled in the main engine room. Fourteen of them lay unconscious on the steel deck; two missile technicians and Petrachkov were dead. It was very hot here so close to the big, steam-driven turbomachinery. The air in compartment eight smelled of oil and hydraulic fluid, but it wasn't yet lethal. Pshenichny looked back at the refugees from the abandoned compartments. "How many OBA canisters do we have?"

A quick count came up with more men than oxygen canisters; there were thirty OBAs altogether, most of them already partly used. There were just six full ones left. Pshenichny took all six and lined them up on the deck.

Belikov and Seaman Preminin showed up, their blue coveralls black with sweat. Belikov's mask was still on, the lenses were still fogged. His OBA canister was nearly empty; the sides of the rubber bladder were sticking together.

Pshenichny reached over and pulled off Belikov's mask. The reactor officer looked frightened, but then realized no one else in compartment eight was wearing a mask, either. He took a long gasp of air. The two protective suits were handed up the line. Belikov noticed the small pile of canisters. "Where are the rest?"

"Those are the last of them," said Pshenichny.

Krasilnikov still hovered by the captain. "Belikov will do the job. But when he comes out," said the chief engineer, "he'll be as sterile as a mule."

"If he doesn't get it done," said Britanov, "it won't matter."

———

"I'll go with you, Lieutenant," said Preminin. He reached for the second antiradiation suit. It was made from heavy silvered rubber.

"No," said Belikov. "One of us in there is bad enough. If I can't get all the baffles down, you'll have to finish it." He put on the OBA mask and tested to be sure he could breathe, then stepped through the hatch to compartment seven. It shut behind him with a solid clang. Security Officer Pshenichny grabbed the locking bar and pulled the dogs tight against the rubber seals.

The lights had almost completely failed inside compartment seven, but Belikov knew every inch of the complex reactor space by feel. He didn't need light to find his way down the ladder to the lower machinery space. When he stepped off the bottom rung he found filthy seawater pooled on the deck. It was oily with brown fluid. A lone battle lamp cast enough yellow light to see that when he disturbed the water with his boot it gave off wisps of smoke. He could hear a steady inrush of water from somewhere forward.

To expect a steel pipe to float had always seemed a little bit unreasonable. Of course, so was asking a man to crawl into a live nuclear reactor.

Both VM-4s were down here on the bottom level, separated from the machinery spaces by heavy shielded bulkheads and accessed through a small, low hatch ablaze with serious warnings. Belikov remembered the story of a cook aboard the *Lenin*, a nuclear-powered icebreaker. A real peasant from the *gubinka*, the deep countryside, he'd seen nothing wrong with using a high-pressure steam tap off the primary reactor coolant loop to scour a crusted pan clean. He suffered radiation burns over his whole body and died soon afterward, but he had very clean pans.

Now Belikov was the cook heading into harm's way.

The high-temperature alarm was still shrieking. He'd stopped hearing it. But then, an hour ago he wouldn't have considered walking into a hot nuclear reactor, either. It was amazing what a person could become accustomed to.

He had to bend as he made his way along the bottom level. Belikov was tall, a full six feet. He kept bumping his head against things, obstructions he couldn't quite see kept snatching at his mask, threatening to pull it off. What was the air like here, anyway? In the dim orange light he could see swirling vapor.

It was like going down to a leaky, dark basement filled with a maze of steam pipes and sparking, damaged electrical conduits. A high-pressure air line hissed where a weld had failed. The heat near the two nuclear cauldrons was intense; even outside the shielded bulkhead it was well over fifty degrees Celsius. Hotter by far than any *banya* Belikov had ever taken, though the heavy rubber suit helped a little.

The tool he needed to crank down the jammed quench baffles was stored in a locker. Water had risen to its bottom lip by the time he found it. Of course it was locked. Of course he had no key. *What do they expect us to do, steal tools and sell them to the fish?*

He felt his way around to where he knew a fire ax was mounted to the bulkhead. His gloved hand closed around the wooden handle. He hefted it and used the heavy blade to pry open the locker.

The special crank resembled an oversized meat

grinder. It was heavy, made of solid steel. He dropped the ax and returned to the small hatch that led into the shielded reactor space. There was a tiny, thick window in the middle of it. Through the leaded glazing he could see the two squat shapes of the reactor domes.

He didn't bother with the warnings. No one in their right mind would come in here with the reactors running. He reached down and unlocked the hatch.

A blast-furnace gust flowed out so strongly he could feel it through the insulated suit. *Better not to waste time.* He folded himself through the small hatch, then stood up inside the reactor space.

The two reactor vessels were before him, two domed cylinders seething with nuclear fire. The heat was intense. There was an odd, ozonelike smell to the air.

A sinking submarine stuffed with nuclear poisons. They should all be paddling from *K-219* as fast as they could swim. Who cared if a reactor blew up right next to America? It wasn't as though they were bobbing off Odessa. What Russian would pay a kopeck to keep enriched uranium from dusting American beaches?

Belikov was paying a good deal more than a kopeck. He knew he was taking a huge dose of radiation by standing here. Enough to sterilize him for sure. To keep America safe. That was what he was sacrificing his manhood for.

It was really a crazy world.

He walked up to the first reactor, the starboard VM-4. Its domed top contained four hexagonal sockets. They operated a worm-gear mechanism that would force one of the quench baffles down.

Here, right next to the sizzling reactor, the temperature was eighty degrees Celsius, nearly one hundred eighty degrees Fahrenheit. Enough to cook flesh. Enough to kill. What the devil was he doing?

Belikov inserted the handle into the first socket and began to crank. He saw at once why the safety system had failed: it took all his effort to move it. The heat had warped the guides badly. And without those baffles down, the heat only became worse, the nuclear fire brighter, hotter. It was a self-sustaining reaction. Eventually, without a flow of coolant to take away the heat, the sphere of uranium fuel would melt through the bottom of the reactor vessel, through the hull of the sub, and detonate when it hit cold seawater. A hydrogen blast, not a nuclear explosion, but for anyone close by the difference would be slight. A hydrogen bubble had burst at Chernobyl just a few months back, and look at the mess *that* made.

He threw himself against the steel bar and the jammed gears began to squeal. He followed the handle around the vessel. Each time his suit touched the reactor he heard a sizzle and smelled burning rubber.

How long is this going to take? He'd performed a manual crankdown on a cold reactor as part of nuclear reactor school. Normally it took less than five minutes for all four baffles to be lowered. Sweat poured down his face as he shoved the crank with all his might. It evaporated the instant it emerged from beneath his mask. It was so hot. So very hot. And the radiation, well, it didn't pay to think about some things. He kept turning until his vision began to blur, until he was gasping. Only then did he look down at his OBA canister.

The rubber air bladder was completely collapsed. How was that possible? He'd barely lowered the first baffle. He'd only been here for . . . for how long?

Spots swam in front of his eyes. He stepped back, fighting the urge to tear off the mask and breathe. Belikov was holding the heavy crank handle. It weighed so much, it pulled his arm down to his side. He was so tired, and he'd barely lowered . . . Air. He needed air. He had to get back to eight.

Shuffling like a drunk, Belikov staggered back to the low hatch in the shielded bulkhead, got through, forgot to close it behind, remembered, stood up, and stumbled aft to the ladder leading up to compartment eight. He still had the heavy crank handle. Somehow he climbed. Somehow he made it back to the hatch. He used the crank as a hammer and pounded on the door. When it opened, he fell through and passed out on the deck at Preminin's feet.

Pshenichny propped Belikov against the bulkhead, ripped off the mask, and splashed his face with water. It was warm water, but it seemed to help. "Are they shut down?" he asked Belikov.

The lieutenant's face was very pale, even though his neck was splotched red. He looked up at Pshenichny and mouthed the word *no*.

"Sergei," said the security officer to Seaman Preminin. "You'll have to—"

"I know." Preminin was already putting on the second, cumbersome radiation suit. He clipped two OBA canisters to his belt.

There were just two more unused canisters left in the whole after section of *K-219*.

Chief Engineer Krasilnikov pulled the circuit breaker for the reactor overtemp alarm. Finally, the blood-chilling screech went silent and the command post team could speak, even think.

"Captain," said Aznabaev. The navigator held up a microphone from his ship-to-ship set. "I have direct contact with the *Fyodor Bredkin*. She's fifty kilometers out. Do you want to speak with her?"

Britanov felt both shame and relief. Shame that he might need some rustbucket of a freighter to save his command; relief that if he did need them, they would at least be here. Fumes were spreading right through sealed hatches. So was fire. So was water. The reactors would have to be shut down or else they would burn a hole right through *K-219*'s belly. Then they would all go up in a cloud of radioactive steam. Even if he did get them shut down, it left him with only battery and diesel power to control damage.

It wouldn't be enough. He knew that he would have to get some of his men off to save them. He shook his head. "I don't want to talk. I want to see him. What speed can he make?"

The sub's navigator spoke into the mike, waited a moment, then said to Britanov, "ETA is two hours forty minutes. He wants to know our condition."

"Tell him so do I."

"Captain!" came a cry from the young man sitting at the radar display. "Aerial contact inbound. He's illuminating us with search radar. It looks like an American patrol plane."

"Zhenya," Britanov said to the navigator, "tell the master of the *Fyodor Bredkin* if he wants to know how we're doing, he can ask the Americans." He picked up the *kashtan*. "Pshenichny! What's happening with those reactors?"

The security officer helped Preminin close the last fastener on his radiation suit. He picked up the *kashtan*. "They're going back in now, Captain," he said as he undogged the hatch leading forward into compartment seven. "The alarm is off."

"We killed the power to it," Britanov said. "We have no readings up here at all. Kapitulsky is ready to start the diesels but you've got to get those reactors secured."

"We'll do our duty, Captain." He looked at Preminin. The young seaman had the heavy crank handle now. Belikov looked too weak to pick it up. Was it heat, the air, or radiation?

"How's Belikov?" Britanov asked.

Belikov was wobbly as he stood. Premmin took the *kashtan* and answered for them both. "We're okay, Captain. Trust us to do the job," he said, then put his mask on, checked the flow from the OBA canister, and together with Belikov went back in.

Any idea that the alarm's silence was a good sign was instantly dispelled by the raging heat inside compartment seven. With the pumps failed, each glowing uranium sphere was dumping heat into an insufficient supply of coolant; the heat radiated through the steel reactor vessels and into the submarine.

Belikov knew it was worse than before. He followed Preminin down the ladder to the bottom.

"Comrade Lieutenant," said Preminin, "let me go in. You can stay by the gauges and relay reports to central command."

Belikov knew it was a polite way of saying that he
didn't look able to help. He nodded. Preminin went
through the low hatch and into the shielded reactor
space.

Belikov picked up the *kashtan* by the gauges. "Comrade Captain. It's Belikov, sir. I'm at the local reactor
control board now in compartment seven."

"Belikov, read me the temperatures off the panel,"
said Kapitulsky. "Start with the highest."

"The temperatures are all redlined. Starboard and
port reactors are both starved for water. Coolant flow
is almost zero in the port reactor. There's still some
circulation in the starboard."

"The readings, they're accurate?" asked Kapitulsky. "What's the air temperature in there, Belikov?"

"Very hot," he said weakly. He knew that as hot as
it was standing out here, inside the reactor space,
right next to those two hellish vessels, it was worse.

Preminin inserted the crank and managed to force the
first quench baffle, the one Belikov had started, all the
way down. Even through the rubber suit it was like
standing under a powerful infrared lamp; the heat
was like nothing he'd ever experienced. "Number one
down!" he shouted.

Belikov had cranked that one down most of the
way himself. Still, it was progress. "Number one baffle down, port reactor," he reported. All four baffles
were needed to surround the uranium sphere.

Preminin inserted the handle into the second socket.
He pushed. It refused to move at all. He pushed harder,
then with all his strength.

The handle bent, threatened to break, then, with a

crack that Belikov could hear all the way outside the reactor space, it moved. Preminin cranked the second baffle down by throwing himself at it, working his way around the blazingly hot steel vessel.

"Second . . . I mean, number two baffle . . . baffle is down," he said through dry, parched lips. He picked up the handle and found it oddly difficult to insert it into the third socket. Sweat streamed down his brow and into his eyes. The intense heat evaporated it instantly, leaving a mask of salt over Preminin's face.

"Preminin!" shouted Belikov. "Check your OBA!"

"I'm . . . I'm not feeling so good, Comrade Lieutenant." He groaned the words as the steel crank fell into the third socket. He pushed. Like the others it required all his strength, all his weight, to budge. He was beyond feeling as he threw himself against the handle. It moved, stubbornly, then moved again, again, and finally stopped. He leaned against it. The steel bent. Only then did he realize the third baffle was fully down. "Number . . . number three is—" He stopped, swaying on his feet next to the steel reactor vessel.

"Preminin!" Belikov dropped the *kashtan* and rushed into the reactor space.

Preminin was on the deck. Belikov picked up the handle and inserted it into the fourth socket. Preminin had broken through the tightest place on the warped guide and it moved more easily. He cranked the last baffle down, then dragged Preminin out through the hatch to the outer reactor space.

"Captain! Belikov . . . here. Port reactor is—" He stopped and felt the heat rising up his body. The spots were back in his eyes. He looked down at his OBA canister. Once again the sides of the rubber bladder were sticking together. He was out of air! "Port reactor is secure! I'm taking Preminin . . . out."

He dropped the mike and dragged Preminin up the ladder. When they opened the hatch leading back to compartment eight, they fell through in a single heap.

"Water!" shouted Pshenichny as he pulled the mask from the lieutenant's face. Belikov's skin was dead white. His eyes bloodshot and bulging. He tried to lift his head so that he might take a sip but Belikov flopped back to the deck like a dead man. Preminin was coming around, slowly, as someone brought a cupful of tepid water. Pshenichny splashed both men, then gave the rest to Preminin to drink.

"What about the starboard reactor?" Britanov's voice boomed in over the loudspeaker.

"We're down to two OBA canisters, Captain," said Pshenichny. "We need more if they're going to both go back in." Though looking at Belikov, he didn't think the lieutenant was going to walk again any time soon, much less go back into the reactors.

"We can't get anyone back through compartment four," said Britanov. "I need that second reactor shut down now, Valery."

Pshenichny was about to tell Britanov that he would have to wait until the two men regained their feet when a small, weak voice interrupted.

"I'll go," said Preminin. He got his legs under him and stood. "Give him the OBA canisters," Pshenichny ordered one of the warrant officers.

"But they're our last ones," the *michman* demurred. There were no other oxygen canisters in the entire after section of the sub. If that poison gas came here they'd all suffocate before—

"Give them to Preminin." He looked at the young seaman. "You have to shut it down by yourself."

"I would have done it before, but it's hot in there," said Preminin as he adjusted the mask over his face. "Count on me."

Preminin grabbed the handle and went back to the hatch. This time when it opened, an acrid whiff of bitter almond wafted through. He stopped for an instant and turned, as though he wanted to say something, but changed his mind.

A stronger smell of poison billowed in from the dark, hot compartment beyond the bulkhead.

Preminin shuffled into the darkness, alone, the last man in compartment seven, the only one left who could shut the runaway reactor down.

"Close that hatch!" Pshenichny bellowed after Preminin disappeared. A warrant officer leaned against the steel door as two sailors dogged it down tight. With poison gas now on the other side and no OBA canisters left, they had to rely on the rubber seals around the hatch to keep them alive. "Seal it!"

The clang of the last dog was loud and final in a way that would come back to haunt Pshenichny. It would come back to haunt them all.

Sergei Preminin was gasping, not breathing, as he went down the long, dark ladder into the bowels of compartment seven. He had to force air into his lungs through the OBA mask; he kept worrying that the canister was empty, but the real reason was the rapid buildup of pressure in the compartment. Between the broken steam line and the intense heat radiated by the reactors, compartment seven had pressurized like a hot-air balloon with the burners on full. A constant hiss of escaping steam could be heard above the gurgle of seeping water. Preminin had never felt so hot in all his life.

The sound of water cooled him. It reminded him of the stream near his home village of Skornyakovo. It was cold and crystal clear, and the fish he caught with his brother were a treat for the family, so much better than the drab tinned meat, old, moldy cheese, and hard bread from the state store. Those fishing expeditions with his brother were what made him interested in the Navy to begin with; if something so clean, so alive as a beautiful fish could be found amidst so much squalor, then a life on the water, or in it, might hold promise. It might give Sergei something, some pride, a job at the local flax mill could never supply.

The rubber suit was very heavy. It was lined with lead foil to protect against radiation. Moving was like swimming in some thick fluid, like being underwater, if the sea had turned hot enough to cook you like a crab in a pot.

At the bottom of the ladder he turned, flashed his light, then walked six meters down a short corridor. The darkness didn't frighten him. But to have it empty, filled with poison gas, to have seawater running down the passage like a stream, to be sealed in seven alone, that was something else.

Preminin turned right, then took the three steps up to the local reactor control area outside the shielded space. The hazy beam of his explosion-proof light swept the panel of gauges.

Coolant pressure was zero on both reactors. Coolant flow, almost zero. The first reactor's temperature was only now beginning to drop; the second VM-4 was pegged, the needle into the far right corner of the red zone. How far? How hot could it be in there? It had to be very close to meltdown. He thought of the men back in compartment eight. Sixty of his mates, fourteen of them unconscious, three already dead. They'd all be killed if that hot radioactive slag melted through and found the cold sea. Everyone was counting on him now. Belikov, Pshenichny, most especially Captain Britanov. No one else could do the job.

It had all come down to Engineer-Seaman Sergei Preminin.

He saw the dangling *kashtan* swinging on its cord. He picked it up and said, "Captain? This is Seaman Preminin. I'm in the local reactor control area in seven." He read the dismal numbers off the gauges, then said, "I'm going back in now."

"You can do it, Sergei," Britanov said, though his worried tone said something else.

"Yes, sir. I will." He groped his way to the small access hatch and unlocked it. The steel door blew back and slammed against the bulkhead as though someone had been trapped inside and now wanted out very badly. The high pressure hissed out through the opening, then subsided.

Beyond the hatch was an inferno. He felt the heat on his knees through the rubber, through the lead, through everything. He folded himself through the low hatch and reentered the reactor space.

He stood up. It was just three steps to the starboard reactor. He inserted the crank into the domed top and began to push.

Preminin gasped for air as he worked. The air pressure made his ears fill and crackle. He kept swallowing. His mouth, his throat, were dry as poured sand.

The first quench baffle squealed as he forced it down into position. He did the same for the second, the third. His head was light enough to float. He realized he was gasping harder now, like a fish brought up from the water. He looked down: the first OBA canister was empty. He took a deep breath.

He unscrewed the oxygen source and threw it away, holding his breath as he threaded on the second, and last, canister. The fittings would not align. They jammed, cross-threaded. His ears began to tingle, his throat burned, a traitorous impulse in his lungs screamed, *Breathe!*

He had to get the second canister connected. The air beyond his mask swirled with poison. He yanked the metal cartridge off the fitting and slowly, deliberately, with all the calmness a man can muster when he is suffocating, twisted it onto the end of his air tube.

The threads lined up. He screwed it on tight, then took a small taste of air.

Something sharp etched his throat as he sucked down the air. Like breathing shards of glass. The strange feeling filled his lungs, then disappeared.

Preminin went back to the reactor. He inserted the crank into the fourth, and last, baffle. He had to push with all his strength. His home village had a communal well that still relied on the steady clopping of an old horse hitched to its handle. Round and round, the horse was always walking but it never got anyplace.

Sergei Preminin was doing the same thing, hitched instead to a ninety-megawatt nuclear reactor. He walked his way around the blazingly hot steel dome. His suit was now scorched black instead of silver. He could smell burnt rubber through his mask. There were holes in the breathing tube, and through those holes he could smell bitter almond. If he took a deeper breath than normal, the sharp, glassy scratch filled his lungs. Each gasp was raw and painful, but a little poison was better than suffocating. He'd never told anyone, not the Navy recruiters, definitely not his mates on board *K-219*, but he had a fear of being trapped. He hated elevators. Let the doors shut and he'd break out in a sweat.

Well, it was too hot now to sweat, even if the steel walls curved in around him, the atmosphere heavy, hot, and lethal.

Preminin went round and round. How many more turns left? Just a few. Then he would leave this space, this oven. The doors would open. He would escape the trap.

Britanov waited with Kapitulsky in central command. There had been no word from Preminin now for too long. "Sergei?" Britanov said into the *kashtan*. "Are they secured, Sergei?"

"They have to be," said Kapitulsky. "It doesn't take that long. It can't."

There was no answer over the intercom.

"Start the forward diesel generator," said Britanov. "We're going to need all the power we can get from it."

"Understood." The propulsion engineer went forward to crank up the emergency generator.

"Captain?" said the radar operator. "Aircraft overhead now. He's circling us."

"Sergei!" Britanov shouted into the mike. "Report!"

Still nothing.

"Captain, this is Pshenichny in eight. Have you heard from Preminin? We haven't seen him since he went in and our intercom won't dial into seven." Pshenichny could talk to central command, but not to Preminin. "He only had two canisters with him. Did he shut the plant down?"

"We don't know," said Britanov as the thrum and clank of the forward emergency diesel began.

"Switching the main power bus to backup," said Krasilnikov. The lights in CCP blinked off, then grew bright. The intercom scratched, then squealed. A weak voice came through the loudspeaker. "Captain?"

"Pshenichny?"

". . . Seaman Preminin."

"Sergei! Where are you?"

"Comrade Commander, the . . ." The weak voice faded.

"Sergei! What is it?"

"Captain, the reactors are secured."

Britanov realized he'd been holding his breath. It went out in a long *whoosh* as a cheer went up in the CCP. "I'm leaving . . . for the exit now."

"Well done, Sergei!" said Britanov. "You're a hero. How do you feel?"

"It's very hot in here. I'm on my last OBA."

"Then get the hell out of there."

The intercom went dead.

"Zhenya!" Britanov called for the navigator. "Tell Moscow our reactors are shut down. They're safe."

"Yes, sir!"

THE DOMAIN OF THE GOLDEN DRAGON

FROM *Spy Sub:*
A Top Secret Mission to the Bottom of the Pacific

by Roger C. Dunham

*I*n 1986, with the Cold War still freezing the waters between the U.S. and the then-U.S.S.R., the story of *K-219* became one of the most polarizing incidents during the face-off. After the Russian nuclear submarine sank with its complement of nuclear missiles still intact, the U.S. submarine *Halibut* was dispatched to the area where *K-219* was lost to see what it could find out about the remains of the Russian submarine. Roger C. Dunham was a nuclear-reactor technician on board the *Halibut*, and his account, told in the book *Spy Sub*, was the only version allowed by the Navy until several years later.

Although I couldn't find out much more about Mr. Dunham, I do know that he tells a very good tale about the true lives of submariners during the Cold War, right down to the drills, boredom, and everything else. Although names (including that of the sub)

have been changed according to naval security proto-
cols, the efforts of the crew of the *Halibut* (or *Viperfish*) shine through on every page, particularly when
one of their own suffers an accident, as in the following excerpt.

In the cockpit of the sail, high above the *Viperfish*, Lieutenant Pintard was waiting for word from the captain. The large and jovial officer of the deck, studying the calm ocean in front of our bow, was on the lookout for any debris that could strike the tops of our periscopes during the submerging operation ahead. Captain Harris stood at his side and scanned the myriad of ships off the west coast of Oahu, while the two lookouts announced the various bearings and distances of the ships passing by. Behind the four men, the American flag flapped vigorously in the wind, the sound blending with the noises of churning ocean water and the distant rumbling sound of our propulsion system.

"All ahead standard," Pintard ordered into the microphone under the rim of the cockpit. His voice carried down to the men at the diving station below and into the engine room's maneuvering area where we monitored the reactor and propulsion system. At the sound of the order, Marc Birken and Jim McGinn immediately began cranking their wheels toward the left to open the throttles.

The whine of the turbines increased in intensity, and we all dutifully placed the black plastic sound guards over our ears to protect our hearing. From that moment on, if anybody in the engine room wanted to talk, he had to shout. For the most part, however, there was no conversation; we just sat in front of our panels and watched the maze of meters displaying the various conditions of the reactor and electrical systems throughout the boat.

At the top of the sail, Captain Harris leaned over the side of cockpit and studied the white wake that began to boil around and behind us as we answered the bell and increased our speed.

"Ten seconds from the order and look at that!" he said, obviously impressed.

"Nuclear power," Pintard said, reflecting on the obvious.

"No clouds of black smoke, no delay."

"Rickover would love it."

"Let's take her down," the captain said. He stepped through the hatch and began the long climb down to the control center.

"Aye, aye, sir," Pintard said as he and the two lookouts made a final scan of the horizon and the world around them.

"Strike the colors and clear the bridge!" Pintard ordered.

The two lookouts immediately lowered their binoculars, removed the American flag, and scrambled down the ladder. Following behind them, Pintard moved his large frame down the sixty-foot ladder with the knowledge that he would not see the sunlight again for at least two months.

Inside the submarine, the captain watched the ocean ahead of us through the starboard periscope as the three men jumped off the ladder into the control room. One of the lookouts reached up to the lanyard attached to the hatch and vigorously pulled on it. With the resounding noise of steel against steel, the hatch slammed tightly against the pressure hull and closed off our last remaining opening to the outside world.

"Control room hatch shut and dogged, sir!" the lookout hollered as he spun the wheel on the underside of the hatch.

The chief of the boat, a short, sandy-haired man named Philip O'Dell, grabbed the microphone hanging near the diving station and announced, "Now, dive! Dive!"

As the chief's voice echoed throughout the submarine, the lookouts eased into their cushioned seats and pushed forward on their airplane-like control wheels. The ballast control panel operator flipped switches across his panel to open valves and flood our external ballast tanks, thereby increasing the weight of the boat and sinking us down into the water. The *Viperfish*'s bow dipped, and we assumed a 20-degree down-angle. The gentle rolling movement of the surface waves changed to the motionless sensation of losing contact with the rest of the world.

"Like hanging in outer space," Svedlow commented from his seat next to me.

"Inner space," Lieutenant Katz corrected him from his engineer's seat behind us. "At least we ain't going to be rolling anymore, and nobody's going to get sick down here."

We moved several hundred feel below the surface, not deep enough to worry about excessively increased ocean pressure but sufficiently deep to keep us below any surface ships. If we suddenly had to surface, collision with a moving ship was not likely. We would hear their engines and screws from several miles away and adjust our course accordingly.

It was vastly more difficult to identify stationary objects on the surface, however, because we couldn't see them and we couldn't use our active sonar, which would give away our position to anybody listening. Our sonarmen, sitting in their "sonar shack" room near the control center, monitored the noises of various cruise liners passing above us. Undoubtedly, the ships were filled with vacationing tourists, admiring the approaching island of Oahu, who did not have a clue that a submarine holding 120 men was tracking them from below.

Once we leveled out at running depth, Richard Daniels relieved me from the reactor control panel watch, and I was free to roam about the boat for the next eight hours. Because three qualified reactor operators were now on board, my life for the next two months would be composed of a seemingly endless number of twelve-hour segments, each consisting of four hours of watching the reactor control panel and eight hours of sleeping or wandering around the boat and wondering what to do next. During this entire time, we would remain submerged, as we waited for the Special Project team to gather whatever information the Fish could find and hoped that something good came of it all.

We had come to accept that the captain and other officers would not tell us in what direction we were heading, where we were going, and what we were going to do when we got there. All of us knew we were going to be searching for something that was extremely secret. Surprisingly, nobody was much bothered by the fact that we were provided with no information. The crew, especially those in the engine room, were to remain almost entirely out of any tiny information loop that might exist. We did not need to know anything about the Special Project in order to do our jobs.

Each man had his own regimen to counteract the

boredom during his hours off watch. I had packed stacks of novels and correspondence courses in French and chemistry from the University of California into my bunk locker, and I planned to spend much of my free time reading or preparing lessons. The *Viperfish* also had about seventy-five full-length motion pictures stored in the dining area; after the evening meal, each movie was shown twice for the men off watch. Many of the movies were first-run features and were thoroughly entertaining, but many others had never reached the ticket-buying public and had subtitles accompanying strange stories that made little sense. Whether the movie was good or bad, we generated the usual continuous observations about everything, from the way an actress walked to the lines her lover whispered in tender moments of love. Nothing occurred in any movie that was too small or too trivial to deserve at least one comment from a member of the crew.

On the second day out, one of the cooks discovered an old, dusty two-hour film reel showing landings of Regulus missiles. The *Viperfish* had previously fired Regulus missiles as her main purpose in life, and there was considerable interest in seeing the results of our boat's old missile days. Prior to the discovery of the movie, nobody on the boat was aware that the Navy ever landed missiles. We logically assumed that once the missile had been fired, it was simply destroyed on impact, along with the target. We all pulled up seats at the dining room "theater," turned out the lights, and hollered for the ancient film to roll.

The entire movie was a repetition—the same thing, over and over. First, we saw the blue sky and an occasional palm tree or two waving in the breeze.

Suddenly, two tiny specks appeared in the distance and approached the island at high speed. After a few seconds, we recognized a winged Regulus missile, with lowered wheels, closely followed by a Navy jet with a pilot struggling to control the Regulus with radio signals. The missile's engine was off as it maintained a high-speed glide in the direction of the runway.

It was a silent movie, and there was no hint as to the source of either the missile or the jet. They both just came out of the sky, from specks to full size in about thirty seconds. No landmarks identified the island, which appeared to be a remote uninhabited coral reef. Throughout each sequence, the pilot of the jet endeavored to keep his slow-flying airplane from stalling, while he worked to bring the Regulus safely to the runway. We guessed it was a reclamation process of sorts, to salvage the Regulus missiles and perhaps to lower the cost of each test firing.

As we silently watched, the first effort failed miserably. The missile, too far to the left of the runway, was aimed almost at the cameraman before it frantically moved to the other side in a manner that landed it straight into the trees. The next missile, controlled by another pilot, had a better chance. It appeared to be lined up correctly; however, just before its tiny wheels touched down, it began to waver and finally nosed into the asphalt in a spectacular crash that disassembled the thing all the way down the runway. The third missile touched down nicely, its wheels spinning furiously, and we all cheered just before it lifted back into the air and began bouncing wildly down to the end of the runway, where it crashed into the lava rocks. The fourth missile appeared briefly and then suddenly disappeared out of sight, presumably crashing into the ocean.

By the time the fifth pair of specks appeared, we were all taking bets on the chances of chaos versus a successful landing.

"He's looking good! He's looking good!" Doc Baldridge hollered.

"He's going to take out the cameraman!" Chief Mathews yelled.

"Five bucks says it'll crash!" the cook called out.

"Five to one!" somebody else said.

"You're on!"

"Oh my God, look at that!"

"Bring it back to the left! It's off course!"

"It's too high!"

"Now it's too low!"

"Dumb goddamn pilot!"

Another Regulus missile bounced and spun its way down the runway and finally disassembled into a heap of smoldering metal.

"Skimmer non-qual puke pilot!" was the usual final observation as money changed hands.

Finally, about five landings later, one missile actually came safely to an upright halt and the ocean around the *Viperfish* reverberated from our cheers. An hour and a half later, five or six more missiles landed safely, and we were left speculating about the award that the photographer must have received for filming so many missiles coming right at him.

The cook finally turned off the projector. Some of the crew drifted off toward their racks for a few hours' sleep, while others wandered out to the far corners of the boat to assume their watches. A half hour later, the next group of men coming off watch assembled in the crew's dining area for snacks and the watching of a special movie, starring the United States Navy, titled *Attempted Landings of Regulus Missiles, Using Jets.*

We continued to move through the ocean toward our mysterious destination, the engine room pulsating with the power of a reactor running at nearly 100 percent to drive the propulsion turbines at top speed. From the plummeting temperature of the ocean water, it was apparent that we were moving in a northerly direction, but none of us knew whether we were heading west toward the Soviet Union or east in the direction of the United States. On the fifth day, that issue was settled as we entered the Domain of the Golden Dragon.

I had not heard of the beast. At the time of the first announcement, I was lying in my rack and studying a lesson related to the conjugation of a long list of French verbs. If I completed ten lessons before our return to Pearl Harbor, there was a good chance that I could soon finish the course and be one step further along the tortuous pathway to a college degree. It would not be difficult, I reasoned—just conjugate the verbs, memorize the vocabulary, pull out my portable typewriter, and assemble the lesson for the professor in his office at Berkeley. Immediately after I memorized the fourth verb on the list, Chief Mathews made the announcement over the ship's IMC loudspeaker.

"Now, attention all hands! We have a sonar contact, bearing 275 degrees, one mile off the port bow, closing on the *Viperfish* at twelve knots!"

I slammed the book shut and yanked back the curtain covering the opening to my rack.

A sonar contact closing on the *Viperfish*? A torpedo?

I stuck my head out into the passageway and looked around, half expecting to see men running to battle stations. Nobody was running anywhere, and the only sign that anyone else had heard the announcement was the presence of several other heads looking out from their racks. I reasoned that it must be some kind of torpedo fire-control drill.

Mathews' voice came out over the loudspeaker system again. "Now, sonar reports the contact has attached to the boat! The contact has attached to the boat!"

This was getting weird very fast. It had to be a strange homing torpedo, I thought, or maybe a type of mine that was somehow attached to the *Viperfish*. I jumped out of my rack in a rush and began to dress quickly, as I listened for a call for surfacing, for battle stations, or for somebody to do something.

"Now, we have entry!" The chief's voice carried the urgency of the situation. "We have confirmed entry of an unauthorized biological form into the wet bilge of the boat."

The opening to the wet bilge, on the decking immediately next to my rack, was covered by a steel grating that spanned the hole. Unfortunately, at that moment, I was standing on top of the steel grating. I froze and slowly looked straight down into the bilge, my mind struggling with the concept of an unauthorized form somewhere below me. Standing at the bottom of the wet bilge was one of our enlisted men, Willie Washington, looking straight up at me, his eyes wide open and filled with fear.

Immediately, he began climbing up the ladder as fast as his arms and legs could move. He was shrieking, "There's a biological something coming in! Lemme outa here!"

I held the grate open for him as he flew out of the wet bilge and disappeared down the passageway without looking back to see what kind of biological form might be chasing him. I lowered the grating and stood directly on top of it. Looking down into the hole, I wondered how anything attaching from outside our boat could migrate through the maze of pipes into the bilge.

And that was when Chief Mathews made his final loudspeaker announcement.

"Now, all scallywags and non-quals, all pukes and others who have not crossed the 180th meridian, I am authorized to announce that the Golden Dragon has gained entry into the *Viperfish*. The Dragon will be immediately convening a golden tribunal in the crew's dining area. All non-quals and other pukes without a certified document granting entry to the Domain lay to the crew's dining area for determination of guilt and justice, according to the Honorable Code of the Golden Dragon!"

The line was long, the trial was short, and the justice was swift. We entered the darkened dining area, one at a time, to find ourselves staring at the face of a huge Golden Dragon with fiery illuminated eyes and a belly that looked remarkably like that of the nuke machinist mate, Joaquin Santos. Paul Mathews had been assigned as the Golden Assistant for the Dragon; there was no defense except useless whimpering pleas for leniency. The creature itself served as the honorable judge, the prosecuting attorney, and the jury; the Dragon's word was absolute and would yield to no appeal.

I was found guilty of all charges. General malfeasance, corruption, multiple gestures of disrespect to the Golden Dragon, and other compelling but undefined improprieties were included, and the sentencing occurred immediately. A quick swig of the Golden Brew was the punishment, a matter ably attended to by the Golden Assistant, Chief Mathews, who provided me with a ladle filled with the foulest, greasiest, oiliest soup I had ever tasted. As I gulped the solution, large quantities spilled onto my dungaree shirt, leaving me with a musty rolling odor unknown to the civilized world. My stomach immediately rejected the entire mess. With cheers from the crew and an identification card certifying me to be now worthy of the Golden Dragon's domain, I was ordered to leave the court before the tribunal reversed its honored and lenient decision. I returned to my rack, where French books took second place to a quick but thorough shower and a change into clean dungarees.

After moving through the Golden Dragon's 180th meridian, Chief Mathews expanded my education in naval lore with his story about the Golden Dragon. Since the time that Greek and Roman sailors guided their fragile vessels on the high seas, the benevolence of mythical gods was believed to be essential for survival and success. As the centuries passed and science advanced, the improved understanding of the challenging forces at sea—weather, waves, and unsettled shiftings within the human mind—diminished the importance of the gods. Only two remain in control of these elements today. Although King Neptune continues to dominate sailors crossing the equator, the more fearful Golden Dragon of the international date line, the supreme serpent controlling the 180th meridian in the mid–Pacific Ocean, generates greater respect from sailors entering its waters. Stretching thousands of miles east of the Kamchatka Peninsula and north to the Aleutian Islands, the violent and turbulent seas within the control of this mythical creature are known by all men of ships and submarines as the Domain of the Golden Dragon.

Continuing our presumably westward journey to enter the icy waters of the Soviet sector, we pushed through the ocean with wide-open throttles for several more days. We finally approached a destination of sorts, somewhere, I guessed, near the Kamchatka Peninsula. The announcement came with an abrupt change in our bell, the first new propulsion order in more than a week, that boiled Marc Birken to attention with the order, "Slow to one-third! Do not cavitate! Do not cavitate!"

Marc rapidly cranked his throttle wheels nearly shut as everybody sitting in the maneuvering area of the engine room looked up at the cavitation indicator lights. The noise from the tiny bubbles spinning off the screw made a cracking sound that could be heard for miles. It was essential, if we were to avoid detection by others, for us to slow the screws and rig the ship for silence.

Since "do not cavitate" was now a standing order for the engine room, it was apparent to me that the captain suspected that somebody, out there in the ocean, might be listening for us.

The captain and executive officer also spread the word for us to do everything possible to maintain silence. Although we could talk, watch movies, and move around the *Viperfish* in a relatively normal manner, we were careful to avoid slamming the steel hatches separating the compartments and to avoid dropping anything on the decking.

Of greatest importance was the garbage. Any light bulbs in the debris ejected from the *Viperfish* would implode with a bomb-like detonation that could be heard for hundreds of miles. Silence was imperative. Garbage bags were checked and double-checked. It was almost as if we had started tiptoeing through the dark spaces of a stranger's house because somebody, probably armed with an arsenal of lethal weapons, could be nearby—awake and listening for the sounds of an intruder.

We shifted in the chairs of our watch stations as these thoughts penetrated our consciousness. The unknown nature of the listening force added to its ominous feel and made it seem more powerful and frightening. Moving slowly and silently through waters that were likely within the Soviet sector, we could almost feel the presence of something or someone above us or around us—listening, waiting, ready to take action against us if we were detected. The crew's morale, already burdened by the problems of the society we had left behind, was further weighted by this new threat. Nobody speculated about what would happen if we were detected, but the subject persistently haunted us while we concentrated on the cavitation monitor and silence.

Chief Morris obviously felt it as much as the rest of us. That evening, he snapped at one of the crewmen,

"There's a flashlight in the engine room with dead batteries. Didn't you guys run the PM [preventive maintenance] last week?"

"I'm sure we did, Chief," the electrician answered calmly. "Which flashlight is it?"

Glaring at the man, the chief stuck out his jaw and said, "I'm not going to tell you. You're going to have to find it yourself."

The man looked at the chief but restrained himself from making any comment. He roamed throughout the engine room as he tested each flashlight one at a time. It took him a half hour, but he finally found the bad light and replaced the batteries.

The rest of us jumped on the chief from that point on. In the subtle manner of submarine crews everywhere, we delivered our message without running afoul of the military chain-of-command structure. When anyone asked where something might be located, the answer, almost always within earshot of Chief Morris, was always an impudent, "I'm not going to tell you. You're going to have to find it yourself."

At that point, we still had almost two more months on patrol. There would be no escape for the chief. He would receive the same message, over and over, wherever he might wander throughout the *Viperfish*. He learned fast, however, and never pulled a "you gotta find it yourself" trick again.

More than a week after leaving Pearl, and nearly two years since the *Viperfish* had started her long journey as a spy submarine, we reached a destination that was unknown to most of us. The SOBs in the hangar compartment prepared for the search. They checked and double-checked our coordinates from the ship's navigation system and compared the data with the information they had been given in Hawaii. Working diligently, they began to prepare the Fish for the complex process required to lower it into the high-pressure ocean.

Finally, they started lowering the Fish down the hole and out through the belly of the *Viperfish*. It was a cooperative effort by Lieutenant Dobkin, Robbie Teague, Captain Harris, and the cluster of civilians. They all tossed out ideas and orders as they eased the Fish, one foot of cable at a time, into the ocean on the start of its journey that would take it miles away from our submarine.

We did not linger around the hangar during this time, so that the SOBs could do their work without our intrusion. Hoping that something worthwhile would come of it, we managed the rest of the boat. It was apparent that our ability to function as a seagoing submarine in matters of military defense was highly limited with the expensive Fish trailing several miles below us. We could not quickly change course, we could not speed up or slow down, and we were unable to change our depth abruptly without destroying the search pattern or damaging the Fish. We were like a military aircraft, flying through the middle of a battle zone at dangerously slow speeds with flaps extended, landing gear down, and controls frozen.

The *Viperfish* was vulnerable, and everybody knew it. Even though the Fish was nearly twenty thousand feet below us, it had to be carefully pulled by its cable so that it would remain only a few feet off the ocean floor. The entire operation was extremely delicate, and its success depended on our moving slowly, systematically, and deliberately at all times.

During the first few days of the search, my biggest worry was the consequences of any flooding. The Fish and its cable likely would be destroyed during any emergency surfacing action or by a sudden loss of propulsion power resulting from any problem in the engine room. I found myself forcing these thoughts from my mind during the long hours of sitting in front of the reactor panel and wondering who was out there listening for us. All of us worked hard to concentrate on the meters spread across our panels.

After two weeks of our quietly moving back and forth across our search pattern, the noise from the first explosion hit our submarine. It was clearly audible to all of us, a distant "whomp!" followed by a long period of stunned silence from our crew.

"What the hell was that?" I asked Brian Lane. Brian and I had been sitting side by side in front of our control panels for the past three hours, as we watched our meters, puffed on cigars, and tried to stay alert despite the monotony and boredom of our tasks.

Lane turned in his chair and looked at me. For a moment, I thought he hadn't heard the noise—his eyes didn't seem to register the enormity of an explosion in the ocean thousands of miles from land. He looked inappropriately relaxed as he spoke the hang-loose Hawaiian vernacular of the day, "Ain't no big thing, bruddah."

I stared at him. "No big thing? Jesus Christ! We're in the middle of the ocean, Brian," I said. "There's not supposed to be anybody else out here."

"It could be from a thousand things," he said, dismissing the more ominous implications.

"Or it could be somebody has found us."

"Survey ships, war games by our guys, fishing fleets detonating fish to the surface, it could be anything."

Glancing back at the reactor control panel, I scanned the meters and looked for anything even slightly abnormal as more explosions went off. I adjusted the reactor control system and shifted around in my chair.

The man of the house is looking for the intruder, I thought.

Behind us, Lieutenant Katz called the control center, asked a couple of questions, and listened carefully. "The captain doesn't know what the sound is," he said, hanging up the telephone. "The sonarmen think the noise is probably coming from a sonobuoy dropped by something—an aircraft, a ship, or maybe even another submarine."

Another explosion went off, and all of us waited for the next one.

"Goddamn!" I said as I put my clipboard down and waited.

"Somebody out there is exploring the thermoclines," Katz said, referring to the layers of water created by virtue of their different temperatures. A layer of cool water next to warmer water causes the deflection of sonar waves; objects, such as submarines hiding on the other side of the thermocline, are concealed from detection by ships on the surface. To improve the chances of finding deeply submerged vessels, floating sonobuoys eject explosive charges that drop deep below the surface. When the charge sinks to a predetermined level, it detonates and the sonobuoy broadcasts any reflected echoes to a receiving ship or aircraft.

It is a tricky business because of the "tunnel effect" that echoes the explosive sound back and forth down the tunnel for many miles and confuses everybody about distances. If we were sitting at the end of a long thermocline tunnel, an explosion from five or ten miles away could sound like it was right outside our hull. Unfortunately, there is no easy way to determine whether or not a tunnel is present. We had no way of knowing if the explosions were from a distant source or right outside our boat.

The explosions, carrying up and down the thermoclines, continued to vibrate the hull of the *Viperfish*, but we tried to ignore the noises and the implications of their presence. Occurring at irregular intervals for several weeks, they disrupted our sleep, frazzled our nerves, and made everybody feel miserable. During this time, we relentlessly pursued our search of the ocean bottom. As the weeks stretched into a full month with no sign of success, morale plummeted even more. The most ominous sign of widespread discontent was the oppressive silence that began to emerge throughout the *Viperfish* as the Fish found nothing, the explosions continued, and our hope for success waned. When the crew was happy, everybody groused about everything; when the crew was depressed, silence prevailed. The *Viperfish*'s crew was becoming silent.

As we roamed our search area, the civilians and Special Project crewmen debated the best way to scan the bottom of the ocean for our target without missing any areas. Some previous experience with towed devices, similar to the Fish, had been documented in the archives of U.S. search projects, such as that by the USS *Mizar*, the oceanographic research ship that had found a nuclear bomb off Spain, but there was almost no experience with a submarine towing miles of cable.

Is it best to move in a straight line back and forth across the search area, they wondered, with the potential of losing the "lineup" during each complicated turnaround procedure? Should the submarine encircle a central point by starting with a huge circle that gradually becomes smaller and smaller? Maybe the circles should start at a central point and expand by ever-increasing diameters. Or would it be better to make equal-sized circles overlapping in a single direction that would result in a wide swath of searched ocean bottom, hopefully performed in such a manner as to rule out any missed areas.

There were no books on the subject and little information beyond the *Mizar* data. Most of us were vaguely aware of the successful operations, which included finding the USS *Thresher* in 1964, but the *Mizar* was fundamentally different from the *Viperfish*: she was a surface craft. Searching the bottom of the ocean in a vessel heaving around on the surface is, in some ways, more of a challenge than it is in a submarine that remains at a fixed depth below the surface.

At least, in a submarine, depth control is usually possible to predict and maintain. Because it was essential for the Fish to remain a specific distance above the bottom of the ocean, in order to prevent its destruction by contact with terrain irregularities, precise submarine depth control was mandatory. Alternatively, if the *Viperfish* pulled the Fish too high above the bottom, its ability to "see" anything below it would be compromised. As long as no emergencies developed that would require sudden changes in depth, a silent submarine was clearly the vessel best suited for a secret search of the ocean's bottom.

The speed of the vessel also dramatically affected the altitude of the Fish above the ocean floor; if the *Viperfish* inadvertently slowed for a few seconds, the Fish could easily sink and be destroyed against rocks or ridges. Cable length had a nearly immediate effect on the Fish's altitude, and careful control of the spool rotation was of top priority. Reactor power and turbogenerator power were essential to operation of the Special Project's computer system that analyzed information from the Fish. Finally, the *Viperfish*'s buoyancy, depth, and direction, which were controlled by the ballast control operator, the planesmen, and the helmsmen, required close communication and teamwork.

Success, however, continued to be elusive. As time passed, we all became increasingly frustrated. We experimented with different methods of moving the boat, and we varied circular patterns and Fish elevations. Each new trial consumed days at a time and resulted in nothing.

After all of these failures, Robbie Teague brought a stack of stunningly clear 8 x 10 black-and-white photographs to the crew's dining area to show us life at twenty thousand feet below the surface, compliments of the Fish. Bizarre bat-like structures stuck out from the bodies of some fish, and others had ornaments clinging to their faces. Other structures resembling slugs lay on the bottom; Robbie called them sea cucumbers. As we passed around the pictures, we expressed appropriate interest in the fauna, complimented Robbie's photography and the clarity of the images, and asked if the civilians had found the object of our search.

Robbie's smile faded. "Not yet, but we're still looking."

"Are we still circling, or have we started a new pattern? If we can't find it here, why can't we look somewhere else?" Richard Daniels asked, his voice sounding tense.

"Because this is where it's supposed to be," Robbie said, almost inaudibly.

"Tell us what it is, and we'll become more enthusiastic. Is it a UFO?" Daniels asked.

"They don't have me in the loop. Can you understand that?"

"A nuclear warhead?"

"It's secret, guys, secret."

"Nobody on the *Viperfish* knows what we're looking for?"

"Nope, nobody I know around here. I just develop the pictures, and—"

"Why is this thing so important?"

"It's classified, it—"

"Right, right, but if we can't find it, then where it's supposed to be doesn't mean much."

"Okay," Robbie said softly, "you're right. However, if we keep looking, we do have a chance. And they tell me it's important."

Robbie gathered his pictures in the silence that followed and, without another word, returned to the hangar compartment—his diplomatic mission of fostering Special Project enthusiasm a notable failure.

As we cruised around and around and back and forth and as morale continued to slide, a shocking event occurred one morning in the crew's dining area. We were all eating freshly cooked oatmeal when one of the forward crew machinists violently spit the cereal all over the dining area table and jolted the men around him.

"Goddamn it all, where's the cook?" the man hollered as everybody began to examine their own cereal.

"Right here," Marty Belmont said, looking concerned as he walked up to the table. "What's the problem?"

Marty was a chubby, pleasant little fellow who worked as hard as anybody on the boat and did a good job. His work was especially important because the meals were almost the only variability in our day-to-day lives, and good food meant a happy, or at least a happier, crew. The budget for food on submarines exceeds that of any other branch of the Navy. Regularly taking advantage of that fact, Marty tried to make the food as tasty as possible.

"Marty, there's goddamn worms in the goddamn cereal!" the machinist hollered, spilling out more food. Immediately, everybody in the dining room, including myself, simultaneously blasted food from our mouths. The tables were covered with a layer of partially chewed cereal.

"Jesus Christ, Marty, don't you check for bugs in the food?" another man yelled.

"Did Robbie give you these animals from the bottom of the ocean?"

I spit out some more food and carefully examined the bowl of cereal in front of me. Thousands of tiny white worms, crawling among the grains of warm cereal, exactly matched the color of oatmeal—a perfect camouflage, unnoticed by the rest of us. It occurred to several of us, as we groused and grumbled and generally felt miserable, that the cereal had actually tasted pretty good, a little meatier than usual perhaps, but the flavor was definitely unique.

Marty gathered up the bowls, his face distressed, as he reflected on the ruins of the morning meal. "I'm sorry, fellas. They must have broken into the grain. I cooked the cereal but I guess I didn't get it hot enough. Damn little buggers shoulda died."

We all stared at the man, speechless.

Finally, one of the men stood up and handed Marty his bowl. "Even *dead* worms don't belong in the cereal."

"I'm doing the best I can," Marty said, wiping down the tables, as a couple of the other galley crewmen joined him to clean up the mess covering most of the tables.

From that day on, the phrase "I'm doing the best I can" became synonymous with the ever-increasing numbers of important things going wrong in spite of the best intentions.

The search continued for another two weeks, until even the normally enthusiastic civilians in the hangar became discouraged. Robbie didn't bring any more pictures to us, and the men throughout the *Viperfish* stopped speculating about the object of our search. A feeling of profound frustration and gloom descended on everybody. The explosions outside our hull were similar to Chinese water-drop torture; each one wasn't that loud but added together, day after day, the noise created a mental state of continuous uneasiness.

As our second month under water began, I found

myself slowly feeling more and more claustrophobic. None of us had seen any sunlight or sky since the day we left Pearl Harbor. After each four-hour watch, the dilemma of nowhere to go and nothing to do became a problem. I had passed the time by completing French lessons and reading a couple of books during the first month at sea, but now I found myself becoming restless after reading just one or two pages—it was getting increasingly difficult to concentrate. My French lessons were becoming much more of a challenge, and it took all the effort I had just to sit down and concentrate on trying to understand bits and parts of the language.

The final blow came shortly after I started working on the last paragraph of a full page of carefully typed French. The typing of my correspondence course work had taken most of my free time during the preceding several days. Moving from one word to the next, I struggled to avoid mistakes, looked up each incomprehensible French idiom, penned in the proper accent marks, and corrected the inevitable errors that slipped through in spite of it all. As I endeavored to clarify the spelling of a particularly strange French word in the last part of the final paragraph, a large hydraulic valve above me abruptly cycled with a loud whoosh. A thick glob of grease dropped from the valve directly onto the part of my typewritten page sticking out of the typewriter.

I stared at the oil as it slithered down the single-spaced sentences. Watching the typewriter ink smear as the oil diluted the letters, I felt my head begin to pound. I ripped the page from the typewriter, shredded the paper into the tiniest pieces I could manage, and cursed France and everybody in Europe. Then,

I steamed down to the crew's dining area to watch another half hour of Regulus missiles crashing down runways on a deserted atoll in the middle of nowhere.

After almost seven weeks of fruitless searching with the background noises of sonobuoy explosions echoing up and down Soviet thermocline tunnels, Captain Harris finally decided to bring in the Fish and head back to Hawaii. We began the prolonged process of reeling several miles of cable into the *Viperfish*. Cruising back and forth with our Fish out—a mother ship with her very long and delicate umbilical cord—was not an exercise that made us feel particularly useful, especially so because we had failed to find anything worthwhile. Most of us looked forward to stowing the miserable device and reconverting the boat into a more maneuverable non–Fish towing vessel. We hoped that we could now at least try to function like the military ship we were supposed to be.

During the hours of reeling in the Fish, a powerful storm began to build in the waters stretching across the North Pacific. We were at a depth of three hundred feet, where surface wave activity should not affect us more than 90 percent of the time; on that day, we entered the 10 percent portion where rules didn't apply. It was a slow-roll type of movement, nothing that would make us think about hunting for Ralph O'Roark but enough to let us know that nature was stirring up the surface. The noises of sonobuoys stopped at the beginning of the storm, and everybody began to feel better as the huge spool outside our pressure hull continued to reel in the Fish. Finally, to our great relief, the civilians stowed the Fish in a corner of the hangar and the captain ordered the

Viperfish to pick up speed and begin clearing out of the Soviet sector.

I relieved Richard Daniels from his reactor watch shortly after we began to accelerate in the direction of Pearl. We had to shout to be heard above the whining of the propulsion turbines and reduction gears, which were thirty feet away from the maneuvering area. I gathered the information from Richard about the reactor, now running at full capacity, and pulled up a seat in front of the control panel. Brian Lane sat next to me, manning his complex electrical control panel. To my surprise and in contrast to his silence of the past several weeks, he now became more talkative.

"We're running low on fuel," I said, as I gathered data from the meters filling the panel in front of me. There is no fuel gauge, per se, to pinpoint when the nuclear reactor requires a new uranium core, but data from multiple operational sources leave no doubt about the remaining fuel.

Brian turned and smiled at me. "Enough to get back?" His smile faded. "Right?"

"Enough to get back," I reassured him. "If my calculations are correct."

"No gas stations out here—"

"No uranium stations," I corrected,

"No shore-power cables to hook up to the battery."

"Nope, gotta rely on the reactor. Lucky for the forward pukes that they have the nukes to get them back."

"Thank God."

Lane then turned in his chair and looked at me. His eyes seemed to stare through me, but he smiled in a way that was strangely out of sync with the general mood throughout the submarine.

"You can't get to me," he said in a matter-of-fact tone. I watched him as he turned back to his panel and began scanning his meters.

The phrase was a familiar submariner idiom. "You can't get to me" speaks the essence of being a submariner. It is a statement that says, even in the cramped quarters and continuous press of close human contact, even when there are worms in the cereal and detonations in the ocean, nothing is allowed to get under the skin. "You can't get to me" said it all: Nothing bothers me, I am a professional, and there is no way anything that is said or done will be a problem for me.

Lane said it at the wrong time, however. He watched his panel while I looked at mine, our ears enclosed by the plastic sound guards that shut out the screaming machinery around us. After noting more data on my log sheet, I glanced sideways at the man and wondered why my friend and shipmate had said something so far out of proper context. I finally dismissed the matter with the speculation that he must have misunderstood—the shrill noise of turbines drowning out what I had said.

About that time, when I was feeling about as grouchy as almost everybody else, the EOOW decided to quiz me. A tall man, Lieutenant George Sanders was moving up through the ranks of nuclear-trained officers, but he had an officer-elitist attitude. His trace of an "I am better than you" approach contrasted sharply with the leadership capabilities and personalities of the other submarine officers who fostered our respect by earning, rather than demanding, it. He

got on my nerves as he paced back and forth behind
Lane and me when we were on watch, and I was
never quite sure what he was going to say next.

On this watch, he was irritating me more than
usual. So, when the quiz began, I clenched my teeth,
crossed my arms across my chest, and stared at the
reactor panel.

"Okay, Dunham," he said from behind me, "you're
cruising along at four hundred feet."

Consistent with the range of appropriate responses
of an enlisted man to an officer, I respectfully answered, "Yes, sir."

"Okay. Now, the ship begins to sink."

"Yes, sir, the ship sinks." This would not be difficult, I thought, just a matter of the ship sinking.

"*Begins* to sink!" he shrieked. "You now have two
choices. You can save the reactor or you can save the
ship."

"Yes, sir." I was sure I would have more choices
than two.

His voice became icy. "Well, Dunham, what are
you going to do?"

"I'll save the ship, sir," I said, not having a clue as
to where his line of speculation was leading.

"Right, that is correct. Very good." I adjusted my
ear protectors in the hope that his voice would blend
in with the turbogenerators.

"However, Dunham," he continued, "you will save
the reactor if I tell you to save the reactor."

With that, Lieutenant Sanders had reached his goal.
Even though I might want to save the ship, he, as an
officer, would force me to do something contrary to
training and common sense. It was a power thing.
What I should have said at that point was something

like, "The choice is yours, sir, because you are the EOOW."

I felt a flash of irritation at the whole line of questioning, so I blurted out, "No, sir, I would not save the reactor."

He stopped pacing the deck and stood directly behind my chair. "You would save the reactor if I told you to," he said forcefully.

My irritation rose. I jotted a couple of numbers from the reactor panel onto my clipboard. "No, sir. I would save the ship, but I would not save the reactor."

His voice climbed an octave. "You would save the reactor if I told you to!"

"No, sir."

I noticed Brian sinking down into his chair. He was trying to be as inconspicuous as possible.

The lieutenant became livid. "You would if I told you to!" he yelled, bits of sputum flying in all directions.

"No, sir," I answered politely. "I would not be inclined to save the reactor, sir."

He began to hyperventilate. A couple of enlisted men standing near the maneuvering area quickly walked away, probably searching for a place to hide. I gnashed my teeth, grabbed the reactor clipboard, and noted some additional information in my logbook as Sanders finally sat down, his face red with anger. I put the clipboard down and wondered if I was going to be court martialed for refusing a hypothetical order. From my perspective, the entire issue was the result of everybody being annoyed about everything, the failure of our search mission, and the effects of nearly two months of submerged duty. But, for Sanders, it was personal, an enlisted man's insolence, and something, by God, that was going to be taken to Lieutenant Pintard immediately after the watch.

Ten minutes after I finished the watch, Pintard took me to the hangar compartment, now quiet, and spoke like a father to an errant son, "Dunham, Dunham, Dunham . . ."

"Well, he was a bit out of line, sir," I said.

Pintard smiled. "Lieutenant Sanders is an excellent officer, and next time just tell him what he wants to hear."

"Hypothetical orders—"

He raised his hands to stop me. "If Mr. Sanders wants you to save a mermaid swimming to the moon, just tell him you will do everything possible to save the bitch, okay? This is a submarine, but there is a military structure that needs to be followed."

I agreed, and that was the end of the issue; however, a new phrase, "You will if I tell you to!" entered the lexicon of the *Viperfish* crew. It was repeated a hundred times during the days ahead, usually within earshot of Lieutenant Sanders and always in the tone of an authoritarian out of control. If somebody said, "I'm really not sure I'd want to swim in the Ala Moana harbor," the immediate, reflexive response would be a hollered, "You would if I told you to!"

Because there is no way that any man on a submarine can escape the "pinging" (verbal barbed wire) of the crew, an early lesson of submarine life, for an officer and enlisted man alike, is that there is a price to pay for being obnoxious. The barrage of pinging from the entire crew can become incessant; when somebody with an inappropriate attitude is trapped with the crew, this can eat him alive. Wherever he walks, from bow to stern, other crewmen (officer and enlisted) are everywhere. They sleep above and below him; they sit at his table; they eat meals and watch movies with him; they use the head and take showers next to him.

If the word is out that he has brought any form of grief to one of the crew, retribution follows—a dig here or there, a phrase, anything that conveys displeasure—and it will not let up.

Two months is a long time, and there is nowhere to hide. Officers are as much at risk as enlisted men. From the cook serving protein-enriched cereal—"doing the best I can"—to the chief ordering his man to "find it yourself" to the officer who orders "you'll do it if I tell you to," they will find no mercy from the crew. The pinging continues, without pause until enough time goes by that everybody finally forgets the issue or until some redeeming act from the accused brings forgiveness and peace.

Two days later, when I passed by the radio shack, one of the crew angrily handed me an official Navy bulletin recently transmitted to the *Viperfish*. The bulletins were passed around the boat on rare occasions and served as a kind of Navy-oriented newspaper. After climbing into my rack and pulling the curtain, I turned on the light and scanned the front page. Anything would be more interesting than French lessons.

The first story reported the tale of an enlisted Navy man who was found guilty of using LSD. The LSD had caused him no problems except for prolonged staring sessions, and he seemed to do fine except for repeated, unpredictable flashbacks. On one

such flashback, the man apparently thought he was
an orange; the accompanying editorial warned of the
dangers to nuclear reactor operators who think they
are becoming fruit.

Because I never used drugs and didn't know of anybody on the *Viperfish* with any kind of a drug habit,
I moved to the second article. This one was written by
the captain of a nuclear submarine somewhere in the
world who had purged most of the nukes on his ship
for various reasons that seemed to have little merit.
The article pointed out, however, that Admiral Hyman G. Rickover was quite satisfied with the action,
was *happy* with the action, and the editorial warned
us to stay on our toes, or we too might be at risk for a
purge. As I remembered the NR Board debacle and
began to feel gloomy at the thought of a Mao Tse-
tung purification on board our submarine, I became
aware of the *Viperfish* sliding into a steep and sustained down-angle.

I have never liked the feeling of our boat pointing
her bow toward the bottom of the ocean. In most
cases, a down-angle is a transient process carrying little risk. The helmsmen push forward on their Repub-
lic Aviation control wheels, and the entire vessel
rotates forward into a downward slide. The duration
of the down-angle affects the psyche of the entire
crew. The steeper the down-angle, the greater the anxiety, until it becomes a waiting game—waiting for the
down-angle to stop and for the submarine to level out.
Depending on speed and buoyancy factors, a submarine can point down for only so long before something
dramatic happens.

Outside the control station, the men had no information about the depth of the submarine during

down-angle maneuvers, and no announcement indicated how much deeper the *Viperfish* was going. It was like being a passenger in a diving airliner that had no windows, with predictable results on the enclosed humans: a fine sweat covering the skin, a hand tightening its grip on the side of the chair, and irritation demonstrated by spontaneous small movements of annoyance.

When is the dive going to stop? How far down are we going to go?

Other thoughts, private thoughts, moved through the minds of the men riding the submarine down, thoughts about test depth and crush depth, thoughts about pressures at the bottom of the ocean, and sobering thoughts about survival. It was essential, we all knew, that the destination depth not fall below the ship's maximum test depth. In a steep dive, the time it takes to pass through the test depth and reach the crush depth is a matter of only a few seconds.

In submarine school, we had been told that submarines in the American fleet will often take steep down-angles under many operational scenarios. It happens all the time, it is normal. "The conning station knows what it is doing, it will not overstress the ship," we had been told, there is no need for panic, everything is under control.

Fine, but how long does the dive continue, and at what point would it be appropriate to start wondering about our depth?

I ripped aside the curtain of my rack. Looking up and down the passageway, I checked for anything that seemed unusual. The boat was definitely pointed in a steeply downward direction, and there was no indication that we were going to level out or move into an up-angle at any time in the near future. The off-watch crew was scattered throughout the berthing area, arms and legs protruding into the dark passageways, mouths rumbling out a symphony of snores. Several of the men began stirring restlessly as the down-angle increased a couple of degrees and the submarine seemed to accelerate her dive.

I swung out of my rack, pulled on my dungarees, and hiked up to the *Viperfish*'s diving station to investigate. At 0300 the control center was only dimly lit by glowing red pinpoints of light on the electronic panels—the compartment was fully "rigged for red." The room was unusually silent, and everybody looked grim. Captain Harris paced back and forth next to the lowered periscopes, Commander Ryack leaned across the railing and scrutinized the gauges over the shoulders of the two helmsmen. Chief Mathews and Petty Officer Michael Davidson, wearing life jackets, stood next to the ladder leading up to the sealed overhead hatch. With thick belts encircling their waists and steel chains, ready to be latched to railings on the outside deck, hanging at their sides, they were preparing to climb the ladder. I stared at them as I tried to understand what they were going to do.

I turned to Sandy Gallivan, standing at my side, and asked him what was going on. He looked at me, his face tense, his words strained.

"Problem with the Fish winch mechanism," he said quickly. "Gotta hold the boat in a down-angle or our Special Project operation is shot. Bates is keeping us steady at this depth with positive buoyancy, and we're moving real slow." He pointed in the direction of Joel Bates, the lanky ballast control panel operator, who was hunched over his chair, his eyes glaring at his depth gauges.

"Aren't we moving pretty deep right now, with the down-angle and all?" I asked.

"Even though we're about four hundred feet," he said patiently, "we're not changing depth because of the positive buoyancy. As we move forward, we float up by an equal amount, holding our depth steady. It is a delicate balance, and Bates is going crazy trying to keep us at four hundred. Mathews and Davidson are going topside to free the hydraulic lock on the Fish's cable reel. In about thirty seconds, we are going to surface."

"We're going to surface with a down-angle?" I asked.

"With a down-angle," Sandy confirmed, looking unhappy. "At least we're not dangling a Fish below us."

Mathews and Davidson rechecked the thick belts holding their rail chains and looked up the ladder at the control room hatch as Philip O'Dell grabbed the microphone to the loudspeaker system.

"Now, surface, surface, surface!" Chief O'Dell's voice bellowed from speakers throughout the submarine.

With the rapid movements of practiced experience, the men in the control center flipped the switches controlling the high-pressure ballast air system. As the roaring compressed air blew water out of our ballast tanks, we rapidly ascended—the bow of the *Viperfish* still strangely pointing down by about 20 degrees. We broke through the surface of the early-morning ocean, and the helmsmen immediately opened the control-room hatch connecting to the sail. The thin form of

Gerry Young raced up the ladder in front of Captain Harris. Both men scrambled to the top of the sail, and two lookouts followed closely behind. Mathews and Davidson remained next to the ladder in the control center, as they waited for orders to move out of the *Viperfish*.

From sixty-five feet above the deck, Young's voice crackled over the loudspeakers in the control center. "Con, Bridge, how do you read me?"

"I read you loud and clear, how me?" Chief O'Dell called into his microphone.

"I hear you same," the speakers replied.

For about ten minutes, the captain and the OOD studied the waves around the *Viperfish* in the early-morning dark as she plowed through the heaving waters. The freezing rain and wind, occasionally carrying blasts of salt-laden sea spray, whipped around the cockpit and blew into their faces.

The boat rolled vigorously from the cross-wave activity. The lookouts watched for lights of any approaching ships. The dark shape of the *Viperfish* would not be visible to the crew of another ship because we were running without lights, and there was always a small chance of collision with some random freighter straying out of the shipping lanes.

Commander Young's major responsibility as the officer of the deck was to establish the best possible course for the *Viperfish* and lead her directly into the driving seas. Swells hitting the bow of the boat were easily traversed, but those striking the superstructure from abeam could cause severe rolling. He ordered several course changes during the first few minutes to move the *Viperfish* into the best direction through the waves. As each wave rolled out of the dark with an almost predictable regularity and approached the bow, we lifted up smoothly to ride over the top.

The captain had a bigger problem. Chief Mathews and Petty Officer Davidson were about to leave the security of the boat to walk on a slippery submarine deck. Everybody was aware that we were more than a thousand miles from the nearest land, and there was nobody nearby to help if we had a problem.

Inside the control room, Mathews and Davidson climbed to the top of the ladder. Dragging their rail chains behind them, they stopped just below the open hatch to the sail. Again, they paused and awaited orders.

"Mathews, Davidson, lay topside, into the sail!" the captain's order finally crackled down from the control room loudspeakers.

The two men quickly disappeared through the hatch into the dark interior of the sail, their chains clattering behind them. Within the sail, they turned on their flashlights to light up the door leading to the outside of the sail structure. The chief yanked up on the handle and swung the door wide. As it slammed against the outside steel, torrents of rain and roars from the black ocean stunned the men.

"Jesus" was all Davidson said, softly under his breath. As the junior enlisted man, he would faithfully follow his chief into the hostile night. He would say nothing more but, rather, concentrate on the job awaiting them and ignore the energy hammering the world around them.

Waiting for their final orders from the captain, Mathews and Davidson clutched the bar inside the open door and tried to see out into the night. High above their heads, the captain, the OOD, and the lookouts continued to scowl at the powerful forces surrounding the boat.

The captain's deep voice finally rumbled down to the sail from the cockpit: "You're clear for the top-side deck!"

The two men immediately stepped out through the sail door and clamped their short chains to the railing carved into the steel deck. Beginning to inch forward slowly and clutching the handrail on the starboard side of the sail, they dragged their chains behind them as they progressed toward the hydraulic pipes ahead.

"I can't see a goddamn thing!" Mathews growled to Davidson as he brushed the rain from his eyes and shined his flashlight into the night.

"Nothing to see but the goddamn freezing rain!" Davidson hollered back over the roar of the ocean. They rounded the front of the sail and prepared to move across the deck, Mathews leading the way in the direction of the hydraulic system's valves.

Without warning, a rogue wave loomed like a huge black mountain two hundred yards in front of the *Viperfish* and began rolling directly at the submarine's heaving deck.

The four men in the cockpit simultaneously saw the massive shape that dwarfed the boat and seemed to become increasingly larger. Driven by the winds and tortured by the forces of the sea pulling up into its face, the black wall of water roared in thunderous slow motion, the crest topped by foaming white water higher than the top of the sail. The lookouts hollered their warning. The OOD and the captain immediately tried to save the men on the deck below.

"Get back inside!" Young's voice blasted urgently from the top of the sail.

"Get into the sail!" the captain hollered. "Get inside, now!"

Young grabbed the microphone communicating into the control center and hollered, "Come right 20 degrees!"

The helmsman in the control center instantly turned the *Viperfish* farther to the right. The bow, moving slightly to the new course, pointed directly into the wave that seemed to grow like a powerful creature, a living thing preparing to devour the vessel and the men who challenged its waters.

"Come right another 10 degrees!" Young screamed into the microphone, as he tried to point the *Viperfish* directly into the powerful wave so that she could bisect and ride over it.

"Right, 10 degrees, aye, aye, sir!" the chief of the boat called back, and the helmsman responded with the rudder change.

The men on the deck turned and raced for the safety of the sail. Davidson reached it first, his chain now ahead of the chief. He frantically unlatched his clamp and leaped through the door, while Mathews hollered, "Go! Go! Go! Go!"

The wave hit the *Viperfish* head-on and consumed her bow. Crashing high over the outstretched bow planes, it foamed across the top of the bat-cave hump and finally roared across the deck toward the sail. Just as Davidson turned to reach for his shipmate, the decking around him shuddered from the wave's impact. Water flooded over the top of the sail and into the cockpit sixty-five feet above the ocean, drenched the four men, and then roared down the long ladder. It almost washed Davidson back out the door.

A solid column of seawater crashed through the

open hatch of the control room, flooded the decking, and soaked everybody in the area of the diving station. On the deck outside the sail, Mathews held his breath as the wall of water crashed into him. Burying him beneath its violence, the wave forced him away from the door and broke his grip on the sail's handrail. It slammed him against the deck and finally accelerated him toward the stern. Frantically, he reached toward his belt to grasp the chain that strained with the weight of his body dragging the clamp along the steel rail.

The clamp suddenly broke free from the rail. As the rush of water carried Mathews into the ocean, he struck the deck with a final glancing blow and disappeared toward the churning screws of the *Viperfish*.

Davidson, scrambling around inside the sail, tried to stand up again. He grabbed the hinges of the door and looked out into the night for Mathews. His broken flashlight washed out the door with the water clearing from the sail. His fingers clutched the inside railing as he leaned outside the door to search behind the *Viperfish* for any signs of a light.

"Paul!" he hollered at the top of his lungs, his eyes moving to the foaming sea that roared past the sides of the boat. He called the chief's name again, but he knew there would be no answer. He took one last desperate look before finally backing into the sail, his mind numb with the shock of losing his shipmate.

"Man overboard, starboard side!" he screamed up to the four men at the top of the sail. "The chief is gone!"

"Man overboard! Man overboard!" Young's urgent voice bellowed down into the control room loudspeakers as the captain and the lookouts shined their lights toward the foaming white water beyond the stern of the boat.

Inside the control room, Young's voice immediately hollered over the loudspeaker, "All back emergency!" to the helmsmen. "Right full rudder!"

We had performed drills like this a hundred times. Remembering the routine, I raced to the starboard corner of the control room to grab the man-overboard bag, a large white duffel bag filled with life vests and other floatation equipment. I dragged it across the deck to the base of the ladder and dropped it into the water pooling in front of the periscope station. It was obvious that the bag would be of no help to anybody.

In the engine room, Billy Elstner spun the ahead throttles shut and rapidly opened the reverse throttles that rotated the screws in the opposite direction.

"Who went over?" a voice called from the other side of the control room.

"Jesus Christ!" Commander Ryack exploded furiously, his voice filled with rage. "It doesn't matter who went overboard, goddamn it! It is one of our shipmates and that's all that counts!"

"Are we answering the back emergency bell?" Young's voice from the cockpit filled the control room.

"Yes, sir!" O'Dell hollered into the microphone. "Answering back emergency."

The lights throughout the boat briefly dimmed as the men in the engine room drained steam energy from the nuclear reactor in their effort to halt the *Viperfish*. Sloshing in the water, I moved away from the ladder in the control center and felt useless. The life vests inside the bag couldn't even be delivered to the ocean, much less to the man in the water, and he was already wearing a life vest. Further, the flashlights in the bag would be immediately lost in the thrashing sea even if we could toss them out.

While Commander Ryack spun the starboard periscope around to search into the night, the four men at the top of the sail, two on each side, leaned over the edge of the cockpit as they scrutinized the waters behind the boat. There was no sign of Mathews or his light in the surrounding darkness.

"I can't see anything out there," the OOD said with frustration.

"He's out there," the captain said. "We'll go ahead with the 'Y' and we'll find him."

"Control, bridge!" Young hollered into his microphone under the steel lip of the sail. "Chief Mathews is in the water behind us! Can you see him through the scopes?"

"Negative!" Ryack shot back. "Nothing!"

The rudder orders came, and we started to make a "Y" turn, a procedure well known to the men at the top of the sail. The object was to back the boat in a light, rotating movement while keeping the man overboard in full view. Our biggest problem was that nobody had seen the chief since the wave had washed him away. Also, now that we were turning in the sea, the waves began hammering at us from directly abeam, steeply rolling the boat from the lateral forces.

A larger wave, fifteen to twenty feet high, slammed into us and hit directly broadside. Roaring through the open sail door, it drenched Davidson with more freezing water. He considered closing the hatch but then decided to leave it open in the hope that he would see the chief as the boat continued to rotate. About that time, however, he realized that Chief Mathews might not be conscious.

"We're tracking the area," Young called down to the control room as the rolls became more prominent. Both lookouts cursed as they scanned the ocean behind the *Viperfish* for any sign of a light in the sea.

"Answering full back emergency!" from the engine room, as we felt the pulsating power of the screws stopping our forward motion.

"Turn on the running lights and set the fire-control watch!" the captain hollered, ordering the men in the control center to man the dead reckoning tracer (DRT).

Another wave slammed broadside against us and rushed through the open door of the sail. Again, a column of seawater roared down the control room hatch and flooded the control center.

"Close the fucking hatch!" the executive officer hollered from the periscope station. One of the enlisted men pulled down on the halyard and slammed the hatch shut. He then activated his microphone to tell the men in the sail that they were sealed outside the *Viperfish*.

"Bridge, control!" he called out. "We've taken water in control! The control room hatch is closed!"

The loudspeakers responded a quick acknowledgment.

At that moment, I was sure that Chief Mathews was lost forever. There was no way we could recover anybody we couldn't see or reach, a man under the pounding waves, probably a mile or more away from us, a man now freezing in the waters of the Soviet sector. Sloshing through the ankle-deep water, I dragged the man-overboard bag away from the base of the ladder. Small waves moved across the flooded decking of the control room with the movements of the boat, and I looked for a bucket to help clear the water.

"Grab some sponges and move the water out!" Chief O'Dell hollered, as we rolled another 30 degrees and salt water splashed into the fire-control panels. The technicians responsible for the electronics systems raced up and down the passageway to turn off everything in danger of salt water contamination.

I grabbed a fistful of sponges and tried to soak up the water. The boat continued rolling, now more violently as we moved across the "Y" and lateral to the seas. More waves of water splashed against the electronic systems. O'Dell and Ryack, each manning a periscope, rotated them back and forth as they scanned the ocean behind the *Viperfish* for any signs of Mathews' light. Staring through the lenses into darkness, they saw nothing but the black of a violent, empty night.

Outside the boat, the metal door on the side of the sail repeatedly crashed against the frame of the superstructure. It sounded hauntingly as if Paul Mathews was out there pounding the *Viperfish* with a hammer and trying to get back inside.

"Do you see anything through the scopes?" the captain's voice called down to the control center.

"Nothing!" Ryack answered. "Goddamn it, nothing." His thumb remained poised on the TBT (target bearing transmitter) button at the base of the periscope handle, his eyes scanning back and forth.

"Bridge, this is the engine room!" Pintard called over the loudspeaker. "We are approaching the maximum bearing temperature limits for our backing turbines!"

"Keep your bell on!" Commander Young's sharp voice yelled down to the engine room.

"Where the hell is he?" Ryack said, moving the handles of his scope. "It's a goddamn hurricane out there—"

"I don't see anything, either," O'Dell said from behind his scope. "He's out there somewhere."

The speakers filled with another call from the engine room, Pintard's voice now more persistent. "We have exceeded our bearing and oil temperature limits for the backing turbines!"

"Keep your bell on!" Young's voice roared through our loudspeakers.

"Gotta get him on the leeward side," Ryack said.

O'Dell rotated his periscope again.

"Gotta see him, first," he said.

"Problem is, we may run over him before we spot him."

"Goddamn it . . ."

"How long have we been backing down?"

"Probably four or five minutes. It took us two minutes just to stop."

The speaker came to life again, the EOOW's voice urgent. "Bridge, engine room, the bearing temperatures are now—"

"Keep your bell on!" Young hollered again from the top of the sail. Although Young was standing the OOD watch, as the boat's engineer, he probably knew the limitations of his turbines better than any other man on board.

I mashed sponges into the water and wrung them into the buckets as we struggled to clear more water from the control center. We are going to do everything we can to save him, I thought—we are even going to burn out our propulsion turbine bearings.

Dipping the sponges into the water again, I cursed the persistent slamming sound of the unlatched sail door. The noise struck blow after blow on the minds of the men in the control center. We heard it as a repetitive call from our man, lost in the howling forces of hell that raged around us, pleading for the crew of the *Viperfish* to bring him back.

The medical consequences of being lost at sea mark a relentless path from initial shock and terror to a final paralysis that destroys the victim's mind and body. The first few seconds, a time when there still might be hope for a rescue, bring a harsh reality—the frantic search into the howling night for the departing ship, the stinging of eyes from the blasting of the water and wind, and the fighting for breath as the foaming ocean tries to invade the lungs.

During this time, the light attached to the life jacket shines a weak beam into the night with an energy that determines nothing less than the fact of survival itself. For when the battery's energy becomes exhausted, the light will fail as the victim himself will fail. And, as more time passes, the victim accelerates his downward slide that weakens the muscles and begins to spread a deadly paralysis throughout his body. He finally moves into a deep and frozen coma as his hypothermic mind is mercifully shielded from being a witness to his own death.

When Chief Mathews' chain had pulled away from the rail and he slammed off the *Viperfish*'s hull into the freezing ocean, his shouts for help were immediately extinguished by the roaring of the ocean and the howling of the wind. He checked his light—

his only lifeline in the night—and his fists formed a death grip on his life jacket. Struggling to hold his head above the pounding ocean, he knew, as a matter of cold and practical reality, that the shouting of his voice and the waving of his arms could be heard and seen by nobody. He knew from the beginning that his chance of survival was nearly zero.

He massaged the light attached to his life jacket and thought about pulling it free so that he could hold it high, but he quickly abandoned the idea. What would he do if he accidentally dropped it into the sea? He looked down at the light frequently, taking some assurance that its white glow could possibly mean survival. Without the light, he would be a dark shape in a dark ocean, a figure that could not be seen and would not be saved from the cold waters. For he knew that when hypothermia develops—the dropping of temperature as the body cannot produce adequate heat—the mind slows, body movements weaken, and survival is no longer possible.

At the periscopes in the control center of the *Viperfish*, Chief O'Dell and Commander Ryack continued their intense search of the waters behind us as the boat shuddered from the waves pounding the hull. Every roll of the submarine generated another wave of seawater rolling across the deck of the control center and crashing against the electronic control panels that lined our bulkheads. Another call from the engine room about bearing temperatures was followed by orders to maintain the bell, continue backing, proceed with the search for Chief Mathews, and the temperatures be damned.

Captain Harris saw the first flash of light. He and the other three men were searching from their vantage point high above the *Viperfish* as the submarine completed her backing bell. By its nature, the "Y" maneuver led to the vessel moving perpendicular to the wave motion, which resulted in the steep rolling that hampered our efforts to clear away the water from the control center.

It was just a flash, a spark and nothing more, from the center of blackness.

"Sixty degrees off the port bow!" the captain shouted and pointed into the night.

"All ahead two-thirds!" Commander Young immediately ordered into the microphone connecting to the engine room.

"Left full rudder."

"The light's gone, sir!" one of the lookouts said, his binoculars aimed at the area several hundred yards away.

"He's probably under water again," the captain said as the *Viperfish* responded to the new bell. "We'll just close in on the area of the light. Bring her around, Gerry," he said to the OOD.

"If we don't see the light again, we're going to take a chance on going right over him," Young said.

"Just keep him downwind of the boat," the captain said patiently.

From the control room, there was almost no information about the events topside. We knew that the chief was gone; we knew that the backing bell had either destroyed or come close to destroying the turbine bearings; and we knew that the *Viperfish* was now starting to move forward. The two men on the periscopes continued their search, but they were greatly hampered by the steep rolls tilting the periscopes from one side to the other, which prevented them from getting a fix on anything around us. Everybody in the control room worked in a state of stunned silence. As we continued to clear water from the decking, we kept hoping that some progress was being made from the top of the sail, but we also knew that a recovery under these conditions was extremely unlikely. After hearing the ahead bell and the rudder changes and then the all-stop bell, we waited for ten minutes while absolutely nothing happened. The final story of Chief Mathews came to us only later, in bits and pieces.

From the top of the sail, the men in the cockpit saw the light again, and then again, as the *Viperfish* completed the "Y" maneuver and came to a halt, upwind of the chief.

"Hang on, Mathews!" the captain yelled as the final approach was made. "We're going to get you!"

There was no answer from the chief as the deck party of lookouts and a thoroughly soaked and freezing Michael Davidson ventured out on the deck for the recovery. They threw lines from the boat in his direction and then threw more lines. Mathews did not reach out for them or move closer to the boat, and he did not respond. In the end, a man went into the ocean to bring him back.

Suddenly, the hatch above our heads opened, and a splash of water dropped into the control center.

"Stand by to bring him down the ladder!" Davidson hollered from inside the sail, and we all gathered around the base of the ladder to help.

Mathews was nearly unconscious when the men carefully lowered him, head first, down the ladder into our waiting arms. He was sobbing, speaking incoherently, and mumbling over and over, "I never saw the boat."

"It's okay, Paul," we told him as Doc Baldridge checked his abrasions, several of which were still bleeding. He had slammed against the boat's superstructure a couple of times when his chain separated, but he had no broken bones or serious head injuries.

We wrapped him in several blankets and moved him down to his rack, where the Doc repeatedly checked on him for the next two days.

He had been in the water only twenty to thirty minutes, but for Mathews, those minutes had been an eternity. While in the ocean, before his mind began to fade and before his muscles developed the malignant paralysis of hypothermia, he was certain that he was going to run out of time. He could not see the boat, he could not know we were closing in on him, and he could not know there was still hope.

"Let's take her down," the captain said softly to the OOD at the top of the sail.

"Clear the bridge! Clear the bridge!" Young called out and the men scrambled down the long ladder into the safety of the *Viperfish*.

"Dive! Dive!" the chief's voice was broadcast throughout the boat as hatches were shut and we angled down again, away from the fury on the surface. Dropping hundreds of feet, we returned to our quiet existence beneath the sea.

IMPROVING THE BREED

FROM *Rising Tide: The Untold Story of the
Russian Submarines That Fought the Cold War*

by Gary E. Weir and Walter J. Boyne

Our last pair of authors takes us deeper inside the minds and strategy of the Soviet submarine captains pitted against the U.S. Navy during the Cold War. Gary E. Weir received his doctorate in history from the University of Tennessee, Knoxville, in 1982. After working as professor of history at the U.S. Naval Academy, Dr. Weir joined the Naval Historical Center, and in 1996 was promoted head of the Contemporary History Branch. His publications include *Building American Submarines, 1914–1940*; *Forged in War: The Naval-Industrial Complex and American Submarine Construction, 1940–1961*, the 1993 winner of the prestigious Theodore and Franklin D. Roosevelt Naval History Prize; and *Building the Kaiser's Navy: The Imperial Naval Office and German Industry in the Tirpitz Era, 1890–1919*. Dr. Weir is also an associate professor of history for the University of Maryland University College, and the recipient of fellowships and grants from the McClure Foundation, the Office of Naval Research, the Woods Hole Marine

Biological Laboratory, and Germany's Deutscher Aka-
demischer Austausch Dienst.

Walter J. Boyne is a former director of the Smithso-
nian's Air and Space Museum, aviation historian, and
bestselling author. He joined the Air Force in 1951
and earned his wings a year later, then flew as a B-50
and B-47 combat crew member in the Strategic Air
Command and later was a nuclear test pilot with the
4925th Nuclear Test Group at Kirtland AFB, flying
both the B-47 and B-52. After serving in Vietnam,
Colonel Boyne retired and joined the National Air
and Space Museum as an assistant curator in 1974
and was eventually appointed as its director. From
1983 to 1986, Boyne oversaw many aspects of museum operations and pioneered numerous projects to
provide the highest level of aerospace education and
information. He began a prolific research and writing
career in 1962. Since then, he has written more than
five hundred articles, twenty-eight nonfiction books,
and four novels, all focusing on aviation, with several
books appearing on the *New York Times* bestseller
list. His recent books include the Jet Air Trilogy,
chronicling the birth and evolution of the jet aircraft
industry.

From the most tragic of circumstances to the best, we
will now see the Soviet Navy and its submarines in
action as their leaders no doubt meant for them to
perform. First, a retired captain takes us on a spell-
binding journey under the Arctic Ocean to the North
Pole, revealing the Soviet feeling upon reaching the

very top of the world, which bears many similarities
to Captain Anderson's account almost twenty years
earlier. Then, they engage in their own game of cat-
and-mouse (or fish, in this instance), showing their
flair for strategy as they launch an operation against
the U.S. Navy designed to reveal their enemies' intentions while concealing the Soviets' own capabilities,
and accomplish their goal with steel nerves and seemingly endless patience.

In the past, the hauntingly brutal concept of mutual assured destruction had prevented war. With both sides possessing nuclear weapons in abundance, no one wished for a nuclear exchange. Nuclear weapons also prevented extreme military measures, like any action by the Soviet army against NATO, because such an action would inevitably provoke a nuclear response. As a result, the United States and the Soviet Union stood like two huge nuclear sumo wrestlers, locked in an embrace that neither could break.

To maintain this absurd balance, both the Soviet Union and the United States created new and better nuclear weapons, and, to all appearances, both would continue to do so for the foreseeable future. The leaders and the populace of both sides had accepted this state of affairs, and eventually accepted the uneasy peace as the normal political situation. Fortunately for everyone but the leaders of the Communist Party, an entirely new situation developed as the result of the confluence of two totally different situations.

By the 1980s, the booming economy of the United States, spurred by the rapid growth in the power and applications of the computer, ushered in an era of entirely new weaponry, one that would enable a departure from the MAD philosophy of military action. This was a true Revolution in Military Affairs (RMA), one that caught the Soviet Union by surprise, and one that also surprised many in the West. Regardless, it revolutionized submarine warfare and increased its level of sophistication.

As the Cold War moved into its fourth decade, the confrontation below the surface of the World Ocean continued unabated. The geopolitical world began to change but Russia continued to control and exercise formidable nuclear forces, including a fleet of submarines of remarkable quality and efficiency, captained by men of great skill and daring. One of the best of these was Captain First Rank Anatoli I. Shevchenko, whose experiences under both Soviet and Russian regimes are worth recounting. He led daring operations that revealed true Soviet submarine capability and their dangerous operations against their American counterparts.

Born in 1941 during the eastern front Nazi nightmare, this redheaded Soviet submariner hailed from Odessa, one of the bustling Black Sea ports of the southern Ukraine. After spending two years as a sailor in the Black Sea Fleet, Shevchenko entered the Black Sea Naval College in Sevastopol, receiving his commission as a lieutenant in 1965. The school trained him in cruise missile technology and prepared him as a watch officer, capable of serving on any vessel in the Soviet Navy.

Like many of his future adversaries learning their trade at the U.S. Naval Academy in Annapolis, Maryland, this Soviet midshipman went on summer cruises while in school, visiting for a time with various fleet units to learn about surface and subsurface warfare as well as aviation. In 1963, the summer cruise took him and his Sevastopol classmates to Gadzhievo, near Polyarni, to visit the submarines of the Northern Fleet. He immediately decided to choose submarines as a career path.

Upon graduation, he joined the crew of a Northern

Fleet Charlie 2 class nuclear submarine commanded by Captain Second Rank Valentin Savitsky, as the propulsion officer. After several years' experience in various capacities, including a year as assistant to the commander, he took the exams to qualify for command himself. With these behind him, he did a three-year tour as executive officer during which he made five combat patrols. In 1977, after passing a course for prospective commanding officers in Leningrad, he received his first command, a Victor 2. He took that boat and her crew to sea for the next five years.

Shevchenko matured as a commander during years that witnessed the Soviet Navy coming of age. Gorshkov projected Soviet naval power on a global scale barely more than a decade after World War II, but the navy struggled to live up to the ambition. The submarine fleet Shevchenko joined had many new designs that could compete on an equal footing with American Sturgeon and Los Angeles class fast attack boats. His fleet now had a history, a reputation, and a generation of pioneers who had taken the Cold War to the Americans. For Shevchenko, command gave him the opportunity to test himself, to live up to the responsibility, to forge a family from the raw material of his crew. It also gave him the opportunity to stand out and add his name to the history of the Soviet Navy. As he recalled many years later, "I tried to do everything in a unique way. I wanted to command in a manner that would not occur to others. I wished to be a true original. I had to know my boat and the men, to make them both my ally, and to teach them to perceive the world as I saw it."

His first chance to test his crew and to display his truly contagious confidence came with a 1977 deployment with his Victor 2 in the Mediterranean Sea, which he already knew well.

On his transit toward Gibraltar he encountered an American Sturgeon class submarine attempting to trail him. Shevchenko, like many of his Soviet ship-mates, viewed this most dangerous of undersea tactics very differently than his American and NATO coun-terparts. As happened so often during the Cold War, the two ships tested each other before Shevchenko ultimately slipped away. He knew that this cat-and-mouse game would reveal a submarine's technical capability, her tactics, and the level of competence of the commander. In many cases the submarines would come dangerously close, and collisions occurred with some regularity.

While Shevchenko expected the Americans occa-sionally to succeed in the game, he and his Soviet col-leagues now felt confident that their submarines could meet the challenge, particularly in quiet opera-tions. He viewed the submariner's world as that of the hunter—patient, deliberate, quiet, cerebral. Soviet and American submariners trailing each other to test skills and gather intelligence served as vital prepara-tion for the shooting war that no one hoped would come.

Very early in his career as a commander, Shevchenko became one of the Soviet Navy's experts on Arctic operations. In this environment the hunt became even more difficult because the acoustics of the frigid ocean quickly betrayed the presence of one submarine to another. The absence of regular commercial traffic left the fish and mammal population and the ice itself as the only acoustic cover.

The forbidding ice was an unavoidable hazard in

the Cold War because of the strategic importance of the Arctic, which provided the shortest trajectories for the intercontinental ballistic missiles available to both sides. By 1979, when Shevchenko made his first polar transit, both the Soviet Union and the United States could launch such missiles from submerged submarines.

Shevchenko knew that he would frequently find American submarines silently waiting for him along his path in the far north. A Los Angeles class submarine would hover in a neutrally buoyant state and acoustically collect operational and technical data on Soviet performance. She would then slide in behind the passing Russian to trail her. Shevchenko expected it and did not find it troubling. He would report all sonar contacts, all confirmed American contacts, and any indication that the adversary had successfully followed him. Sometimes he would pursue the American intruder to drive her out of the region, then return to the standard missile boat escort mission.

Rather than feeling compelled to play cat-and-mouse, Shevchenko regularly used active sonar to focus on any detected submarines, saying, "I used active only. If I detected a submarine I always assumed that the commander of that vessel had already detected me. Most of the submarines on both sides by that time had roughly equivalent detection capabilities. For me to assume that I might still mask my presence when I already had an American on my sonar was foolish."

Shevchenko's first journey to the North Pole took place in 1979, after his command, the *K-513*, received an award as the best boat in his squadron from Deputy Defense Minister Marshal Kirill Moskalenko.

K-513 was then scheduled for maintenance, and he planned to go on leave. But a summons arrived from the headquarters of the deputy commander of the submarine flotilla, Rear Admiral Eugene Chernov, a man whom Shevchenko greatly admired for his confidence, competence, and style. Chernov possessed that special personality, self-discipline, and professional behavior known as "charisma." As a commander, he displayed the quick mind and combative personality that Shevchenko sought to emulate. Chernov, who was short, had to project size rather than physically display it. For Shevchenko, observing Chernov was a lesson in leadership, teaching him a commander's responsibility to educate his crew, to prepare them for every task, to make the essential decisions, and to take responsibility.

In the spring of 1979, the Northern Fleet commander Admiral of the Navy Georgi Egorov visited the *513*. He listened to Shevchenko's report on the status of his submarine, his crew, and the tests planned for his relatively new Victor 2, all in the presence of the new submarine squadron commander, Captain First Rank V. Anokhin. When the inspection concluded, the admiral asked Shevchenko if he had any questions. He would never presume to present the admiral with questions he had not cleared first through his chain of command, but he saw an opportunity and decided to take it. Based on the admiral's favorable estimate of the *513*, he asked Egorov to provide *513* with a newly developed narrow-band, low-frequency acoustic analysis system to improve the capabilities of the submarine.

Egorov ordered the head of the radio-technical department of the Northern Fleet, Captain First Rank Boris Novi, to provide *K-513* with the requested equipment. Novi quickly promised delivery and installation the very next week.

In preparing for the polar transit, Captain Shevchenko went back to the very beginning, to the fundamentals of ship-handling and command.

His primary mission was to cruise under the Arctic ice and surface at the North Pole. In addition, he would add to their knowledge of the Arctic region so that nuclear submarines could operate more safely. He would open the operation by practicing cruises under the ice both solo and with other submarines. *K-513*'s crew also studied the bathymetric conditions in the Arctic Ocean, to gather data on the features of the ice, to practice ways of establishing the submarine's exact location at any time and that of a patrolling partner, to take regular fathometer readings, and to lose no opportunity to carefully observe NATO naval forces. Shevchenko scheduled his departure for August 1, 1979. *K-513* would set out for the Arctic Ocean from Zapadnaya Litsa at a course and speed that would place her at the edge of the ice pack by August 24. Three days later the boat would begin a short-range practice cruise of twelve hours' duration in the company of the Charlie class submarine *K-320*, an ocean tug, and an icebreaker. Then *K-320* would take her turn on August 28, practicing in the region for fifteen hours with the aid of *K-513* and two surface vessels. If the exercises proved successful, *K-513* would then cruise under the ice into the Arctic Ocean via the deep canyons of Franz-Victoria and Saint Anne's Troughs, approaching latitude 83°30' north. *K-320* would accompany Shevchenko on this first leg to 83°30' and would then depart for home, leaving *K-513* to complete the journey to the North Pole. If everything went according to plan, Shevchenko would surface at 90° north on September 1.

As their preparations approached completion, Gorshkov called the senior officers of the *K-513* and *K-320* to Moscow, along with Vice Admiral Rudolf Golosov, Shevchenko's superior, and Rear Admiral Chernov. Shevchenko had never visited Gorshkov's inner sanctum before and was terribly nervous. When he met the Soviet Navy's most senior officer, Shevchenko reported on his preparations for the voyage. Both the presentation and the question session went well.

Shortly after 0900 on August 24, the *513*'s crew cast off the boat's lines and put to sea. The trip to the rendezvous point went smoothly and the presence of Rear Admiral Golosov on board as senior commander helped the crew focus on both their tasks and Shevchenko's orders. *K-513* met her companion vessels on August 27 at latitude 78°00' north, longitude 42°24' east, 143 miles away from the edge of the ice pack.

Shevchenko quickly implemented his cruise plan by submerging to 450 feet and proceeding north at 20 knots toward the edge of the polar ice. While in contact with the icebreaker *Dobrinya Nikitich* he explored the outer reaches of the Arctic ice cover at approximately 80° north latitude. His log reflects a close call that revealed the nature and power of the Arctic ice.

———

1905 hours, I arrived in the region where the submarine was supposed to practice and slowed down to 5 knots. According to our reconnaissance data there was no ice yet in sight. The sonar complex designed by Rubin showed a clear horizon. I brought K-513 to periscope depth. I could see an empty horizon through the periscope; 1.87 nautical miles away on a bearing of 238° the radar showed a spot which presumably was a single iceberg.

1920 hours, Speed, 7 knots; submerged to 120 feet; I brought the submarine around to starboard and maneuvered toward the iceberg. My sonar picked up noises seemingly made by the iceberg; the detection resembled the sound made by the rising tide, a brook, or the sound of water poured from one glass to another.

1930 hours, I twice used low-power active sonar to measure the thickness of the iceberg at distance. There was no echo. Therefore, we assumed it didn't have a big draught. We were 1.6 nautical miles away. I used the mine detection sonar to control our distance as we approached the iceberg.

1934 hours, Our sonar screen showed the ice at a bearing of 219° at 1.1 nautical miles. I slowed to 3 knots to permit ice reconnaissance devices to work.

1944 hours, NOK-1 [the navigation ice detector] detected that the nearest edge of the iceberg exhibited two oval ledges. I kept the boat moving at 2.5 knots.

1945 hours, The device measuring ice thickness showed nothing, so I took 513 under the first ledge.

1947 hours, NOK-1 detected the second ice ledge at 10 to 15° relative; the whole iceberg was drifting to starboard. Suddenly, the sonar detected what was probably the right blade of my forward dive planes brushing against the ice surface. *513* held its depth at 130 feet while the gyrocompass showed a drift to starboard. I changed the rudder angle to move the stabilizers and propeller away from the ice and took the boat down to 180 feet.

2004 hours, Course, depth, and speed unchanged. The stern planes worked well. To discover the extent and effect of the damage sustained by our contact with the iceberg, I tested the dive planes at 12 knots and carefully examined the attitude of the boat at all times. The boat responded well. As a result, I made a decision to examine the outer hull and the dive planes when we arrived at the surface rendezvous.

Shevchenko did not surface until 0346 on August 28. He encountered moderate waves at force one and foggy conditions that limited visibility to one nautical mile. His crew immediately went topside to examine the bow, finding the blade of the starboard dive plane a few degrees off with a dent approximately one foot from its tip. The axle by which the dive plane moved leaned over at a 15-degree angle and would not budge. It had obviously brushed against the second ledge of the iceberg. The bow and the outer hull showed no marks at all and the dive plane forward on the port side worked very well. Given that a malfunctioning starboard plane would have no impact on the boat at speeds up to 20 knots submerged, Shevchenko decided to continue the mission and report on the damage when they returned to base. On August 28, the Northern Fleet sent Shevchenko a report that *K-513* was proceeding north into a region with a very high iceberg count, some with a draught of 210 feet. He decided to negotiate the ice field carefully, staying submerged well below the massive subsurface sections of the icebergs. He reached the edge of the ice pack at latitude 80°23' north.

That same day Shevchenko analyzed his progress so far, concluding that submarines en route to the Arctic via the Saint Anne's and Franz-Victoria Troughs should cruise for safety at or below 450 feet.

Careful acoustic analysis with new sonar equipment demonstrated that he could relate certain noises to the icebergs. Readings taken by the low-frequency acoustic analyzer revealed unique sounds when the boat moved at seven knots or less and remained relatively shallow at a depth of approximately 120 feet. Icebergs emerged clearly from the sonar at ranges of two or three nautical miles at a frequency of 5 kilohertz. He resolved to make sure the officers under his command studied this phenomenon carefully. While the active sonar permitted him to gauge the distance to these icebergs, it made sense to stay 450 feet down and rely on the NOK for further information. This instrument displayed the physical limits of the iceberg captured imperfectly by the active sonar. With it Shevchenko could see how easily the iceberg could have damaged his diving plane. He knew that he would remember his first encounter with the monstrous iceberg for the rest of his life.

On August 29 at 0100, *K-320* and the *513* prepared for their joint run toward the Pole. As *K-320* sat on the surface two miles away, both submarines tested every device on board, from communications to detection to navigation, to ensure a safe collaboration. They even submerged for a time to accept instructions from the Northern Fleet under different conditions to verify their ability to receive essential communication. Both submarines reported to the fleet that the exercise could begin.

At 0145 they began their voyage and both submarines began to dive. *513* descended almost immediately to 450 feet, leveling and adjusting trim at a speed of 12 knots.

All during the exercise the two boats constantly checked their course as well as their relative positions. In addition, Shevchenko had his navigation and control room personnel continually take readings for depth, sonar contacts with undersea formations, the configuration of the ice overhead, and the occasional *polinya*. For the next ninety-seven hours, the two crews learned, recorded data, and helped one another over a distance of 972 miles. At 0735 on August 30, *K-320* turned and set a course for home. Now on her own, *K-513* set her sights on the Pole, proceeding 450 feet down at 12 knots.

Surfacing presents one of the most daunting challenges of the polar experience for submariners. It requires common sense combined with the careful use of the precision data provided by advanced technology. Shevchenko intended to practice the surfacing maneuver as soon as a suitable location above presented itself. The need to practice became even more apparent as the overhead ice cover changed to a maximum thickness of up to 12 feet.

During the afternoon of August 31, Shevchenko decided to make the final run to the Pole. He began looking for a suitable *polinya* in a region of ice with a relatively smooth underside 1,500 feet long in order to practice surfacing. This would allow his communications gear to safely break the surface without damaging his rudder and dive planes.

His first surfacing exercise is recorded in his log as follows:

> 1317, course 0°, speed 12 knots, depth 450 feet; the mine detection device showed a plane ice zone, presumably a *polinya*. I slowed down to 3 knots; the ice-thickness measuring device was on, the officer observed the under ice surface through the periscope and over the television monitors.
>
> 1327, course 10°, depth 450 feet, speed 3 knots; I cruised under the center of an ice zone 4500 feet long with a relatively flat underside. The ice was 12 feet thick.

Shevchenko carefully maneuvered the boat to the center of the chosen area, approaching at a depth of 270 feet, completely level and parallel to the ice above. He stopped *K-513* and began to hover. The actual surfacing would take place without propulsion. He had to choose the correct speed of ascent by pumping water out of the submarine's ballast tanks, increasing positive buoyancy, and monitoring the rate of his rise. He would also adjust the angle of the boat slightly to protect his stern dive planes and his rudder from any collision with the underside of the ice. A slight down angle at the stern would place the bow slightly higher as the vessel rose to meet the surface ice.

He activated the training alarm, sending all of the

relevant crewmen to their posts and focusing their attention on the next step in the exercise process. Shevchenko's log again picks up the story:

1336, depth 270 feet, deferent 0°. *513* in position for vertical surfacing. I kept the image of our target location on the television monitor.

1345, Resumed hovering at 255 feet. Initiated ascent via ballast release. The boat began to rise at 9 feet per minute. The vertical surfacing system worked perfectly. The huge ship responded well to each command from the diving officer Boris Dyachkov.

1359, depth 120 feet. Surfacing maneuver continued. As the boat came close to the ice, I slowed to 6 feet per minute. To protect the dive planes and the rudder I effected a 2° stern deferent (stern down) by pumping ballast water from the bow tanks to the stern.

1426, depth 45 feet. The stern deferent was 5°. The television complex clearly showed that the submarine was drifting with the current and with the ice. With a 1.2 feet per minute surfacing speed *513* touched ice projecting 15 feet below the surface with her bow. The contact immediately decreased the stern deferent to 3° and caused the boat to drift 30° to starboard with the under-ice current. The depth stabilizer was switched off and the television went white. To prevent the submarine from sliding along the underside of the ice, I pressed her to the ice by expelling 16 tons of ballast. The positive buoyancy pinned the boat to the underside of the ice and arrested the drift, avoiding damage to the stern dive planes, rudder, and

the sail-mounted antennae. We proceeded to receive
communication from base through the ice without
any interference. Initially, errors in the signals received via the Marshrut radio-navigation system
caused the navigators to make an 8-mile mistake in
their estimation of the surfacing point location.

With this first exercise successfully completed,
Shevchenko prepared the crew for the delicate diving
process. Pulling away from the underside of the ice
also required care. When the crew finished all of the
planned activity near the surface, including a trash
drop, Shevchenko ordered an increase in the ballast,
and *K-513* successfully cleared the ice after spending
twenty-nine minutes near the surface.

Due to temperature, pressure, and natural hydro-
dynamic forces, the boat began to descend quicker as
depth increased. At about 150 feet the speed of descent
increased to 30 to 36 feet per minute. Now timing became important. The diving officer had to pump water
out of the trim tanks at about 300 feet, while the propulsion came on line to move the vessel forward. At
that depth, the odds in favor of colliding with ice
under the surface approached zero and the slowly
increasing forward motion of the vessel would return
maneuvering control to the helm. On board *K-513*,
the propulsion officer, Captain Second Rank Vladimir
Katomin, was responsible for performing this underwater ballet. At 430 feet, *K-513* resumed her course
for the Pole.

For the rest of the journey to the Pole, the crew
attentively observed the instrument readings and
the television screens. Above them, there were oc-

casional breaks in the ice, the size of a football field
at most, on the surface. In addition, the underside
of the floating ice displayed many ledges arranged
like layers, some jutting out as much as thirty feet.
At the North Pole, their fathometer showed a huge
projection of the ice perpendicular to the surface
down to 125 feet. Other areas had ice showing only
a 6- to 8-foot draught underneath a smooth thick
surface extending horizontally for 2,700 feet. Everywhere they looked the natural conditions awed
them.

At 1832 on August 31, 1979, Shevchenko informed
the crew that the navigator now placed them at the
North Pole. The entire ship's complement received
the news with cheering and excitement, for they had
joined a rather exclusive Soviet and American club.
Shevchenko congratulated his crew on their achievement and quickly set them to work finding a *polinya*
so they could open their hatch at the top of the world.

He defined a search area of 360 degrees with the
Pole as the center, and divided it into four quadrants.
The boat then systematically surveyed each quadrant
at 5 knots, looking for a suitable *polinya*. At 1815 the
mine detector showed a distinct edge with a plane surface at a modest distance. Shevchenko set his course
accordingly and felt almost instinctively that he had
his *polinya*.

He carefully recorded the ascent and his achievement. He ordered his watch engineer Sergey Topchiev
to stop the turbine and at his order the boat began its
ascent. According to his log, at 1820 *K-513* rose to
180 feet; the boat's attitude and trim were checked.
The periscope and instruments showed clear water

above. The *polinya* was approximately 675 feet long and 300 feet wide.

Shevchenko leveled the boat at 180 feet without propulsion, using his trim tank to adjust the ballast. The boat continued to rise at a rate of 12 to 15 feet per minute, and he kept the stern slightly lower than his bow, protecting his rudder, screws, and aft dive planes from the impact with the ice. He kept *513* in the center of the *polinya* by occasionally using his emergency slow-speed propulsion shaft driven by the turbine, making sure that neither the stern nor the dive planes came into contact with the ice.

By 1833, the boat reached 170 feet and continued to rise. With all of the reporting and ordering completed, everything became strangely quiet. Only the boatswain's voice, calling out the depth, broke the silence. In his memory, Shevchenko can still clearly hear the last call, ". . . depth, 12 feet; . . . the boat has stopped." Everyone felt the stern deferent suddenly disappear and the submarine commenced rocking gently on a clear surface. Smiling, Shevchenko turned to Admiral Golosov and asked permission to raise the periscope.

Nothing prepared him for this first glimpse of the polar region. As he recalls it:

I didn't expect to see what I saw through the periscope! There was pure white and serene ice around the submarine. There was a wonderful rainbow stretched through the eastern part of the sky, which was shining with all the colors as if it had multi-shade diamonds. It was gorgeous! Golosov went to the periscope. A minute after, having opened the hatch, I was standing at the bridge. I really wanted the crewmen to see this beauty, and then to report to the commander-in-chief on the surfacing. Having prepared the machinery and devices for the stop-over in the *polinya* and the communication means for the report to the base, the crewmen had a chance to admire the pure Arctic beauty, to feel the terrific ice silence, and to collect memories with their cameras. We had a meeting on the bow of the submarine and raised the Soviet and Naval Flag to the melody of the Soviet hymn. Then there were salute shots to commemorate the surfacing at the North Pole. The report on the surfacing of the *K-513* was sent at 1925. The men stayed on the upper deck for more than an hour. At 2000 the men of the second shift went to the upper deck. The sun was still above the horizon, but the area changed daytime colors for darker and deeper ones, all the while keeping the greatness of its silence.

As night descended, the crew took the flags down and the submarine began preparations to submerge. Shevchenko had the hatch closed at 2130 and imme-diately gave orders to dive the boat. At 120 feet the crew pumped water out of the trim tank to slow the speed of descent. Otherwise the effect of temperature and pressure in the depths would make the boat so negatively buoyant that the descent would proceed far too quickly. At 360 feet, Katomin, "the choreogra-pher," once again brought main propulsion on line just in time. In those late summer days of 1979, *K-513* spent two hours and thirty-seven minutes on the sur-face at the top of the world.

At 450 feet, Shevchenko ordered the helm to make turns for 8 knots and then, handing the bridge over to his executive officer, he retired to the navigator's plot and laid in the course for their return trip. Later that evening he reported to Golosov on their probable time of arrival and extended an invitation for a midnight dinner to celebrate their conquest of the North Pole. A few hours later they turned for home, depth 450 feet, speed 12 knots.

Anatoli Shevchenko built a solid naval career, including chases with American attack submarines, but that was only a glimpse of what lay in store for him when he conducted possibly the Soviet Navy's most audacious sting operation at sea, the large-scale operations Aport and Atrina of the mid-1980s.

Without complete secrecy, these plans would never have worked. Complacency and routine on the part of the U.S. Navy would also play a critical role in this endeavor. Seemingly secure behind their constantly probing attack submarines, stealthy missile boats, powerful battle groups, and the SOSUS acoustic detection system, the U.S. Navy needed to feel in control of the GIUK gap, the North Atlantic, and the approaches to its own shores. As President Ronald Reagan preached the gospel of American military and naval strength arrayed against the "evil empire," Admiral of the Fleet of the Soviet Union Sergei G. Gorshkov prepared a secret exercise, a sting operation, that he hoped would quietly demonstrate Soviet naval capability and betray American practice and intention while leaving his old adversary none the wiser.

And now seemed the perfect time to do it. Gorshkov knew that his tenure as commander in chief of the Soviet Navy, initiated by Khrushchev in 1956, would conclude in December 1985. In his seventy-fifth year, this old destroyer sailor could not think of a better parting shot than asking his Northern Fleet submariners to lead the Americans and their NATO allies into a trap. Furthermore, the possibility of conducting a successful operation while Secretary Gorbachev prepared to meet Ronald Reagan in Geneva in November 1985 made it the perfect time to act on a plan conceived by one of the admiral's more promising and energetic subordinates. Reagan needed to know what the Soviet Navy could do, but not until the First Secretary of the Communist Party of the Soviet Union wanted him to know.

In his second year commanding the Thirty-third Division of the Northern Fleet, Captain First Rank Anatoli I. Shevchenko had his own memorable style and personal manner. An imposing figure of roughly six feet in height with a commanding presence, Shevchenko still has his penetrating stare and easy smile. His personality as an operational commander quickly filled any room he entered with a determined manner, a preoccupation with significant detail, and a carefully applied sense of humor. Like an artist in the act of creation, he enjoyed the process of command, from the conceptual sketch, through the details and brush strokes, to the application of his unique style and signature to the finished product. This time his agile mind had concocted an operation that he felt sure would lead the Americans to betray themselves.

After pulling strings to have his plan approved by

higher authority, Shevchenko launched the preparations but kept everything to himself. Neither he nor his superiors informed the KGB or the GRU. None of the security services knew about the plan or the timing of the operation. Indeed, he employed a variety of stories to provide sufficient cover for the orders that arrived from Moscow instructing five submarines of the Victor 2 and Victor 3 classes to prepare for sea. He wanted to demonstrate that the Soviet submarine force could acquire as much significant operational intelligence about the American fleet using ingenuity and sheer determination as the latter could about the Soviets with SOSUS and all of their other varied and vaunted ASW surveillance methods. Shevchenko also wanted to remind the Americans that Soviet submarines, some with missile capability, could still operate off the American coast, as they did in the early years of the Cold War, with nuclear warheads at the ready. Given the policies and the rhetoric of the Reagan administration and the increasing economic weakness of the Soviet Union, the geopolitical situation seemed to call for an operation that could give Gorbachev some authority at the conference table. Shevchenko and his fellow submariners did not like the First Secretary's inclination to redraw Soviet defense policy, but they understood the hard line coming out of Washington. They recognized that adversary all too well.

Just before he left for Cuban waters to take command of this secret operation, Shevchenko went to the head of Northern Fleet Security and presented for his signature the paperwork authorizing the operation. The plan carried the curious code name "Aport," a meaningless collection of letters selected deliberately to avoid betraying the essence of the plan. The submarines involved would leave for the Atlantic coast of the United States and Canada the next day. Rather than having an opportunity to complain about the lack of both information and prior consultation, the security officer found the document already approved by the most powerful flag officers in the Soviet Navy. Left with no choice, he signed on the dotted line. Shevchenko smiled and took all copies of the completed documents with him. He would leave no trail.

The only other officers briefed on this plan prepared their submarines and crews for immediate departure. Shevchenko himself set off for Cuba on board a Project 705 Lira-type nuclear attack submarine, the type NATO referred to as Alfas. The swift and deep-diving Alfa, very much like the one Captain Boris Kolyada took to sea, would transport Shevchenko and his operations staff to a position east of Fidel Castro's island at speeds approaching 45 knots submerged. There they would transfer to the Moma class hydrographic research vessel *Kolguyev*. This scientific and intelligence-gathering surface vessel would enable Shevchenko to control the entire operation from the Caribbean Sea via satellite link.

Shevchenko designed Aport to present the U.S. Navy with a confusing, unexpected, and powerful Soviet submarine presence near the American coast. He gambled that this situation would force the NATO Atlantic command to respond immediately in ways that would reveal some SSBN patrol areas, the current tactical habits of fast attack submarines, the response time of ASW surveillance aircraft, and the extent of SOSUS capability and coverage. It helped considerably that the John Walker spy ring in the United States

had already betrayed NATO sufficiently to give the
Victors a fair chance to penetrate undetected into the
North Atlantic.

On the morning of May 29, 1985, the four submarines put to sea. Departing from West Litsa on the
Kola Peninsula, they moved out into the Barents Sea
and headed for the "corner," the name given to the
North Cape, where the submarines began their turn
south and west into the Norwegian Sea. A fifth boat,
the Victor 1 class *K-147*, left from Gremikha, the
Northern Fleet base situated farthest to the east on
the Kola, carrying a new onboard detector designed
to search for submerged radioactive wake traces from
the nuclear propulsion systems of American submarines. They all dropped down through the Iceland-
Faeroes gap into the North Atlantic on their way to
the Aport staging area Shevchenko had selected in
the Newfoundland Basin off the Canadian coast.

Shevchenko knew that his Victors might not make
it undetected through the American and NATO surveillance constantly focused on the choke points between Greenland, Iceland, and the United Kingdom.
Neither would the presence of a lone Soviet hydrographic vessel in the Caribbean, placed there for his
use as a command ship, go unnoticed at Atlantic Fleet
Command in Norfolk. Of course, an operator of his
experience knew all too well that you did not pin
strategies on hope.

He had something else in mind. In this case, one
has to look not at submarines, weapons, platforms,
and sensors for the source of his confidence, but at
the ocean itself. While the ocean environment might
present regular dangers, it also provides the stealth
that submarines need to succeed. If you look at a map

of the northwestern Atlantic Ocean, examine carefully the coast of Maine and the Canadian Maritime Provinces just to the north. Off that coast, to the east and north, lie the Newfoundland Grand Banks, one of the busiest fishing grounds in the world. Slightly farther to the east, the continental shelf ends and the bottom drops away into Shevchenko's chosen Newfoundland Basin. In this area the powerful Atlantic warm-water anomaly called the Gulf Stream turns east and north after its long journey from the Florida Straits, ready to become part of the North Atlantic Current before it proceeds across the ocean to the United Kingdom.

NATO scientists and ASW officers constantly sought better ways to examine the Gulf Stream because its warm waters profoundly affected the behavior of passing acoustic signals, whether generated by whales or by Victor class boats on their way to provoke the Americans into revealing valuable operational intelligence. Shevchenko hoped he might slip through the NATO surveillance network, but he did not worry too much. He knew the presence of the Victors would stir the NATO pot. When it did, he intended to hide his boats in the warm waters of the Gulf Stream. In this region, the ocean would provide physical and, even more important, intermittent acoustic cover. He would use the natural characteristics of the ocean, eternally reliable, to confuse the technology available to the Americans just long enough to win his prize.

The operation began with a signal from Shevchenko on June 18. Beginning at a point barely west of the Newfoundland Grand Banks, two of the Victors began following one another, clockwise, in a gigantic circle, while two others did the same in a different but concentric circle moving counterclockwise. At the same time, four Tu-142M aircraft took off from the San Antonio air base in Cuba to join the operation by performing ASW sweeps of the Newfoundland Basin with sonobuoys and surveillance gear designed to detect American submarines and to intercept communications. Once the Soviet boats began their pattern running, the Americans reacted just as Shevchenko's plan had predicted. The Soviets observed at close range American and NATO ASW aircraft operating regular flights from Maine, the Canadian Maritimes, Bermuda, and the Azores at all hours of the day looking for the four Victors. In the meanwhile, the Russians looked for American submarines.

Gulf Stream waters populated by an increased number of Soviet submarines presented a terrible danger to the United States and a very perplexing problem for the U.S. Navy. While the boats clearly and often showed up on air, surface, and subsurface surveillance systems, they also disappeared with a disturbing regularity, often for many days without any indication of their activity or the timing of their return to base. Not unlike Tom Clancy's fictional Soviet commander, Marko Ramius in *The Hunt for Red October*, Shevchenko intended to use the Gulf Stream as intermittent cover, cover that would potentially permit him to move his boats from the Newfoundland Basin in the north as far south as the American submarine bases at Charleston, South Carolina, and King's Bay, Georgia. Ramius had a silent propulsion system, the dream of every submariner, and detailed undersea maps of the canyons of the Reykjanes Ridge, a mountain range projecting south and west of Iceland. Shevchenko's

Victors could not operate with complete silence, but the warm waters of the Gulf Stream, an anomaly in the usually frigid North Atlantic, might hide their presence, almost on demand, for days or weeks at a time. Warm water temperatures would inhibit the detection capabilities of the passive sonar systems used by the Americans to track Soviet boats. For Shevchenko, that was enough.

Captain Peter Cressy, commanding officer of Patrol Wing Five based at the Naval Air Station in Brunswick, Maine, lost sleep because of Shevchenko's tactics. He found the increase in Soviet submarine activity disturbing and their regular tendency to disappear from his sonar absolutely maddening. Not a man to admit defeat and determined to discover the conditions that prevented his ASW patrol aircraft from regularly tracking Shevchenko's boats, he relentlessly exercised all technical and human means at his disposal for finding the Victors. This distinguished 1973 graduate of the U.S. Naval War College concluded that the dilemma had nothing to do with his aircraft, the ability of his aircrews, or the technology at his disposal. The ocean itself presented the problem, especially the most powerful dynamic force in the segment of ocean he patrolled, the Gulf Stream. As an ASW officer, he knew how easily the behavior of sound in seawater could change, and especially the critical role temperature played. He quickly asked one of his staff to produce the best Gulf Stream scientist the navy could find. In 1985, only two men fit that description: Henry Stommel of the Woods Hole Oceanographic Institution and Allan Robinson of Harvard University. Robinson quickly found himself in a car and on his way to Maine.

On hearing the problem of the lost Victors, this Massachusetts native, oceanographer, and physicist immediately realized he could help Cressy. Assisted by his postdoctoral colleagues and graduate students, Robinson had just finished formulating the first part of a computer modeling system designed to predict environmental change in the ocean. The first part of this "Harvard Ocean Prediction System," or HOPS, naturally—and in this case fortuitously—focused on one of Robinson's favorite Atlantic forces, the Gulf Stream. When Cressy and Robinson began to look for Shevchenko's Victors through the digital lens provided by HOPS, Patrol Wing Five detections via sonobuoy improved significantly. While not the ultimate answer to the acoustic fog generated by the Gulf Stream, Robinson's work helped predict the behavior of the stream in much the same way that an evening news show meteorologist would predict the week's weather. The process was not perfect, but it gave the hunters a better chance to flush their target with sonobuoys.

As far as Shevchenko knew, his submarines had remained undetected throughout the operation, and only the *K-488* appeared on American surveillance devices in the vicinity of Iceland during the return voyage. Below the surface and frequently hidden in the temperature variations and the gyres of the Gulf Stream, *K-324* detected American SSBNs and fast attack submarines on three different occasions, maintaining a combined contact time of twenty-eight hours. Another of Shevchenko's sub captains reported that he had trailed an American SSBN for five days.

In the hierarchy of targets for the Soviet submariners, only the SSBNs surpassed the American aircraft carriers in importance. Victors and all of the advanced Soviet boats existed to gather this kind of intelligence and every Soviet submarine commander lusted after the moment when he had the upper hand against an American ballistic missile submarine. Practical experience had already demonstrated that American SSBNs, operating in a patrol quiet mode at a very low speed, could remain so silent that a Victor would have to be within a mile of the American missile boat in order to be sure of detecting her. Shevchenko guessed that the SSBNs operated at one-tenth the noise level generated by the quietest Soviet submarines. Shevchenko's efforts provided the Soviet Union with up-to-date intelligence on SSBN locations and operational areas, on attack submarine tactics and habits, and on the latest air search techniques employed by NATO and the United States. The operation concluded on July 1 and the boats involved returned safely to the Northern Fleet.

From Shevchenko's point of view, the operation succeeded beyond his expectations. The Americans had greater wealth, a larger navy, and amazing technical assets, at times making secret Soviet submarine missions nearly impossible. In response, he chose to gather intelligence with the best weapons available to him and on site, as a hunter might. With the Aport strategy Shevchenko flushed his quarry, and forced a reaction. As he directed operations from his ship in the Caribbean, the Victors sharply prodded the Americans and came prepared to observe and capitalize on the results. While more difficult, dangerous, and certainly less subtle than many of the methods employed by the Americans and NATO, the captain and the Soviet naval command considered the outcome and the lessons learned well worth the risk. They could move up and down the American Atlantic coast, keeping themselves concealed for much of the time. It became a first step in a much more ambitious application of a similar technique.

Aport provided a preface to a more elaborate plan, an effort to keep the Soviet Navy active, politically influential, and seemingly on par with NATO. Only weeks after the Reagan-Gorbachev summit in Reykjavik, Iceland, in October 1986, the new commander in chief of the navy, Gorshkov's successor, Admiral of the Fleet Vladimir Chernavin, decided that Captain Shevchenko needed to go to sea once again. Chernavin wanted to establish his reputation as a strong and aggressive leader, while giving the political leadership confidence in their ability to challenge the Americans in their own waters. This time, the techniques used in Aport, supplemented by lessons learned from the U-boat strategy employed with significant effect early in World War II by German Grand Admiral Karl Doenitz, gave birth to a more complicated hunt. Once again, Shevchenko would try to sting NATO. He would call this venture "Atrina."

He turned once again to five Victor class attack submarines. Using communication wavelengths more frequently employed by merchant vessels and ocean tugboats, all five boats carefully masked their communication with the Northern Fleet. They also tried to drown the acoustic signature generated by each submarine in a noisy sea. Given the traffic through the GIUK gap, both natural and man-made, they had

their choice of using either inbound Soviet submarines or scores of noisy surface vessels as ponderous
but relatively efficient cover. Each boat moved deliberately with the ship traffic through the Iceland-Faeroes
region into the North Atlantic and then dispersed to
predetermined locations scattered over that immense
body of water.

Only the submarine commanders now taking up
station in far-flung parts of the Atlantic received
highly classified briefings on the operation. As with
Aport, Shevchenko kept the number of informed men
to a bare minimum, once again denying even the naval security services access to his plans. From the Soviet vantage point, Aport had worked flawlessly and
Shevchenko had no reason to depart from a tried-
and-true approach. Of all the boats chosen for the
new operation, only one had experienced Aport. All
five Victor 3s possessed the first Soviet operational,
stern-deployed, towed sonar array that would enable
them, like the Americans, to extend from a stern vertical stabilizer a very sensitive set of hydrophones
towed well behind the noise made by the boats' own
screws.

The Atrina strategy clearly followed the lessons
that Aport had taught, namely, that NATO would
obviously respond with all of its most critical assets if
strategically important regions seemed threatened.
Therefore, borrowing from Grand Admiral Doenitz's
wolfpack technique of World War II, Shevchenko
planned to stage smaller-scale versions of Aport at
various strategically important areas in the Atlantic.
With a critical mass of Soviet submarines gathering in
any given region, NATO would respond aggressively,

pursuing with both air and subsurface assets. The Soviet strategist planned to converge and then disperse
at repeated but irregular intervals at various points in
the Atlantic, revealing each time the nature of the
NATO presence in the area.

The first convergence, for example, took place near
the base used by the British and occasionally the Americans near the port of Hamilton in Bermuda. The Soviet boats came together, vectored at Shevchenko's
command by satellite and aircraft communication, to
a location in the Sargasso Sea, once again a warm-
water area that played havoc with acoustic detection.
When one or more of the boats had been detected, the
others observed and often pursued the American fast
attack submarines tracking individual Victors. This
time Admiral Chernavin assisted Shevchenko with
ASW surveillance aircraft not only from Cuba, but
also from the Northern Fleet air bases on the Kola
Peninsula.

NATO's swift and strong countermeasures only
ended up serving the operation's strategic goals. According to Soviet sources, the American Atlantic Submarine Command, or "SubLant," dispatched six
nuclear submarines in search of Shevchenko's group of
five Victors, and the U.S. Atlantic Fleet used ASW surveillance aircraft and SURTASS ships of the Stalwart
class to perform aerial and sonar sweeps. Atrina repeatedly demonstrated the Soviet ability to explore
NATO intentions and capabilities, while displaying the
Northern Fleet's transatlantic reach. Along with the
obviously important results of the sting operations,
they needed to demonstrate for the Americans and
NATO that the Soviet fleet could still operate at considerable distance, close to American shores, and in

coordination. In spite of the geopolitical circumstances, Chernavin used Atrina to remind NATO that he had inherited and would use Gorshkov's formidable fleet in the interests of the Soviet Union.

Submarine Books of Note

Silent Victory by Clay Blair, Jr. (Philadelphia: Lippincott, 1975)

Wahoo by Richard H. O'Kane, RADM, USN (Ret.) (Novato, CA: Presidio Press, 1987)

Clear the Bridge by Richard H. O'Kane, RADM, USN (Ret.) (Chicago: Rand McNally, 1977)

Thunder Below by Eugene B. Fluckey, RADM, USN (Ret.) (Urbana: University of Illinois Press, 1992)

The Luck of the Draw by C. Kenneth Ruiz, Captain, USN (Ret.) (St. Paul, MN: Zenith Press, 2005)

Silent Running by James F. Calvert, VADM, USN (Ret.) (New York: J. Wiley, 1995)

Blind Man's Bluff by Sherry Sontag and Christopher Drew (New York: HarperCollins, 1998)

Dark Waters by Lee Vyborny and Don Davis (New York: New American Library, 2003)

The Silent War by John Pina Craven (New York: Simon & Schuster, 2001)

The Death of the Thresher by Norman Polmar (Philadelphia: Chilton Books, 1964)

The Rickover Effect by Theodore Rockwell (Annapolis, MD: Naval Institute Press, 1962)

An explosive new thriller from
New York Times bestselling authors

LARRY BOND
& JIM DeFELICE

LARRY BOND'S
RED DRAGON RISING

EDGE OF WAR

In this second book in Bond's latest gripping series,
CIA agent Mara Duncan faces her most grueling assignment:
get scientist Josh MacArthur and a seven-year-old witness to the
Chinese atrocities in Vietnam out of the country safely. With a
relentless Chinese monk and the entire Chinese secret service in
Vietnam at their back, it will be no easy task.

"A superb storyteller...Larry Bond seems to know
everything about warfare, from the grunt in the
foxhole to the fighter pilots far above the Earth."
—*The New York Times Book Review*

Hardcover: 978-0-7653-2138-1 | eBook: 978-1-4299-6062-5   tor-forge.com